RED, WHITE, and BLACK

SECOND EDITION

RED, WHITE, and BLACK

The Peoples of Early America

Gary B. Nash

University of California at Los Angeles

Prentice-Hall, Inc., Englewood Cliffs, New Jersey 07632

Library of Congress Cataloging in Publication Data

NASH, GARY B.
　　Red, White and Black.

　　Bibliography: p.
　　Includes index.
　　1. United States—History—Colonial period,
ca. 1600-1775.　2. America—Discovery and
exploration.　3. United States—Race relations.
I. Title.
E188.N37 1982　　　973.2　　　81-13804
ISBN 0-13-769794-5　　　AACR2
ISBN 0-13-769786-4 (pbk.)

Cover engravings by permission of The Bettmann Archives, Inc.
(left and right figures) and Dover Publications, Inc. (center figure).

Editorial/Production supervision
　and interior design by Edie Riker
Cover design by Mark Binn
Manufacturing buyer: Edmund W. Leone

©1982, 1974 by Prentice-Hall, Inc., Englewood Cliffs, N.J. 07632

Printed in the United States of America

10　9　8　7　6　5　4　3　2　1

ISBN 0-13-769786-4 {P}

Prentice-Hall International, Inc., *London*
Prentice-Hall of Australia Pty. Limited, *Sydney*
Prentice-Hall of Canada, Ltd., *Toronto*
Prentice-Hall of India Private Limited, *New Delhi*
Prentice-Hall of Japan, Inc., *Tokyo*
Prentice-Hall of Southeast Asia Pte. Ltd., *Singapore*
Whitehall Books Limited, *Wellington, New Zealand*

FOR BROOKE, ROBIN,
JENNIFER, AND DAVID

CONTENTS

FOREWORD xi

ACKNOWLEDGMENTS xv

INTRODUCTION 1

1 **BEFORE COLUMBUS** 7

Cultural Evolution, 8
Pre-Contact Population, 16
The Iroquois, 17
The Native American World View, 25

2 **EUROPEANS REACH THE AMERICAS** 29

Spanish and Portuguese Expansion into the New World, 30
English Entry into the Colonial Race, 32

3 CULTURES MEET ON THE CHESAPEAKE 43

The Re-establishment of Virginia, 45
Reorganization and Tobacco, 49
English-Indian Relations, 53
The War of 1622 and Its Aftermath, 60

4 CULTURES MEET IN THE NORTHEAST 67

Puritanism, 67
The Elusive Utopia, 71
Puritans and Indians, 75
The Question of Land, 79
The Pequot War, 81

5 PATTERNS OF INDIAN-EUROPEAN INTERACTION 87

Dutch-Indian Relations, 88
Quaker-Indian Relations, 95
French-Indian Relations, 104
Spanish-Indian Relations, 111

6 THE COASTAL SOCIETIES: RESISTANCE, ACCOMMODATION, AND DEFEAT 115

Metacom's War, 116
Bacon's Rebellion, 121
The Colonization of South Carolina, 126
Carolina-Indian Relations, 128
The Tuscarora and Yamasee Wars, 132

7 EUROPE, AFRICA, AND THE NEW WORLD 141

The Atlantic Slave Trade, 142
The Development of Slavery in the English Colonies, 147
Slavery in North and South America, 152

8 THE AFRICAN RESPONSE TO SLAVERY 165

Capture and Transport of Slaves, 166
Adjustment to Slave Life, 170
Regional Variations of American Slavery, 172
Slave Resistance and Rebellion, 178
Black Culture in Colonial America, 185

9 THE TRANSFORMATION OF EUROPEAN SOCIETY   **199**

    The Eighteenth-Century European Immigrants,   199
    Land, Growth, and Changing Values,   206
    The Cities,   210
    Changing Social Structure,   213
    The Great Awakening,   219

10 WARS FOR EMPIRE AND INDIAN STRATEGIES FOR SURVIVAL   **223**

    Iroquois Diplomacy,   224
    Creek Diplomacy,   230
    Cherokee Diplomacy,   234
    Transformations in Indian Society,   235
    Cultural Persistance,   244

11 THE SEVEN YEARS WAR AND ITS AFTERMATH   **247**

    Population Increase,   247
    The Seven Years War,   248
    Indian Strategy in The Seven Years War,   251
    Indian-White Relations After 1763,   258
    The Colonizers Society After 1763,   264
    Abolitionism,   268

12 THE MIXING OF PEOPLE   **273**

    Indian-European Contact,   275
    White-Black Intermixture,   280
    African-Indian Contact,   285
    Cultural Interaction of Red, White, and Black,   291

BIBLIOGRAPHICAL ESSAY   **299**

INDEX   **323**

FOREWORD

The uniqueness of this study is apparent at the very outset. Unlike the traditional approach to early American history, Gary Nash begins neither with
the first English footholds at Plymouth Rock and Roanoke Island nor with
Christopher Columbus's voyage, but some 20,000 years before Christ when
the first Americans spread themselves over the continent. By the time the
Europeans managed to find their way to the old "New World," a diversity of
native cultures had existed for thousands of years. Challenging the ethnocentric focus of traditional history, Nash views the Europeanization of the
New World as only one crucial stage in the evolution of colonial society. The
history of the American people is not primarily the story of European settlers but the complex interaction of three major cultural groups—white, red,
and black: "the story of a minority of Englishmen interacting with a majority
of Iroquois, Delawares, Narragansetts, Pequots, Mohicans, Catawbas,
Tuscaroras, Creeks, Cherokees, Choctaws, Ibos, Mandingos, Fulas, Yorubas,
Ashantis, Germans, French, Spanish, Swedes, and Scotch-Irish." That the
Europeans should have emerged as the dominant group was in large measure a tribute to their organizational skills, military know-how, and expertise
in the arts of duplicity and repression.

When, in the 1630s, the hand of God sifted from among the English people a chosen company of men and directed them to this new Canaan, Peter
Bulkeley, a Puritan clergyman, made his classic pronouncement that, "we,

the people of New England, are as a City set upon a hill, in the open view of all the earth, the eyes of the world are upon us, because we professe our selves to be a people in Covenant with God." Utopias, model societies, and wilderness Zions tend to breed a strange variety of man. Like most recent historians, Nash rejects the notion that the Puritans were the drab, color-less, humorless, sexually-inhibited creatures that could prompt Henry L. Mencken to define Puritanism as "the haunting fear that someone, some-where, may be happy." But neither does he view the Puritans as immune to totalitarianism, intolerance, or violence. (This is not necessarily to suggest, as did one United States senator, that the Puritan and frontier traditions must bear some of the responsibility for the assassination of President John F. Kennedy.) Of course, as Nash demonstrates, New England did not re-main the homogeneous society some of its founders had envisioned but evolved into a region where the spirit of commerce, speculation, and busi-ness distracted new generations from the righteous path to salvation. Rather than confine himself to internal politics and the often strange manifestations of religiosity, however, Nash examines with particular care how the Puritans interacted with the several Indian tribes who were initially in their midst. For the Puritans, after all, the Indian represented a substantial challenge, not only because he possessed the land they coveted but also because he appeared to be the very "counter-image of civilized man, thought to be lack-ing in what was most valued by the Puritans—civility, Christian piety, pur-posefulness, and the work ethic." For the Indians, on the other hand, the Puritan Commonwealth familiarized them with the white man's potential for deceit, arrogance, broken trust, and savagery. "It was deemed wiser," Nash writes, "to urge war against threatening Indians than to punish fellow Eng-lishmen who had initiated the violence." That enormous sense of mission that pervaded the Puritans, and the felt need to protect their internal secur-ity from "the demons of the invisible world," victimized Quakers, heretics, fortune tellers, and Indians alike, though with varying degrees of ferocity.

The tragic story of Puritan-Indian relations, although comprising only a small portion of Gary Nash's treatment of European-Indian contact, illus-trates the way in which he has chosen to view traditional subjects (like the Puritans) in a much broader perspective. Few, if any, general studies of early American historians devote as much attention as does *Red, White, and Black* to the impact of the Indians and ethnic and cultural conflict. How Englishmen first perceived the Indians, the contradictory images that evolved out of their relationships, the initial expectations of the European settlers and the Indians, and the insatiable appetite of the white man for more territory and wealth provide the necessary background for examining the violence and brutality that ensued until the elimination of the Indian could be rationalized as the extinction of an inferior, cultureless, and savage people. English-Indian relations, as Nash demonstrates, differed from region to region; the ways in which the interior tribes—the Creeks, Cherokees, Iroquois, and others—interacted with the English colonists, for example, provide some strikingly different patterns from those which characterized Puritan New England. Although the coastal Indian cultures eventually lay shattered, Nash shows how the prolonged resistance of those tribes gave the interior Indian cultures the necessary time "to adapt to the European presence and to devise strategies of survival as the westward-moving frontier approached them." And he makes one other point quite explicit. Many of the early colonists had envisioned a virtuous society organized around concepts of "reciprocity, spirituality, and community." With the passage of time, and with the steady growth of the white population, however, "the only people in North America who were upholding these values, and organizing their society around them, were the people who were being driven from the land."

If the Indian provoked among white men a violent response to his presence and cultural differences, the African excited even greater antipathy among a people who had come to view blackness as the very incarnation of evil and ugliness and as synonymous with heathenism, savagery, and bestiality. In examining the origins of racism and slavery, Nash critically examines and synthesizes the most recent scholarship. The result of several centuries of experience with African labor in North America helped to sustain and reinforce the initial impressions of blacks and created what Nash rightfully terms one of the great paradoxes of American history. "In the land heralded for its freedom and individual opportunity the practice of slavery, unknown for centuries in the mother country, was reinstituted." While addressing himself to why this happened, Nash also examines the Afro-Americans as "active participants in the cultural process" and describes their response to enslavement. Viewing the Africans and their enslavers as "an encounter or interaction of two cultures," he suggests that "the acculturation of slaves involved not only adaptation to the death-dealing daily toll of the plantation but education in strategies of survival, resistance, and rebellion."

Throughout this volume, Nash focuses our attention on the "historically voiceless," not only the slaves and Indians but white indentured servants, involuntary white immigrants, and those who came to America with high hopes but remained in the lower stratum of white colonial society. Whatever the legend of American success and unlimited opportunity, Nash finds equally compelling the story of those who struggled and lost. Even as political democracy expanded in colonial society, economic democracy appeared to be waning. "An open society," Nash argues, "with ample opportunities in the eighteenth century for entrepreneurship and with relatively few restraints imposed by government, was leading, paradoxically, to a growing gulf between rich and poor and to a concentration of economic power in the hands of a thin upper layer of society. Culturally committed to a society in which the individual, and not the community, was the central concern, the white population of colonial America was transforming what they thought to be uniquely American into what was more and more resembling the European conditions that they had fled." Synthesizing the work of recent demographers, Nash finds that the steady growth of the population and economic developments resulted in a less even distribution of wealth, more social stratification, and a marked increase in propertylessness in virtually every community. If American society on the eve of the Revolution still remained a land of opportunity for most people, Nash reminds us that some one-fourth of the population was in bondage or had been evicted from their lands and that "the promise of American colonial society was intimately and unforgettably intertwined with the exploitation of African labor and Indian land."

To the reader expecting a traditional treatment of traditional subjects, this volume suggests an altogether different perspective and approach. But to say that this is an "uncommon" view of early American history is only to underscore the extent to which historians have defined that experience all too narrowly and provincially.

Leon F. Litwack
1974

ACKNOWLEDGMENTS

The pages that follow began to take form in my mind in 1970 when I participated in redesigning the introductory course in American history at the University of California, Los Angeles. This effort was directed at making American history more understandable to an ethnically, socially, and intellectually diverse undergraduate audience by studying it as the process of change that occurred when people of widely varying cultural backgrounds interacted over a period of four centuries. Although this does not sound like a startling innovation, I discovered that it required me to read broadly in areas that had largely escaped my notice during fifteen years of studying and teaching colonial American history—anthropology, ethnohistory, African history, and Latin American history. To say that they "escaped my notice" is to put the point obliquely, for one of the thrusts of this book is that we read, think, and write selectively and in ways that reflect our cultural biases. Nothing more than changing my "angle of vision" was required to make it apparent that early American history and the early history of the American peoples were two different subjects and that the latter was comprehensible only by vastly widening the scope of my reading and thinking about the subject.

In revising this book for this second edition I have been informed, aided, corrected, inspired, and sustained in various degrees by Richard Beeman,

Francis Jennings, Michael McGiffert, Walter Williams, David Sweet, Neal Salisbury, and especially John Howe, as well as by countless undergraduate and graduate students at the University of California, Los Angeles, whose insights and interest have helped me pursue this work.

Gary B. Nash

"A people without history is like wind upon the buffalo grass"

Old Teton Sioux saying

INTRODUCTION

"God is English." Thus John Aylmer, a pious English clergyman, exhorted his parishioners in 1558, attempting to fill them with piety and patriotism.[1] That thought, though never so directly stated, has echoed ever since through our history books. As schoolchildren, as college students, and as presumably informed citizens, most of us have been nurtured on what has passed for the greatest success story of human history, the epic tale of how a proud, brave offshoot of the English-speaking people tried to reverse the laws of history by demonstrating what the human spirit, liberated from the shackles of tradition, myth, and oppressive authority, could do in a newly discovered corner of the earth. For most Americans, colonial history begins with Sir Walter Raleigh and John Smith and proceeds through John Winthrop and William Bradford to Jonathan Edwards and Benjamin Franklin. It ends on the eve of the Revolution with wilderness-conquering settlers preparing to pit themselves against a mother country that had grown tyrannical.

This is ethnocentric history, as has been charged frequently and vociferously in the last decade, both by liberal white historians and by those whose citizenship is American but whose ancestral roots are in Africa, Asia,

[1]Quoted in Carl Bridenbaugh, *Vexed and Troubled Englishmen, 1590–1642* (New York: Oxford University Press, Inc., 1968), p. 13.

Mexico, or the native cultures of North America. Just as Eurocentrism made it difficult for the early colonizers and explorers to believe that a continental land mass as large as North America could exist in the oceans between Europe and Asia, historians in this country have found it difficult to understand that the colonial period of our history is the story of a minority of English colonizers interacting with a majority of Iroquois, Delawares, Narragansetts, Pequots, Mahicans, Catawbas, Tuscaroras, Creeks, Cherokees, Choctaws, Ibos, Mandingos, Fulas, Yorubas, Ashantis, Germans, French, Spaniards, Swedes, Welsh, and Scots-Irish, to mention only some of the cultural strains present on the continent.

Recently, American historians, most of them educated in the post-World War II era, have tried to provide a corrective to the white-oriented, hero-worshipping history of the high school textbooks. But in the main their efforts have amounted to little more than a restocking of the pantheon of national heroes with new figures whose skin is not so pale. Thus pedestals have been erected for Crispus Attucks, the half-Indian, half-black fisherman of Boston who fell first at the Boston massacre; for Ely Parker, the Seneca general who helped the North win the Civil War and later served his friend, Ulysses Grant, when the latter attained the presidency; and for Caesar Chavez, the leader of the United Farm Workers, who has brought major gains to the Chicano agricultural workers of this country.

This kind of historical revisionism does not serve us very well. To be sure the old mythology has been altered slightly by including new figures in the national drama. But has American history been rewritten if the revisionism consists primarily of turning a monochromatic cast of characters into a polychromatic one with the story line unchanged? Vine Deloria, Jr., an outspoken Indian leader, has charged that much of the "new" history still "takes a basic 'manifest destiny' white interpretation of history and lovingly plugs a few feathers, woolly heads, and sombreros into the famous events of American history."[2] What is revisionist about a history that still measures all events of our past in terms of the values of white society, that views American history through an Anglo-American lens, and that regards Indians and Africans in the colonial period as inert masses whose fate was wholly determined by white settlers?

The pages that follow proceed from the belief that to cure the historical amnesia that has blotted out so much of our past we must reexamine American history as the interaction of many peoples from a wide range of cultural backgrounds over a period of many centuries. For the "colonial period" this means examining not only how the English and other Europeans "discovered" North America and transplanted their culture there, but also how societies that had been in North America and Africa for thousands of years were actively and intimately involved in this process. Africans were not

---

[2]Vine Deloria, Jr., *We Talk, You Listen: New Tribes, New Turf* (New York: The Macmillan Co., 1970), p. 39.

merely enslaved. Indians were not merely driven from the land. As Ralph Ellison, the black American writer, has reasoned: "Can a people . . . live and develop for over three hundred years by simply *reacting*? Are American Negroes simply the creation of white men, or have they at least helped to create themselves out of what they found around them?"[3] To include Africans and Indians in our history in this way, simply as victims of the more powerful Europeans, is hardly better than excluding them altogether. It is to render voiceless, nameless, and faceless people who powerfully affected the course of our historical development as a nation.

To break through the notion of Indians and Africans being kneaded like dough according to the whims of the invading European societies, we must abandon the notion of "primitive" and "civilized" people. There is still some utility in pointing out differences in technological achievement—the Europeans' ability to navigate across the Atlantic and their ability to process iron and thereby to manufacture guns, for example. But if we take these achievements as constituting the marks of a "superior" culture coming into contact with an "inferior" one, we will unconsciously entrap ourselves in a mental construct in which Europeans are the active agents of history and the African and Indian peoples are the passive victims.

Africans, Indians, and Europeans all had developed societies that functioned successfully in their respective environments. None thought of themselves as inferior people. "Savages we call them," wrote Benjamin Franklin more than two centuries ago, "because their Manners differ from ours, which we think the Perfection of Civility; they think the same of theirs."[4] To think of Indians simply as victims of European aggression is to bury from sight the rich and instructive story of how Narragansetts, Iroquois, Delawares, Pamunkeys, Cherokees, Creeks, and many other tribes, who had themselves been changing for centuries before Europeans touched foot on the continent, responded creatively and powerfully to the newcomers from across the ocean and in this way shaped the course of European settlement.

This book adopts a cultural approach to our early history. By this I mean that we will look at the land mass which we know as "North America" as a place where a number of different cultures converged during a particular period of history—between about 1550 and 1750, to use European methods of measuring time. In the most general terms we can define these cultural groups as Indian, African, and European, though, as we will see, this oversimplification is itself a Eurocentric device for classifying cultures. In other words, this book is not about colonial American history as usually defined, but about the history of the *peoples* of eastern North America during the two centuries that preceded the American Revolution.

Each of these three cultural groups was exceedingly diverse. In their

[3]Ralph Ellison, *Shadow and Act* (New York: New American Library, 1964), p. 301.
[4]"Remarks Concerning the Savages of North America" (1784), in *The Writings of Benjamin Franklin*, ed. Albert H. Smyth (New York: The Macmillan Co., 1907), X: 97.

cultural characteristics Iroquois were as different from Natchez as English from Egyptians; Hausas and Yorubas were as distinct as Pequots and Creeks. Nor did the subgroups in each of these cultural blocs act in concert. The French, English, and Spanish fought wars with each other, contending for power and advantage in the seventeenth and eighteenth centuries, just as Hurons and Iroquois or Creeks and Cherokees sought the upper hand in their respective regions. Our task is to discover what happened when peoples from different continents, diverse among themselves, came into contact with each other at a particular point in history. It is social and cultural *process* and *change* that we are primarily concerned with—how societies were affected and their destinies changed by the experience of contact with other cultures. Anthropologists call this process "transculturation" and historians call it "social change." Whatever the terms, we are studying a dynamic process of interaction that shaped the history of American Indians, Europeans, and Africans in North America in the seventeenth and eighteenth centuries.

It is well to remember that when we speak of "cultural groups" or "societies" we are referring to abstractions. A *society* is a group of people organized together so that their needs—the sustaining of life at the most basic level—can be met. *Culture* is a broad term that embraces all the specific characteristics of a society as they are functionally related to each other—technology; modes of dress and diet; economic, social, and political organization; religion; language; art; values; methods of child-rearing; and so forth. Simply stated, "culture" means a way of life, the framework within which any group of people—a society—comprehends the world around it. But "culture" and "society" are also terms which imply standards or norms of behavior. This is what is meant by "cultural traits" or "group behavior." To employ such terms is to run the danger of losing sight of the individual human beings, none of them exactly alike, who make up a society. Culture is a mental construct which we employ for the sake of convenience so that highly varied and complex individual behavior can be broadly classified and compared. Because we are Americans, belonging to the same nation, speaking the same language, living under the same laws, participating in the same economic and political system, does not mean that we are all alike. Otherwise there would be no generation gap, no racial tension, no political conflict. Nonetheless, taken collectively, Americans typically organize their lives differently than do people in other parts of the world. While we must be aware of the problems of a cultural approach to history, it at least provides us with a way of understanding the interaction of the great mass of individuals of widely varying backgrounds who found themselves cohabiting one part of the "New World" several centuries ago.

One other cautionary note is necessary. Though we will often speak of racial groups and racial interaction, these terms do not refer to genetically different groups of people. For half a century anthropologists poured their intellect and energy into attempts to classify all the peoples of the world, from the pygmies of Borneo to the Aleuts in Alaska, according to genetic differences. Noses were measured, cranial cavities examined, body hair noted, lips described, and hair and eye color classified in an attempt to define scientifically the various physiological types of man and then to demonstrate that these characteristics coincided with degrees of "cultural development." It should come as no surprise that this massive effort of Western white anthropologists resulted in the conclusion that the superiority of the Caucasian peoples of the world could be "scientifically" proven.

Today, genetic sciences have wiped away this half-century effort, and we are now far less convinced that significant genetic differences separate "racial groups" as previously classified by anthropologists. It is now apparent that Europeans in the New World fashioned different codes of race relations based upon their own needs and upon attitudes concerning how people should be classified and separated. "Negro" in Brazil and in the United States, for example, came to have different meanings that reflected conditions and values, not genetic differences. As Sidney Mintz wisely reminds us, "The 'reality' of race is thus as much a social as a biological reality, the inheritance of physical traits serving as the raw material for social sorting devices, by which both stigmata and privileges may be systematically allocated."[5]

Thus we gain little insight into the historical process by distinguishing cultural groups at the biological or physiological level. We are not considering genetically different groups but human populations from different parts of the world, groups of people with cultural differences. Most of all, we will be inquiring into the way these peoples, brought into contact with each other, changed over the course of several centuries—and changed in a manner that would shape the course of American history for generations to come.

[5]Sidney Mintz, "Toward an Afro-American History," *Journal of World History*, 13 (1971): 318.

1

BEFORE COLUMBUS

The history of the American peoples begins not in 1492, the date which most of our history books take as their point of departure, but more than 350 centuries before the birth of Christ. It was then that humans first discovered what much later would be called America. Thus American history can begin with some basic questions: Who were the first inhabitants of the "New World"? Where did they come from? What were they like? How had their societies changed over the millennia that preceded the arrival of Europeans.

Almost all the evidence suggesting answers to these questions comes from archaeologists who have excavated ancient sites of early life in North America. By unearthing objects of early material culture—pots, tools, ornaments, and so forth—and establishing the age of skeletal remains of the "first Americans," they have dated the arrival of man in America to about 35,000 B.C.

Anthropologists generally agree that these first inhabitants of the continent were men and women from Asia. Nomadic peoples from the inhospitable environment of Siberia, they migrated across the Bering Straits between Siberia and Alaska in search of more reliable sources of food. Geologists have determined that Siberia and Alaska were connected by a land bridge only during the two long periods when massive glaciers covered the northern latitudes, locking up most of the world's moisture and leaving the floor of the Bering Sea exposed. These two long periods were from 32,000 to

36,000 years ago and again from 20,000 to 28,000 years ago. At other times the melting glaciers raised the level of water in the Bering Straits, inundating the land bridge and thus blocking foot traffic to North America. So when Europeans found a way to reach North America in ships less than 500 years ago, they encountered a people whose ancestors had come on foot between 20,000 and 36,000 years ago.

Although most anthropologists agree that the migration was of Asian peoples, particularly from northeast Asia, the skeletal remains of these migrants also reveal non-Asian characteristics. It is probable that they represent a potpourri of different populations in Asia, Africa, and Europe, which had been mixing for thousands of years. But whatever the prior infusion of genes from peoples of other areas, these first Americans were Asiatic in geographical origin.

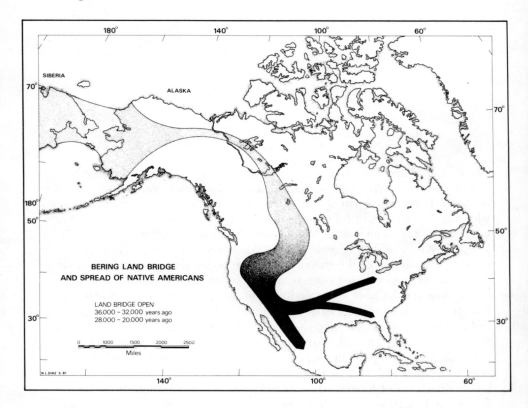

CULTURAL EVOLUTION

Once on the North American continent, these early wanderers began trekking southward and then eastward, following vegetation and game. Generations passed before these nomads reached the Pacific Northwest. The migratory movement, taking thousands of years, ultimately reached the tip of South America and the east coast of North America. American history traditionally emphasizes the "westward movement," but for hundreds of generations in North America the frontier moved southward and eastward. The distances were immense—15,000 miles from the Asian homeland to Tierra del Fuego, the southernmost limit of South America, and 6,000 miles from Siberia to the eastern edge of North America.

During the centuries spanned by these long migrations, the first Americans became widely dispersed over an immense land mass. One band in search of new food sources would split off from another. This process, repeated many times in many areas, marked the emergence of separate cultures, numbering in the hundreds on the continent. Cultural differences over a period of thousands of years became more distinct as people in different ecological regions organized their lives and related to the land in ways dictated by their natural habitats. Europeans would later indiscriminately lump together a wide variety of native cultures under a single rubric "Indian." But in reality myriad ways of life had developed by the time Europeans found their way to the very old "New World." If Europeans had been able to drop down on native villages from the Atlantic to the Pacific coasts and from Alaska to the Gulf of Mexico in 1492 they would have found "Indians" living in Kwakiutl rectangular plank houses on the Northwest Coast, in Gothic domed thatched houses in Wichita territory, in earth lodges in Pawnee prairie country, and in barrel-roofed rectangular houses in Algonkian villages in the Northeast woodlands. Different societies had developed a great variety of techniques for providing basic shelter because they lived in areas where building materials and weather conditions varied widely. The same diversity marked the ornaments and clothes they fashioned, the tools they employed, and the natural foods they gathered.

This diversity of native culture is also evident in the languages they spoke. Linguistic scholars divide Indian languages, at the point when Europeans first arrived in North America, into twelve linguistic stocks, each as distinct from the others as Semitic languages are from Indo-European languages. Within each of these twelve linguistic stocks, a great many separate languages and dialects were spoken, each as different as English from Russian. In all, about two thousand languages were spoken by the native Americans—a greater linguistic diversity than in any other part of the world.

How can we account for this striking diversity of Indian cultures? The explanation lies in an understanding of environmental conditions and the way in which bands of people adapted to their natural surroundings, molding their culture in ways that allowed for survival in their region. As elsewhere in the prehistoric world, human beings were basically seed gatherers and game hunters. They were dependent for life on a food supply over which they had little control. They struggled to master their environment but were frequently at its mercy. Thus, to take a single example, as great geologic changes occurred in North America about 8000 B.C., vast areas from Utah to the highlands of Middle America were turned from grasslands into desert. Big game and plants requiring plentiful water could not survive these changes and Indian cultures in these areas either had to move on to find new sources of food or modify their cultures to the new conditions.

Another way of understanding the process of cultural change and the proliferation of culture groups is to focus on agriculture—the domestication of plant life. Like all living organisms, human beings depend ultimately on plants to survive. For both man and animals plants are the source of life-sustaining fuel. The ultimate source of this energy is the sun. But to tap this solar energy humans and animals must rely on plants because they are the only organisms capable of producing significant amounts of organic material through the photosynthetic process. Plant food was—and still is—the strategic element in the chain of life. It nurtured humans and it sustained the animals that provided them with their second source of food.

When humans learned to control the life of plants—*agriculture* is the term we give to the process—they took a revolutionary step toward controlling their environment. It was the domestication of plants that began to emancipate human beings from oppression by the physical world, facing extinction if the food supply decreased or vanished through forces beyond their control. To learn how to harvest, plant, and nurture a seed was to assume some of nature's functions and to gain partial control over what had been uncontrollable. In the wake of this acquisition of partial control over nature's forces came vast cultural changes.

Dating the advent of agriculture in the New World is difficult, but it is estimated at about 8000 to 5000 B.C. Agriculture was also developing in Europe, Asia, and Africa during this period. Where it occurred first, a much debated subject, is not as important as the fact that the "agricultural revolution" began independently in several widely separated parts of the world.

When the production of domesticated plant food replaced the gathering of wild plant food, dramatic changes occurred in the life of societies. First, plant domestication allowed for a more sedentary as opposed to nomadic existence. Secondly, it spurred great population growth, for even putting as little as 1 percent of the land under cultivation produced enormous increases in the food supply. Thirdly, the cultivation of plants reduced the amount of time and energy needed to obtain a food supply and thus created more favorable conditions for social, political, and religious development; aesthetic expression; and technological innovation. Lastly, it led in most areas toward a sexual division of labor, with men clearing the land and engaging in the hunt for game while women planted, cultivated, and harvested crops.

Thus the agricultural revolution began to reshape the cultural outlines of native societies. Population growth and the beginnings of sedentary village life were accompanied by more complex social and political organization. Bands evolved into tribes, and tribes evolved into larger political entities.

Tasks became more specialized, and a more complex social structure took form. In some societies the religious specialist became the dominant figure, just as in other parts of the world where the agricultural revolution had occurred. The religious figure organized the common followers, directed their work, and exacted tribute as well as worship from them; in return he was counted on to protect the community from hostile forces.

When Europeans first reached the "New World," Native Americans were in widely different phases of this agricultural revolution, and thus their cultures were marked by striking differences. A glimpse at several of the societies with which Europeans first came into contact in the early sixteenth century will illustrate the point.

In the Southwest region of North America, Hopi and Zuñi cultures had been engaged in agricultural production and a sedentary village life for some 4,000 years before the Spanish first arrived in the 1540s. By about 700 to 900 A.D. these tribes had begun to abandon the ancient pit houses dug in cliffs and to construct rectangular rooms arranged in apartmentlike structures. By about 1200 A.D. "Pueblo" culture, as it was termed by the Spanish, had developed planned villages composed of large terraced buildings, each with many rooms. These apartment-house villages were often constructed on defensive sites—on ledges of massive rock, on flat summits, or on steep-sided mesas, locations that would afford the Hopis and Zuñis protection from their northern enemies, the Apaches. The largest of them, at Pueblo Bonita, contained about eight hundred rooms and may have housed as many as a thousand persons. No larger apartment-house type construction would be seen on the continent until the late nineteenth century in New York City.

By the time of Spanish arrival, the Hopis and Zuñis were also using irrigation canals, check-dams, and hillside terracing as techniques for bringing water to what had been for centuries an arid, agriculturally marginal area. At the same time, the ceramic industry became more elaborate, cotton replaced yucca fiber as the main clothing material, and basket weaving became more artistic. In its technological solution to the water problem, its artistic efforts, its agricultural practices, and its village life, Pueblo society on the eve of Spanish arrival was not radically different from peasant communities in most of the Euro-Asian world.

Far to the east of the Zuñis and Hopis, other Indian cultures were evolving. From the great plains of North America to the Atlantic tidewater region a variety of tribes belonging to three main language groups—Algonkian, Iroquoian, and Siouan—were growing in strength. Their existence in eastern North America, which has been traced as far back as 10,000 B.C., was based on a mixture of agriculture, food gathering, game hunting, and fishing. Like other tribal groups that had been touched by the agricultural revolution, they gradually adopted semi-fixed settlements and developed a trading network linking together a vast region.

Finely-crafted combs and decorative objects such as these, recovered from Hopewell moundbuilder sites, were fashioned centuries before European arrival. (Courtesy the Ohio Historical Society.)

Among the most impressive of these societies were the so-called Moundbuilders of the Ohio River Valley, who constructed gigantic sculptured earthworks in geometric designs, sometimes in the shapes of huge humans, birds, or writhing serpents. When colonial settlers first crossed the Appalachians, after almost a century and a half on the continent, they were astounded at these monumental constructions, some reaching as high as seventy feet. Their stereotype of eastern Indians as forest primitives would not allow them to believe that these were built by native peoples, so myths were invented to explain how survivors of the sunken islands of Atlantis or descendants of the Egyptians and Phoenicians had wandered far from their homelands, built these mysterious monuments, and then disappeared. Archaeologists and anthropologists now conclude that the Moundbuilders were the ancestors of the Creeks, Choctaws, and Natchez. Their culture evolved slowly over the centuries and by the advent of Christianity had developed considerable complexity. In southern Ohio alone about ten thousand mounds, used as burial sites, have been pinpointed. Another one thousand earth-walled enclosures have been excavated, including one enormous fortification with a circumference of about three and one-half miles, enclosing about one hundred acres, or the equivalent of fifty modern city blocks. Archaeologists know that the Moundbuilders participated in a vast trading network covering the eastern half of the continent because a great variety of items found in the mound tombs can be traced to other parts of the continent: large ceremonial blades chipped from obsidian from rock formations in what is now Yellowstone National Park; embossed breastplates, ornaments, and weapons fashioned from copper nuggets from the Great Lakes region; decorative objects cut from sheets of mica from the southern Appalachians; and ornaments made from shark and alligator teeth and shells from the Gulf of Mexico.

By about 500 A.D. the Moundbuilder culture was declining, perhaps because of attacks from other tribes or perhaps because of severe climatic changes that undermined agriculture. To the west another culture, based on intensive agriculture, was beginning to flourish. Its center was beneath present-day St. Louis, and it radiated out to encompass most of the Mississippi watershed from Wisconsin to Louisiana and from Oklahoma to Tennessee. Thousands of villages were included in its orbit. By about 700 A.D. this Mississippian culture, as it is known to archaeologists, began to send its influence eastward to transform the life of most of the less technologically advanced woodland tribes. Like the Moundbuilders of the Ohio region, these tribes, probably influenced by Meso-American cultures through trade and warfare, built gigantic mounds as burial and ceremonial places. The largest of them, rising in four terraces to a height of one hundred feet, has a rectangular base covering nearly fifteen acres and containing 22 million cubic feet of earth, larger at its base than that of the Great Pyramid of Egypt. Built between 900 and 1100 A.D., this huge earthwork faces the site of a palisaded Indian city which contains more than one hundred small artificial mounds marking burial sites. Spread among them was a vast settlement, called "America's first metropolis" by one archaeologist. This Mississippi Valley city, known as Cahokia, is estimated to have had a population of 35,000.

The finely crafted ornaments and tools recovered by archaeologists at Cahokia include elaborate ceramics, finely sculptured stonework, carefully embossed and engraved copper and mica sheets, and one funeral blanket fashioned from 12,000 shell beads. These artifacts indicate that Cahokia was truly an urban center, with clustered housing, markets, and specialists in toolmaking, hide dressing, potting, jewelry making, weaving, and salt making.

Several centuries before Europeans arrived on the Atlantic seaboard the Moundbuilder and Mississippian cultures had passed their prime and, for reasons not yet clear, were becoming extinct. But their influence had already passed eastward to transform the woodlands societies along the Atlantic coastal plain. Although the widely scattered and relatively fragmented tribes that were settled from Nova Scotia to Florida never matched the earlier societies of mid-continent in architectural design, earthwork sculpturing, or artistic expression, they were far from the forest primitives that Europeans pictured. Changed by contact with the Hopewell and Mississippi cultures, they added limited agriculture to the skills they had already acquired in exploiting a wide variety of natural plants for food, medicine, dyes, flavoring, and smoking. In the mixed natural economies that resulted, they utilized all the resources around them—open land, forests, streams, shore, and ocean.

For the most part, these people of the Northeast Woodlands, on whose lands European fishermen began camping to dry their codfish in the late fifteenth century, lived in villages, especially after they had been influenced by the agricultural traditions of the Ohio and Mississippi Valley societies. Locating their cornfields near fishing grounds and learning to fertilize the young plants with the heads of fish, they settled into a more sedentary pattern of life. Domed wigwams of birch and elm, copied in the early years by Europeans, were clustered together in villages which were often palisaded. The birch-bark canoes, light enough to be carried by a single man from stream to stream, gave them a means of trading and communicating over a vast territory. The extent of development among these Eastern Woodlands societies on the eve of European contact is indicated by the archaeological evidence of a Huron town in the Great Lakes region which contained more than one hundred large structures housing a total population of between four and six thousand. Settlements of this size were larger than the average European village of the sixteenth century and larger than all but a handful of European colonial towns in America a century and a half after colonization began.

Along the Atlantic seaboard, from the St. Lawrence Bay to Florida, Europeans encountered scores of local tribes of the Eastern Woodlands

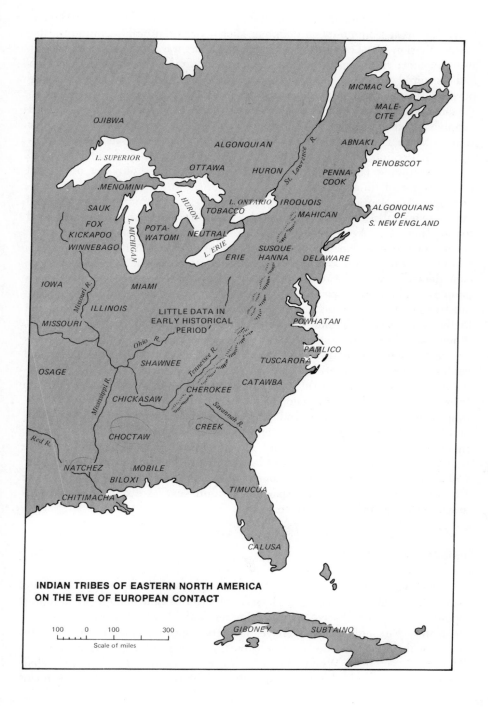

INDIAN TRIBES OF EASTERN NORTH AMERICA
ON THE EVE OF EUROPEAN CONTACT

100   0   100   300
Scale of miles

15

groups. Each maintained cultural elements peculiar to its people, although they shared in common many things such as agricultural techniques, the sexual division of labor, pottery design, social organization, and toolmaking. But the most important common denominator among them was that each had mastered the local habitat in a way that sustained life and ensured the perpetuation of their people. In the far north were Abenakis, Penobscots, Passamaquoddys, and others, who lived by the products of the sea and supplemented their diet with maple sugar and a few foodstuffs. Farther south, in what was to become New England, were Massachusets, Wampanoags, Pequots, Narragansetts, Niantics, Mahicans, and others—small tribes occupying fairly local areas and joined together only by occasional trade. South of them, in the Mid-Atlantic area, were Lenni Lenapes, Susquehannocks, Nanticokes, Pamunkeys, Shawnees, Tuscaroras, Catawbas, and others, who subsisted on a mixture of agriculture, shellfish, game, and wild foods. They, too, were settled in villages and lived a semi-sedentary life.

One of the most heavily populated regions of the Atlantic coast was the Southeast, where rich and complex cultures, some of them joined in loose confederacies, were located. Belonging to several language groups, these peoples could trace their ancestry back at lease 8,000 years. Some of the most elaborate pottery-making in the eastern half of the continent occurred in the Southeast, beginning about 2000 B.C. Hopewell burial mound techniques were also integrated into these cultures, and a few hundred years before De Soto marched through the area in the 1540s, grandiose ceremonial centers, whose construction involved earthmoving on a vast scale, had become a distinct feature of this area. In touch with Mississippian culture, the tribes of the Southeast evolved elaborate ceramic and basket-weaving techniques, long-distance trade, and in some cases, as with the Natchez, hierarchical and authoritarian social and political organizations. These people included the powerful Creeks and Yamasees in the Georgia and Alabama regions, the Apalachees in Florida and along the Gulf of Mexico, the Choctaws, Chickasaws, and Natchez of the lower Mississippi Valley, the Cherokees of the southern Appalachians, and several dozen smaller tribes scattered along the southeast coast.

PRE-CONTACT POPULATION

On the eve of European contact how many Native Americans inhabited North America? Anthropologists have argued for decades about pre-conquest population levels and have searched for methods that might provide reliable estimates. But only recently have scholars conceded that most estimates made in the past have been affected by the estimator's conception of Native American societies. When Indian culture is viewed as "savage," characterized by nomadic hunters and gatherers, it is difficult to think in terms of large populations in North America. But if these societies are seen as sedentary, agriculturalist, and complex in their social organization, then larger numbers seem possible.

Until a few years ago, the accepted population of Native Americans north of Mexico in the immediate pre-contact period was one million, an estimate made a half century ago by the greatly respected anthropologist James Mooney. This figure has now been severely challenged, primarily on the basis of research demonstrating that Mooney greatly underestimated the demographic disaster that occurred when Native Americans came into contact with European diseases. Mooney based his estimates on rough tabulations of Indians made in various areas several decades or more after initial contact. But he failed to recognize the precipitous population decline, approaching 90 percent in many regions, that occurred very rapidly when pathogens carried by Europeans infected Native Americans and spread like wildfire through their villages. It is now believed that the pre-contact population north of Mexico may have been as high as 10 million, of whom perhaps 500,000 lived along the coastal plain and in the piedmont region accessible to the early European colonizers. Even if the most liberal recent estimates are scaled down by half, we are left with the startling realization that Europeans were not coming to a "virgin wilderness," as some called it, but were invading a land which in some areas was as densely populated as their homelands.

THE IROQUOIS

Among the Eastern Woodlands cultures we may focus briefly on the Iroquois peoples in order to gain a more vivid impression of how life and society were organized in at least one Indian society. The Iroquois were to become not only one of the most populous but also the most powerful of the northeastern tribes. Their territory stretched from the Adirondack Mountains to the Great Lakes and from what is now northern New York to Pennsylvania. Five tribes—the Mohawks ("People of the Flint"), Oneidas ("People of the Stone"), Onondagas ("People of the Mountain"), Cayugas ("People at the Landing"), and Senecas ("Great Hill People")—composed what was later called by Europeans the League of the Iroquois or in Iroquoian language *Ganonsyoni*, "The Lodge Extended Lengthwise" or that which spreads far. The Iroquois confederation was a vast extension of the kinship group that characterized the northeastern woodlands pattern of family settlement and the *Ganonsyoni* embraced perhaps 10,000 people at the beginning of the seventeenth century.

The origin of the League of the Iroquois has fascinated historians for more than a century. Some argue that the Iroquois were weak and disorganized when English and French settlement began in the early 1600s and infer that the League was forged as a means of responding to the European presence. But earlier studies, which have regained acceptance, show that the League was formed in the late fifteenth century and derived from the Iroquois' own attempts to solve a difficulty that had plagued them for generations in their "loosely organized ethnic confederacy"—the problem of blood feuds and chronic small-scale violence with neighboring Algonkian tribes. Population increase in the northeast, triggered by more extensive development of agriculture, had heightened the need for hunting during this period. This brought tribes which had previously made little contact with each other into more frequent conflict situations. Iroquois villages were palisaded in the fifteenth century, a sign of intensifying conflict, and the males of the villages apparently became more and more preoccupied with war. When Jacques Cartier sailed up the St. Lawrence River in 1534 he heard from members of Algonkian tribes that their enemies, the Iroquois, had been driven from the Laurentian region several generations earlier.

Legend has it that the unification of Iroquoia was led by Hiawatha, a Mohawk sachem. About 1450 Hiawatha lost several of his relatives and in his bereavement wandered off into the wilderness. In what was probably a hallucinatory state Hiawatha had a vision in which a supernatural creature named Dekanawidah appeared and appointed him as his agent. Dekanawidah, writes Anthony Wallace, "dictated a code for the revitalization of Iroquois society," and Hiawatha carried it from village to village, recruiting disciples who regarded him as a prophet.[1] Hiawatha's visions gradually took the form of a plan for a new and strong confederacy of the loosely affiliated Iroquois villages. The key to the plan was a prohibition of blood revenge by any Iroquois against any member of the five tribes. In the event of a killing, a ritualized condolence ceremony was to perform the function of relieving bereavement depression, which before could only be satisfied by blood revenge. A council of forty-nine chiefs, delegated by the five nations and meeting at Onondaga, was granted power to make decisions for all the villages. Thus a political structure was erected to maintain intra-Iroquois peace and gradually to draw surrounding tribes into the confederacy.

As Hiawatha's preaching of the visions of Dekanawidah gained acceptance, a loose ethnic confederacy was transformed into a more cohesive political confederacy. The prohibition of intra-Iroquois blood feuds allowed population to increase, villages to gain stability, and the Iroquois to develop the political mechanisms for solving their internal problems and for presenting a more unified front in negotiating with their Algonkian neighbors for the use of hunting territories to the north or in admitting dependent tribes to settle on their territory. That all of this was occurring during the century before European arrival was fortuitous because it facilitated the development of a coordinated Iroquois policy for dealing with the European newcomers.

[1] Anthony F. C. Wallace, "The Dekanawidah Myth Analyzed as the Record of a Revitalization Movement," *Ethnohistory,* 5 (1958): 126.

In most respects this "revitalization movement" was similar to those that have sprung internally from societies in stress in other parts of the world at widely separated times. The appearance of a messianic figure who touches off a new wave of morality, codifies a new approach to life, and thus revitalizes the society in a time of troubles was a story that should have been familiar to Europeans, with their own Christian mythology. The message of Dekanawidah expressed the sense of social compact and communitarianism that would be a hallmark of Puritanism in New England several centuries later. "We bind ourselves together," said Dekanawidah "by taking hold of each other's hands so firmly and forming a circle so strong that if a tree should fall upon it, it could not shake nor break it, so that our people and grandchildren shall remain in the circle in security, peace and happiness."[2]

In the period before European arrival, then, the minimum purpose of the League of the Iroquois was to strengthen the villages, bind them together, and strengthen Iroquoia against attack from without or division from within. The philosophers of the League later expounded a maximum purpose that again found a parallel in the Puritan sense of mission: "the conversion of all mankind, so that peace and happiness should be the lot of the peoples of the whole earth," and so that all people should blend together in one human confederacy. Dekanawidah is alleged to have said, "The white roots of the Great Tree of Peace will continue to grow, advancing the Good Mind and Righteousness and Peace, moving into territories of people scattered far through the forest."[3]

If some aspects of Iroquois culture were shared by Europeans, others were different enough to convince the colonists that their society had little in common with that of the indigenous people. For example, work in the villages of Iroquoia was done communally and land was owned not by individuals but by all in common. An individual family might till their own patch of land, but it was understood that this usage of land in no way implied private ownership. Likewise, hunting was a communal enterprise. Though individual hunters differed in their ability to stalk and kill deer, the collective bounty of the hunting party was brought back to the village and divided among all. Similarly, several families occupied a long house, but the house itself, like all else in the community, was regarded as common property. For the Iroquois the concept of private ownership of property— the idea that each person should own his own land or house—would have struck at the heart of the most important theme in their value system—the cooperative or communal principle. "No hospitals [poorhouses] are needed among them," wrote a French Jesuit in 1657, "because there are neither mendicants nor paupers as long as there are any rich people among them. Their kindness, humanity and courtesy not only makes them liberal with

[2]Anthony F. C. Wallace, *The Death and Rebirth of the Seneca* (New York: Alfred A. Knopf, Inc., 1970), p. 42.

[3]*Ibid.*, p. 42.

what they have, but causes them to possess hardly anything except in common. A whole village must be without corn, before any individual can be obliged to endure privation." About the same time a Dutch missionary wrote: "The chiefs are generally the poorest among them, for instead of their receiving from the common people as among Christians, they are obliged to give to the mob."[4]

Village settlement was organized by extended kinship groups. Contrary to European practice, the Iroquois family was matrilineal, with family membership determined through the female line. Thus a typical family was composed of an old woman, her daughters with their husbands and children, and her unmarried granddaughters and grandsons. Sons and grandsons remained with their kinship group until they married; then they joined the family of their wife. Divorce was also the woman's prerogative; if she desired it, she merely set her husband's possessions outside the long house door. Thus Iroquois society was organized around the matrilineal "fireside." In turn, several matrilineal kinship groups, related by a blood connection on the mother's side, as between sisters, formed a *ohwachira*, or a group of related families. These *ohwachiras* were grouped together in clans. A village might be made up of a dozen or more clans. Villages or clans combined to create a nation (or "kinship state," as it has been called) of Senecas or Mohawks.[5]

Iroquois society was not only matrilineal in social organization, but invested the women of the community with a share of the political power. Political authority in the villages derived from the *ohwachiras* at whose heads were the senior women of the community. It was these women who named the men representing the clans at village and tribal councils and who named the forty-nine sachems or chiefs who met periodically at Onondaga as the ruling council for the confederated Five Nations. These civil chiefs were generally middle-aged or elderly men who had earlier gained fame as warriors but now "forsook the warpath for the council fire."[6] The political power of the women was not limited to the appointment of male representatives to the various ruling councils. When individual clans met, in a manner resembling the later New England town meeting, the senior women were fully in attendance, caucusing behind the circle of men who did the public speaking, lobbying with them, and giving them instructions. To an outsider it might appear that the men ruled, because it was they who did the public speaking

[4]Reuben Gold Thwaites, ed., *The Jesuit Relations and Allied Documents; Travels and Explorations of the Jesuit Missionaries in New France, 1610–1791* (Cleveland: Burrows Brothers, 1899), XLIII: 271; Johannes Megapolensis, Jr. "A Short Account of the Mohawk Indians," (1644), in J. Franklin Jameson, *Narratives of New Netherland, 1609–1664* (New York: Charles Scribner's Sons, 1909), p. 179.

[5]William N. Fenton, "The Iroquois in History," in *North American Indians in Historical Perspective*, eds. Eleanor Burke Leacock and Nancy Oestreich Lurie (New York: Random House, Inc., 1971), p. 139.

[6]*Ibid.*, p. 138.

and formally reached decisions. But their power was shared with the women. If the men of the village or tribal council moved too far from the will of the women who had appointed them, they could be removed, or "dehorned." Only so long as they satisfied the will of the women who had placed them in office were they secure in their positions.

The division of power between male and female was further extended by the role of the women in the tribal economy. While men were responsible for hunting and fishing, the women were the primary agriculturists of the village. In tending the crops they became equally important in sustaining the community. Moreover, when the men were away on hunting expeditions, which frequently required long treks away from the village over a period of weeks, women were left entirely in command of the daily life of the community. Even in military affairs women played an important role, for it was the women who supplied the moccasins and food for warring expeditions, and a decision to withhold these supplies was tantamount to vetoing a military foray. Thus power was shared between the sexes, and the European idea of male dominancy and female subordination in all things was conspicuously absent in Iroquois society.

In attempting to understand the nature of the Iroquois–European interaction it is also useful to inquire into the development of the Iroquois "personality" and patterns of individual behavior. Psychologists tell us that most of our personality traits, our way of responding to people and events, are firmly rooted in our early upbringing. The modes of child-rearing adopted by a society are important in understanding collective behavior. The Iroquois and other woodlands people, no less than Europeans, designed child-rearing practices that would impart to their children knowledge and skills necessary for survival. They also passed down an understanding of their cultural and historical heritage in order to inculcate group identity and a strong feeling of loyalty and responsibility to the group. Thus Iroquois parents taught their children how to hunt, make tools, grow crops, and identify plants and animals, just as Englishmen taught their children the rudiments of everyday survival. Similarly, both societies worked to fill their children with a sense of their heritage and instilled group loyalty through rituals and ceremonies.

One aspect of child-rearing on which European and Iroquoian cultures differed was in the attitude toward authority. In Iroquois society the autonomous individual, loyal to the group but independent and aloof, was the ideal. "Liberty in its fullest extent becomes their ruling passion," a Quaker observed in the early nineteenth century, and his description echoed the earliest Jesuit accounts of two centuries before.[7] Boys were expected to become good hunters and loyal, selfless members of the clan. They were not respected if they were dependent, submissive, or unduly cowed by authority. They were trained early in life "to think for themselves but to act

[7]Quoted in Wallace, *Death and Rebirth of the Seneca*, p. 38.

for others."[8] They were being prepared to enter an adult society which was not hierarchical, as in the European case, but in which individuals lived on a more equalitarian basis, with power more evenly distributed among men and women or old and young than in European society. Because material possessions were not prized and private ownership of property was of no importance, the competitive principle operated only insofar as the prestige of a hunter or warrior was concerned. The pursuit of worldly goods at the expense of a fellow clansman would have gained an Iroquois male only scorn in his village, and deference to fellow villagers would have been out of place. In European society, where material possessions were greatly coveted and where the social structure made elaborate distinctions between rich and poor, godly and ungodly, literate and nonliterate, male and female, and politically enfranchised and unenfranchised, far more attention was given to maintaining proper respect for authority. Submission to authority and the maintenance of hierachical lines became principles around which child rearing was organized.

In raising children Iroquois parents were more permissive than their European counterparts. They did not believe in harsh physical punishment. They encouraged their young to imitate adult behavior and were tolerant of fumbling early attempts. In the first months of a baby's life the mother nursed and protected the child and at the same time hardened it by baths in cold water. Weaning was not ordinarily begun until the age of three or four. Rather than beginning strict regimens of toilet training at an early age the child was allowed to proceed at its own pace in achieving control over natural functions. Early interest in the anatomy of the body and in sexual experimentation was accepted as normal. All this was in sharp contrast to European child-rearing techniques, which stressed the importance of accustoming the child to authority from an early age and backed this up by taking the child from the breast at about two years, by toilet training at an early age, by making frequent use of physical punishment, by condemning early sexual curiosity, and by emphasizing obedience and respect for authority as central virtues. Iroquois parents would have regarded as misguided the advice of John Robinson, the Pilgrims' pastor, to the parents of his congregation: "And surely there is in all children . . . a stubbornness, and stoutness of mind arising from natural pride, which must, in the first place, be broken and beaten down; that so the foundation of their education being laid in humility and tractableness, other virtues may, in their time, be built thereon. . . . For the beating, and keeping down of this stubbornness parents must provide carefully . . . that the children's wills and willfulness be restrained and repressed. . . . Children should not know, if it could be kept from them, that they have a will of their own, but in their parents' keeping."[9]

[8]Ibid., p. 34.

[9]Quoted in John Demos, A Little Commonwealth: Family Life in Plymouth Colony (New York: Oxford University Press, Inc., 1970), pp. 134–35.

The approach to authority also differed for adult members of the society. Iroquois society, like most Indian societies of North America, had little of the complicated machinery that Europeans developed to direct and control the lives of its members. No laws and ordinances, sheriffs and constables, judges and juries, or courts or jails—the apparatus of authority in European societies—were to be found in the Northeast Woodlands prior to European arrival. Yet boundaries of acceptable behavior were firmly set. Though priding themselves on the autonomous individual, the Iroquois maintained a strict sense of right and wrong. Rather than relying on formal instruments of authority, however, they governed behavior by inculcating a strong sense of tradition and attachment to the group through communally performed rituals. It was this sense of duty, bolstered by a fear of gossip and a strongly held belief in the power of evil spirits to punish wrongdoers, that curbed antisocial behavior among the Iroquois. In European society a crime or unethical act might be dealt with by investigation, arrest, prosecution, sentencing, and imprisonment, involving at various steps along the way the authority of a number of people and institutional devices. In Indian society a simpler system operated to transform the aberrant individual. He who stole another's food or showed cowardice in war was "shamed" by his people and ostracized from their company until he had atoned for his actions and demonstrated that he had morally purified himself.

The Iroquois and other Woodlands societies also employed a form of psychotherapy to resolve personal and group problems. Believing that dreams were "the language of the soul," they paid close attention to them and "deliberately sought the answers to many of life's problems in them."[10] More than two centuries before Freud's development of psychoanalytic theory, northern Indian cultures recognized that the mind had both conscious and unconscious levels; that unconscious desires and fears were often expressed symbolically in dreams; that these desires and anxieties, if unfulfilled or unresolved, could cause psychic and psychosomatic illness; and that those suffering from nightmares or haunting dreams could often find relief by recounting their dreams to a group, whose members attempted to help the individual find the meaning of and the cure for the subconscious problem.

An incredulous Jesuit priest, Father Ragueneau, described this theory of dreams as he witnessed it in Huron villages in 1649. The Indians, he reported, believed that

> in addition to the desires which we generally have that are free, or at least voluntary in us, . . . our souls have other desires, which are, as it were, inborn and concealed. These, they say, come from the depths of the soul, not through any knowledge, but by means of a certain blind transporting of the soul to certain objects; these transports might in the language of philosophy be called *Desideria innata*, to distinguish them from the former, which are called *De-*

---

[10]Bruce G. Trigger, *The Children of Aataentsic: A History of the Huron People to 1660* (2 vols.; Montreal and London: McGill-Queen's University Press, 1976), I, 81.

sideria Elicita. Now they believe that our soul makes these natural desires known by means of dreams, which are its language. Accordingly, when these desires are accomplished, it is satisfied; but, on the contrary, if it be not granted what it desires, it becomes angry, and not only does not give its body the good and the happiness that it wished to procure for it, but often it also revolts against the body, causing various diseases, and even death. . . . In consequence of these erroneous ideas, most of the Hurons are very careful to note their dreams, and to provide the soul with what it has pictured to them during their sleep. If, for instance, they have seen a javelin in a dream, they try to get it; if they have dreamed that they gave a feast, they will give one on awakening, if they have the wherewithal; and so on with other things. And they call this *Ondinnonk*—a secret desire of the soul manifested by a dream.[11]

It would be mistaken to romanticize Iroquois culture or to judge it superior to the culture of the European invader. To do so would only be to invoke the same categories of "superior" and "inferior" that Europeans used to justify the violence they unleashed when they arrived in the New World and to forget that exercises in ranking cultures depend almost entirely on the criteria employed. Instead of grading cultures, almost always an exercise of expansionist societies attempting to subjugate other people, we must understand that Iroquois society, like English or French society, was a total social system that had evolved over a long period of time before Europeans arrived. In dynamic relationship with their environment and with neighboring peoples, the Iroquois had become more populous, more sedentary in their mode of settlement, more skilled in agricultural techniques, more elaborate in their art forms. They had also emerged as one of the strongest, most politically unified, and militaristic societies in the Northeast Woodlands. Even after the formation of the League of the Iroquois, which had as one of its objectives the abatement of intertribal warfare, an impressive amount of fighting seems to have occurred between the Five Nations and surrounding Algonkian peoples. Many of these conflicts involved a quest for glory and some of them may have been initiated to test the newly forged alliance of the five tribes against lesser tribes which could be brought under Iroquoian domination. Whatever the reasons, the Iroquois on the eve of European arrival were feared and sometimes hated by their neighbors for their skill and cruelty in warfare.

Of course the Iroquois were not the only Indian tribes that Europeans encountered in the early seventeenth century. Along the Atlantic seaboard, from the St. Lawrence Bay to Florida, the English, Spanish, Dutch, and French met a vast number of tribal groups. These groups varied in population and power, but even in areas of low population density, dynamic cultures had evolved. In several regions intertribal conflict had resulted in political unifications or confederacies with which Europeans would have to reckon. As was to become evident, even small numbers of Indians could present a considerable problem for those intent on occupying their land.

[11]Quoted in Anthony F. C. Wallace, "Dreams and the Wishes of the Soul: A Type of Psychoanalytic Theory among the Seventeenth-Century Iroquois," *American Anthropologist*, 60 (1958): 236.

THE NATIVE AMERICAN WORLD VIEW

While Native American and European cultures were not nearly so different as the concepts of "savagery" and "civilization" imply, societies on the eastern and western sides of the Atlantic had developed different systems of values in the centuries that preceded contact. Underlying the physical confrontations that would take place when European and Native American met were incompatible ways of looking at the world. These latent conflicts can be seen in contrasting European and Indian views of man's relationship to his environment, the concept of property, and personal identity.

In the European view the natural world was a resource for man to use. "Subdue the earth," it was said in Genesis, "and have dominion over every living thing that moves on the earth." The cosmos was still ruled by God, of course, and supernatural forces, manifesting themselves in earthquakes, hurricanes, drought, and flood, could not be controlled by man. But a scientific revolution was under way in the early modern period, which gave humans more confidence that they could comprehend the natural world—and thus eventually control it. For Europeans the secular and the sacred were distinct, and man's relationship to his natural environment fell into the secular sphere.

In the Indian ethos no such separation of secular and sacred existed. Every part of the natural world was sacred, for Native Americans believed the world was inhabited by a great variety of "beings," each possessing spiritual power and all linked together to form a sacred whole. "Plants, animals, rocks, and stars," explains Murray Wax, "are thus seen not as objects governed by laws of nature but as 'fellows' with whom the individual or band may have a more or less advantageous relationship."[12] Consequently, if one offended the land by stripping it of its cover, the spiritual power in the land—called "manitou" by some woodlands tribes—would strike back. If one overfished or destroyed game beyond one's needs, the spiritual power inhering in fish and animals would take revenge because humans had broken the mutual trust and reciprocity that governed relations between all beings—human and nonhuman. To exploit the land or to treat with disrespect any part of the natural world was to cut oneself off from the spiritual power dwelling in all things and "was thus equivalent to repudiating the vital force in Nature."[13]

Because Europeans regarded the land as a resource to be exploited for man's gain it was easier to regard it as a commodity to be privately held. Private ownership of property became one of the fundamental bases upon which European culture rested. Fences became the symbols of exclusively

[12]"Religion and Magic," in *Introduction to Cultural Anthropology: Essays in the Scope and Method of the Science of Man,* James A. Clifton, ed. (Boston: Houghton Mifflin Company, 1968), p. 235.

[13]Calvin Martin, *Keepers of the Game: Indian-Animal Relationships and the Fur Trade* (Berkeley and Los Angeles: University of California Press, 1978), p. 34.

held property, inheritance became the mechanism for transmitting these "assets" from one generation to another within the same family, and courts provided the institutional apparatus for settling property disputes. In a largely agricultural society property became the basis of political power. In fact, political rights in England derived from the ownership of a specified quantity of land. In addition, the social structure was largely defined by the distribution of property, with those possessing great quantities of it standing at the apex of the social pyramid and the mass of propertyless individuals forming the broad base.

In the Indian world this view of land as a privately held asset was incomprehensible. Tribes recognized territorial boundaries, but within these limits the land was held in common. Land was not a commodity but a part of nature that was entrusted to the living by the Creator. John Heckewelder, a Moravian missionary who lived with the Delawares in the eighteenth century, explained that they believed the Creator "made the Earth and all that it contains for the common good of mankind; when he stocked the country that he gave them with plenty of game, it was not for the benefit of a few, but of all: Every thing was given in common to the sons of men. Whatever liveth on the land, whatsoever groweth out of the earth, and all that is in the rivers and waters . . . was given jointly to all and every one is entitled to his share. From this principle hospitality flows as from its source."[14] Thus, land was a gift of the Creator, to be used with care, and was not for the exclusive possession of particular human beings.

In the area of personal identity Indian and European values also differed sharply. Europeans were acquisitive, competitive, and over a long period of time had been enhancing the role of the individual. Wider choices and greater opportunities for the individual to improve his status—by industriousness, valor, or even personal sacrifice leading to martyrdom—were regarded as desirable. Personal ambition, in fact, played a large role in the migration of Europeans across the Atlantic in the sixteenth and seventeenth centuries. In contrast, the cultural traditions of Native Americans emphasized the collectivity rather than the individual. Because land and other natural resources were held in common and society was far less hierarchical than in Europe the accumulative spirit and personal ambition were inappropriate. "In contrast to the exalted position of man in Judeo-Christian tradition," writes Calvin Martin, the Native American "cosmology conferred upon the Indian a rather humble stature."[15] Hence, individualism was more likely to lead to ostracism than admiration in Indian communities.

[14]John Heckewelder, *Account of the History, Manners, and Customs of the Indian Nations* . . . (Philadelphia: American Philosophical Society, 1819), p. 85, reprinted in Wilcomb Washburn, *The Indian and the White Man* (Garden City, N.Y.: Doubleday & Company, Inc., 1964), p. 63.

[15]Martin, *Keepers of the Game*, p. 74.

In spite of these differences it was not inevitable that the confrontation of European colonizers and Native Americans should lead to mortal combat. Inevitability is not a satisfactory explanation for any human event because it implies that man's destiny is beyond human control and thus relieves individuals and societies of responsibility for their actions. Inevitability, in fact, is a winner's rationalization for historical clashes; it is a mode of explanation rarely advanced by the losing side. And we shall see that the clash of cultures took many forms in the New World, with nothing predetermined but with everything dependent upon the complex interweaving of many factors in particular places and at particular times.

2

EUROPEANS REACH
THE AMERICAS

From the fifteenth to the twentieth centuries one of the dominant themes of history has been the militant expansion of European peoples and European culture into other continents. Only in the last half century has this process been reversed, as colonized people have struggled to regain their autonomy through wars of national and cultural liberation. For Western historians this global expansion has been closely equated with the spread of "civilization," the carrying of an allegedly superior European culture to so-called "primitive" areas of the world. As various cultures were engulfed by colonizing Europeans, the notion grew that "progress," in the form of the growing outreach of European civilization, was being served.

Yet the cultural superiority of Europeans at the time they reached the western hemisphere is far from clear in retrospect. The very notion of "superior" and "inferior" cultures is a construct of imperialist nations, and it is now time to abandon this concept in our study of history. More to the point is that it was the "New World," placed at the service of colonizing Europeans, that catapulted Europe out of a prolonged period of stagnation and regression. For more than a century before the Atlantic Ocean was turned into a familiar body of water Europe had suffered population decline because of epidemic disease and prolonged wars; economic lassitude as reflected by withering production and trade; and cultural inertia as evident in the absence of progress in the natural sciences, the decay of the universities, and the crumbling of the Holy Roman Empire. Islamic culture was the most dynamic force in Europe in the fourteenth and fifteenth centuries, expanding deep into Africa and edging in upon Europe from the East. Western Europe before the "age of discovery" was characterized by pessimism, cynicism, and despair. It was the resources of Africa, Asia, and the Americas—precious metals, vital new foodstuffs such as maize and potatoes, land, and people—that provided a basis for a commercial revival and launched an epoch of European expansion and development. In attempting to find a water route to the oldest parts of the Old World, Columbus stumbled upon what was a new world only in the European imagination. But this fortuitous error sparked the imagination of Europeans—one of their most valuable qualities—and touched off a revival of enterprise and overseas expansion that lasted for more than four hundred years.

SPANISH AND PORTUGUESE EXPANSION INTO THE NEW WORLD

Columbus thought he had reached India when he made a landfall on the island of Hispaniola in 1492. This was precisely his quest—to find an all-water route to the Orient so that European traders, who trafficked in the indispensable spices that made European food palatable, could avoid paying tribute to the Middle–Eastern middlemen who skimmed the profits off overland trading ventures. It is customary to focus on the navigational and geographical importance of Columbus's voyages, but his sea wanderings would have been written off as an expensive failure, once it was realized that he had not found the illusive water route to India, had it not been for the discovery of gold on Hispaniola in 1493. Without their gold and other precious minerals, the new-found lands would have been only obstacles on the water road to the Far East.

But, while his discovery was accidental, Columbus was still an archetypical figure of European expansion. Thoroughly medieval in his patterns of thought, he was also ambitious, adventuresome, ready to translate an idea, however ridiculed, into action, and audacious enough to maintain his course even when his sailors were ready to mutiny in despair of ever seeing dry land again. Capitalizing on great advances in marine technology and on the Portuguese oceanic explorations of the previous century, Columbus, like the Vikings five hundred years before him, discovered that the ocean west of Europe had its limits. He amply possessed the European quality of arrogance that in the centuries ahead was to prove so valuable in colonization—and so destructive of human life.

Once gold and silver were found, a wholesale rush of enterprising young men from the lesser nobility in Spain began the transatlantic adventure. By the 1550s they had explored, conquered, and claimed for their Queen the Isthmus of Panama, Mexico, most of South America except Brazil and the far southern plains, and the southerly reaches of North America from California on the Pacific Coast to the Floridas on the Atlantic Coast. Led by military figures such as Cortez, Pizarro, and Coronado, they established the authority of Spain and the Catholic Church over an area which dwarfed their homeland in size and population. By the end of the sixteenth century the Spanish had conquered the major centers of native population, established a thriving transatlantic trade, were carrying African slaves by the thousands to their colonies, and were supervising the extraction of gold and silver in fabulous quantities from the lands under their domination.

From the 1490s to the 1590s, the colonization of the Americas was dominated by Spain. Her only rival was Portugal, whose energies first went into colonizing the Atlantic islands—Azores, Madieras, and Canaries—that lay off the coast of Portugal and northwest Africa, and establishing centers of trade on the east and west African coasts. Not until the 1550s did Portugal stake out a claim in Brazil, destined to become the center of her New World activities. By the end of the century sugar production claimed the labor of most of some 25,000 Portuguese colonists and perhaps an equal number of African slaves in Brazil.

Closely tied to the economic strivings of Europe's emerging nation-states were the religious goals of colonization. Both Catholics and Protestants looked upon the occupation of the New World, at least in part, as a religious crusade. Spain had been involved for centuries in conflict with the "infidel" Moors; in fact, it was only in the same year that Columbus reached Hispaniola that Christian Spain completed the expulsion of the Moors. Conquest of the New World fulfilled not only national dreams of glory but also offered the opportunity to convert a continent filled with "heathen" people to Christianity.

The religious motive was complicated by the Catholic–Protestant division within Christianity. For Europeans heathens were heathens; but whether their conversion would be to Catholicism or to Protestantism depended upon which European nation achieved domination over them. That Christians could be so bitterly divided, engaging in religious wars for several centuries and inflicting mass destruction in the name of God, may seem puzzling to those raised in a secular society. But the intensity of this conflict within Christian Europe becomes more understandable when we remember that for men and women of this age—as in the centuries before—religion was the organizing principle of life. Man's mastery of the environment was slight since science and technology had not yet proceeded far enough to control the natural forces. Thus people attributed to supernatural forces what could not be understood or governed. Faith, not reason, dominated life, and thus people of different faiths found themselves passionately committed to defending their ideology and attacking those with variant views.

These "isms"—Protestantism and Catholicism—can be understood, then, as prescribed codes of living, as ways of ordering and imparting meaning to one's world and one's place in it. Such ideological commitments did not differ markedly from the "isms" of today—communism, socialism, democracy—in terms of their power to compel allegiance. These too are systems of values and beliefs, ways of organizing societies. They, too, give meaning to what we do and provide us with a sense of identity. Twentieth-century wars, fought with far greater ferocity and technological ruthlessness than the religious wars of the early modern era, provide a way of understanding why Christians and Moslems or Catholics and Protestants would fight so relentlessly to spread their particular faith to the native inhabitants of the lands they were invading.

ENGLISH ENTRY INTO THE COLONIAL RACE

By the time England awoke to the promise of the New World, the two Iberian powers were firmly entrenched there. England was the most backward of the European nations facing the Atlantic in exploring and colonizing the Americas. Only the voyages of John Cabot (who was in reality the Genoa-born Giovanni Caboto) gave England any title to a place in the New World sweepstakes. Moreover, Cabot's voyages in the 1490s were never followed up. Even the famous expeditions of John Hawkins in the 1560s must be dismissed as unimportant in the expansion of Europe into America because Hawkins was primarily involved in piracy—raiding Spanish trade in the Caribbean with the backing of Catholic-hating English merchants, who hoped to induce their government to sponsor their occasional attempts to challenge the New World monopoly of Spain and Portugal. England's only significant contact with North America had been in connection with the Newfoundland fisheries where, since the 1520s, English fishing fleets had competed with the French, Portuguese, and Spanish for the valuable cod—a vital protein source in the diet of most Europeans.

But England too sought New World colonies, for colonies provided new markets, new sources of raw materials, and, if they contained gold and silver, added to the total supply of specie by which the strength of nations was then measured. England, at the end of the sixteenth century, was understandably eager to establish a foothold on the North American coast, for Spain and Portugal already dominated the South American continent and parts of the Caribbean, and had laid claim to the southern portions of the North American landmass as well. If the English did not move soon, it would be too late. By the same token, Spain was intent upon resisting English incursions into her sphere of influence. As Englishmen took the first tentative steps toward empire, the Spanish planned seaborne attacks on any English settlement that might dare to exist on the Atlantic coast of North

America. The first known map of the tiny English settlement at Jamestown, Virginia, drawn by an Irish Catholic sailor on an English ship that delivered colonists to the Chesapeake settlement, was smuggled back to Spain. It was highly prized because it provided the necessary information for a surprise attack on this first English foothold on the North American coast.

English entry into the colonial race had its origins not only in the desire to share in the exploitation of New World resources but also in the ideological war that raged in Europe throughout the last half of the sixteenth century. All the western European powers facing the Atlantic with the exception of the Scandinavian countries were involved in this struggle between those who professed Catholicism and those who adhered to Protestantism. This national and religious conflict was a continuation of issues and interests first raised in the Reformation and Counter–Reformation.

During much of the sixteenth century England swayed back and forth between religious ideologies, living first under the Protestant regimes of Henry VIII and his sickly son, Edward VI, and then under the Catholic reign of his daughter Mary Tudor, who had married Philip II of Spain—the chief pillar of Catholic power in Europe. When Mary Tudor died and Henry's second daughter, Elizabeth, took the throne in 1558, England returned to Protestantism. Like her father, Elizabeth favored Protestantism primarily as an expression of national independence. First and foremost, she meant to create the conditions for national growth and prosperity. Although in economic matters she enjoyed some success, the religious question always hung above her head. Philip II of Spain, her brother-in-law, regarded her as a Protestant heretic and plotted against her incessantly.

In 1587 the smoldering conflict between Catholic Spain and Protestant England broke into open conflict. England braced itself for the seaborne attack that was expected from the Spanish armada, regarded as the most powerful navy in the world. The battle that ensued is known simply as the Spanish Armada. In the spring of 1588 the Spanish fleet set sail for England, reaching its destination late in July. For two weeks a battle raged at sea. To the amazement of most of Europe the English, aided by the Dutch, prevailed. The Spanish defeat did not establish English superiority at sea or bring England any overseas territory in recognition of her victory. It did not even propel England into the overseas colonial race. But it did prevent a crushing Catholic victory in Europe and temporarily ended Spanish dreams of European hegemony. The Armada brought a temporary stalemate in the wars of religion and made clear for a generation—until 1618, when the beginning of the Thirty Years War again threw Europe into open religious conflict—that religious uniformity was not to be imposed by force. England was free to pursue her own destiny, free from the domination of other European powers.

With the way clear for overseas expansion, the "westward fever" began to catch hold in England at the end of the sixteenth century. One unsuccessful and inconsequential effort had already been made—the planting of a small settlement on Roanoke Island, off the coast of North Carolina, in the 1580s. But after the Armada the English gentry and merchants began to sense the profits that beckoned from the New World. Their capital and experience would be indispensable in the decades ahead.

Urging their countrymen on were two Richard Hakluyts, uncle and nephew. In the last quarter of the sixteenth century they devoted themselves to explaining the advantages of settling the remote regions on the other side of the Atlantic. In a number of pamphlets they set forth the arguments in favor of colonization. Glory, profit, and adventure awaited everybody: for the nobility at court colonization promised an empire in the New World and a source of new baronies, fiefdoms, and feudal estates; for the merchant there were new markets and a landmass filled with exotic produce that could be marketed at home; for the clergymen there awaited a continent filled with "savages" to be converted for the greater glory of Christ; for the commoner there beckoned a field of adventure and limitless economic opportunity; for the impoverished laborer there was the prospect of starting life anew amidst boundless land and opportunity. The Hakluyts publicized the idea that the time was ripe for planting English stock across the Atlantic. Shakespeare contributed his bit to the national excitement by writing a play, *The Tempest*, about those who crossed the ocean to further the greatness of their country.

English participation in the age of exploration and colonization began with a generation of adventurous seadogs and gentlemen such as Walter Raleigh, Francis Drake, Humphrey Gilbert, and Richard Grenville. With limited capital and minimal support from the Crown, they attempted much and ended mostly in failure. We give their exploits much room in our history books because they were the first to try. But England could not become a serious colonial power in the New World until the government, as in Spain and Portugal, gave active support to colonizing schemes, and, more important, until the merchant community and the rising middle class in England began plowing investment capital into overseas colonizing experiments. Thus all the early efforts came to little or nothing: the voyages of Hawkins in the 1560s on the Spanish Main; the Roanoke voyages of 1585 to 1588, which ended in failure; the Sagadahoc settlement on the coast of Maine in 1607, which lasted only a year; and even the settlement of Jamestown, Virginia, in 1607, which limped along for a generation before securing a viable economy.

In these feeble first efforts the leaders of English colonization lacked the principal ingredients of the successful Spanish and Portuguese colonial efforts. They had little backing in the form of subsidies, ships, and naval protection from the national government. They had minimal support from the Church of England in contrast to the extensive participation of the Catholic Church in the Spanish and Portuguese colonies. And they lacked the participation of citizen investors—a broad mass of middle- and upper-class people who would risk money in colonizing experiments. As long as English colonization rested in the hands of the English nobility—restless sons of aristocrats and favored courtiers of the Crown—nothing much was achieved. It took far more than outfitting a few ships and gathering up a few hundred adventurous or desperate individuals to surmount the obstacles inherent in overseas colonization. It was one thing to reach the New World in small wooden ships and land several hundred men with supplies for several months; but it was quite another to organize these people into a social and economic organization that could survive in a frightening new environment, much less successfully exploit the resources locked in the earth.

What was especially needed in launching English colonization was the wealth and support of the rising middle class of English society. Such men, who at the beginning of the Tudor period had been relatively insignificant, had been making enormous strides forward in the second half of the sixteenth century. This redistribution of economic and political power, which historians call the "rise of the gentry," was indispensably important to the successful settlement of North America. The colonization movement would probably never have succeeded in the hands of the English nobility unsupported by this much broader segment of English society. This support came grudgingly in the first half of the seventeenth century, and even then English investors were far more drawn to the quick profits of sugar cultivation in the West Indies than to the uncertainties of mixed farming, lumbering, and fishing on the North American mainland.

To the difficulties of generating adequate financial and political support was added the reality that whether they focused on the North American continent or the Caribbean islands, English colonizers squarely confronted rival claims of other European nations—claims that in many cases were backed up by actual occupation of territory. By the early seventeenth century Portugal and Spain already had about 150,000 colonists in their overseas possessions, and although most of them were in Peru and Mexico, where major population centers had been established at Potosi, Mexico City, and Cartagena, they had also planted frontier outposts in southwestern North America and at various points along the Atlantic coast from Florida to the Chesapeake Bay. Spanish claims extended as far north as Newfoundland. The English, as they approached the North American mainland, were well aware of the Spanish presence. Nothing testified so poignantly to this as the fact that after initial settlements were planted the English built their forts facing the sea—to fend off Spanish attacks—rather than facing inland where Indian danger lay. It was the prudent work of those who knew they were engaged in semi-piratical intrusions on the established colonies of Spain.

Englishmen were also approaching a continent occupied by Frenchmen. Since 1524, when Giovanni da Verrazzano had explored the eastern edge of North America, the French had dreamed of finding cities of gold and the

Northwest Passage to China. The French could settle, however, only where the Spanish had no use for the land. Thus, after abortive attempts to plant colonies in Florida and Brazil, which were wiped from the map by the Spanish and Portuguese, the French contented themselves with developing the northerly expanses of Canada. French fishermen had been working the coasts of Newfoundland and Nova Scotia since the early sixteenth century and the development of a sporadic fur trade with the Indians of the area began in 1534 with Cartier's exploration of the gulf of St. Lawrence. These efforts convinced the French that the St. Lawrence River area could be profitable, even if the climate was inhospitable. Only the St. Lawrence and Hudson rivers provided access by water into the interior of the northern parts of the continent and in 1603 the French wisely chose to plant their first settlements near the mouth of the St. Lawrence. They thus pushed forward their quest for another form of New World gold—the skins of fur-bearing animals.

Englishmen approaching the North America coast, therefore, had to reckon with Spain and France, whose prior efforts and established claims dictated that the English look to the middle part of the Atlantic seaboard for a toehold on the continent. But it was another people, the indigenous inhabitants of the land, that claimed English attention most forcefully. What did men like Gilbert and Raleigh know about the native occupiers of the land as they approached the forbidding coast of North America in the 1580s? How would they be received by these people whom Columbus, thinking he had reached India, mistakenly called Indians? How would Englishmen obtain the use or possession of land these Indians occupied? And how were ideas about the nature of Indian peoples influenced by the thorny question of obtaining sovereignty over the land?

English Images of the Native Americans

We can be sure that the first English colonizers experienced the apprehensions that regardless of time or place fill the minds of those who are attempting to penetrate the unknown. But they were far from uninformed about the Indian people of the New World. Beginning with Columbus's description of the New World, published in several European capitals in 1493 and 1494, a mass of reports, stories, and promotional accounts had been circulating among sailors, merchants, geographers, politicians, and churchmen who were participating in the early voyages of discovery, trade, and settlement. These became the basis for an understanding of the New World by any adventurer approaching the eastern edge of land in the West Atlantic Ocean.

From this considerable literature, the early colonists were likely to have derived a split image of the natives of North America. On the one hand they had reason to believe that the Indians were a gentle people who would be receptive to those who came not to harm them but to live and trade with them. Columbus had written of the "great amity towards us" that he encountered in San Salvador in 1492 and described the Arawak Indians there as "a loving people without covetousness," who "were greatly pleased and became so entirely our friends that it was a wonder to see." The Indians "brought us parrots and cotton thread in balls, and spears and many other things, and we exchanged for them other things, such as small glass beads and hawks' bells, which we gave to them."[1] Verrazzano, the first European to navigate the eastern edge of the continent, wrote with similar optimism from the Bay of New York in 1524. The natives were graceful of limb, tawny colored, with black alert eyes, and "dressed in birds' feathers of various colors, and they came toward us joyfully, uttering loud cries of wonderment, and showing us the safest place to beach the boat."[2]

From this time on, accounts of natives of the New World included many such enthusiastic descriptions of native people and their eagerness to receive European explorers and settlers. This positive side of the image of the Indians not only reflected the friendly reception which Europeans apparently received in Newfoundland, parts of Florida, and elsewhere in the Caribbean and South America, but also represented a part of the vision of the New World as an earthly paradise—a Garden of Eden where war-torn, impoverished Europeans could find a new life amidst nature's bounty. That Columbus thought he had found the Gihon, one of the Biblical rivers flowing from Eden, when he reached the Orinoco River in 1498 is vivid testimony to this strain in the European mentality.

Another reason existed for drawing a favorable image of the North American natives. The English, like other European colonizers, hoped that trade with native peoples would become a major source of profit on the other side of the Atlantic and in other ways needed the aid of indigenous people. The early English voyages were not primarily intended for the purpose of large-scale settlement and agricultural production. Trade with the Indians, the search for gold and silver, and discovery of the Northwest Passage were the principal goals. Land had been a key element for the Spanish and Portuguese colonizers in the New World. But land conquest did not figure importantly in the English mind in the early stages of colonizing activity. The intention, rather, was to establish well-fortified trading posts at the heads of rivers where the natives would come to trade. In this mercantile approach to overseas adventuring the English promoters of the late sixteenth and early seventeenth centuries were influenced by earlier English participation in the Levantine and Muscovy trade where English merchants had operated profitably for half a century, not invading the land of foreign

[1]Quoted in Wilcomb E. Washburn, ed., *The Indian and the White Man* (Garden City, N.Y.: Doubleday & Co., Inc., 1964), p. 4.

[2]Lawrence C. Wroth, *The Voyages of Giovanni da Verrazzano, 1524–1528* (New Haven: Yale University Press, 1970), p. 137.

peoples and driving them from it, but "trafficking" among them without challenging their possession of the land or attempting to subjugate them. So a special incentive existed for seeing the Indian as something more than a "savage." It was only a friendly Indian who could be a trading Indian. If trade was the key to overseas development, then it is not surprising that English promoters would suggest that the Indian might be receptive and generous—a person who could be wooed and won to the advantages of trade.

However, a counterimage of the Indian was also firmly lodged in the minds of Englishmen approaching the coast of North America. This negative picture of the native imagined a savage, hostile, beastlike person. Such a depiction was firmly established in the Spanish and French literature of colonization. As early as the first decade of the sixteenth century Sebastian Cabot had paraded in England three Eskimos taken captive on his voyage to the Arctic in 1502. A contemporary described the natives as flesh-eating, primitive specimens, who "spake such speech that no man coulde understand them, and in their demeanour like to bruite beasts."[3] A flood of pamphlets in the second half of the sixteenth century described the natives in terms that could have caused little optimism concerning the reception Europeans would receive. These accounts were filled with portraits of the Indians as crafty, brutal, loathsome half-men whose cannibalistic instincts were revealed, as one pamphleteer wrote in 1578, by the fact that "there is no flesh or fishe, which they finde dead, (smell it never so filthily) but they will eate it, as they finde it, without any other dressing [cooking]."[4] Other accounts limned the natives as bestial, living in sexual abandon, and in general moved entirely by passion rather than reason.

Apart from tales of travel and adventure in the New World, the English had a far more striking reason for imagining that all would not be friendship and amiable trading when they encountered the native occupants of the North American coast. For years they had been reading accounts of the Spanish experience with Indian peoples in Mexico and Peru—and the story was not a pretty one. Chief among these Spanish accounts was the work of the Dominican friar Bartholomé de Las Casas, whose *Brevissima Relacion de la Destruccion de las Indias* was translated into English and published in 1583 as *The Spanish Colonie, or Brief Chronicle of the Actes and Gestes of the Spaniards in the West Indies*. On the one hand, Englishmen could delight in Las Casas's gory descriptions of Spanish cruelty and genocide, for such stories confirmed all the worst things that the Protestant English believed about the Catholic Spaniards with whom they were about to go to

---

[3]Richard Hakluyt, *Divers Voyages touching the discoveries of America, and the Ilands adjacent unto the Same* (1582), Hakluyt Society *Publications*, 1st Ser., 7 (London: The Hakluyt Society, 1850): 23.

[4]Vilhjalmur Stefansson, ed., *The Three Voyages of Martin Frobisher* (London: The Argonaut Press, 1938), 2: 23.

war. The Hakluyts eagerly contributed to the "Black Legend" concerning the Spanish colonizers, labeling them "hell-hounds and wolves."

Such accounts, useful in fueling anti-Spanish and anti-Catholic prejudices, also suggested that when Europeans met "primitive" people, slaughter was inevitable. Moreover, Las Casas was rebutted by a host of Spanish writers who justified Spanish behavior by insisting that the Indians had precipitated bloodletting and, because of their unalterably bestial nature, could be dealt with in no other way. However useful accounts of Spanish cruelty might be for Protestant pamphleteers, Englishmen embarking for the New World must have wondered whether the same experience awaited them. Few doubted that they enjoyed the same technological superiority as the Spanish. If they desired, they could presumably lay waste the country they were entering. In addition, the English experience with the Irish, in whose country military officers like Gilbert and Raleigh had gained experience in the subjugation of "lesser breeds" for several decades, suggested that the English were fully capable of every cruelty contrived by the Spanish. However tractable and amenable to trade the Indian might appear in some of the English literature, the image of a hostile savage who awaited Christian adventurers could never be blotted from the English mind. The English knew from their own invasions of Ireland and the Netherlands in the late sixteenth century that indigenous peoples did not ordinarily accept graciously those who come to dominate them. To imagine the Indian as a savage beast was therefore a way of predicting the future, preparing for it, and justifying what one would do, even before one caused it to happen.

A third factor nourishing negative images of the Indian related directly to the native possession of land coveted by Europeans. For Englishmen, as for other Europeans, the Indian occupation of the land presented problems of law, morality, and practicality. As early as the 1580s, George Peckham, an early promoter of colonization, had admitted that some Englishmen doubted their right to take possession of the land of others. In 1609 the thought was raised again by another promoter of colonization, Robert Gray, who asked rhetorically, "By what right or warrant can we enter into the land of these Savages, take away their rightfull inheritance from them, and plant ourselves in their places, being unwronged or unprovoked by them?"[5] It was an appropriate question to ask, for Englishmen, like other Europeans, had organized their society around the concept of private ownership of land and regarded this concept as important evidence of their superior culture. They were not blind to the fact that they were entering the land of another people, who by prior possession, could lay sole claim to the entire continent.

To some extent the problem could be resolved by arguing that Englishmen did not intend to take the Indians' land but wanted only to share with

---

[5]*A Good Speed to Virginia* (1609), quoted in Wesley Frank Craven, "Indian Policy in Early Virginia," *William and Mary Quarterly*, 3rd Ser., 1 (1944): 65.

them what seemed a superabundance of territory. In return, they would extend to the Indians the advantages of a richer culture, a more advanced civilization, and, most importantly, the Christian religion. It was this argument that the governing council in Virginia used in 1610 when it advertised in England that the settlers "by way of marchandizing and trade, doe buy of them [the Indians] the pearles of earth, and sell to them the pearles of heaven."[6] It did not matter that the Chesapeake tribes had indicated no desire to exchange their land for such Christian instruction as a ragged band of Englishmen could provide.

A second and more portentous way of answering the question of English rights to the land was to deny the humanity of the Indians. Thus, Robert Gray, who had asked rhetorically if Englishmen were entitled to "plant ourselves in their places," answered by arguing that the Indians' inhumanity disqualified them from the right to possess land. "Although the Lord hath given the earth to children of men," he wrote, "the greater part of it [is] possessed and wrongfully usurped by wild beasts, and unreasonable creatures, or by brutish savages, which by reason of their godles ignorance, and blasphemous Idolatrie, are worse than those beasts which are of most wilde and savage nature."[7] This line of reasoning was filled with danger for the Indian, for while many leaders of colonization would avow, as one of them put it, that "every foote of Land which we shall take unto our use, we will bargayne and buy of them," others would find it more convenient to suggest that Indians, merely by being "Godless" and "savage," as defined by English invaders, had disqualified themselves from rightful ownership of the land.[8] In this sense there was much to be gained by projecting deeply negative images of native peoples. The darker the image—the more it defined aboriginal peoples in nonhuman terms—the stronger was the European claim to the land of the New World. Defining the Indian as a "savage" or "brutish beast" or "tawny serpent" did not give Europeans the power to dispossess Indians of their land. But it gave them the moral force to do so if and when physical force became available. The Spanish, Portuguese, Dutch, French, and English did not differ much in this regard.

A pamphlet published in London as the first English expedition was preparing to embark for Roanoke Island illustrates how both the positive and the negative images of the Indian operated in the English mind. Written by Sir George Peckham, who had accompanied Humphrey Gilbert on a voyage to Newfoundland in 1583, *A True Report, of the late discoveries, . . . of the*

---

[6]*A True Declaration of the Estate of the Colonie in Virginia* . . . (1610), in *Tracts and Other Papers, Relating Principally to the Origin, Settlement, and Progress of the Colonies in North America* . . . , Peter Force, comp. (Washington, D.C., 1884), 3: No. 1, p. 6.

[7]*A Good Speed to Virginia* (1609), quoted in Gary B. Nash, "The Image of the Indian in the Southern Colonial Mind," *William and Mary Quarterly*, 3rd Ser., 29 (1972): 210.

[8]William Strachey, *The Historie of Travell into Virginia Britania* (1612), eds. Louis B. Wright and Virginia Freund, Hakluyt Society *Publications*, 2d Ser., 103 (London: The Hakluyt Society, 1953): 26.

Newfound Landes clearly expressed the emerging formula for English colonization: formal expressions of goodwill, explanations of mutual benefits to be derived from contact between English and Indian peoples and yet, lurking beneath the surface, dark images and the anticipation of violence. Peckham's pamphlet began with an elaborate defense of the rights of maritime nations to "trade and trafficke" with "savage" nations and assured Englishmen that such enterprises would be "profitable to the adventurers in perticular, beneficial to the Savages, and a matter to be attained without any great daunger or difficultie." Some of the natives, he allowed, would be "fearefull by nature" and disquieted by the "straunge apparrell, Armour, and weapons" of the English, but "courtesie and myldnes," along with a generous bounty of "prittie merchaundizes and trifles as looking Glasses, Bells, Beades, Braceletts, Chaines, or collers of Bewgle, Christall, Amber, Jett, or Glasse" would soon win them over and "induce their Barbarous natures to a likeing and mutuall society with us."[9]

With this explanation of how he hoped the English might act, and how the Indians might respond, Peckham proceeded to reveal what he must have considered the more likely course of events:

> But if after these good and fayre meanes used, the Savages nevertheless will not be heerewithall satisfied, but barbarously wyll goe about to practise violence either in repelling the Christians from theyr Portes and safe Landinges or in withstanding them afterwardes to enjoye the rights for which both painfully and lawfully they have adventured themselves thether; Then in such a case I holde it no breache of equitye for the Christians to defende themselves, to pursue revenge with force, and to doo whatsoever is necessary for attayning of theyr safety; For it is allowable by all Lawes in such distresses, to resist violence with violence.[10]

With earlier statements of the gentle and receptive qualities of the Indians almost beyond recall, Peckham reminded his countrymen of their responsibility to employ all necessary means to bring the Indians from "falsehood to truth, from darkness to light, from the highway of death, to the path of life, from superstitious idolatry, to sincere christianity, from the devill to Christ, from hell to Heaven."

Thus two conflicting images of the Indian wrestled for ascendance in the English mind as the first attempts to colonize in the New World began. At times the English tended to see the native as a backward but receptive person with whom amicable and profitable relations might be established. But the negative image, filled with visions of violence and bloodshed, reverberated even more strongly in the minds of those who were sailing toward land already occupied by people of a different culture.

---

[9]David Beers Quinn, ed., *The Voyages and Colonizing Enterprises of Sir Humphrey Gilbert*, Hakluyt Society *Publications*, 2nd Ser., 84 (London: The Hakluyt Society, 1940): 450–52.

[10]*Ibid.*, 453.

3

CULTURES MEET
ON THE CHESAPEAKE

England's first real attempt to establish colonizers in the New World came in 1585, when Walter Raleigh, a favorite at the court of Queen Elizabeth, organized a major expedition of ships and men. A year before, Raleigh had dispatched two ships on a reconnaissance voyage to the lower latitudes of the North American coast, for the English at this time still knew virtually nothing about the climate and natural resources of the area between French-claimed territory in the St. Lawrence region and Spanish-held Florida. Relying upon a Portuguese pilot who had accompanied an earlier Spanish voyage along the coast, Raleigh's ship captains made landfall on the Outer Banks of the Carolina coast and established contacts with the local Indians on Roanoke Island. Two of the Indians had been induced to return to England. Displayed in London, they were an invaluable part of the publicity campaign that Raleigh launched for a large expedition in 1585.

It was this second Roanoke voyage that marked the first extended encounter between Indians and the English-speaking, Protestant variety of European. Some 600 men in seven ships sailed from Plymouth in April of 1585 and reached the Outer Banks that summer. About 100 of the men were left on Roanoke Island with promises that a relief expedition would return the next spring. For Indians of the Chesapeake region what then occurred helped to fix impressions of who and what these Englishmen were. Likewise, the accounts of the Roanoke experience later published in London helped to plant in the minds of other Englishmen coming to America in the early seventeenth century ideas of the people they were likely to encounter.

Though differing in detail, all accounts agree that the Indians of the Carolina coast were receptive to the English in 1585. Arthur Barlow, a member of the first expedition, wrote that "we were entertained with all love, and kindness, and with as much bountie, after their manner, as they could possibly devise. We found the people most gentle, loving and faithful, void of all guile, and treason." Barlow remarked that the Indians were "much grieved" when their hospitality was shunned by the suspicious English.[1] Other accounts, while less complimentary to the Indians, also averred that the indigenous people were eager to learn about the artifacts of English culture and, though wary, extended their hospitality. Since the English came in small numbers, the Indians probably did not regard them as much of a threat. No conflict occurred until the English discovered a silver cup missing and dispatched a punitive expedition to a nearby Indian village. When the Indians denied taking the cup, the English, deciding to make a show of force, burned the village to the ground, and destroyed the Indians' supply of corn. After that, relations deteriorated. Aware of their numerical disadvantage and convinced that the local Indian leader was organizing mainland tribes against them, the English employed force in large doses to convince the local Indians of their invulnerability. As one member of the expedition admitted, "Some of our companie towardes the ende of the yeare, shewed themselves too fierce, in slaying some of the people, in some towns, upon causes that on our part, might easily enough have been borne withall."[2] Given this course of events, the coastal tribes must have concluded that the English were untrustworthy, quick to resort to arms, and dangerously unpredictable.

The 1585 Roanoke settlers scanned the horizon for sight of the relief expedition in the early summer of 1586. But the ships that finally appeared belonged to Sir Francis Drake, who had been conducting predatory raids on the Spanish Main and only incidentally dropped in on the Roanoke colony. Discouraged at the failure of the relief expedition to appear and short of food, the colonizers clambered aboard Drake's ships for a ride home. About six weeks later the relief expedition arrived, only to find the colony abandoned. Less than twenty men were now left to guard the fort that had been erected on Roanoke Island. They were nowhere to be found when still another relief expedition arrived in 1587 with 110 adventurers, led by John White. These were to become the famous "Lost Colonists," for when the next relief expedition finally reached Roanoke in 1590—earlier attempts at sending out ships had been aborted by the Spanish Armada—no trace could

[1]David Beers Quinn, ed., *The Roanoke Voyages, 1584–1590*, Hakluyt Society *Publications*, 104 (London: The Hakluyt Society, 1955): 108.
[2]*Ibid.*, 381–82.

be found of them. Given the previous hostility between settlers and Indians, it is likely that they had succumbed to the attacks of local tribes.

The Roanoke voyages were never large enough nor fully capitalized enough to have led to permanent and self-sustaining colonies. They served only as a symbol of the English challenge to Spain in North America, but they were useful in accumulating knowledge about the region that was to become the focus of English overseas colonization. In terms of the first sustained contact between English and Native American cultures they were a resounding failure. "What was lost in this famous lost colony," we have recently been reminded, "was more than the band of colonists who have never been traced. What was also lost and never quite recovered in subsequent ventures was the dream of Englishman and Indian living side by side in peace and liberty."[3]

For two decades after the Roanoke experiment, Englishmen launched no new colonial adventures. A few English sea captains, representing merchants who dabbled in the West Indies trade, looked in on the coast of North America and attempted to barter with the Indians. They reported that their relations were generally friendly. But no further English attempts at colonization would come until after the death of Queen Elizabeth in 1603 in whose reign so much had been done to propagandize American colonizing and to obtain for it the backing of the Crown and the mercantile wealth of the nation. North America, so far as it was an arena of European colonization, still belonged to the Spanish and French.

THE RE-ESTABLISHMENT OF VIRGINIA

The first permanent English settlement in the New World was founded at Jamestown, Virginia in 1607. But properly speaking it was not a colony at all, at least in the sense of being a political unit governed by the mother country. Rather it was a business enterprise, the property of the Virginia Company of London, made up of stockholders and a governing board of directors which answered directly to James I. Its primary purpose in the eyes of its founders was to return a profit to its shareholders—merchants, political figures at the royal court, and others who had invested their capital in the hope that the English could duplicate the remarkable success of the Spanish and Portuguese in Mexico, Peru, and Brazil.

The King's charter to the Virginia Company of London began with the suggestion that the company was to concern itself with bringing the Christian religion to such people "as yet live in darkness and miserable ignorance of the true knowledge and worship of God." Christianizing the Indians of the Chesapeake area no doubt concerned many Englishmen in an era when

---

[3]Edmund S. Morgan, "Slavery and Freedom: The American Paradox," *Journal of American History*, 59 (1972–73): 16.

the rivalry with Spain for the uncommitted peoples of the earth was analogous to the ideological struggle for the uncommitted people of the Third World by communist and capitalist countries after World War II. But far more important in the minds of those who subscribed to shares in the Virginia Company was the desire to receive a return on their investment. As Captain John Smith, who was to become a central figure in the drama unfolding in Virginia, later wrote: "We did admire how it was possible such wise men could so torment themselves and us with such strange absurdities and impossibilities: making Religion their colour, when all their aime was nothing but present profit. . . . For I am not so simple to think that any other motive than wealth will ever erect in Virginia a Commonweale."[4]

How would the Virginia Company enrich its stockholders? Nobody was quite sure, but it was assumed that profits in the New World would come in a variety of ways: through the discovery of gold and other minerals; by trade with the Indians; by production of pitch, tar, potash, and other products of the forest needed by the English navy; through the development of a fishing industry; and, best of all, by discovering the illusive passage through the American continent to Cathay. Some of these objectives had been realized in other English joint-stock ventures: by the Muscovy Company in Russia, the Levantine Company in the Middle East, and the East India Company in the Far East. Why not in North America?

Once sufficient capital was obtained, the principal problems were to recruit laborers who would go to the colony as employees of the Virginia Company and to establish the kind of administration and authority that would channel their energies toward the desired goals. Both of these problems proved thorny in the early years.

The tiny fleet that set sail for Virginia in December 1606 was the final fruit of a year's planning in London by investors and the board of governors of the Virginia Company. Three ships carrying about 120 colonists embarked under the command of Captain Christopher Newport. Sixteen weeks later, after stopping in the West Indies for water and provisions, a landfall was made on the Chesapeake Bay. Men and provisions were put ashore; a few weeks later the ships disappeared over the horizon, leaving the small band of Englishmen alone in an unknown land.

What followed in the next nine months, before Captain Newport returned with supplies and additional settlers, is a dismal tale of human weakness and misfortune. Attempts were made to explore the area, to build a fort and shelters within it, to plant crops, and to organize a bit of fishing. But the colonists seemed to have spent much of their time dividing into factions and organizing plots against each other. The supplies quickly dwindled and the men were soon on starvation rations. Some deserted to the Indian villages where food was plentiful. Dysentery, caused by the brackish water of the

[4]Edward Arber and A. G. Bradley, eds., *Travels and Works of Captain John Smith* (Edinburgh: J. Grant, 1910), 2: 928.

Jamestown area, plagued the settlement. One of the members of the resident council of governors was expelled by his exasperated colleagues. A second was sentenced to execution as a spy of the Spanish, who were thought to be planning the elimination of the colony. A third was saved from hanging only by the arrival of the reprovisioning ships from England. When Newport returned in January 1608 only thirty-eight of the original settlers were still alive. Three days later fire destroyed most of the crude buildings in Jamestown and most of the freshly unloaded supplies.

Twice in 1608 and once in 1609 the Virginia Company of London sent out ships with new settlers and supplies. But the "starving time" continued and, as one of the leaders later wrote: "dissentions and jarrs were daily sowne amongst them [the settlers], so that they choaked the seed and blasted the fruits of all men's labors."[5] Although more than 900 settlers were sent to Virginia in the first three years, by the winter of 1609–10 only sixty survivors remained in the colony and some among them had resorted to cannibalism in their distress. In London, while the directors of the Virginia Company circulated promotional pamphlets such as *Good Speed to Virginia and Virginia Richly Valued,* the street talk rumored that the colony was a dismal failure, and investors glumly counted the money they had wasted on this ill-starred enterprise. Men asked what had gone wrong with the plan to establish English presence in North America.

One of the flaws in the plans of English promoters of colonization was that they had badly miscalculated the reality of the North American coast. Most investors and participants in the colony were hoping to duplicate the Spanish experience in Mexico and Peru. They dreamed of dragging from the earth the precious minerals which would make them wealthy. They hoped to utilize a native labor force or at least to profit from trade with the Indians. But Virginia was not Mexico or Peru. Its earth contained neither gold nor silver, and thus all the frantic digging that was done in the early months and all the loading of ships with mica-speckled dirt, which the colonists thought must be gold, brought only a depletion of energy and shattered dreams. "Our gilded refiners, with their golden promises," wrote John Smith, "made all men their slaves in hope of recompence. There was no talke, no hope, nor worke, but dig gold, wash gold, refine gold, load gold [in order to load] a drunken ship with so much gilded [mica-filled] durt."[6]

Doubling the disappointment was their inability to utilize the labor of the Indians of the region. Most Englishmen who came to Virginia in the initial stage of colonization probably assumed that without undue effort they could exploit the Indians of the New World. Upon their backs could be built a prosperous society. Cortez had conquered the mighty Aztec empire with a

[5]John Rolfe, *A Relation of the State of Virginia* (1616), quoted in Perry Miller, "Religion and Society in the Early Literature: The Religious Impulse in the Founding of Virginia," *William and Mary Quarterly,* 3d Ser., 6 (1949): 29.

[6]Arber and Bradley, eds., *Works of Smith,* 1: 104.

few hundred men and then turned the labor of thousands of Indians to Spanish advantage. Pizarro had done the same in Peru. Why should it not be so in Virginia?

But in the Chesapeake region the English found that the indigenous people were not so densely settled and could not be so easily subjugated. Smith later wrote that the Spaniards were fortunate enough to colonize "in those parts where there were infinite numbers of people who had manured the ground so that food was provided at all times."[7] Moreover, the Spanish got the "spoil and pillage" of the well-developed regions they colonized because they brought with them a military force capable of overpowering the native society. But the English settled in Virginia where there was no wealthy Indian empire to conquer. Nor could some 20,000 Indians of the Chesapeake region be molded into a labor force at the Europeans' command, for the English brought with them neither an army of conquistadors nor an army of priests to convert Indians to the European religion. Unable to exploit or utilize the native population, the Virginia settlers found the New World paradise far from utopian.

A third flaw in the English plan of settlement related to the composition of the original settlers at Jamestown. Of those who arrived in the early years, many were gentlemen-adventurers who were ill equipped to undertake the rugged work of colony building and proved to be only a drain on the tiny settlement's resources. By the same token there were far too few laborers and farmers—men who could cut trees, build houses, and farm the soil. John Smith complained that a small number of adventure-seeking gentlemen would have been well enough; but "to have more to wait and play than worke, or more commanders and officers than industrious labourers" was foolishness, "for in Virginia a plaine Souldier that can use a pickaxe and spade, is better than five Knights."[8] Those who had been bred to a life of labor were not much better. "A more damned crew hell never vomited," growled the president of the Company, and his opinion was echoed and embellished by one of Virginia's first historians, who described the original colonizers as "unruly Sparks, packed off by their Friends, to escape worse Destinies at home . . . , poor Gentlemen, broken Tradesmen, Rakes and Libertines, Footmen, and such Others, as were much fitter to spoil or ruin a Commonwealth, than to help to raise or maintain one."[9] This inappropriate selection of colonists not only created manpower problems but also led to chronic social tension. Men of high social standing were regarded in England as essential to the strength and stability of society. But in a

---

[7]Quoted in Sigmund Diamond, "From Organization to Society: Virginia in the Seventeenth Century," *American Journal of Sociology*, 63 (1958): 460.

[8]*Ibid.*, 461.

[9]George Sandys to John Ferrar, 1623, in Susan M. Kingsbury, ed., *The Records of the Virginia Company of London* (Washington, D.C.: Government Printing Office, 1906–35), 4: 23; William Stith, *The History of the First Discovery and Settlement of Virginia* (New York: Joseph Sabin, 1865), p. 103.

wilderness settlement on the edge of a vast, unknown continent they only created resentment, unwilling to work themselves and unable to command the respect of those under them.

The most enlightening example of the social tension created when Englishmen moved to a new environment on the opposite side of the Atlantic Ocean is the case of Captain John Smith. Smith claimed no aristocratic blood; his father was a simple west country tenant farmer. Concluding at sixteen that life as a merchant's apprentice held nothing for him, Smith embarked on war as a career. Before he had reached his mid-twenties he had traveled and fought his way across Europe and back as a professional mercenary in the employ of various local warlords who purchased his services. He fought duels in Transylvania, battled the Turks on the plains of western Hungary, was captured and enslaved for several years in Istanbul, escaped into Russia, and worked his way back to England by way of North Africa. Because of his military experience, his skill as a cartographer, and because he had friends in London who were interested in the Virginia enterprise being mounted in 1606, Smith was recruited as a member of the first Jamestown expedition. His experience suggested that he would be a good man to have along when the going got rough.

Even on the ocean voyage Smith had fallen out with some of the leaders of the expedition, men with gentry blood flowing in their veins, and had been clapped in irons on the *Susan Constant*. When the secret orders were opened upon arrival on the Chesapeake, Smith discovered that he had been named a member of the Virginia governing council. This aroused further resentment. Smith had little patience with men who reckoned that their social origins excused them from manual labor, and he did not hesitate to say so. As it happened, he was one of the few who possessed the courage and ability to explore and map the region around Jamestown, establish contact with the Indians, negotiate with them, and attempt rational organization of the colony's slender human resources. The net effect of his exertions, however, was to alienate the gentlemen councilors around him. They saw his aggressiveness and disdain for their social superiority as a calculated attempt to gain control of the colony and to depose them in the process. They attempted to eliminate Smith as a dangerous influence at Jamestown but by September 1608 Smith had outlasted most of his enemies and for a year he ruled the colony as president of the council.

REORGANIZATION AND TOBACCO

After three years of near anarchy and failure to find ways of exploiting the Chesapeake region, the directors in London perceived that what was needed in the colony were not soldiers of fortune but ordinary farmers who could extract from the land the necessary food supplies to sustain the colony and begin the cultivation of a staple crop. They therefore reorganized the company in 1609 and enticed a large number of settlers to Virginia with promises of free land at the end of seven years' labor for the company.

Under this new system of recruitment about 1,200 new emigrants came to Virginia in 1610 and 1611. But even with this manpower the Virginia Company could not develop staple crops or find a way of returning a profit to its investors. The colony limped along and the company barely remained afloat. By 1616 death and re-emigration to England had reduced the population to 350. Again the company raised the inducements for going to the Chesapeake. This time 100 acres of land were offered outright to anyone in England who would journey to the colony. Instead of pledging limited servitude for the chance to become sole possessor of land, an Englishman trapped at the lower rungs of society at home could now become an independent landowner in no more time than it took to reach the Chesapeake.

Under this new program, the Virginia Company gave up, once and for all, the hope of rewarding its shareholders through the employment of a work force, either native or English. Now the company operated simply as an organization for the promotion and sale of land. Its aim was to encourage as many Englishmen as possible to come to Virginia to pursue their fortunes independently. In time, if the colony proved itself valuable, its vast land resources could be sold profitably. Other concessions were made. In 1619 the company allowed the election of a representative assembly, which would participate in governing the colony and thus bind the colonists emotionally to the land. In the same year the company shipped a boatload of unmarried women to the colony in order to improve morale and touch off a small population explosion.

In response to these concessions more than 4,500 colonists arrived between 1619 and 1624. They came no longer as employees of the Virginia Company of London or as individuals to be governed entirely at the discretion of the resident council and the governing council in London. Through its failures, the company had learned that only by promising immediate ownership of land and by allowing a degree of local government could it hope to keep the colony alive and growing. The colony had been initiated not by men seeking political or religious freedom but by profit-seeking investors in England, fortune-hunting adventurers, and common riffraff from the back alleys and prisons of England. After almost two decades the original plans had been abandoned as men adjusted unrealistic expectations to the realities of the New World.

The reorganization of the Virginia Company and the new inducements to settlement helped to lift the colony out of the depths of social disorder and unprofitability in the early years. But also crucial to Virginia's revival was the discovery that tobacco grew exceptionally well in the soil of the Chesapeake region. Widely used in the seventeenth century as a mild narcotic, tobacco had been first brought to Portugal from Florida in the

1560s. But it was Francis Drake's boatload of the "jovial weed," procured in the West Indies in 1586 and then popularized among the upper class by Raleigh, that converted it from medicinal purposes to a social addiction. By the early seventeenth century England was swept with the smoking craze. Young bloods in English society developed various tricks and affectations as a part of the smoking cult: the "Ring," the "Whiffle," the "Gulp," and the "Retention" became a part of the new social habit. Even the violent opposition of King James could not arrest the popularity of smoking tobacco. Sounding like a modern physician, James anonymously published *Counterblast to Tobacco* in which he described smoking as "a custom loathsome to the eye, hateful to the nose, harmful to the brain, dangerous to the lungs, and in the black stinking fumes thereof, nearest resembling the horrible stygian smoke of the pit that is bottomless." It was to no avail, however, as English society imported more and more tobacco leaf from the New World. At first the West Indies supplied the bulk of the crop, but experiments with tobacco culture in Virginia proved phenomenally successful and profitable. Virginia's first crop was shipped to England in 1617; seven years later 200,000 pounds of leaf were exported, and by 1638 the crop exceeded 3,000,000 pounds. Tobacco became to the Chesapeake region what sugar was to the West Indies and silver to Mexico and Peru.

Tobacco, of course, would not grow by itself, and as the demand grew, English planters on the Chesapeake sought a source of cheap labor. In the Spanish and Portuguese colonies the settlers had been able to incorporate the native populations into a forced labor system that approximated slavery. But the English lacked the power in the early years to enslave the local tribes. So it was to England that the tobacco planters looked for their labor supply—and particularly to the most depressed segment of the population, made up of young men who were willing to sell their labor for four to seven years in exchange for passage across the Atlantic and a chance, after they had served their time, to become independent landowners and tobacco planters in the New World. England was full of such men, for population growth and the enclosure of land had created an army of unemployed. "Our country [is] overspread," wrote a magistrate in Kent, "not only with unpunished swarms of idle rogues and counterfeit soldiers but also with numbers of poor and weak but unpitied servitors."[10] Such impoverished immigrants were called indentured servants because they had committed themselves to serve a master for a specific period of time. They differed from the earlier employees of the Virginia Company only in that they had contracted their labor to an individual rather than to a company. Put to work in the tobacco fields, an indentured servant could tend about 1,000 to 2,000 tobacco plants, which could be expected to yield tobacco worth about £100

[10]Quoted in Peter Clark, "The Migrant in Kentish Towns, 1580–1640," Peter Clark and Paul Slack, eds., *Crisis and Order in English Towns, 1500–1700* (Toronto: University of Toronto Press, 1972), p. 117.

to £150 a year. Few men in England could generate an equivalent income for a year's labor.

After tobacco proved successful in Virginia, a fairly small number of landowners clamored for indentured servants in order to increase the amount of land under cultivation. Brought to the colony by the shipload, these servants were auctioned off at the dock to the highest bidder. The more servants a landowner could purchase, the greater the crop he could produce; larger crops brought more capital with which to purchase more land and additional servants. Thus, Edmund Morgan writes, "Virginia differed from later American boom areas in that success depended not on acquiring the right piece of land but on acquiring men. Land that would grow tobacco was everywhere, so abundant that people frequently did not bother at first to secure patents for the amounts they were entitled to. Instead men rushed to stake out claims to men, stole them, lured them, fought over them—and bought and sold them, bidding up the prices to four, five, and six times the initial cost."[11]

Life for these indentured servants was nightmarish. If malarial fevers of the swampy Chesapeake area did not kill them within a few years, then the work routine imposed by masters, who treated them like cattle, usually did. Virginia's servants were the personal property of a small group of tough, ambitious planters in whom political and social power was so concentrated that they would brook no restraints on their behavior. What might happen to a man who challenged a system controlled by the few became apparent to an ordinary immigrant named Richard Barnes in 1624. His tongue loosened by alcohol in a local tavern, Barnes uttered some "base and detracting" words against the resident governor. For this it was ordered that he "be disarmed [and] have his armes broken and his tongue bored through with an awl [and] shall pass through a guard of 40 men and shalbe butted [with muskets] by every one of them and att the head of the troope kicked downe and footed out of the fort; that he shalbe banished out of James Citye and the Island, that he shall not be capable of any priviledge of freedome of the countrey . . . [hereafter]."[12]

Barnes was not an indentured servant but a freeman; for indentured servants who defied the will of the ruling group of tobacco planters life could be even more hazardous, for servitude in early Virginia was different from early chattel slavery only in degree. Unrestrained by the courts, which in the mother country protected the rights of servants against unduly oppressive masters, servant owners treated their bondsmen as pieces of property. John Rolfe, one of the leading figures of the colony, reported in 1619 that the "buying of men and boys" and even the gambling at cards for servants in Virginia "was held in England a thing most intolerable." Six years later, an

[11]Edmund S. Morgan, *American Slavery, American Freedom: The Ordeal of Colonial Virginia* (New York: W. W. Norton & Co., 1975), pp. 114–15.
[12]*Ibid.*, 124.

English merchant refused to take a boatload of indentured servants to Virginia because, as he explained, "servants were sold here up and down like horses." What occurred in "boomtime Viriginia," Morgan concludes, was "not only the fleeting ugliness of private enterprise operating temporarily without check, not only greed magnified by opportunity, producing fortunes for a few and misery for many," but also the beginning of "a system of labor that treated men as things."[13] It is no wonder, then, that of some 10,000 persons transported to Virginia between 1607 and 1622, only about 2,000 were still alive at the end of that period. "In steed of a plantacion," wrote one English critic, Virginia "will shortly gett the name of a slaughter house."[14]

ENGLISH-INDIAN RELATIONS

While Virginia's promoters were adapting their plans to the realities of the Chesapeake environment, the settlers were not only devising means of exploiting the land and immigrant labor but also encountering the native people of the region. Will it or not, they could not develop the region's resources without directly confronting the original inhabitants of the land. From the time that the first Jamestown expedition touched shore, Indians and Englishmen were in continuous contact in North America. Moreover, permanent settlement required acquisition of land by white settlers—land that was in the possession of the Indians. That single fact was the beginning of a chain of events which governed the entire sociology of red-white relations.

It is not possible to know exactly what Englishmen expected of the Indians as they approached the Chesapeake Bay in the spring of 1607. Nor is it possible to be certain whether the Indian destruction of a Spanish mission in the same area a generation before bespoke a generalized hostility toward Europeans. But it is likely, given the English belief that the Roanoke colony had been reduced to a pile of bones by the Indians a generation earlier, and given the Indians' sporadic experience with Europeans as a militaristic people, that neither side was very optimistic about the receptiveness of the other. The pessimistic view of the English must have been greatly intensified when the Jamestown expedition was attacked near Cape Henry, the most seaward point of land in the Chesapeake Bay region, where the first landfall was made. From this point on, the English proceeded with extreme caution, expecting violence and treachery from the Indians, even when they approached in outwardly friendly ways. When the one-armed Captain Newport led the first exploratory trip up the newly named James River, just

[13]*Ibid.*, 129.

[14]Francis Jennings, *The Invasion of America: Indians, Colonialism and the Cant of Conquest* (Chapel Hill, N.C.: University of North Carolina Press, 1975), p. 79.

RAPPAHANNOCK RIVER

POTOMAC RIVER

CHESAPEAKE BAY

77°

76°

38°

38°

MONACAN

TERRITORY

CHICKAHOMINY RIVER

POWHATAN

HENRICO

CHICKAHOMINY TRIBE

WEROWOCOMOCO

PAMUNKEY RIVER

PASPAHEGH

Jamestown

POWHATAN'S CRESCENT

Cape Charles

37°

37°

JAMES RIVER

KECOUGHTAN

Cape Henry

Approximate Boundary of Powhatan Confederacy

NANSEMOND

0   10   20
Miles

THE EARLY
CHESAPEAKE

N.L.DIAZ 5-81

77°

76°

54

weeks after a tiny settlement had been planted at Jamestown, he was confused by what he encountered. The Indians, a member of his group wrote, "are naturally given to trechery, howbeit we could not find it in our travell up the river, but rather a most kind and loving people."[15] This account describes how the English were wined and dined by the Indians, who explained that they were "at oddes" with other tribes, including the Chesapeake tribe that had attacked the English at Cape Henry, and were willing to ally with the English against their enemies.

It is now known that the Indians of the region were accurately describing their situation when they said they were "at oddes" with other tribes. Some forty small tribes lived in the Chesapeake Bay region. Powhatan was the paramount chief of several dozen of these and for years before the English arrived had been consolidating his hold on the lesser tribes of the area, while warding off the inland tribes of the Piedmont. In this kind of situation Powhatan may have seen an alliance with the English as a means of extending his power in the tidewater area while simultaneously neutralizing the power of his western enemies. At the same time, his unpleasant experience with Europeans, including a clash just three years before with a passing English ship whose crew had been hospitably entertained but then had killed a local chief and kidnapped several Indians, probably made Powhatan extremely wary of these newcomers.

John Smith and others were quick to comprehend the intertribal tensions as well as the linguistic differences among the Indians. But apparently they could not convince themselves that some tribal leaders could find their arrival potentially to their advantage. Perhaps because their position was so precarious, with dysentery, hunger, and internal strife debilitating their tiny settlement, they could only afford to regard all Indians as threatening. Hence, hostile and friendly Indians were seen as different only in their outward behavior. Inwardly they were identical—"savage," treacherous men who only waited for a chance to drive the English back into the sea from which they had emerged.

During the first months of contact, the confusion in the English mind surfaced again and again. In the autumn of 1607, for example, when food supplies were running perilously low and all but a handful of the Jamestown settlers had fallen too ill to work, the colony was saved by Powhatan, whose men brought sufficient food to keep the struggling settlement alive until the sick recovered and the relief ship arrived. Many saw this as an example of Powhatan's covert hostility rather than as an attempt of the chief to serve his own interests through an alliance with the English. "It pleased God (in our extremity)," wrote John Smith, "To move the Indians to bring us Corne, ere it was halfe ripe, to refresh us, when we rather expected . . . they would

---

[15]Philip L. Barbour, ed., *The Jamestown Voyages Under the First Charter, 1606–1609,* Hakluyt Society *Publications*, 2d Ser., 136 (London: The Hakluyt Society, 1969), 103–4.

destroy us."[16] As a man of military experience among "barbarian" people in other parts of the world, Smith was not willing to believe that the Indians, in aiding the colony, might have found the survival of the English in their own interest. Another leader of the colony could only attribute the Indians' generous behavior to the intervention of the white man's God. "If it had not pleased God to have put a terrour in the Savages heart," he wrote, "we had all perished by those wild and cruell Pagans, being in that weake estate as we were."[17]

In December 1607 Smith was captured during one of his exploratory incursions into Powhatan's country and marched to Werowocomoco, the seat of Powhatan's confederacy. Powhatan seems to have wanted to employ this opportunity to impress the English with his power and arranged a mock execution ceremony for Smith. At the critical moment, as the executioners prepared to deliver the death blows, the chief's favorite daughter, Pocahontas, threw herself on Smith to save him. About twelve years old, Pocahontas had been a frequent visitor to Jamestown, undoubtedly as an emissary of her father, and was well known to Smith. But rather than understanding the rescue in symbolic terms, as Powhatan's way of indicating his strength but also his desire to forge a bond with the newcomers, Smith and other Virginians took Pocahontas's gesture as a spontaneous outburst of love for the English—an un-Indian-like act attributable to English superiority or perhaps to God's intervening hand. Hostility was on the English mind, sporadic hostility had already occurred, and Powhatan's deliverance of the English leader, at a time when the colony was almost defenseless, was thus not conceived as a conciliatory act.

In the aftermath of the incident, Pocahontas became a kind of ambassador from Powhatan to the struggling Jamestown colony, an agent who became fluent in the English language and kept her father informed on the state of the internally divided Englishmen. By late 1608, more colonists had arrived in Jamestown, and Smith, as the new president of council, adopted an aggressive stance, burning Indian canoes, fields, and villages in order to extort food supplies and to cow Powhatan and his lesser chiefs into submission. Fully aware that Virginia could not be resupplied from England every few months and that the colonists were unable to sustain themselves in their new environment, Smith sought a forced trade with Powhatan. By the end of 1608 the chief had determined to let the Englishmen starve, a policy made manifestly clear not only by his refusal to trade corn but by his withdrawal of the Pocahontas emissary. On penalty of death the young Indian daughter of the chief was forbidden to enter the English settlement. "Captain Smith," intoned Powhatan at a confrontation of the two leaders in January 1609, "some doubt I have of your coming hither, that makes me not so kindly seek to relieve you as I would [like]. For many do inform me your

[16]Arber and Bradley, eds., *Works of Smith*, 1: 8–9.
[17]Barbour, ed., *Jamestown Voyages*, 136: 144–45.

coming is not for trade, but to invade my people and possess my country."[18]

Smith's response, as the leader of a colony where some men were deserting to the Indians while others starved, was to raid Indian villages for provisions. Powhatan's response was to attack the English wherever he could. Even the arrival of fresh supplies and several hundred new colonists in July and August did not help, for the provisions were quickly exhausted, the men ravenously consuming more than they produced. When the relief ships departed in October 1609, with John Smith aboard one of them, Virginia embarked upon a winter of despair. Under the surveillance of Powhatan, who ambushed foraging colonists whenever he could, the death toll mounted. George Percy, Smith's successor, wrote that after the horses had been eaten, the dysentery-racked Virginians "were glad to make shift with [such] vermin as dogs, cats, rats, and mice." When these were exhausted, men resorted to "things which seem incredible, as to dig up corpses out of graves and to eat them—and some have licked up the blood which hath fallen from their weak fellows. And amongst the rest, this was most lamentable, that one of our colony murdered his wife, ripped the child out of her womb and threw it into the river, and after chopped the mother in pieces and salted her for his food, the same not being discovered before he had eaten part thereof."[19]

Powhatan's policy of withdrawing from trade with the encroachers had succeeded. By the spring of 1610 the Spanish ambassador to England, Alonso de Velasco, reported accurately that "the Indians hold the English surrounded in the strong place which they had erected there, having killed the larger part of them, and the others were left, so entirely without provisions that they thought it impossible to escape." Virginia could be easily erased from the map, Velasco counseled his government, "by sending out a few ships to finish what might be left in that place."[20] What the Spanish ambassador did not know was that two relief ships had reached Jamestown in May 1610 but found the situation so dismal that Sir Thomas Gates, arriving to assume the governorship of the colony, decided to embark the remaining sixty survivors, set sail for England, and admit that Englishmen could not permanently inhabit the shores of the Chesapeake. On June 7, 1610, Gates ordered the forlorn settlement stripped of its meagre possessions, loaded the handful of survivors aboard, and set sail down the James River for the open sea. The ships dropped anchor for the night after reaching the Chesapeake Capes and planned to start the return ocean voyage on the following day.

On the next morning three ships hove into sight. They carried 150 new

[18]Quoted in Philip L. Barbour, *Pocahontas and Her World* (Boston: Houghton Mifflin Company, 1970), p. 46.

[19]Quoted in *ibid.*, pp. 64–65.

[20]Quoted in Grace Steele Woodward, *Pocahontas* (Norman, Okla.: University of Oklahoma Press, 1969), p. 120.

recruits sent out by the Virginia Company and a new governor, Sir Thomas West, Lord De la Warr. Jamestown, at its moment of extinction, was reborn.

Newly armed and provisioned, the revitalized Jamestown colonists revived and extended their militaristic Indian policy. The new attitude toward the Powhatan Confederacy was apparent in the orders issued in 1609 for governing the colony. Three years before, the Virginia Company had instructed, "In all your passages you must have great care not to offend the naturals, if you can eschew it."[21] Now the governor was ordered to effect a military occupation of the region between the James and York rivers, to make all tribes tributary to him rather than to Powhatan, to extract corn, furs, dyes, and labor from each tribe, and, if possible, to mold the natives into an agricultural labor force as the Spanish had done in their colonies. As the English settlement gained in strength, Smith's successors continued his policy of military foraging and intimidation. From 1610 to 1612 Powhatan attacked the colonists whenever opportunities presented themselves and the English mounted attacks that decimated three small tribes and destroyed two Indian villages. Most of the corn that sustained the colony in these years seems to have been extracted by force from Powhatan's villages.

In 1613 the English kidnapped Pocahontas in a move designed to obtain a return of English prisoners and a quantity of weapons that the Indians had acquired over the years and to force payment of "a great quantitie of Corne," as Pocahontas's abductor, Captain Samuel Argall put it.[22] Understanding that his daughter was not in harm's way, Powhatan made limited concessions to the English but refused to satisfy all the ransom conditions. In the following year, when the widower John Rolfe vowed to marry Pocahontas, Powhatan reluctantly assented to the first Anglo-Indian marriage in Virginia's history and signed a humiliating peace treaty. Pocahontas became the instrument of an uneasy truce between the two societies and returned to England with Rolfe and other members of Powhatan's Confederacy in 1616 in order to promote further colonization of the Chesapeake. She died on the eve of her departure for Virginia in 1617 after helping to raise the money that pumped new lifeblood into the Virginia Company and consequently sent hundreds of new fortune-seekers to the Chesapeake as part of the population buildup that would lead to a renewal of hostilities five years after her death.

Notwithstanding misconceptions, suspicion, and violence on both sides, the English and the Powhatans lived in close contact during the first decade of English settlement and cultural interchange occurred on a broad scale. Although it has been a commonplace in the popular mind since the moment when Europeans and Native Americans first met that the Europeans were

[21]E. G. R. Taylor, ed., *The Original Writings of Correspondence of the Two Richard Hakluyts,* Hakluyt Society *Publications,* 2d Ser., 77 (London, 1935): 494.

[22]Quoted in Woodward, *Pocahontas,* p. 156.

"advanced" and the Indians were "primitive," the technological differences between the two cultures, as anthropologist Nancy Lurie has recently reminded us, were equaled or outweighed by the similarities between these two agricultural societies.[23] The main technological advantages of the Engglish were their ability to traverse large bodies of water in wooden ships and their superiority in the use of iron to fashion implements and weapons. But the Indians quickly incorporated such iron-age items as kettles, fishhooks, traps, needles, knives, and guns into their material culture. In return they provided Englishmen with an understanding of how to use nets and weirs to catch the abundant fish and shellfish of the Chesapeake waters and introduced Europeans to a wide range of agricultural products that were unknown in Europe before the New World was reached. Englishmen in Virginia learned from the natives how to cultivate tobacco, corn, beans, squash, pumpkins, and other food products. Indians also introduced the English to a wide range of medicinal herbs, dyes, and such important devices as the canoe.

Such cultural interaction proceeded even while hostility and sporadic violence was occurring in the early years. It was facilitated by the fact that some Indians lived among the English as day laborers, while a number of settlers fled to Indian villages rather than endure the rigors of life among the autocratic English rulers and oppressive tobacco planters. This kind of interchange brought a knowledge and understanding of the other culture. Thus, even while the English pursued a policy of intimidation in the early years, they recognized the resilience and strength of the Indians' culture. Smith marveled at the strength and agility of the Chesapeake tribesmen, at their talent for hunting and fishing, and admired their music and entertainment. He noted that they practiced civil government, that they adhered to religious traditions, and that many of their customs and institutions were not unlike those of the Europeans. "Although the countrie people be very barbarous," he wrote, "yet have they amongst them such government, as that their Magistrats for good commanding, and their people for due subjection, and obeying, excell many places that would be counted very civill." Other Englishmen, such as the Anglican minister, Alexander Whitaker, who proselytized among the Indians, wrote that it was a mistake to suppose that the Indians were merely savage people, "for they are of body lustie, strong, and very nimble: they are a very understanding generation, quicke of apprehension, suddaine in their dispatches, subtile in their dealings, exquisite in their inventions, and industrious in their labour."[24] So, while both sides adjusted uneasily to the presence of the other, both were involved in

[23]Nancy Lurie, "Indian Cultural Adjustment to European Civilization," in *Seventeenth-Century America: Essays in Colonial History*, ed. James M. Smith (Chapel Hill: University of North Carolina Press, 1959), pp. 38–45.

[24]Arber and Bradley, eds., *Works of Smith*, 1: 43–84; Whitaker, *Good News from Virginia* (1613), quoted in Roy H. Pearce, *The Savages of America: A Study of the Indian and the Idea of Civilization* (Baltimore: The Johns Hopkins University Press, 1953), p. 13.

cultural borrowing. It was a process between two peoples separated by a cultural gap that was not nearly so large as the Europeans found it convenient to imply by labeling one culture "savage" and the other "civilized."

THE WAR OF 1622 AND ITS AFTERMATH

After the increase of population that accompanied the rapid growth of tobacco production, relations between the two peoples underwent a fundamental alteration. While giving Virginia an important money crop, the cultivation of tobacco created an enormous new demand for land. As more and more men pushed up the rivers that flowed into the Chesapeake Bay to carve out tobacco plantations, the Indians of the region perceived that what had previously been an abrasive and sometimes violent relationship might now become a disastrous one. Powhatan had retired in 1617, just as the cultivation of tobacco was beginning to expand rapidly. His kinsman, Opechancanough, who assumed leadership of the tidewater tribes, concluded that he must embark upon a program of military renaissance and spiritual revitalization.

Opechancanough was battling not only against land-encroaching Englishmen but against the diseases they were spreading among the Indian population. The deadliest of all European weapons were the microorganisms brought ashore in nearly every immigrant. In Europe these bacteriological infections—smallpox, diphtheria, scarlet fever, yellow fever, and others—had wrought demographic disaster in the fifteenth and sixteenth centuries. But infected populations had gradually built up immunities against them. The Indians of the New World, however, had no such immunity when the Europeans arrived as human carriers of these pathogens. The effects were therefore swift and deadly. Whole tribes could be wiped out in a few years, leaving vast areas depopulated. The greater the density of Indian population, the swifter the spread of the disease. In Mexico and other parts of the densely populated Spanish empire the Indian population losses were far more catastrophic than in more sparsely settled coastal North America. But in the Chesapeake region minor epidemics had taken their toll in the 1580s and again in 1608. Between 1617 and 1619 another epidemic decimated the Powhatan tribes.

In leading a reorganization of his people, Opechancanough relied heavily on Nemattanew, a war captain and religious prophet whom the English called "Jack of the Feathers" for the "fantastick Manner" in which "he wou'd often dress himself up with Feathers . . . as though he meant to flye."[25] A shadowy figure who came often to the English settlements, Nemattanew had convinced his tribesmen that he was immortal and that they would be

[25]J. Frederick Fausz, "The Powhatan Uprising of 1622: A Historical Study of Ethnocentrism and Cultural Conflict" (Ph.D. dissertation, College of William and Mary, 1977), pp. 346–49.

immune to musket fire if they rubbed their bodies with a special ointment. In March 1622, as Opechancanough was piecing together plans for a unified attack on the Virginia settlements, Nemattanew was murdered by the English. His death triggered the famous Indian assault two weeks later that dealt the colony a staggering blow; but the highly combustible atmosphere generated by a half-dozen years of white expansion and pressure on Indian hunting lands was the fundamental cause of the attack.

Although it did not achieve its goal of ending English presence in the Chesapeake area, the Indian attack of 1622 wiped out almost one-third of the white population. Included among the victims was Opechancanough's nephew by marriage, John Rolfe. It was the final straw for the Virginia Company of London. Shortly thereafter it declared bankruptcy, leaving the colony to the governance of the Crown. The more important result was that those who survived the attack were left free to pursue a ruthless new Indian policy. Even though several leaders in the colony confided to men in England that the real cause of the Indian attack was "our owne perfidious dealing with them," it was generally agreed that henceforward the colonists would be free to hunt down the Indians wherever they could be found. No longer would it be necessary to acknowledge an obligation to "civilize" and Christianize the native. A no-holds-barred approach to "the Indian problem" would now be taken. One Virginian wrote revealingly after the attack:

> Our hands which before were tied with gentleness and faire usage, are now set at liberty by the treacherous violence of the Sauvages. . . . So that we, who hitherto have had possession of no more ground than their waste and our purchase at a valuable consideration to theire owne contentment gained; may now by right of Warre, and law of Nations, invade the Country, and destroy them who sought to destroy us; whereby wee shall enjoy their cultivated places, turning the laborious Mattacke into the victorious Sword . . . and possessing the fruits of others labours. Now their cleared grounds in all their villages (which are situate in the fruitfullest places of the land) shall be inhabited by us, whereas heretofore the grubbing of woods was the greatest labour.[26]

A note of grim satisfaction that the Indians had succeeded in wiping out one-third of the English population can be detected. Now the colonizers were entitled to devastate Indian villages and take rather than buy the best land. John Smith, writing from England two years after the attack, noted that some men held that the attack "will be good for the Plantation, because now we have just cause to destroy them by all meanes possible." Another writer expressed the genocidal urge that was prevalent when he reasoned that the Indians had done the colonists a favor by sweeping away the previous English reluctance to annihilate the Indians. He enumerated with relish the ways that the "savages" could be exterminated. "Victorie," he wrote, "may be gained many waies: by force, by surprize, by famine in burning their

---

[26]Edward Waterhouse, "A Declaration of the State of the Colony and Affaires in Virginia . . ." (1662), in Kingsbury, ed., *Records of Virginia Company*, 3: 556–57.

Corne, by destroying and burning their Boats, Canoes, and Houses, by breaking their fishing Weares [weirs], by assailing them in their huntings, whereby they get the greatest part of their sustenance in Winter, by pursuing and chasing them with our horses, and blood-Hounds to draw after them, and Mastives to teare them."[27]

Once the thirst for revenge was slaked, the only debatable point was whether the extermination of the Indians would work to the benefit or disadvantage of the colony. One prominent planter offered "reasons why it is not fittinge utterlye to make an exterpation of the Savages yett" and then assured his neighbors that it was not genocide he was against but the destruction of a people who, if properly subjugated, could enrich all Virginians through their labor. But both subjugation and assimilation required more time and trouble than the Virginians were willing to spend. The simpler course, consistent with instructions from London to "root out [the Indians] from being any longer a people," was to follow a scorched earth policy, sending military expeditions each summer to destroy villages and crops.[28] In 1629 a peace treaty was negotiated but then rejected because it was decided by the council that a state of "perpetual enmity" would serve the colony better. It was a policy predicated on the belief that acculturation of the two peoples, even if possible, was not desirable.

In the aftermath of the Indian attack of 1622 an unambiguously negative image of the Indian pervaded the Virginian mentality. Words such as "perfidious," "cunning," "barbarous," and "improvident" had been used earlier to describe the natives, but their culture had still commanded considerable respect in English eyes. After 1622 the Indians' culture was seldom deemed worthy of consideration. More and more abusive words crept into English descriptions of the Indians and negative qualities were projected onto them with increasing frequency. Whereas John Smith and others of the first decade had described the Indians as "ingenious," and "industrious," and "quick of apprehension," the author of a history of the massacre, writing just after the event, asserted that the Chesapeake Indians "are by nature sloathfull and idle, vitious, melancholy, slovenly, of bad conditions, lyers, of small memory, of no constancy or trust . . . by nature of all people the most lying and most inconstant in the world, sottish and sodaine: never looking what dangers may happen afterwards, lesse capable than children of sixe or seaven yeares old, and lesse apt and ingenious."[29] Hereafter, the elimination of the Indians could be rationalized far more easily, for they were now seen as cultureless, unreconstructible savages rather than merely as hostile people whose culture, though different in some respects from the English, fitted them admirably for survival in the Chesapeake area.

[27]*Travels and Works of Smith,* 2: 578–79; Waterhouse, "State of the Colony," in Kingsbury, ed., *Records of Virginia Company,* 3: 557.

[28]John Martin, "The Manner Howe to Bringe the Indians into Subjection," in Kingsbury, ed., *Records of Virginia Company,* 3: 705–7.

[29]Waterhouse, "State of the Colony," in Kingsbury, ed., *Records of Virginia Company,* 3: 562–63.

In the two decades that followed the Indian attack of 1622 Virginia grew to about 8,000 settlers. By 1662 the population had swelled to 25,000 and the colony was shipping seven million pounds of tobacco a year to England. Although the Crown appointed a royal governor to rule in conjunction with an appointed council and an elected House of Burgesses, the real power in the colony lay at the local level where each tobacco planter operated autonomously with little regard for centralized authority. Men like Governor John Harvey, appointed in 1626, could complain that these planters acted "rather for their owne endes than either seekinge the generall good or doinge right to particuler men."[30] But there was little he could do to foster a spirit of community or to curb the appetites of the land-hungry, profit-conscious tobacco planters. When he proposed that a lasting peace be negotiated with the Indians and the Chesapeake tribes be left unmolested on the land they were occupying, the planters refused to cooperate. These were men who had clawed their way to the top of the rough-hewn frontier society, and they had no intention of allowing the governor to interfere with their engrossing of large tracts of land or their continuation of an aggressive Indian policy. When Harvey tried again in 1635 to impose his will, a coterie of Virginia's leaders plotted against him, provoked violence, and evicted him from the colony while sending petitions back to the mother country complaining of his arbitrary and unreasonable policies.

It was such tough, self-made, ambitious men as these, unhindered by religious or humanitarian concern for the Indians and unrestrained by government, that the Chesapeake tribes had to confront after 1630. They also had to face the rapidly shifting population balance—the drastic decline of their numbers by disease and war during the first quarter-century of English presence and the rapid increase of English colonists after 1624. These factors were beyond the control of the Chesapeake tribes. Even so, the natives continued to follow their traditional way of life. Years of contact with European culture had done little to convince them that they should remodel their religion, social and political organization, or values and beliefs on English patterns. Only the technological innovations and material objects of the newcomers were incorporated into Indian culture; the other aspects of European culture were resisted or rejected.

The Indian uprising of 1644 is additional proof "that the Indians' method of adjusting to changes wrought by the Europeans continued to be an attempt to prevail over or remove the source of anxiety—the settlers—rather than to adapt themselves to foreign culture." Though fewer in number than in 1622, the tribesmen attacked under the leadership of the aged Opechancanough, who was carried into battle on a litter. That the young warriors were willing to risk an all-out attack, knowing the grim reprisals that would rain down on them if they were defeated, is an indication of "the stubborn

[30]Quoted in Bernard Bailyn, "Politics and Social Structure in Virginia," in Smith, ed., *Seventeenth-Century America*, p. 97.

resistance of the Indians to cultural annihilation."[31] The Powhatan tribes were again the losers in the war of 1644, partially because the aid they expected from white Marylanders, whose relations with Virginia had always been abrasive, did not materialize. But their determination apparently convinced the Virginians that Indians could rarely be cowed into submissiveness. Rather than risk future wars, the colonists reversed the policy of the 1620s and in 1646 signed a formal treaty with the survivors of the Powhatan Confederacy that drew a line between red and white territory and promised the Indians safety in their areas. It was the beginning of the modern reservation system, for it recognized that assimilation of the two peoples was unlikely and guaranteed to the indigenous people a sanctuary from white land hunger and aggression. In return the Powhatan tribes agreed to render military assistance in the event of an attack by tribes outside the Chesapeake area and promised a yearly tribute to the Virginia colony in beaver skins.

When a census was taken in Virginia in 1669, only 11 of the 28 tribes described by John Smith in 1608 and only about 2,000 of the 20,000 Indians present when the English arrived were still left in the colony. The English victory in the clash of cultures was partly due to the continued immigration of new settlers to the colony during an era when disease drastically thinned the Indian ranks. The waning strength of the Powhatan Confederacy also related to the technological inferiority of their weapons, although the bow and arrow could be as effective as the musket in forest fighting. More important in the Indians' decline was their inability to unite against the incoming European peoples. They outnumbered the English during the first two decades of settlement and might have expected to be further aided by the fierce internal divisions that gripped the Virginia colony for years. But in times of military crisis the colonists were better able to unite, if only momentarily, than the tribes of the Chesapeake region.

A more indirect factor in the decay of Indian strength was the functionlessness of the Chesapeake tribes within the English economic and social system. This can be best understood by looking comparatively at the English and Spanish systems of colonization. In the Spanish colonies, the densely settled Indians had been utilized effectively as a subjugated labor force, both in the silver mines and in agriculture. The Spanish had unerringly located the native population centers in Mexico and Peru and made them the focal points of their colonizing efforts. The Indians supplied the bulk of the labor for Spanish extractive and productive enterprises in the early decades; hence it was not only desirable but necessary to assimilate them into the European culture. Moreover, the Spanish church had a vested interest in the Indians. It sent hundreds of missionaries to the colonies with the express purpose of obtaining as many conversions as possible for the greater glory of the church. Thirdly, because the Spanish immigrants were disproportionately

[31]Lurie, "Indian Cultural Adjustment," in Smith, ed., *Seventeenth-Century America*, pp. 51–52.

male, Indian women came to serve the function of mistress, concubine, and wife. Though they were regarded as inferior to Spanish women, thousands of them became the sexual partners, inside and outside marriage, of Spanish men and in this way were of the utmost importance to the colonizers. Of course none of these functions could be fulfilled until the native societies had been subordinated to Spanish authority. And the most merciless forms of mass killing and terrorization were employed by the Spanish to ensure their ascendancy in the first period of contact. Thereafter, however, the native people were seen not primarily as a threat to Spanish colonization, though the possibility of native uprisings was always present, but as a population that could answer the economic, religious, and biological needs of the Europeans. Important incentives existed for drawing the natives into Spanish culture, for mixing with them, and protecting them. In spite of the catastrophic spread of European diseases, which may have reduced the Indian population by as much as 75 percent in the first century of contact, an impressive degree of acculturation and assimilation took place in the Spanish colonies.

In English Virginia none of these factors pertained except in the most limited way. The English brought no military force comparable to the conquistadors to subjugate the sparsely settled Chesapeake tribes and drive them into agricultural labor. The Anglican Church sent only a handful of clergymen to the colony and they made only token efforts to mount a missionary campaign. Their power over local settlers so far as relations with the Indians was concerned was minimal. Nor was there any significant sexual conjoining of English males and native women, partly because of English squeamishness about women of another culture but probably even more because Indian women, living in tribes not subjugated by the English, had no inclination to consort with men of the intruding culture. Interracial marriages were almost unknown in Virginia and the few contacts between white men and Indian women that did take place were limited to the frontier areas where trappers and traders occasionally made liaisons with native women.

The only way in which the Indian served the needs of the white colonist was in the fur trade where the Indian acted as trapper and hunter. But the fur trade was always of negligible importance in the early Virginia settlements, and by the 1620s tobacco dominated the Virginia economy. What the colonists primarily wanted from the Indian was his cleared land, as was made manifest in the aftermath of the 1622 attack. Within the first generation of European settlement, it was demonstrated that neither side possessed the military capacity to subjugate the other. But for the English subjugation was unnecessary. The Indian, it was understood, had little to contribute to the goals of English colonization and was therefore regarded merely as an obstacle. Once defined in these terms, the Chesapeake tribes became the subject not of assimilative policies but apartheid plans which called for separation or removal. In almost a perfect reversal of Spanish

Indian policy the English in Virginia after 1622 worked to keep the two cultures apart. Like the Spanish policy, this plan was based on calculations of self-interest. Differences in the exploitable resources of the Spanish and English colonies, in the density of Indian population, in the demographic composition of the colonizing and colonized societies, and in the social backgrounds of the colonists, rather than differences in national character, attitudes toward the indigenous people, or in national policy, were chiefly responsible for the pursuit of assimilation in Spanish America and the pursuit of racial separation in Virginia.

4

CULTURES MEET
IN THE NORTHEAST

While Indians of the Powhatan confederacy were planning their attack on the white settlements of Virginia in 1622, Englishmen were mounting an "invasion" of Indian territory five hundred miles to the north. The word "invasion" is used not so much because Puritans, like other Europeans, were entering land occupied by indigenous people but because for Puritans life itself was a militant campaign against the Devil. The initial arrival of the Pilgrims on the western edge of the Atlantic in 1620 marked the beginning of a movement of English Protestants whose ideas, values, and institutions did more to shape the contours of colonial society than any other group. Yet in their relationships with people of other cultures Puritans were not significantly different from their countrymen of other religious persuasions.

PURITANISM

Puritanism was, among other things, a religious reform movement. Since the reign of Henry VIII, when England had turned toward Protestantism, Catholic–Protestant tensions had racked the country. When Elizabeth ascended the throne in 1558 she attempted to effect a religious compromise. But avowed anti–Catholics regarded the Church of England that flourished under her reign as at best a halfway house between a corrupt and a pure church and at worst barely distinguishable from the Church of Rome with its liturgy, vestments, rituals, and oppressive bureaucracy. Some Englishmen wanted greater purity in the church, a more radical cleansing of Catholic elements. They became known as Puritans.

Puritanism was also a political and social response to long-range changes that had been occurring in English society. Men and women of this era were living at a time when the traditional feudal society was giving way to a more modern social order. England was entering the modern age. This brought the overturning of the traditional church, the growth of cities, enclosure of land, an increase in trade, and the rise of a capitalistic society in which the individual had far more autonomy. The most visible social effects of these long-term trends were uprooted peasants cast off the land, an increase in vagabondage and poverty, and frightening increases in urban crime as people crowded into the cities, particularly into London, which grew from about 75,000 in 1550 to 200,000 in 1600 and to 325,000 in 1650.

Some of the changes overtaking English society impinged upon values and individual behavior. In the older medieval ethos people were arranged in a fixed system of hierarchies in church, government, economic organizations, and family. Life in an English rural village reflected this emphasis on rank and order. Every individual was contained within a web of elaborate relationships which conferred duties and responsibilities on each member of the community. There was the manorial hierarchy with lord, steward, and tenants; the parish hierarchy with vicar, churchwardens, and overseers of the poor; the hierarchy of the established church with archbishop, bishops, deans, canons, and visitors; and the hierarchy of economic enterprise with corporations, guilds, masters, journeymen, and apprentices. But in the period of modernization individuals gradually worked themselves free of the authority of corporate groups. Little by little inroads were made on the religious authority which dictated individual belief; on the political authority which strictly governed civil behavior and defined political rights in a limited way; and on the economic authority by which guilds and monopolies granted by the Crown closely regulated prices, wages, and conditions of work. Thus "protesters" or Protestants began challenging the authority of the Church of Rome; individual entrepreneurs challenged the right of the guilds to regulate work; individual enterprises challenged monopolies that excluded outsiders from areas of economic activity; and agricultural operators began buying small farmsteads and consolidating them into larger agricultural units, dislocating tenant farmers in the process.

To Puritans, the sight of individuals breaking free of traditional restraints was fearsome. In religion this could be applauded because it involved an attempt to place the individual in a more direct relationship with God, removing the traditional intermediaries—especially the Catholic Church. But Puritans deplored individualism in other areas of life because it left people to their own devices, where they promptly acted out the worst fantasies of social anarchy. Social order, respect for authority, morality—all seemed to be crumbling amidst the new social and economic order. Everywhere "idle and masterless men," as one social critic phrased it, roamed the land.

The concept of "every man alone," the individual operating freely in time and space, is at the core of our modern system of beliefs and behavior. But to intellectuals, social critics, and religious leaders of the late sixteenth century this conjured up only frightening visions of chaos. Individualism as a mode of behavior threatened the concept of community—of people bound together by obligations and responsibilities. In the older conception of society each person gained rights not as an individual but as a participating member of a corporate group. It was upon these corporate entities—religious, political, economic, and social—that rights were conferred. Now, under a newer ethic, the individual rather than the group became the conceptual unit of thinking. To Puritans this conjured up a frightening vision of anticommunity.

As a social and political movement Puritanism intended to address itself to this problem of the individual versus the community. Puritans intended to reverse the march of disorder, wickedness, and "masterlessness" which they saw burgeoning in English society. Through a new discipline the Puritans hoped to create a regenerated social order and thus to restore the lost equilibrium of their society. Their method or plan was to prescribe an ethic which stressed work or industriousness, in whatever one's calling, as a primary way of serving God. One did not have to occupy a high station or follow a profession; one had only to work hard in whatever station one found oneself, be that lawyer, blacksmith, or common laborer. Each "calling" was equally worthy in God's sight and, if followed assiduously, would lead the individual toward spiritual grace. One of the Puritan leaders wrote: "If thou beest a man that lives without a calling, though thou hast two thousands to spend, yet if thou hast no calling, tending to publique good, thou art an uncleane beast. God sent you unto this world as unto a Workhouse, not a Playhouse."[1]

Secondly, the Puritans sought to organize themselves into religious congregations where men and women could labor together, discipline themselves, and work for mutual salvation. Virtuousness would be fostered by a group concern, with each member not only working for his or her own perfection but also scrutinizing the behavior of others for signs of waywardness. Thirdly, the Puritans believed that in order to reform their society at large, they would have to assume responsibility—moral stewardship—over all those around them. In a chaotic and criminal world God's "elect" must save not only themselves but must also assume the burdens of civil government

---

[1]Quoted in Perry Miller and Thomas H. Johnson, *The Puritans* (New York: American Book Company, 1938), pp. 325–26.

so as to reform society at large. Others who could not find Christian truth in their hearts might have to be coerced and controlled, directed and dominated. Thus, all would be bound together in covenant to do God's work. In this sense Puritanism was an instrument of radical politics designed to capture the machinery of civil government and to bring about the conversion of the whole society. A mass movement with an ideological vision was to rule the land—a radical departure from traditional thought, which held that kings ruled by divine right and delegated their authority to those below them.

The rise of Puritanism during Elizabeth's reign, and the subsequent persecution of Puritans by her successor, James I, is a familiar story. For our purposes it is enough to understand that despite their initial successes, Puritans were increasingly harassed under James. By the 1620s many were convinced that in order to reform English society, the crusade for a new design in living would have to be first carried out in another part of the world. Economic opportunity also beckoned, at a time when many Puritans were feeling the effects of depression in England and thus was an important part of their decision. But their ideological commitment marked them off from the colonizers in Virginia. These were men and women fired by a vision of building a Christian utopia, dedicated to organizing themselves around the concept of community, and possessed of the belief that industriousness and self-discipline were indispensable parts of worshipping their God. In Virginia, by contrast, the spirit of communalism and an ideological vision were conspicuously absent. Economic ambitions, rather than being contained and limited within a set of moral prescriptions, were pursued in and of themselves.

The Puritans were by no means the first Europeans to reach the shores of what was to be called New England and what was the homeland of a number of Algonkian-speaking tribes. Fishermen of various European nationalities had been working the Newfoundland Banks and drying their catches on Cape Cod and the coast of Maine since the late sixteenth century. Hundreds of fishing ships had visited the New England coast and made contact with local Indians before 1607 when the first English attempt at colonization was made in the region. The attempt at settlement in that year was short-lived, for the small number of men who disembarked on the coast of Maine were beset with food shortages, fire, and inhospitable winds. Not until 1620 was another attempt at colonization made, this time by several hundred English Pilgrims who had earlier fled to Holland and now decided to establish themselves in the New World. Slowly, in the 1620s, other fur-trading and fish-drying settlements took root along the coast. But none of these could compare with the great Puritan migration which began in 1630 when eleven ships and some seven hundred passengers set out from England. They were the vanguard of a movement that by 1640 had brought about 12,000 people to New England's shores.

THE ELUSIVE UTOPIA

Led by John Winthrop, a member of the English gentry, the Puritans set about building their "Citty on the Hill" as they called their experiment in utopia building. The hope was to establish communities of pure Christians who collectively swore a covenant with God that they would work for his ends, knowing that in return he would watch over them. The individualistic impulses that had flowered in England were to be brought under control as all worked for the common good. To accomplish this the Puritans agreed to employ what today we might call totalitarian means. There could be no diversity of opinion concerning religious orthodoxy in the new communities. Government would be limited to those who were visibly filled with God's grace as determined by those already in the church. Offenders, both civil and religious, would be rooted out and punished severely. Every aspect of life was to be integrated into the quest for utopia—economic activity, political activity, intellectual activity, and religious activity. The Puritans were attempting to integrate all the elements of their culture into one unified quest at a time when contemporary European society was characterized by greater diversity and individualism. Participants in the experiment, at least initially, agreed to give up some of their freedoms in order to accomplish greater goals. Homogeneity, not diversity, was sought, and achieving the goals of the community rather than protecting the rights of its individual members was the main concern. This was to be a society consensual in origin but authoritarian in operation. The Puritans in England had formulated an ideology of rebellion which was now to be employed as an ideology of control.

As in Virginia, the early months were difficult. More than two hundred of the first seven hundred immigrants perished and a hundred more, chronically depressed by their first winter in the forbidding New England climate, returned to England the next spring. But Puritans kept coming. They began "hiving out" along the shores of Boston's Back Bay, along the rivers that emptied into it, south into what was to become Connecticut, and north along the Massachusetts coast. Crops were planted, fishing begun, and Massachusetts quickly achieved the viable economic base which had been so sorely lacking in Virginia in the early years. This success can be explained not only by the militant work ethic and self-discipline shared by most of the settlers, but also by the quality of leadership exercised by such men as Winthrop, John Cotton, John Eliot, Richard Mather, and Thomas Shepard, who were experienced in local government, law, and the uses of exhortation. The typical early leader in Virginia was a soldier of fortune or a roughneck adventurer whose instincts were almost entirely predatory. Massachusetts was led in the early years by university-trained ministers, experienced members of the English lesser gentry, and men compulsively determined to

Intensity and purposefulness suffused the personality of John Winthrop, leader of the Puritan migration to New England. (Courtesy American Antiquarian Society.)

fulfill what they regarded as God's prophecy for New England.

Nevertheless, Massachusetts experienced dissension and conflict in the early decades, both within its communities and in contact with the natives of the region. Even on the voyage across the Atlantic some inkling that the sun would not always shine on the Puritan experiment appeared. In the middle of the voyage Winthrop was compelled to remind some of the less submissive members of the expedition that respect for authority was to be a fundamental part of this new venture. Once on firm ground, and surrounded by boundless land, it proved difficult to squelch acquisitive instincts or to keep people closely bound in covenanted communities. Restless souls began moving away from the center of authority. Others, remaining at the center, agitated for a broader-based political system and a decentralization of authority that would give the individual towns the right to manage their own affairs. After only two years Winthrop wondered if the Puritans had not gone "from the snare to the pit." Thirteen years later he was still struggling to convince those around him that "if you stand for your natural corrupt liberties, and will do what is good in your own eyes, you will not endure the least weight of authority, but will murmur and oppose, and be always striving to shake off that yoke."[2]

Winthrop's troubles multiplied. In 1633 Roger Williams arrived in New England and now the established leaders were faced with a contentious and visionary man who defined religious orthodoxy in terms different from theirs and had no intention of changing his views to conform with those already pronounced orthodox. Williams preached that the Puritans were not truly pure because they would not proclaim complete separation from the Church of England. He argued that their interpretation of the Bible was incorrect. Perhaps most discomfiting, he charged that the colonists were intruding on Indian soil and illegally depriving the natives of their rights. By 1635 Williams had resisted all who struggled to make him retreat from his views and defied the civil magistrates to try or punish him for his teachings. Convinced that Williams would split the colony into competing religious groups; destroy all stability, cohesion, and authority; and bring about the disintegration of the colony through his religious perfectionism, the Massachusetts magistrates banished him from the colony and attempted to ship him back to England. But Williams escaped and trekked southward where he started a small settlement of his followers—the seed of the colony of Rhode Island.

Even as Williams was being banished to his personal Eden, the authorities were confronted with another preacher of unorthodoxy—Anne Hutchinson. Brilliant and charismatic, she had proven her value to the community as a midwife, healer, and spiritual counselor after she arrived in 1634. But in the next two years she emerged as more than a counselor. She gathered many in the community around her for religious discussions and then took to dissecting the previous Sunday's sermons, raising points of criticism concerning the theological interpretations of John Wilson, Boston's minister. Before long she was the center of a movement call Antinomianism—a variant interpretation of Puritan doctrine which stressed the mystical elements of God's grace and the futility of applying rules and regulations to govern the process by which each individual came to terms with his or her God. By 1636 Boston was dividing into two camps and Anne Hutchinson was drawing to her circle not only those who believed in her theological views

[2]Quoted in Richard S. Dunn, *Puritans and Yankees: The Winthrop Dynasty of New England, 1630–1717* (Princeton: Princeton University Press, 1962), p. 24.

but most of the discontented in the community—merchants who were disgruntled with the government's price controls, young people who disliked the rigid rule of their elders in church and government, women chafing under male authority, and artisans who resented wage controls imposed to arrest the inflationary trend that had begun.

Determined to rid themselves of this second threat to uniformity of opinion, the clergy and the magistrates tried Anne Hutchinson in 1636. After two long and symbolic interrogations she was excommunicated from the Boston church and banished from the colony for preaching eighty-two erroneous theological opinions. The sentence read to her at the trial's end conveys the fear that had been aroused in Boston and the determination of the magistrates to squelch further division within the community. "Forasmuch as you, Mrs. Hutchinson, have highly transgressed . . . and offended and troubled the Church with your Errors," intoned the judge, "and have drawn away many a poor soule, and have upheld your Revelations; and forasmuch as you have made a lye. . . . Therefor in the name of our Lord Jesus Christ . . . I doe cast you out . . . and deliver you up to Satan . . . and account you from this time forth to be a Hethen and a Publican . . . and I command you in the name of Jesus Christ and of this Church as a Leper to withdraw your selfe out of the Congregation."[3] With a number of her followers, Anne followed the route of Roger Williams to Rhode Island. The colony's leaders, the guardians of the dream of a Christian utopia, had demonstrated the lengths to which they were prepared to go to ensure homogeneity.

New England could not really remain homogeneous, no matter how many nonconformists were banished from its midst. Nor could the acquisitive instincts which ate at the concept of community be forever dampened. The work ethic inevitably brought material gains, and with worldly success individuals developed the ambition to reach still higher—precisely what the Puritan leaders feared would destroy the stable harmonious system they were trying to build. Population increase, geographical expansion, and trade with the outside world all worked against the idea of a closed corporate community suffused with religiosity. In spite of the leaders' admonitions that "the care of the public must oversway all private respects," Massachusetts, even in the early years, demonstrated the difficulty, if not the impossibility, of setting down land-hungry immigrants in the New World and expecting them to restrain their appetites and individualistic urges. The centrifugal forces of the environment were more than a match for the centripetal forces of religious ideology.

---

[3]Quoted in Emery Battis, *Saints and Sectaries: Anne Hutchinson and the Antinomian Controversy in the Massachusetts Bay Colony* (Chapel Hill: University of North Carolina Press, 1962), p. 246.

PURITANS AND INDIANS

Given the Puritan ideal of community and the centrality of the idea of reforming the world in their image, it might be thought that the conflict and limited acculturation that characterized Anglo-Indian contacts on the Chesapeake would have been replaced in New England by less hostility and greater interaction. But this was not the case.

Descendants of nomadic hunters who had come to the region 10,000 years before, the Indians of New England lived on the margin of the agricultural zone. Therefore, their economy combined hunting, fishing, and agriculture, though the latter, by the time Europeans arrived, was their primary subsistence activity. Efficiently utilizing their environment according to the season, they engaged in winter hunting, spring stream fishing and clearing of fields, summer cultivation of crops and sea fishing, and autumn harvesting and hunting. "Seasonality," writes Neal Salisbury, "provided the basis for a rudimentary but regularly recurrent annual cycle."[4]

The sexual division of labor was marked among the Algonkian tribes of New England. Men hunted but women were responsible for all phases of agriculture—planting, maintaining, and harvesting crops—as well as for fishing and gathering wild plant products. Since agriculture had become the most important component of the economy, a distinct imbalance had evolved in the productivity of the two sexes. This did not lead, as in the case of the Iroquois, to the adoption of a matrilineal kinship system or the conferring of a degree of political power upon women. In New England kinship remained patrilineal, and men continued to dominate political and religious life.

Political leadership of Algonkian tribes in New England was held by single individuals, called "sachems" in the southern region and "sagamores" in the northern region. The sachem's role was to coordinate, at the village level, activities that concerned the group as a whole—hunting, trade, the administration of justice, and diplomacy. The sachem's authority depended heavily on maintaining the consent of his people. This, in turn, depended greatly on the sachem's ability to communicate with the spiritual forces that controlled the fate of the tribe. "Their authority is most precarious," wrote one Frenchman among the Abenaki, "if indeed, that may be called authority to which obedience is in no wise obligatory."[5] Sachems and sagamores were not chiefs or lords whose title was inherited and authority unquestioned, but "coordinators and ceremonial representatives for their people."[6]

In the pre-contact period the Algonkian-speaking people of New England were more densely settled than in the Chesapeake region, probably num-

[4]Neal E. Salisbury, *Manitou and Providence: Indians, Europeans, and the Making of New England, 1500–1643* (New York: Oxford University Press, forthcoming).

[5]Reuben Gold Thwaites, ed., *The Jesuit Relations and Allied Documents . . . 1610–1791* (Cleveland: The Burrows Brothers Company, 1896), II, 73.

[6]Salisbury, *Manitou and Providence.*

bering more than 100,000 between the Kennebec River and Cape Cod. Among them, the most numerous were the Abenaki, Pawtucket, Massachuset, Narragansett, Pequot, and Wampanoag. All of these groups had been in contact with Europeans for many generations. Fishermen who dried their catches and engaged in minor trade had provided the more northerly tribes with knowledge of European culture since the first quarter of the sixteenth century, and short-lived French and English attempts at settlement in the first decade of the seventeenth century gave them further understanding of the people from across the sea.

A series of English exploratory incursions and small-scale attempts at settlement occurred in the early seventeenth century. All of them had to contend with the fact that the French had already established permanent settlements and a trading network that extended from Nova Scotia to Cape Cod. This economic hegemony had been built upon a system of reciprocal relations with the natives of the region. None of the first English attempts at settlement fared well, for the English adopted a far more militaristic stance toward the Indians, typified in John Smith's formula of deception, intimidation, and unbridled force, which he recommended following his voyage to the New England coast in 1614. English expeditions attacked and kidnapped coastal Indians on a number of occasions. In 1614 one of Smith's captains captured more than twenty Indians and sold them into slavery in Malaga, Spain. Such a predatory approach guaranteed that the English, when they came in larger numbers in the 1620s, would not be welcomed as a people with whom amicable relations could be expected.

It was not brute force or superior numbers, however, that paved the way for a permanent English presence in New England. Rather it was disease. In 1616 English fishermen stopped on the coast and triggered a "virgin soil epidemic"—the implantation of viruses into a population with no immunological defense. Tens of thousands of Indians died within a single year along the New England coast. Especially hard hit was the area from Massachusetts Bay to Plymouth Bay where entire towns were swept away or abandoned. Five years later an Englishman moving through the area wrote that the Indians had "died on heapes, as they lay in their houses, and the living that were able to shift for themselves would runne away and let them dy, and let there Carkases ly above the ground without buriall. . . . And the bones and skulls upon the several places of their habitations, made such a spectacle . . . that as I travailed in that Forrest nere the Massachussetts [tribe], it seemed to mee a new found Golgotha."[7] Three-quarters or more of the native inhabitants of southern New England probably succumbed to the disease.

When the Pilgrims arrived in 1620, they disembarked in an area that had

[7]Thomas Morton, "New English Canaan," in *Tracts and Other Papers Relating Principally to the Origin, Settlement and Progress of the Colonies in North America*, Peter Force, comp. (Washington, D.C., 1836), II, No. 5: 19.

suffered catastrophic population losses just a few years before. This was crucial not only in opening up the land for them but also in greatly weakening the Indians' ability to resist the encroachers. It was the further good fortune of the English to encounter Squanto, a Wampanoag who had been kidnapped by an English ship captain in 1614. Squanto had been sold by his abductor in Spain but somehow had made his way to England where he joined an English captain on several trips to the New England coast. On the second of these trips Squanto found that most of his tribe had been killed by the plague, but he remained in the Cape Cod area and was there when the Pilgrims landed. Through Squanto's friendship the Pilgrims were rendered important assistance in the early years.

A decade after the initial settlement, William Bradford, the leader of the Pilgrim colony, wrote that the English had come anticipating the "continual danger of the savage people, who are cruel, barbarous, and most treacherous"—characteristics that made "the very bowels of men to grate within them and make the weak to quake and tremble."[8] But given the record of kidnapping and broken trust which the English had established in their periodic visits to the coast before 1620, the characterization better fitted the English than the local tribes. The local Indians were probably deeply suspicious of the Pilgrims, but no incident of violence at Plymouth occurred until after the newcomers discovered the natives' underground cold-storage cellars and stole as much of the corn, placed there for winter use, as they could carry off. Even then the Indians chose to minimize contact with the settlers, though after death had reduced the Plymouth colony to about fifty persons in the spring of 1621 the vulnerability of the English invited Indian attack.

The need of the local Wampanoags for a military ally to aid them in their struggle with the neighboring Narragansetts probably explains why they tolerated English abuses and even signed a treaty in 1621 that formed the basis for trade and mutual assistance with the precariously situated English. The logic of the Wampanoag diplomacy was revealed when Miles Standish and other Pilgrims aided them in a dispute with their enemies in 1621. The Wampanoags regarded the treaty as an alliance of equals but the English, regarding themselves as culturally superior, saw it as the submission by the Indians to English domination.

This surface amity lasted only a year, however. In 1622 the arrival of about sixty non–Pilgrim newcomers to the colony brought serious friction. The new colonists settled themselves at Wessagusset, some distance from the Pilgrim colony, stole corn from the neighboring Massachusets, and planned attacks on them when they refused to trade with the needy, but arrogant, newcomers. Under cover of a story that the Indians were conspiring against both white communities, Standish, who had long harbored

[8]William Bradford, *Of Plymouth Plantation, 1620–1647*, ed. Samuel Eliot Morison (New York: Alfred A. Knopf, Inc., 1966), p. 26.

grudges against several insulting Massachusets, led an offensive against the friendly Indians, killing eight of them and impaling the head of the sachem Wituwamet on top of the fort at Plymouth as a symbol of white power. Hearing of the deterioration of relations, John Robinson, formerly the Pilgrims' minister in Holland, wrote Governor Bradford in dismay, asking why the English indulged in needless violence. What was happening to "civilized" men in the wilderness? asked Robinson. Were they beginning to act like "savages," forgetting that they were supposed to represent order and piety? Robinson singled out Miles Standish, the militia captain of Plymouth, who had adopted John Smith's formula of inspiring fear and submission rather than mutual respect and harmonious relations. "It is . . . a thing more glorious, in men's eyes, than pleasing in God's, or convenient for Christians, to be a terrour to poor barbarous people. And indeed I am afraid lest, by these occasions, others should be drawn to affect [this kind of behavior] in the world."[9] As for the Indians, they "could not imagine, from whence these men should come," wrote Thomas Morton, a friend of the Indians, "or to what end, seeing them performe such unexpected actions." From that time on the English colonists were called "Wotowquenange, which in their language signifieth stabbers or Cutthroates."[10]

When the Puritan migration began in 1630, natives of the New England coast had more than a generation of experience with English ways. Little that they had encountered could have rendered them optimistic about future relations, although their own intertribal hostilities continued to make the settlers potentially valuable allies, and their desire for trade goods persisted. As for the Puritans, they were publicly committed to interracial harmony but privately preparing for the worst. The charter of the Massachusetts Bay Company spoke of the commitment to convert the Indians to Christianity. The "principall ende of this plantacion," it pronounced, was to "wynn and incite the natives of [the] country, to the knowledg and obedience of the onlie true God and Savior of mankinde, and the Christian fayth."[11] But the instructions of the Company to John Winthrop revealed more accurately what was anticipated. According to these orders, all men were to be trained in the use of firearms; Indians were prohibited from entering the Puritan towns; and any colonists so reckless as to sell arms to the Indians or instruct them in their use were to be deported to England where they would be severely punished. While ordering that the Indians must be fairly treated, the Company reflected the garrison mentality that settlers, once landed and settled, would manifest even more strongly. No missionary activity was to be initiated for thirteen years.

[9]*Ibid.*, p. 375.

[10]Thomas Morton, "New England Canaan," p. 76, quoted in Neal E. Salisbury, "Conquest of the 'Savage': Puritans, Puritan Missionaries, and Indians, 1620–1680" (Ph.D. dissertation, University of California, Los Angeles, 1972), p. 86.

[11]Nathaniel B. Shurtleff, *Records of the Governor and Company of the Massachusetts Bay in New England*, 5 vols. (Boston: W. White, 1853–54), I: 17.

In the first few years of settlement the Indians did little to arouse Puritan wrath. Their sachems made overtures of friendship; they supplied the colonists with corn during the difficult first winter; and a minor trade was started. It was with surprise that one Puritan leader recounted that during the first winter, when the Puritans "had scarce houses to shelter themselves, and no doores to hinder the Indians access to all they had in them, . . . where their whole substance, weake Wives and little ones lay open to their plunder; . . . yet had they none food or stuffe diminished, neither Children nor Wives hurt in the least measure, although the Indians came commonly to them at those times, much hungry belly (as they used to say) and were then in number and strength beyond the English by far."[12]

This state of coexistence lasted only a few years. Smallpox struck the eastern Massachusetts bands in 1633 and 1634, killing thousands as far north as Maine and as far south as the Connecticut Valley. For the colonists it was proof that God had intervened in the Puritans' behalf at a time when the expansionist impulses of the settlers were beginning to cause friction over rights to land. The town records of Charlestown, for example, state that "without this remarkable and terrible stroke of God upon the natives, [we] would with much more difficulty have found room, and at far greater charge have obtained and purchased land."[13] As in Virginia, it was the need for land that provided the incentive for steering away from rather than toward equitable relations between the societies. That the population buildup came so quickly in Puritan New England only hastened the impulse to regard Indians as objects to be removed rather than subjects to be assimilated.

THE QUESTION OF LAND

Puritan theories of land possession help to clarify this tendency to classify Indians in such a way that only violence rather than assimilation or coexistence could occur. Like other Europeans, Puritans claimed the land they were invading by right of discovery. This theory derived from the ancient claim that Christians were everywhere entitled to dispossess non–Christians of their land. A second European legal theory, called *vacuum domicilium*, bolstered Puritan claims that land not "occupied" or "settled" went by forfeit to those who attached themselves to it in a "civilized" manner. Before he set foot in the New World John Winthrop wrote:

As for the Natives in New England, they inclose noe Land, neither have any setled habytation, nor any tame Cattle to improve the Land by, and soe have noe other but a Naturall Right to those Countries, soe as if we leave them

---

[12]Edward Johnson, "Wonder-Working Providence," quoted in Salisbury, "Conquest of the 'Savage'," pp. 63–64.

[13]Quoted in Alden T. Vaughan, *New England Frontier: Puritans and Indians, 1620-1675* (Boston: Little, Brown and Company, 1965), p. 104.

sufficient for their use, we may lawfully take the rest, there being more than enough for them and us.[14]

Thus, in Puritan eyes, entitlement to the land of New England required nothing more than the assertion that because their way of life did not conform to European norms, the Indians had forfeited all the land which they "roamed" rather than "settled." By European definition the land was *vacuum domicilium*—unoccupied. To this mental picture of an unoccupied land the awful epidemic of 1616–18 had made an important contribution.

Given the slender power of the disease-ravaged coastal tribes of the Massachusetts Bay region and the legal principles invoked under the concept of *vacuum domicilium,* the Puritans were ideally situated to establish their beachhead in the New World. The remnants of the formerly populous Massachuset and Pawtucket peoples were in no position to resist and in fact willingly consented to the settlement of their lands by the Puritan vanguard that inhabited Naumkeag (renamed Salem) in 1629 and the 3,000 settlers who came in the next four years. In return for land, of which they now had a great surplus, the Indians gained the protection of the English against their Micmac enemies to the north. Hence the Puritans quickly acquired the notion that the local Indians were properly regarded as domesticated subjects, who lived in separate villages but were to answer to Puritan concepts of government and law.

Nonetheless, by about 1634 the land question had begun to assume a central place in Puritan-Indian relations. Another epidemic in 1633 had struck down many native people throughout a wide area from the St. Lawrence River to Long Island. Once more the English saw the divine hand intervening in their behalf and Indians trembled at the power of the English God. This may have temporarily lessened the Indian sense of being overwhelmed by the steady flow of English colonists into the area. But pressure on available land resources was mounting rapidly.

The land question also became critical because in 1633 the radical separatist, Roger Williams of Salem, disputed the claim of the Massachusetts Bay leaders that their royal patent entitled them to occupy Indian land without first purchasing it from the natives. Williams had become inmersed in Indian culture shortly after his arrival in 1631—one of the few Englishmen to do so—and by the next year was absorbed in learning their language. Williams argued that the Puritans had illegally and sinfully grabbed Indian land and would have to answer for this before God and the English authorities. He also argued that the natives of the region used the land in rational and systematic ways, thus directly challenging the random use of land supposed in the legal concept of *vacuum domicilium.* The Massachusetts magistrates indignantly dismissed these ideas, ceremoniously burned the tract in which Williams advanced his arguments, and shortly thereafter

[14]"Generall Considerations for the Plantation in New England . . . " (1629), in *Winthrop Papers,* 5 vols., ed. Allyn B. Forbes (Boston: Massachusetts Historical Society, 1929–47), 2: 118.

banished him from the colony. Traveling to Rhode Island with some of his followers, Williams was offered land by a Narragansett sachem and found "among the savages," as he wrote, a place where he and his followers could peaceably worship God according to their consciences. Winthrop's response to Williams's argument was that "if we had no right to this lande, yet our God hathe right to it, and if he be pleased to give it us (takinge it from a people who had so long usurped upon him and abused his creatures) who shall controll him or his terms?"[15] By claiming that God directed all Puritan policy, Winthrop thus charged anyone who murmured dissent with opposing not only Puritan policy but God himself.

Nevertheless, the practice of purchasing Indian land progressed slowly as settlement continued. But the purchases were usually made in order to obtain a favorable settlement in a situation where the same tract of land was coveted by rival groups of settlers. In such cases a deed to the land in dispute from an Indian seller was the best way to convince a court of one's claim. Even in those cases where intra–European rivalry necessitated the purchase of Indian land, the sale could be accomplished through a variety of stratagems designed to reduce the cost to the white settler. Turning livestock into cultivated Indian fields over a period of time was an effective way of convincing an Indian that his land was losing its value. Alcohol was frequently used to reduce the negotiating skill of the Indian seller. Another method was to buy the land at a rock-bottom price from an Indian sachem who falsely claimed title to it and then take to court any disputing sachem who claimed ownership. Before an English court, with its white lawyers, judges, and juries, the Indian claimant rarely won his case. Perhaps most effective of all was fining an Indian for minor offenses of English law— walking on the Sabbath or illegally entering a town, for example—and then "rescuing" him from the debt he was unable to pay by discharging the fine in return for a tract of his land. None of these tactics worked in areas where Indian tribes were strong and unified. But among the decimated and divided tribes of southern New England they were highly effective.

THE PEQUOT WAR

All the factors that operated in Virginia to produce friction between the two societies—English land hunger, a deprecatory view of native culture, and intertribal Indian hostility—were to be found in New England. They were vastly augmented by another factor not present on the Chesapeake—the Puritan sense of mission. For people of such high moral purpose, who lived daily with the anxiety that they might fail in what they saw as the last chance to save corrupt Western Protestantism, the Indian stood as a direct challenge to the "errand into the wilderness." The Puritans' mission was to

[15]Quoted in *ibid.*, 534n.

tame and civilize their new environment and to build in it a pious common-wealth that would "shine like a beacon" back to decadent England. But how could order and discipline be brought to the new environment unless its inhabitants were tamed and "civilized"? Governor William Bradford of Plymouth tellingly described the land he was entering as "a hideous and desolate wilderness full of wild beasts and wild men."[16] Land, beast, and man must all be brought under control. To do less was to allow chaos to continue when God's will was that Christian order be imposed. As Roy H. Pearce has explained, the Indian stood as a vivid reminder of what the English knew they must not become. The native was the counterimage of civilized man, thought to be lacking in what was most valued by the Puritans—civility, Christian piety, purposefulness, and the work ethic. If such people could not be made part of the Puritan system, then the Puritans would have demonstrated their inability to control this corner of the earth to which God had directed them. God would surely answer such a failure with his wrath. So Puritans achieved control of themselves—internal control—through controlling the external world containing forests, fields—and Indians.[17]

The greater one's doubts about the success of this utopian experiment, doubts magnified by internal dissension, the greater the inner need to stifle self-doubt through repression and extension of control. Thus in New England, Indians became obstacles in two senses: as in Virginia and elsewhere they represented a physical barrier since they possessed the land and could not easily be subjugated so as to serve English ends; and they were a psychological obstacle since, while they remained "savages," they threatened the identity of individual Puritans and the collective success of the Puritan Way.

To eliminate "savagism" one did not necessarily have to eliminate the "savages." From their writings it appears that Puritans would have preferred to convert the "heathen" to Christianity. But this could only be accomplished through great expenditure of time and effort. The Spanish and Portuguese had sent hundreds of missionaries along with the conquistadors and settlers. But the Puritans came only with their own ministers and these men had more than enough to do to maintain piety, unity, and moral standards within the white community. Proselytizing the natives of New England never received a high priority. Much was written about foiling Satan, who had "decoyed those miserable savages hither, in hopes that the gospel of the Lord Jesus Christ would never come here to destroy or disturb his absolute empire over them," but little was done in saving the Native Americans from Satan.[18]

[16]Bradford, *Plymouth Plantation*, p. 62.

[17]Roy H. Pearce, *The Savages of America: A Study of the Indian and the Idea of Civilization* (Baltimore: The Johns Hopkins Press, 1953), pp. 3–24.

[18]Cotton Mather, *Magnalia Christi Americana* (Hartford, Conn., 1853), II, 556.

Rather than convert the "savages" of New England, the Puritans attempted to bring them under civil government, making them strictly accountable to the ordinances that governed white behavior in Massachusetts. Insofar as Indians were willing to subject themselves to the new white code of behavior, usually out of fear, the Puritans could prevail, keeping a close eye on all Indians within the areas of white settlement and bringing them to court for any offenses against white law. Many of the smaller bands of eastern Massachusetts, disastrously weakened by European disease or living in fear of strong and hostile neighbors, did what was necessary to satisfy the newcomers. But the question of control became a military problem when the Puritans encountered a tribe that was sufficiently strong to resist the loss of its cultural identity and political sovereignty.

Such were the Pequots—a strong and aggressive people who had migrated to southern New England in the century before English arrival. By the 1630s they had built a trading network of tributary groups and viewed the Narragansetts as their main rival in southern New England. The Pequots worked hard to convince the neighboring Narragansetts that only by uniting against the English could either tribe survive. But their arguments went unheard. Following the advice of Roger Williams, the Narragansetts agreed to ally themselves with Massachusetts Bay, leaving the Pequots virtually alone in their determination to resist the English.

Hostilities between the Pequots and English were ostensibly triggered by the murder of two white ship captains and their crews. One of the mariners, John Stone, was cordially hated among the English, for he had attempted to murder Governor Prence of Plymouth and had later been banished from Massachusetts for other misdeeds. Two years after Stone's death in 1634, John Oldham was found murdered on his pinnace off Block Island. Using these incidents as justification for a punitive expedition against the unsubmissive Pequots, a joint Connecticut-Massachusetts force marched into Pequot country and demanded the murderers (who, as it turned out, were not Pequots) as well as a thousand fathoms of wampum, and some Pequot children as hostages.

The Pequots understood that the issue was broader than the death of several English mariners, that in fact they were embroiled in a complicated set of disputes over land and trade. These were the real causes of the war that shortly would break out. At the center of the tensions was the English–Dutch trade rivalry and intertribal Indian hostilities. Since 1622 the Dutch in New Amsterdam had controlled the Indian trade of New England through their connections to both the Pequot and the Narragansett, the region's two strongest tribes. After the arrival of the English and their rapid expansion in the early 1630s, the Dutch perceived that their trading empire was greatly threatened. Hence, they purchased land on the lower Connecticut River—an area on which several English groups had their eyes—and built a trading post there to defend their regional economic hegemony. Some of the Pequots' discontented client tribes, however, were already breaking away, signing separate trade agreements with and ceding land to the English. Amidst such fragmentation, expansionist New England was ready, with the aid of its Narragansett allies, to drive the Dutch traders from southern New England and to subdue the Pequots who occupied some of the area's most fertile soil. The Pequots first tried to placate the English; when this proved impossible, they chose to resist.

In the war that ensued, the English found the Pequots more than a match until they were able to surround a secondary Pequot village on the Mystic River in May 1637. The English and their Narragansett allies attacked before dawn, infiltrated the town, and set fire to the Pequot wigwams inside before beating a fast retreat. In the meleé about twenty Narragansetts suffered wounds at the hands of the English, who found it difficult to distinguish between Indian enemies and allies. Retreating from the flame-engulfed village, the English regrouped and waited for fleeing survivors from the inferno. Most of the victims were noncombatants since the Pequot warriors were gathered at another village about five miles away. Before the day was over a large part of the Pequot tribe had been slaughtered, many by fire and others by guns. Those who escaped or who were not at the fort were enslaved and sold to other tribes or shipped to the West Indies in chains. One of New England's first historians, William Hubbard, wrote that dozens of captured Pequots were put on board the ship of Captain John Gallup, "which proved [to be] Charon's ferry-boat unto them, for it was found the quickest was to feed the fishes with 'em."[19] One of the militia captains wrote that at Mystic Fort "God . . . laughed [at] his Enemies and the Enemies of his People to Scorn, making them as a fiery Oven . . . [and] filling the Place with Dead Bodies." William Bradford wrote that "it was a fearful sight to see them thus frying in the fire and the streams of blood quenching the same, and horrible was the stink and scent thereof; but the victory seemed a sweet sacrifice, and they gave the praise thereof to God, who had wrought so wonderfully for them, thus to enclose their enemies in their hands and given them so speedy a victory over so proud and insulting an enemy."[20] In 1638, at the Treaty of Hartford, the Pequot nation was declared dissolved. Two generations later Cotton Mather, a pillar of the Puritan ministry, reiterated: "in a little more than *one* hour, five or six hundred of these barbarians were dismissed from a world that was *burdened* with them."[21]

Such savagery as the "civilized" Puritans demonstrated at Mystic Fort was shocking to the Narragansett "savages" who fought with the Puritans. According to one English officer, they came after the victory and "much rejoiced at our victories, and greatly admired the manner of Englishmen's fight, but cried Mach it, Mach it; that is, It is naught, it is naught [bad or wicked] because it is too furious and slays too many men." It was a poignant comment on the different styles and functions of warfare in the two societies.[22]

For the Puritans the extermination of the Pequots was proof of their political and military ascendancy. Its additional function was to provide a response to anxiety and disunity that had become widely diffused throughout the colony. These fears were associated not only with the threat of the Pequots but also with the dissensions within Puritan society. It is well to remember that the war came on the heels of three years of intense internal discord centered around the challenges to the power of the magistrates by Roger Williams and Anne Hutchinson. These challenges, in turn, involved not only theological questions but economic restrictions, the distribution of political power, and competing land claims among English settlers in Massachusetts, Connecticut, and Rhode Island. Their colonies beset with contro-

---

[19]William Hubbard, *A Narrative of the Troubles with the Indians in New England* (1677), quoted in Carolyn T. Foreman, *Indians Abroad, 1493–1938* (Norman: University of Oklahoma Press, 1943), p. 29.

[20]John Mason, "A Brief History of the Pequot War," *Massachusetts Historical Society Collections*, 2d Ser., 8 (Boston: 1826): 140–41. Bradford, *Plymouth Plantation*, p. 296.

[21]Cotton Mather, *Magnalia Christi Americana: or, The Ecclesiastic History of New England* (New York: Russell & Russell, 1967), II: 558.

[22]John Underhill, "News from America," quoted in Salisbury, "Conquest of the 'Savage'," p. 81.

versy, the Puritan leaders talked morbidly about God's anger at seeing his chosen people subvert the City on the Hill. In this sense, the Puritan determination to destroy the Pequots and the level of violence manifested at Mystic Fort can be partially understood in terms of the self-doubt and guilt that Puritans could expiate only by exterminating so many of "Satan's agents." Dead Pequots were offered to God as atonement for Puritan failings.

Victory over the Pequots decisively established English sovereignty over all the Indians of southeastern New England except the Narragansetts and removed the one remaining obstacle to expansion into the Connecticut River Valley. The tribes of southern New England, reduced to about one quarter of their former population, adjusted as best they could to the realities of Puritan power. The fur trade kept the two societies in touch with each other and provided the means by which English iron goods became incorporated into the material culture of the Indians. But the trade, which flourished in the 1630s, petered out by mid-century as the beaver supply in New England became depleted. In spite of these trade contacts, most of the remnant groups that had survived the coming of the English struggled to maintain their native way of life. Some of the weaker and more demoralized groups followed the handful of missionaries, finally spurred to action in 1643 by English critics, who rightly charged that conversion had been studiously ignored for more than a decade. After ten years of effort less than a thousand Indians of the region were settled in four villages of "praying Indians" and fewer than one hundred of these declared their conversion to the Puritan form of Christianity. Even among these, defections would be numerous in the 1670s when war broke out again in Massachusetts. As in the case of Virginia, the natives incorporated certain implements and articles of clothing obtained in the European trade into their culture, but overwhelmingly, even after major military defeats, they preferred to resist acculturation when it meant adopting English religion, forms of government, styles of life, or patterns of social and economic organization.

For Puritans and non–Puritans who migrated into New England in increasing numbers after mid-century, the Indians served no useful purpose. The rough balance of English males and females eliminated the need for Indian women as sexual partners. The church took only a minor interest in the Indian, who in any event could rarely satisfy the qualifications that Puritans placed upon their own people for church membership. The Indian trade withered to relative unimportance, as fishing, lumbering, shipbuilding, and agriculture became the mainstays of the colonizers' economy. This lack of function within English society, combined with the special tendency of Puritans to doubt the Indians' capacity for meeting the standards required in the New Jerusalem, made close and reciprocal contacts between the two societies all but impossible.

5

PATTERNS
OF INDIAN-EUROPEAN
INTERACTION

The history of colonial America has been written primarily as the record of the English in North America. This makes it easy to overlook the fact that for most of the seventeenth century the eastern edge of the continent was the scene of bitter intra-European rivalry. The English were periodically pitted against the Dutch, Swedes, French, and Spanish. Conflict did not stop there, for the English themselves were locked in a series of disputes and insurrections which plagued colonization in the first two-thirds of the seventeenth century and led to armed conflict up and down the seaboard in the last third of the century. In many instances, native groups were able to capitalize on these intra-European and intra-English hostilities in fashioning strategies of adaptation and survival. But they were also confronting the invasion of a bewildering variety of Europeans who, despite linguistic and cultural diversity and competitive strivings, kept growing in number and were often able to bury their differences when the threat of Indian resistance scented the breeze.

How did Dutch, French, and Spanish colonizers relate to the Indian societies they encountered? Did differences in national character and historical experience with "outside" people shape their encounter with the indigenous people of North America? Was the colonizers' religion the crucial variable?

Or did the number of settlers and the type of society they were trying to build figure most importantly in the way intergroup relations evolved? By adopting a comparative approach to European-Indian relations in the seventeenth century we can better understand the uniqueness or typicality of the English experience in Virginia and New England. And we can test certain classic generalizations made by historians such as that of the famous Francis Parkman, who wrote a century ago that in North America "Spanish civilization crushed the Indians; English civilization scorned and neglected him; French civilization embraced and cherished him."[1]

DUTCH-INDIAN RELATIONS

For both the English and the Indians who inhabited the Middle Atlantic region—the area for which the Delaware and Hudson River valleys served as focal points—it was the Dutch who posed the biggest problem from the 1620s until the 1670s. Hollanders had achieved independence from their own colonial masters, the Spanish, only in 1609. But even by then they had become the principal carriers of seaborne commerce in Western Europe and had begun interloping in the Spanish and Portuguese trade to the New World, trading illegally with settlers who were glad to violate the commercial policies of their own countries in order to get more favorable prices from the Dutch in the cloth and slave trade. Then, in a generation of spectacular achievement, the Dutch forged into the forefront of the race for wealth in the New World. In 1621 the Dutch West India Company, impressively capitalized and fully supported by the government, was launched. Its goals were commerce and conquest—to gain control of as much of the European-African-New World trade as possible and to plant colonies wherever the opportunity arose. Success came quickly. Within a few decades the Dutch company had acquired such a staggering acquisition of power that perhaps even American megacorporations in the late twentieth century could not be said to exert the influence that the Dutch West India Company did in the second quarter of the seventeenth century. In 1628 its fleet intercepted and captured the entire annual Spanish flotilla, homeward bound from the Caribbean. Enough gold was scooped up in this single exploit—about fifteen million guilders—to pay a 50 percent dividend to the Company's shareholders with enough left over to finance a military campaign against the Portuguese settlements in northeastern Brazil. For the next half century the Dutch controlled shipping to the New World and in the process reduced the Spanish and Portuguese trade to insignificance.

---

[1]Quoted in Mason Wade, "The French and the Indians," in *Attitudes of Colonial Powers toward the American Indian*, ed. Howard Peckham and Charles Gibson (Salt Lake City: University of Utah Press, 1969), p. 61.

At the same time the Dutch began to take over the African slave trade of their competitors. They had built bases of their own on the African coast as early as 1611, but in the 1620s and 1630s they began assaulting Portuguese forts and trading posts. By 1637, when they captured the center of Portuguese slaving activities, Elmina Castle, on the Gold Coast, they had all but driven the Portuguese from the Atlantic slave trade. Bases on the African coast were linked to bases in the Caribbean which had been seized from the Spanish—Curaçao, Saba, St. Martin, and St. Eustatius. This was accompanied by assaults on Portuguese Brazil, culminating in 1630, when the Dutch overwhelmed the Portuguese and took control of their highly profitable sugar plantations on the northeast coast, the most important source of sugar for the kitchens of Europe. Other arms of the vast Dutch trading empire reached the East Indies, India, Ceylon, and Formosa.

The mighty Dutch were also active on the North American mainland. They had initiated a trade in furs with the Indians in 1609 on the first voyage of Henry Hudson, who sailed as an employee of the Dutch East India Company. Five years later they established a tiny trading post high on the Hudson River near Albany. Shortly after the chartering of the West India Company in 1621 a permanent settlement was planted on the present site of New York City. Called New Amsterdam, it became the center of Dutch colonization in North America for the next half century. Furs rather than sugar or gold were the source of profit for the colony of New Netherland, and as early as 1628 the small Dutch settlement was sending home 8,000 furs a year. The Dutch radiated out in small numbers from this center in the Hudson River Valley for the next four decades. They planted settlements to the north in the Connecticut River Valley, to the south in the Delaware River Valley, across the Hudson River in what was to become New Jersey, and to the east on Long Island. Their numbers were not large and in time they would be overwhelmed by the more numerous English. But their power at sea was never to be underestimated, as the Virginians found out as late as 1667, when Dutch raiders captured twenty tobacco ships in the James River, and in 1672 when they repeated this success. While the Dutch never settled more than 10,000 people in their Middle Atlantic colonies, they were able to exert a strong influence on English affairs. In time the English became far more numerous, and when three Anglo-Dutch wars were fought in Europe between 1650 and 1675, the colony at New Netherland became a target of English attack. It was captured by the English in 1664, recaptured by the Dutch in 1673, and then was almost immediately retaken by the English. This marked the end of Dutch political authority in North America.

For the Dutch, so long as the fur trade was thriving and represented the primary source of profit in New Netherland, relations with the Mahicans of the Albany area and the local tribes in the vicinity of New Amsterdam remained amicable. The Dutch did all in their power to preserve the Indians' goodwill, because they were vastly outnumbered and dependent upon trade for profit. They needed the Indians far more than the Indians needed them. Unlike the Virginians on the Chesapeake or the Puritans in New England, they had immigrated in small numbers and their principal goal was not farming but simply the profitable bartering of European trade goods for the skins of the beaver, otter, and deer. From the Indian point of view there was little to fear from the Dutch presence, for they were few in number, did not have voracious appetites for land, and were eager to trade commodities that Indians wanted and could obtain by trapping animals which existed abundantly in their territory.

As desirable as exchanging furs and skins for European trade goods seemed to the Indian tribes, it contained a hidden danger of utmost significance. Prior to the arrival of Europeans, Indians had hunted for subsistence; because their needs were not great this perpetuated the conservation of game. But once the skins of fur-bearing animals had been incorporated into the international Atlantic market, the Indian began hunting relentlessly in what became a process of game extermination. Under such conditions the beaver supply was quickly exhausted in particular areas. When this occurred, as it did to the Mahican suppliers of the Dutch during the first quarter of the seventeenth century, the fur merchants of the Dutch West India Company began to cultivate their enemies, the Mohawks, the easternmost of the Iroquois tribes whose territories stretched westward to the Great Lakes. The Iroquois eclipsed the Mahicans, became the major suppliers of pelts to the Dutch, and were transformed into a formidable power in the Northeast.

The tendency of the fur trade to trigger or intensify intertribal hostilities became more pronounced in the second quarter of the seventeenth century. To the north of the Dutch settlements the French were also building a fur trade with the powerful Hurons, who commanded the territories north of the Great Lakes. In time, the depletion of furs in the tribal territories under Iroquois control enticed them into attacking the Hurons. If successful, the Iroquois could divert the vast fur resources of the Canadian north from Montreal, the center of French trading activities, to Albany, the main Dutch trading post. Within the context of inter-European rivalry this was a commercial effort to make Amsterdam rather than Paris the major recipient of North American beaver skins. For the Dutch it could be accomplished entirely through diplomacy—the cultivation of ties with the Iroquois—and the supplying of their trading partners with the firearms necessary to destroy the Hurons. Within the context of inter-Indian rivalry, diplomacy was the beginning of a process that often moved immediately to a second stage in which intense warfare occurred. The Iroquois desire to obtain control of more distant hunting grounds, assuming the role of middlemen who received pelts from more westerly hunters and transported them eastward to the Dutch at Albany, became intense. In a period of a few decades an ancient smoldering Iroquois-Huron hostility intensified greatly and led to what amounted to a war of extermination against the Hurons in the 1640s. As one Canadian historian has written: "Before the coming of the Europeans, the Indians' wars had been limited; their motivation and their primitive weapons had precluded too heavy casualties. Afterward their wars became wars of extermination—total war fought for economic ends, and increasingly for ends sought by Europeans."[2] Fighting for individual prestige or blood revenge was replaced by fighting for control of trade.

What is all the more remarkable about the transforming nature of the European presence on the largest and most powerful Indian societies of the Northeast was that so few Europeans were involved. In the second quarter of the century the great Huron nation, comprising 30,000 people or more, was nearly destroyed by European disease and the attacks of Iroquois enemies inspired by the desire for Dutch trade goods. At the same time the victorious Iroquois used the European trade connection vastly to increase their power. All this was triggered by tiny Dutch and French settlements and trading posts scattered along the waterways of the St. Lawrence and Hudson River valleys whose total population, even after almost a half century of settlement, totaled no more than three thousand.

What could happen to smaller Indian tribes, which had neither the strength nor the geographical advantage to play a role in the all-important fur trade, was amply illustrated by the fate of the dozen or so Indian bands that lived in the vicinity of New Amsterdam in the 1640s. A few years before, the Dutch West India Company had begun recruiting more settlers in order to build up the agricultural base of the society. Between 1638 and 1643 the population doubled from one to two thousand. This required land purchases from local Indian bands such as the Rockaways, Canarsees, Massapequas, and Merrics. Having sold their land, however, the Indians saw no reason to leave it until Dutch farmers took it up. Now agriculturalists from both societies lived side by side in areas such as Long Island, Rockaway, and Staten Island. When Dutch cattle trampled Indian fields or the Indian dogs attacked Dutch cattle, tempers flared. The resident governor of the Dutch West India Company, Willem Kieft, added to the tension by attempting to repair the sagging finances of the colony through taxing all local Indians. The Indians resisted this attempt to extract tribute and were not reluctant to venture the opinion that Kieft "must be a very mean fellow to come to live in this country without being invited . . . and now wish to compel them to give him their corn for nothing."[3]

Dutch expansionism and sharp trading with Indian bands in the region inevitably brought sporadic violence. When this involved loss of life among the Dutch, they demanded the surrender of the responsible Indians to their

[2]William J. Eccles, *The Canadian Frontier, 1534–1760* (New York: Holt, Rinehart and Winston, Inc., 1969), p. 59.

[3]Quoted in Allen W. Trelease, *Indian Affairs in Colonial New York: The Seventeenth Century* (Ithaca, New York: Cornell University Press, 1960), p. 66.

system of justice. As permanent settlers and agriculturalists, the Dutch, like the Puritans in New England, sought unequivocal recognition of their sovereignty.

Once the question became one of political and legal authority, the Dutch did not long resist the temptation to use military force. In 1642 a band of Hackensacks, across Newark Bay from New Amsterdam, murdered two Dutch farmers whose cattle had been trampling Indian corn and who allegedly had swindled the Indians in trade. The Hackensack sachems offered to pay the widow of one victim a wampum atonement to "wipe away her tears," the normal procedure according to Indian custom. But they refused to yield up the murderers, which would be tantamount to recognizing that they lived under Dutch law. A year later, the Dutch responded by establishing by force what they could not secure through exhortation or negotiation. Eighty Dutch soldiers fell upon two encampments of Wecquaesgeeks, who had been granted refuge from their Indian enemies by the Dutch. The Dutch soldiers butchered women and children as well as men, as if to match the ferocity of the Puritans' attack on the Pequot village six years before. Through this genocidal attack Governor Kieft made unmistakably clear to all tribes within New Amsterdam's orbit that they must accept Dutch trading terms, pay tribute when required, and recognize Dutch authority.

Dutch-Indian relations in the New Amsterdam region were not significantly different from English contacts with native societies in New England and on the Chesapeake. After the first few years, little was to be gained from trade since the beaver in the area had been exhausted and the Dutch depended upon their Albany traders to tap the rich fur resources of the interior. Nor could the local Indians serve any useful purpose as potential converts to the Dutch form of Christianity, for the Dutch West India Company had little interest in sending over missionaries to convert the local Indians, who were looked upon as ignorant, brutish people separated from the Dutch by an unbridgeable gulf. Neither did the Dutch require Indian wives, for they were plentifully supplied with women from their homeland almost from the outset.

In this situation, with land settlement replacing trading as the dominant economic activity, the local tribes became only obstacles to Dutch expansion and Dutch authority. Since the native people were composed of separate bands of Wappingers, Hackensacks, Wecquaesgeeks, Tappans, Nyacks, Canarsees, and others it was all the easier for the Dutch to fix upon a military solution to the "Indian problem." Unlike the Mohawks of the upper Hudson region, upon whom the Dutch depended for the all-important fur trade, the Indian bands of the lower Hudson served no function in the Dutch hierarchy of needs. Only so long as they possessed greater strength than the Dutch were friendly relations with them preferable to unfriendly relations. The Indians staunchly resisted Dutch authority, and hostilities continued into the 1660s. But their strength was ebbing after decades of attritional warfare, and, while the Dutch were resupplied in men and arms from Europe, the Indians had only their own dwindling resources to call upon. When the English overpowered the Dutch in New Netherland in 1664, they encountered only demoralized remnants of an earlier Indian population.

By contrast Dutch-Indian relations at Albany were peaceful and profitable. Probably not more than one hundred Dutch resided there in the 1640s but they neither attacked nor were attacked by the powerful Mohawks, for both peoples admirably served each other's needs. Even though they were greatly outnumbered, the Albany settlers did not hesitate to sell arms and ammunition to their Indian trade partners. By contrast, in New Amsterdam, where the colonists were far more numerous than the Indians and the Indians far more divided, the Dutch enforced strict regulations against the sale of firearms. This policy is not difficult to understand when the competition for land in the New Amsterdam region is compared with the cooperative activities of Dutch and Mohawks in the Albany region. Firearms were provided to the Mohawks in the knowledge that they would be used by the Indians to gain control over Huron tribesmen aligned with the French. In this sense, every gun in Indian hands contributed to the profitable flow of beaver skins to Amsterdam by way of the Hudson River rather than to Paris by way of the St. Lawrence River. Such a lucrative trade did not necessarily bring mutual respect and admiration between Dutch and Mohawks. Thefts, attacks on animals, and trampled fields were also common in the mixing of the two societies. But as the most careful historian of Indian relations in seventeenth-century New Netherland has written, "Peace was maintained because both sides had everything to lose and nothing to gain by hostilities. . . . The two races regarded each other less often as corn thieves, trespassers, or Indian givers than as sources of economic prosperity; what they thought of each other personally was beside the point."[4]

When England, after a generation of civil conflict culminating in the restoration of Charles II in 1660, decided to make a second great effort in colonizing the West Indies and the North American mainland, the Dutch colony of New Netherland was one of the first objectives. Anglo-Dutch commercial rivalry had intensified after mid-century and the Dutch colony, situated between the English colonies on the Chesapeake and those in New England, was an inviting target. To take it would remove the Hollanders entirely from the eastern seaboard and consolidate the English empire in North America. To this end a military expedition led by Richard Nicholls seized New Netherland in 1664 almost without resistance from the Dutch, who had only a tiny garrison to stand in the way. New Netherland became New York and its Dutch inhabitants were obliged to incorporate themselves into the English colonial system. Though several generations would pass before the English made up even half the population of New York, political

---

[4]*Ibid.*, p. 115.

authority, trade, and military affairs were now securely contained within the British imperial system.

For the Indians of New York, the change of political authority had little significance. Insofar as their relations with Europeans were concerned, Dutch and English were hardly distinguishable. Nothing in the takeover of the English could change the fact that disease and war had already decimated the Algonkian tribes on the lower Hudson. Nor were the English inclined to alter matters since they had now taken over a European administration upon which the local Indians had become pathetically dependent. The English undoubtedly counted it as their good fortune that they were the new masters in an area where the work of subjugating the indigenous population had already been accomplished. Nor were they more inclined than the Dutch to proselytize among the local tribes when more important commercial matters laid claim to their energies.

The last third of the seventeenth century in New York witnessed the further decline of the small tribes in the area of Manhattan, Long Island, and the lower Hudson River Valley. The Indian population dwindled as the natives struggled for existence through a mixture of hunting, fishing, farming, and day labor in white settlements. Their relationship to the Europeans became almost entirely servile. A Long Islander summed it up in 1670: "There is now but few upon the Island, and those few no ways hurtful but rather serviceable to the English, and it is to be admired, how strangely they have decreast by the Hand of God, since the English first setling of those parts."[5]

Hostile Indians had become friendly Indians, but the friendliness was only the outward expression of internal social and political disorganization and the cultural dependency that accompanied it. In this state of demoralization alcohol became ever more important to the local tribes. But while serving as a painkiller for the eroded quality of life, it contributed further to the Indians' demise. Selling alcohol to Indians was prohibited, "yet every one does it," remarked one observer in 1679.[6] Two years later a Minisink sachem bitterly remonstrated that alcohol had caused the death of sixty of his people in three years. The provincial council was several times obliged to affirm in the next decade that Indians in the colony "are free & not slaves" and should not be made lifetime servants against their will. This was poignant proof that the dwindling Indian population was losing not only its cultural autonomy but its physical freedom as well.

At Albany the advent of the English brought no significant change in Indian relations. The Iroquois continued to deal with merchants who were primarily Dutch, to negotiate through interpreters who were Dutch, and to receive European trade goods in return for their furs. The furs, of course,

[5]Daniel Denton, A *Brief Description of New York* (1670), quoted in *ibid.*, p. 179.

[6]*Journal of Jaspar Danckaerts, 1679–1680*, ed. Bartlett B. James and J. Franklin Jameson (New York: Charles Scribner's Sons, 1913), p. 79.

after passing through New York, traveled to English rather than Dutch markets and the goods they received originated in a different part of the European world; but this was of little consequence to Iroquois trappers. Far more important than the substitution of English for Dutch political administration was the fact that the fur trade itself had been in a state of long-term decline since about 1660 and that nothing in the English conquest of the colony could reverse this trend. The decline was caused by the exhaustion of beaver east of the Great Lakes and the difficulties of outwitting the French for control of the western beaver sources.

QUAKER-INDIAN RELATIONS

To the south of New York at the time of the English takeover of New Netherland a colonizing experiment was taking shape that suggests how differently European-Indian relations could be. A mere handful of colonizers had settled in the fertile region between the Hudson River and the Chesapeake Bay before the 1660s, most of them Swedes, Dutch, and Finns under the control of the Dutch West India Company. Then, in the 1670s and 1680s, a wave of English settlers came to the Delaware River valley, which comprised what would become the colonies of East and West Jersey, Pennsylvania, and Delaware. These were the tribal homelands of a loose collection of small tribes of which the Delaware was the largest.

Among all the tribes of the coastal plain, the Delaware had retained their land and way of life the longest. This was primarily because only a small number of Europeans settled in their region during the half century when the populations of Massachusetts, Connecticut, Maryland, and Virginia were growing rapidly. When Europeans did arrive in large numbers, they came as devotees of a religious philosophy called Quakerism that was dedicated to the principle of nonviolence and just relations among people of all religions and races. As long as this philosophy of the Society of Friends held sway, interracial relations in the Delaware River valley stood in sharp contrast to other parts of North America. When migrants who were not Quaker flooded the colony, the Quaker commitment to pacifism wavered, and when Quakers lost political control of the area, the last chance for an autonomous Indian existence along the coastal plain of North America quietly disappeared.

The Quaker emigration focused first in the 1670s on East and West Jersey, formerly a part of New Netherland, and then in the 1680s shifted to Pennsylvania, which was to become the center of the Quakers' hopes for a utopia in the New World. Like their Puritan cousins, Quakers burned with the bright heat of religious conviction. Like the Puritans, they regarded the English Protestant Church as corrupt and renounced its formalistic elements. But they carried the Puritan revolt against Anglicanism to its extreme, decrying all intermediary institutions standing between the individual believer and God. In this sense, the Quaker was essentially a mystic, persuaded that every believer might find God's grace within one's heart through one's own power, unaided by priests, ministers, liturgy, or other devices.

Quakers had been severely persecuted in England after the rise of their movement in the 1650s and therefore began to formulate plans for founding overseas colonies of their own. They sent their advance agents to many of England's colonies where they were often reviled, mutilated, deported, and even hanged for practicing their faith. Then, in 1681, Charles II granted an immense territory to William Penn, one of the most important English Quakers. Penn vowed to make it a refuge for the persecuted of the world. In Pennsylvania, according to his vision, people of all colors, religions, and national backgrounds would live together in peace. However much war and violence might be regarded elsewhere as unavoidable aspects of carving out English settlements among Indians or other European colonizers, peace and interracial harmony would reign in Pennsylvania.

Quakers arriving in the Delaware River valley, therefore, threatened no violence to the Indians. However, the natives of the area had little reason to believe that these Europeans would be different from others they had known for three quarters of a century. From exposure to Dutch, Swedes, Finns, and English the local tribes had learned of European technology, material culture, and values. By the time the Quakers arrived, the Delawares had extensive experience with European firearms and alcohol, two key commodities in the trade they conducted in beaver, otter, and deerskins. Like almost every other tribe that came in contact with the Europeans, they had suffered a major population decline. On the eve of the Quaker arrival the Delaware warrior strength was about 1,000, less than half what it had been before three smallpox epidemics struck the tribe between 1620 and 1670.

The Quakers who emigrated to Penn's new colony were primarily agriculturalists, which meant that, like other colonists, they gave primary importance to the acquisition of adequate amounts of land. Nor did they differ from other English immigrants in seeking material success. Like Puritans, Quakers had been recruited in England from the rising middle groups of society; as their success in Pennsylvania over the next few generations was to demonstrate, the economic urge pulsated in them as vigorously as in others on the continent. But offsetting these built-in potentialities for friction was the Quakers' ideological vision. They believed that despite a historical record that seemed to prove otherwise, people of different cultures and beliefs could live together in friendship and peace. Their optimism was not the product of ignorance, for they were fully aware of what had occurred when Europeans and Indians met in other parts of North America, including two bloody conflicts in New England and Virginia just a few years before Penn received his grant for Pennsylvania. Yet they were ideologically committed to pacifism, eager to avoid the conflict which had beset other colonies, and convinced that what others had not achieved could be accomplished in the Quaker "Holy Experiment."

Even before he set foot in Pennsylvania, Penn laid the groundwork for peaceful relations. In a letter to be transmitted by his commissioners who preceded him to Pennsylvania he wrote to the Delawares: "The king of the Countrey where I live, hath given unto me a great Province therein, but I desire to enjoy it with your Love and Consent, that we may always live together as Neighbours and friends. . . . "[7] In this single statement Penn recognized the Indians as the rightful owners of the territory and gave notice that only with their consent would he allow settlers to establish their farms and towns. As proprietor, Penn had been granted title to all the lands within the bounds of his charter. Colonists must purchase land from him. But he in turn sent advance notice that he would sell no land until he had first purchased it himself from the local chiefs. Penn strengthened his commitment by pledging that the injustices suffered previously by the Indians would no longer be tolerated. Strict regulation of the Indian trade and a ban on the sale of alcohol were promised. Voltaire was later moved to write (though not with strict accuracy) that this was "the only league between those nations [Indian] and the Christians that was never sworn to, and never broken."[8]

When the first Quaker settlers arrived, they immediately began land negotiations with the Lenni Lenapes, as the Delawares called themselves. The Indians may have been suspicious of Penn's promises, which must have sounded like other European expressions of goodwill that had not lasted much beyond their initial enunciation. But the Delawares were no doubt impressed with the lavish supply of trade goods offered for the land along the Delaware River north of the site of what was to become the capital city of Philadelphia. Included were quantities of wampum, blankets, duffels, kettles, hoes, axes, knives, mirrors, saws, scissors, awls, and items of clothing. Also included were rum, powder, shot, and twenty guns, indicating that even those who professed nonviolence and wished to ban the sale of alcohol as a way of stabilizing relations could not afford to deny to Indians the trade goods they most desired.

Penn's arrival in 1682 brought him face to face with the Delawares. It was amity, not violence, that was on his mind and the Indians may have detected this in his eagerness to learn about their language and culture. "I have made it my business to understand [their language]," he wrote, "that I might not want an Interpreter on any occasion. And I must say, that I know

[7]C. A. Weslager, *The Delaware Indians: A History* (New Brunswick, N.J.: Rutgers University Press, 1972), p. 156.

[8]Quoted in Thomas E. Drake, "William Penn's Experiment in Race Relations," *Pennsylvania Magazine of History and Biography*, 68 (1944): 372.

not a language spoken in Europe that hath words of more sweetness in Accent and Emphasis, than theirs."[9]

Another factor conducive to peaceful relations was the absence of an extensive Indian trade. The fur trade flourished north of Pennsylvania and though Penn made efforts to divert the interior trade so that it would pass through Philadelphia rather than Albany and New York, he was singularly unsuccessful in this. This was disappointing to Penn and his merchant friends, but in the long run it minimized the chances for misunderstanding and hostility between Pennsylvanians and Indians. As for trade with more westerly Indians, the timing of the Quaker arrival made this impossible until well after the first generation of settlement. A thriving mid-Atlantic fur trade had existed between the Susquehannocks, who hunted in the regions inland from Delaware Bay, and the Dutch and Swedish traders, who had been established in the area since the 1620s. But the Susquehannocks had been weakened by competition and battle with the Iroquois to the north and then on the eve of the Quakers' arrival by hostilities with Marylanders and Virginians during Bacon's Rebellion. Thereafter the remnants of the tribe had migrated northward where they placed themselves under the protection of their former enemies, the Iroquois. This had left eastern Pennsylvania inhabited only by small local tribes; even as late as 1702 a prominent officeholder remarked that Penn's colony seemed "quite destitute of Indians."[10]

So long as Penn's influence was strong in his colony, Indian relations remained generally harmonious, aided by the absence of competition for land and the presence of only a meager fur trade. Penn resided only briefly in his colony and after 1712, when he suffered several disabling strokes, played almost no role in its affairs. Coinciding with the end of his influence was a development that sent Indian relations in Pennsylvania reeling in the direction they had taken in other colonies: the arrival of waves of land-hungry and decidedly non-pacifist European settlers.

Ironically, the Quaker policy of toleration for all religious and ethnic groups attracted to Pennsylvania in the early eighteenth century the very European groups whose land hunger and disdain for the Indians under-mined the Quaker attitude of trust and love for the natives. In 1710 and 1711 came the first of these, a group of Swiss Mennonites who settled on a tributary of the Susquehannah River sixty miles inland from Philadelphia. In 1717 a much larger group of German Protestants arrived, the vanguard of an influx of Palatinate immigrants who by mid-eighteenth century constituted about 40 percent of the colony's population. In the following year the first of another wave of immigrants poured in—this time Scots-Irish, who began to locate near the present-day Pittsburgh. None of these groups shared Quaker

[9]Weslager, *Delaware Indians*, p. 166.

[10]Francis Jennings, "The Indian Trade of the Susquehanna Valley," *Proceedings of the American Philosophical Society*, 110 (1966): 410.

idealism about interracial harmony. They had been driven from their home-lands by chronic economic depression and were concerned only about build-ing a new life, centered around tilling the soil, in the remote regions of Penn's colony. To obtain land cheaply and live in a colony where they were free to practice their religion was all they asked. But they were not prepared in return to accommodate themselves to the local tribes, particularly if land speculators and government officials in Philadelphia cooperated with them in defrauding the Indians of their land.

A second irony was that many of the Indians whom these refugees from European oppression confronted were also recent refugees from oppression. In the late seventeenth and early eighteenth centuries the valleys of Penn-sylvania drained by the Susquehannah River became a sanctuary for a number of tribes that migrated from the south and west after hearing of the benevolent Quaker Indian policy, which they believed might offer a way out of desperate situations in which they found themselves as a result of contact with European society. From Maryland came the Nanticokes and Conoys to escape war and enslavement that had decimated their tribes for several decades. "The People of Maryland," the Pennsylvania government was told by one Indian spokesman, "do not treat the Indians as you & others do, for they make slaves of them & sell their Children for Money."[11] From Virginia and North Carolina came the Tuscaroras and Tutelos for similar reasons. From the southwest came the Miamis and Shawnees, who had formerly lived in the Ohio Valley and traded with the French. For the Europeans who arrived later in the early eighteenth century it was an unanticipated stroke of good fortune because the migrating Indians facilitated later white settlement by clearing the land for crops, settling village sites near water transportation, and establishing trails for hunting. When Germans and Scots-Irish immigrants pushed into the interior they reaped the advantages of this preparatory work, using the Indian routes to advance west, occupying Indian town sites, and taking over the cleared fields.

The Delawares and other refugee tribes watched their situation deterior-ate even as William Penn lay dying in England in 1718. They brought bitter complaints to the government in Philadelphia that new settlers were build-ing mill dams downstream from them, thus blocking the fish from coming upstream to spawn. Settlers poured in, squatting on land that had not been sold to the proprietary government. Bestowing alcohol liberally upon Indian bargainers, along with intimidating them became the practice of white land policy where Quaker fairmindedness had once reigned. But rather than fight, the tribes preferred to vacate their land, knowing what had happened in Virginia and New England when Indians resorted to violence. By 1724 the main branch of the Delawares had migrated westward, part of them to an area not far beyond the limits of white settlement but others all the way to the Ohio River. They left heavy with resentment. A generation later,

[11]Quoted in Weslager, *Delaware Indians*, p. 182.

when they allied with the French and attacked their former English allies, the Pennsylvanians would reap the wind they had earlier sown. A leading Pennsylvanian wrote of their displacement: "These poor People were much disturbed . . . yet finding they could no longer raise Corn there for their Bread they quietly removed up the River Sasquehannah, though not without repining at their hard usage. . . . Tis certain they have the same reason to resent this as all those other Indians on this Continent have had for the foundation of their Wars that in some places they have carried on so terribly to the destruction of the European Inhabitants."[12]

The process of emptying eastern Pennsylvania of its Indian population was completed in the second quarter of the eighteenth century. Pennsylvanians gained some Delaware land by assigning settler rights in the immediate proximity of Indian villages—a tactic that usually accomplished the desired goals of driving Indians away. Other Delaware land was acquired by conniving with other Indians. In this case it was the Iroquois to whom the Pennsylvanians turned for help in expelling the last of the local tribes. The provincial government proposed an alliance with the Iroquois under which the powerful northern confederacy would assume suzerainty over all smaller tribes residing in Pennsylvania. The object of the alliance, according to the white accounts, was interracial peace—obtainable only when stronger Indian nations assumed the responsibility for managing the affairs of lesser Indian groups. But the real purpose of the alliance was to drive the Delawares from their homelands without having to resort to force. Thus in 1732 the Iroquois pressured one band of the Delawares to give up their lands at Tulpehocken, about sixty miles from Philadelphia, and migrate higher up the Susquehannah River to Shamokin where they were to live under the supervision of a minor Iroquois chief.

Within ten years the process of dispossessing the Delawares had been completed. Fraud deprived them of their last land preserve, the area between the Lehigh and Delaware rivers, known as the Forks of the Delaware. In 1735 James Logan, Pennsylvania's largest land speculator, produced what he alleged was a copy of an old deed signed in 1686 by which the forebears of the present Delaware leaders had ceded this land to William Penn. But the inability of Logan to produce an original copy, the lack of any reference to the transaction in the land records at Philadelphia, and the rarely mistaken oral tradition of the Indians, by which land transactions were scrupulously passed from generation to generation, all point to the conclusion that by now the Pennsylvanians were confident enough of their strength to force from the Delawares what they could not get by agreement.

Though the Delaware chiefs challenged the validity of the deed, they were faced with the combined opposition of the Pennsylvanians and the Iroquois. Finally they signed a confirmation of the alleged 1686 document,

[12]Quoted in Francis Jennings, "The Delaware Interregnum," *Pennsylvania Magazine of History and Biography*, 89 (1965): 178.

Lapowinsa, a Delaware chief, sat for his portrait in 1735. Two years later he gave up a vast tract of land to William Penn's sons in the disreputable "Walking Purchase." (Courtesy the Historical Society of Pennsylvania.)

Tomochichi, who was born before the first Englishman set foot in the Carolinas, sat for his portrait with his nephew in 1734. (Courtesy Smithsonian Institution, National Anthropological Archives, Bureau of American Ethnology Collection.)

This Mohawk chief journeyed to England in 1710 to treat with the English government. His grandson, Joseph Brant, made the same trip 65 years later and joined the British in the American Revolution. (Courtesy Library of Congress.)

bowing to veiled threats that resistance would only lead to abrasive contacts followed by violence, as incoming squatters encroached on their lands. Two years later, in 1737, the Quaker government arranged to "walk off" the bounds of the Indian deed, which granted William Penn's heirs all the land from a specified point in Bucks County westward as far as a man could walk in a day and a half. The walk itself provided another opportunity for defrauding the Indians. Two of Penn's sons, who had recently arrived in Pennsylvania to bolster their sagging estates through the sale of land, personally participated in sending secret parties scouting through the woods to blaze a trail so that three specially trained walkers, operating as a relay team, could cover ground as swiftly as possible. By this device the Penns extended their claim under the infamous "Walking Purchase" almost sixty miles into Delaware territory, far beyond the limits intended by the Delaware chiefs.

Nearly 1,200 square miles now became the property of the Penns. Ten square miles were graciously set aside as an Indian reservation. But the Delaware leaders, bitter at this latest evidence of white dishonesty, refused to move off their land. White settlers began pouring in after purchasing small tracts of land from the Penns and James Logan, who had foresightedly made large purchases in the area. The solution to impending conflict was to pay the Iroquois to remove the Delawares. "We now expect from You," signaled Pennsylvania's governor to the Iroquois in 1741, "that you will cause these Indians to remove from the Lands in the forks of the Delaware and not give any further Disturbance to the Persons who are now in Possession."[13]

A year later Iroquois representatives gathered with the Delaware chiefs in Philadelphia to fulfill their pledge. At a grand council the Iroquois signified a fundamental fact in Indian-white relations: that while English colonists sometimes had the power to swindle, dominate, or subjugate native peoples singlehandedly, they often relied on intertribal hostility and the avidity of Indians for European trade goods to obtain the support of powerful tribes in contests against weaker tribes. "Cousins," the Iroquois orator intoned to the Delawares,

> Let this Belt of Wampum serve to Chastize You; You ought to be taken by the Hair of the Head and shaked severely till you recover your Senses and become Sober; you don't know what Ground you stand on, nor what you are doing. . . . We have seen with our Eyes a Deed signed by nine of your Ancestors above fifty years ago for this very Land, and a Release Sign'd not many Years since by some of yourselves and Chiefs now living to the Number of 15 or Upwards. But how came you to take upon you to Sell Land at all? We conquer'd You, we made Women of you, you know you are Women, and can no more sell Land than Women. Nor is it fitt you should have the Power of Selling Lands since you would abuse it. This land that you Claim is gone through Your Guts. You have been furnished with Cloaths and Meat and Drink by the Goods paid you for it, and now You want it again like Children as you are. . . . For all these reasons we charge You to remove instantly. We don't give you the liberty to think about it. You are Women; take the Advice of a Wise Man and remove immediately. . . . Depart the Council and consider what has been said to you.[14]

With this withering blast the Delawares were stripped of their options. For several generations they had recognized themselves as subordinate to the Iroquois. But the tie had been reciprocal, for if the Delawares recognized the authority of the Iroquois in matters of war and diplomacy, the Iroquois also counted on the Delawares as one of the southern "posts" of their league and respected Delaware management of their own land affairs. Now the Delawares left Philadelphia humiliated by their former protectors and bereft of autonomy in their internal affairs. The Iroquois, lavishly entertained for their intercession, departed Philadelphia with a train of borrowed horses and wagons burdened down with shoes, stockings, hats, blankets, hatchets, hoes, and other goods. James Logan and the proprietors of Pennsylvania left with title to enough land to provide them with handsome incomes for years. The retreating Delawares would not forget, however. The taunts of the Iroquois that they were women and children still

[13]Weslager, *Delaware Indians*, p. 190.

[14]*Minutes of the Provincial Council of Pennsylvania* (16 vols.; Philadelphia and Harrisburg, 1851–53), 4: 578–80.

rang in their ears a dozen years later when they were among the first of the western tribes allied to the French to deliver a series of devastating strikes along the Pennsylvania frontier at the outset of the French and Indian War. The Indian friends of the Society of Friends had been turned into bitter enemies, as William Penn's dream of interracial harmony collapsed under the weight of population buildup, speculator greed, and the acquiescence of the second generation of Quakers.

FRENCH-INDIAN RELATIONS

The French, like the Dutch, were a force in the New World before the English. And like the Dutch, their activities in the late sixteenth and early seventeenth centuries were confined to harrying Spanish and Portuguese shipping, trading surreptitiously with Iberian settlers in the Caribbean and South America, and planting tiny fishing and trading settlements on the North American mainland. The French had first probed North America in 1524 when Giovanni da Verrazzano, sailing for Italian bankers in Lyons, charted the Atlantic coast between Florida and Newfoundland. Verrazzano called the region Nova Gallia or New France. Cartier's voyage in 1535–36 improved the French claim and their knowledge of the St. Lawrence region. Some unsuccessful attempts at planting settlements followed in the 1540s, but the French soon discovered that the real wealth of the northern regions lay not in gold or diamonds but in fish and furs, particularly the latter. By the end of the sixteenth century the French were most numerous among the hundreds of European fishing ships that came annually to Canadian waters. When French settlements at the mouth of the Rio de Janeiro and on the southeastern coast of North America were wiped out by the Portuguese and Spanish respectively in 1560 and 1565, the French decided to concentrate to the north where their commercial activities would be free from Spanish and Portuguese molestation.

As valuable as fishing was, the fur trade turned out to be vastly more profitable. Nothing more was required than to bring trade goods desired by Indians across the Atlantic, anchor a few ships in a sheltered bay of the St. Lawrence, and wait for Indian traders to arrive with pelts. Military conquest was unnecessary and in fact would only adversely affect the trade nexus with the Indians. Even large settlements were not required, for the fur trade involved a simple barter relationship between the French and the Indians.

In time the French decided to plant permanent settlements in North America because they realized that without a colonial population base their trading posts would be subject to the predatory raids of the Dutch, English, or any other colonizing nation. Thus a colony was settled in 1604 at Port Royal, Nova Scotia, and in 1608 a second settlement was planted at Quebec. This determination not only to trade and fish but to solidify claims to the northern part of the continent was enough to induce the English, a thousand miles to the south, to mount a campaign of extermination against the French. Although England and France were not at war, the governor of Virginia, Sir Thomas Dale, commissioned a seasoned explorer and Atlantic seadog, Samuel Argall, to attack the French settlements in 1613. Just a few months after he had abducted Pocahontas in Virginia, Argall wiped out the French settlement at Port Royal. For the next few decades the French struggled to plant tiny settlements and maintain them in the face of growing English opposition centered in New England. But France was preoccupied with the Thirty Years War in Europe and could spare neither men nor money for overseas development. By 1643, after almost half a century of colonization, there were still fewer than four hundred Frenchmen in New France. Most of them were Indian traders or Jesuit priests, who had come in considerable numbers to convert the Indians. As one royal governor of Canada later remarked, only two kinds of business existed in New France— the conversion of souls and the conversion of beaver.

It was under the leadership of Samuel de Champlain, backed by the Company of New France, that New France was established on a more permanent footing. By offering free land the company lured settlers from France to establish a permanent agricultural society. By 1660, though only two thousand Frenchmen lived in the colony as compared with twenty times that number in New England, scattered towns were appearing along the St. Lawrence River.

While the Dutch and English typically used military force or guile to wrest land and political submission from their Indian neighbors, the French in the north were forging relations of a much different kind with Indian societies of the St. Lawrence River valley and the upper Great Lakes region. For the French the Indians were absolutely vital, and this dependency upon the indigenous people, along with a pronounced difference in the attitude of the Catholic church, led to Indian relationships in the seventeenth century that set most French colonies apart from other Europeans in North America. The differences began with numbers. The French were so few in number that they could not have entertained the slightest hope of survival without the friendship of the native peoples surrounding them. In 1640, after four decades of colonizing activity, the entire French population in North America was about 270, hardly equal to any of a number of New England towns. Even a generation later, in 1663, the French population had increased only to 3,000, not much more than that of several Huron towns on the upper Great Lakes.

A high proportion of these Frenchmen were male, which added to the dependency on Indian neighbors. In contrast to the English and Dutch settlements, where the sex ratio among Europeans was far more balanced, Frenchmen took Indian mistresses, concubines, and wives with equanimity. They exhibited no embarrassment at this mixing of blood and were hard put to understand English qualms about interracial relations. In Nova Scotia, where French women were uncommonly scarce, intermarriage was so common that one authority believes that by 1676 virtually all French families had Indian blood in their veins. In the more settled areas of the St. Lawrence River valley, where the Algonkian tribes were less sedentary and Jesuit priests raised some objections to racial mixing, interracial fornication rather than interracial marriage was more customary. The Jesuits frowned on church marriages between the two cultures, but they could do nothing about the sexual urges of their parishioners. "In the Night time," wrote Baron de Lahontan, "all of them, barring the Jesuits, roll from House to House to debauch the Women Savages." Farther west at the trading posts, "miscegenation between the *coureurs de bois* and the Indian women was the rule rather than the exception."[15]

The practice of racial intermixture became official government policy in the 1660s when Colbert, Louis XIV's architect of imperial reorganization, called for a full-fledged integration of the races. Colbert ordered the French settlers "to civilize the Algonquins . . . and the other savages who have embraced Christianity, and dispose them to come and settle them in community with the French, live with them, and bring up their children in their manners and customs." In spite of opposition from the Catholic church, Colbert also encouraged intermarriage and urged the governor of New France to bring about a mingling of the cultures "in order that, having but one law and one master, they may form only one people and one blood."[16] It was a policy contrived to bring the Indians under stricter French control. At the same time it was designed not to destroy or weaken, but to assimilate, the indigenous population. A half century later, two lettered Virginians, William Byrd and Robert Beverley, pondered this "Modern Policy" adopted by France in Canada (and in Louisiana) and lamented that English "false delicacy" in the early years on the Chesapeake had kept them from making a "prudent Alliance" through intermarriage, as the French had done.[17]

It is true that when miscegenation occurred, it was almost always between French men and Indian women and that the offspring of these liaisons followed the mother. This meant that Indian blood was rarely added to the French gene pool. But despite this evidence of French ethnocentrism, frequent intermixing brought contacts of the most intimate nature between the two peoples, and this intimacy could not help but bring about greater mutual understanding. New France was both undermanned and "under-

---

[15]Alfred G. Bailey, *The Conflict of European and Eastern Algonkian Cultures, 1504–1700; A Study in Canadian Civilization* (Sackville, N.B.: The Tribune Press, 1937), p. 112.

[16]Quoted in *ibid.*, p. 107.

[17]William K. Boyd, ed., *William Byrd's Histories of the Dividing Line betwixt Virginia and North Carolina* (Raleigh: North Carolina Historical Commission, 1929), pp. 3–4; Robert Beverley, *The History and Present State of Virginia . . .* , ed. Louis B. Wright (Chapel Hill: University of North Carolina Press, 1947), pp. 38–39.

womaned," two important reasons for forging amicable and intimate relations with the native peoples of the St. Lawrence region.

Equally important in the establishment of nonviolent relations was the fact that virtually every man in New France during the first half century was there either to trade furs or to evangelize among the Indians. Both tasks required Indian cooperation; only rarely could either be accomplished through coercion. Thus French traders traveled hundreds of miles into the remote Great Lakes regions of the Hurons, establishing trading posts, learning the language and customs of the tribes, and engaging in a process of mutual acculturation. In the English and Dutch settlements the Indian trader was the exception rather than the rule, since the vast majority of the settlers, especially after the first few years, were agriculturalists engaging in an activity to which Indians had nothing to offer once their techniques of cultivating crops indigenous to the region were understood by the Europeans.

Those who were not traders in New France were generally Jesuit priests. They established missions, martyred themselves in hostile Indian country, and worked for the greater glory of their God by converting Indians to Catholicism. Fur trading and missionary work often went hand in hand, with missions established at important river junctions where the fur trade took place. Jesuits trekked northward to the farthest shores of the Gulf of St. Lawrence and westward as far as Lake Huron. Their main efforts were concentrated among the 20,000 Hurons who were settled in the Great Lakes region in towns of several thousand. The Jesuits were more willing than the Puritans to believe that Indian beliefs in a supreme being, in the immortality of the soul, and in supernatural forces could be revised sufficiently to find acceptance from their Christian God. Whereas the Puritans insisted that Indians of the New England area erase their values, renounce their way of life, and abandon their religious beliefs as a starting point in accepting Christianity, the Jesuits studied the Indian structure of belief and attempted to slowly change it rather than wholly to replace it. The statement of Father Ragueneau in 1647, which would have struck the Puritan clergy as the work of the Devil, reveals the ethnocentrism of the French—but an ethnocentrism tempered by respect and affection.

> One must be very careful before condemning a thousand things among their customs, which greatly offend minds brought up and nourished in another world. It is easy to call irreligion what is merely stupidity, and to take for diabolical working something that is nothing more than human; and then, one thinks he is obliged to forbid as impious certain things that are done in all innocence, or, at most, are silly but not criminal customs.[18]

This greater flexibility and willingness to accept native culture on its own terms, even while demeaning it, led to a far greater degree of cultural interaction in New France than in New England. Where Puritans settled,

[18]Quoted in Eccles, *Canadian Frontier*, p. 48.

the meager missionary activity that was undertaken was focused on the weakest tribes, those that had lost or were losing their political autonomy and cultural self-sufficiency. Weakened by disease and warfare and demoralized by the rapid growth of the English population, they abandoned some of their traditional ways and attempted to refashion themselves in the white man's image. Living in "praying villages," they conformed to English clothing styles, work habits, and forms of worship. In contrast, the greatest successes of the Jesuits in New France were among the most powerful Indian societies. Like the English Protestant clergy, the French Catholic *recollets* believed that true conversion to Christianity ultimately required giving up "savage" ways. But the Jesuits adopted a more gradualist approach, and, as important, they worked within a colonizing society that was not pursuing a militantly aggressive policy of establishing political domination over native people.

The different nature of French relations with the Algonkians is also revealed in the Gallic attitude toward Indian sovereignty. In all European-Indian contacts the concept of sovereignty was used to connote political authority and can be regarded as a kind of litmus test of the balance of power between the two cultures. In relations with Indians, whom all Europeans regarded as inferior, sovereignty was the ultimate goal to be obtained, for it meant recognition by native peoples that they were no longer strong enough to maintain their political autonomy. Whenever sovereignty was surrendered, subjugation was not far behind if not already present. When the New Englanders fought the Pequots in 1637 the goal was to exterminate or at least bring under English jurisdiction a powerful tribe that refused to accept Puritan sway in this region. Similarly, as soon as the Chesapeake colonists were strong enough they forced the Indians to recognize their sovereignty, a process that began with John Smith's attempts to exact tribute from the tribes of the Powhatan Confederacy. But in New France, the governing council was debating as late as 1664 whether or not an Algonkian Indian who had raped the wife of a French settler should be prosecuted in the French court of justice—a telltale argument revealing that French sovereignty had not yet been established.

Of course declaring sovereignty and implementing it were two different matters, and all European colonizers, having judged their strength sufficient to pronounce their sovereignty, still faced the job of imposing it. In New France in 1664 it was decided to consult with the chiefs of nearby tribes about the rape. The Indian spokesman pointed out that friendly relations had been maintained for decades in spite of individual acts of crime and violence on both sides and agreed that each side must do its best to control its members. The French in this case agreed with the Indians that the offender should not be prosecuted. A half century later, in 1714, when Indians declared that the French had no right to jail or punish them for drunkenness, since they were not subject to the laws of the colony and believed that the liquor, not the drinker of it, was responsible for breaches of conduct, the official reply was acquiescence along with the admission from the French that "the matter is extremely delicate." The French, assenting to the Indians' assertion that they were individually autonomous and collectively sovereign, passed laws prohibiting the sale of alcohol to the Indians. When crimes were committed by Indians under the influence of alcohol, the French courts attempted to discover the illegal supplier, prosecute him for violating French law, and charge him with damages committed by the drunken Indian.

The French policy did not always reflect greater humanitarianism, understanding of the Indians, or acceptance of their culture. First and foremost it was a policy born of weakness. "The French were unable to impose their law on the Indians, and for one good reason; to have attempted to do so with any degree of vigor would have alienated the Indians, and this the French could not afford to do."[19] But from this policy founded on weakness, ironically, came the most lastingly amicable relations between Europeans and native Americans on the continent. By regulating their own subjects in relations with Indians and by continuing to recognize the sovereignty of the Algonkians, the French were able to coexist peacefully with native societies to a degree unprecedented elsewhere in North America. That their settlements were so small and competed so little for cleared land doubtless helped in this regard.

In spite of the relatively pacific character of French-Algonkian relations, the Indians were not altogether spared the ravages that beset other native societies after European arrival. Epidemic diseases were not a matter of policy or national character and they struck the Hurons as mortally in 1649 as they had the Indians of New England three decades earlier. Nor could the French, however good their intentions, avert the attacks on their Huron allies by the Iroquois after the European rivalry for the fur trade began. Once the beaver supply in the traditional Iroquois hunting grounds was exhausted, the Five Nations sought to assume the role of middlemen between the Albany traders and the Huron and Ottawa tribes of the Great Lakes region. When this could not be accomplished through diplomacy, as in the late 1640s, the Iroquois resorted to war. Within a few years they had virtually destroyed the Hurons, Petuns, and Eries living around Lake Erie. War raged intermittently thereafter, as the Iroquois exploited the remaining beaver in their newly conquered territories and perfected the art of hijacking fleets of fur-laden canoes from the Ottawa country to the north as they headed for French markets at Montreal.

Although Catholicism and the French national character helped shape the relationship with Indian societies, economic and demographic factors were often equally important. This is amply demonstrated by French relations

[19]*Ibid.*, pp. 78–79.

with the Natchez of the lower Mississippi region in the early eighteenth century, which stand in stark contrast to the French experience in Canada. The Natchez were a highly stratified and ritualistic people, the southernmost descendants of the ancient Moundbuilders. In their social hierarchy, theocratic authority, hereditary class system, and celebration of war they more closely approximated European culture than any other group in eastern North America. After De Soto had passed through their country in 1542, they experienced little contact with Europeans until the arrival of Robert de La Salle, the French explorer, who laid claim to the lower Mississippi valley for France in 1682. For another three decades, until the French established a small trading post on the Mississippi River in 1713, they had only occasional contact with French missionaries and French and English traders.

When the French began a permanent fortification in Natchez country in the second decade of the eighteenth century—part of their plans to seize control of the interior of the continent—they brought soldiers, women, and black slaves with them. Trade with the Natchez was only incidental to the French purposes. When the Indians killed five traders in retaliation for the ill treatment they had received, the French executed several minor chiefs they had captured. When tension flared again in 1722, Bienville, the French governor, burned three Natchez villages to the ground and demanded that the Natchez emperor, Tattooed Serpent, send him the head of one of the minor chiefs though this violated tribal custom by which all chiefs were immune from the death penalty.

The draconic policy of the French led to further hostilities. In 1729, when the French demanded land cessions without compensation, including the site of an important Indian village, the Natchez responded by mounting an offensive designed to eliminate their oppressors. It was clear by this time that the French had found the Natchez useless for their purposes in the lower Mississippi and felt no qualms about attempting to intimidate them. Though the Natchez were successful in overpowering the French at Fort Rosalie in 1729, killing several hundred of the French and taking prisoner many women, children, and black and Indian slaves, the French were only temporarily beaten back. Reinforcements arrived in 1731 and with the aid of Choctaw allies they stormed the Natchez strongholds with cannon. More than 1,000 Natchez were killed, many captives were burned at the stake, and some 400 were sold into slavery in St. Domingue, just as captured Pequots had been dispatched to the West Indies by Puritans nearly a century before. The surviving Natchez, scattering in small bands, sought refuge among other southeastern tribes. By the end of the year the Natchez nation, once nearly 5,000 strong, had ceased to exist as a sovereign people. Finding no way of utilizing the Indians to their own advantage, the French had worked toward the elimination of these ancient sun-worshipping people with a thoroughness that would have aroused the envy of the English in New England, the Dutch in New Amsterdam, or the Spanish in Mexico.

SPANISH-INDIAN RELATIONS

The manner in which the goals and cultural characteristics of the colonizing group blended with the nature of the Indian society they encountered to produce distinctive kinds of Euro-Indian relations can also be seen in the case of the Spanish borderlands of North America. The main objects of Spanish colonizing zeal were silver-rich Mexico and Peru; secondary regions were Chile, New Granada, Cuba, and Jamaica. A distant third in value to the Spanish were the southernmost reaches of the present-day United States—Florida, the Gulf region, Texas, New Mexico, Arizona, and Baja California.

Although of tertiary concern, these borderland areas were nonetheless valuable as a buffer zone between the Spanish New World empire and the French and English zones of colonization to the north. Spanish explorers had been charting the southeastern and Gulf regions of North America since the early sixteenth century, beginning with Juan Ponce de Leon's expeditions to Florida in 1515 and 1521. By the latter date the Florida tribes must have been fully aware of the dangers inherent in contact with Europeans, for in that year Lucas Vasquez de Ayllón, a Spanish imperial officer and member of the Royal Council of Hispaniola, lured some fifty Indians aboard his ships and whisked them away into slavery in the West Indies. "By such means," wrote a contemporary writer, Peter Martyr, "they sowed hatred and warfare throughout that peaceful and friendly region, separating children from their parents and wives from their husbands."[20]

For the next half century Spaniards planted small settlements on the southeastern coast of the continent, engaging in minor trade with the Indians of the area and establishing missions manned by Franciscan fathers. Several attempts were made to bring the entire Gulf region under Spanish control. From 1539 to 1542 Hernandez De Soto led an expedition deep into the country of the Creek tribes, several hundred miles from the coast, and in 1559 Spaniards drove northward from Mexico in an attempt to establish their authority in the lower Gulf region. Everywhere they went the Spanish enslaved Indians and used them as provision carriers. On occasion, as in 1597, the various coastal tribes concerted themselves in an attempt to wipe out the Spanish missions and trading posts on the Atlantic coast and drive the Spaniards back to Florida. But the Franciscans kept returning as if God had meant for them to settle all the Indians of the region within the sound of the mission bell.

In 1565 the Spanish made a more concerted effort to establish themselves in Florida. Inspired by the construction of a fort by the French at the mouth of the St. John's River in that year, they founded St. Augustine, the oldest

---

[20]Quoted in John R. Swanton, *Early History of the Creek Indians and their Neighbors,* Smithsonian Institution, Bureau of American Ethnology, Bulletin 73 (Washington, D.C.: Government Printing Office, 1922), p. 33.

continuously inhabited town in the continental United States. They evicted the French, and the mission town became thereafter the center of the religious frontier. Meanwhile, New Mexico became a second region of missionary activity. Francisco Vàsquez de Coronado had explored the area in 1540–1542, and missionary activity began within the next half century. Santa Fe, founded only three years after Jamestown, became the administrative center of Spanish colonization in the Southwest.

With little mineral wealth to exploit, these Spanish borderlands were chiefly interesting to the Jesuit and Franciscan missionaries. Presidios, or garrisons, were established in these far-flung territories, and they attracted some Indian laborers and women. But the primary institution of the border-lands was the Catholic mission, which in many cases served also as presidio and administrative center. Hence, the Spanish presence in Florida and in the Southwest was numerically insignificant. Even as late as 1700 probably no more than 4,000 Spaniards lived in the borderland areas claimed by Spain. With no fur trade to conduct or minerals to extract and with no fertile lands available to incoming immigrant farmers, the Spanish related to the Indian peoples of the Southeast and Southwest predominantly in terms of the efforts to convert the native people to Christianity.

Sharp differences existed in the Spanish missionaries' methods. In Florida and California, they gathered Indians within mission complexes where every aspect of life was closely supervised. This was accomplished by persuasion, in some cases mixed with force. To the Spanish priests, supremely indifferent to difficulties, this semi-incarceration of native people was essential to the primary goal, for they viewed religious conversion "as a broadly civilizing process" and thus attempted to bring about a "full social and cultural reorientation of native life."[21] The missions, bearing some of the marks of forced agricultural labor, were instituted in areas where Indian peoples were widely scattered and lived a semi-nomadic existence. In New Mexico, however, Pueblo people had lived in settled villages along the Rio Grande for centuries, practicing agriculture extensively. Here the Spanish missionaries made no attempt to gather native people within the mission walls, but instead built their churches on the edges of settled towns. This led to a division of life "between a town-oriented secular aspect and a church-oriented religious aspect."[22]

The lack of a mutually advantageous economic tie such as united French and Algonkians in New France tended to place the full emphasis in Spanish-Indian relations on religious conversion. Since this often involved a determined effort by the colonizers to effect a wholesale cultural change among the Indians, tension was inherent from the outset. This can be seen in the persistent outbreaks of violence against the Franciscan missionaries of Florida by Guale, Apalachee, and Timucua Indians. Similarly, in New Mexico,

[21]Charles Gibson, *Spain in America* (New York: Harper & Row, 1966), p. 196.
[22]*Ibid.*, p. 197.

where the Spanish attempted to graft Catholicism onto Pueblo culture by building churches in ancient native villages, the Spanish world view was staunchly resisted. Although the Spanish were able to overlay Pueblo culture with a thin veneer of Catholicism beginning in the late sixteenth century, they met fierce resistance in the 1670s when they attempted to restrict traditional Indian religious activities by forbidding Pueblo dances, destroying masks and prayer sticks, and imprisoning and flogging Pueblo priests and medicinemen. These attempts to undermine traditional culture were met by a concerted effort, involving every pueblo north of El Paso, to drive the Spanish out of the region altogether. Called Popé's Rebellion after the Pueblo leader who coordinated it, the revolt was a kind of holy war against the attempt of foreigners to undermine forcibly the Pueblo religion and way of life. The Pueblo rebels destroyed nearly every church in New Mexico, singling out priests for special vengeance. Indians of the Rio Grande were willing to borrow the material culture of the Spanish, but their well-integrated communities fought with great determination against the attempts to impose upon them a religion and culture that required the abandonment of their own ancient cultural identity.

Whether the zone of interaction was in the St. Lawrence River valley, the Hudson River valley, the southeastern coastal sea islands and marshlands, the lower Mississippi River valley, Florida, or New Mexico; whether the Europeans involved were French, Dutch, Spanish, or English; whether the Indians involved were Hurons, Mohawks, Narragansetts, Westos, Creeks, Pueblos, or Natchez; European-Indian relations revolved around one basic axis. For the Europeans the essential components of colonization were land, trade, and physical security. For Indians land, trade, and physical security also were primary goals, but to these must be added the preservation of political and cultural sovereignty. In the zones of interaction where Europeans came in small numbers to pursue trade and did not threaten the Indian land base, relations were generally amicable. In Dutch Albany and French Canada, Europeans and Indians followed mutually profitable pursuits. The Europeans did not threaten the political sovereignty, land base, or cultural integrity of native societies; Indians, in turn, had no desire to attack those who provided greatly coveted trade goods.

But in areas where Indian land, political autonomy, or way of life was at stake or where an Indian slave trade was desired, widespread conflict occurred irrespective of the national origins of the Europeans involved. Europeans were usually the vanquishers in these encounters, but native groups resisted with a determination that far exceeded their numbers.

In the end, we are best equipped to understand the pattern of interaction and conflict between the various Indian and European societies by appreciating that each group pursued its own interests as steadfastly as it could, limited primarily by the resources available to it and restricted partially by conditions and attitudes that predated European arrival. Europeans of all nationalities took what they could get in North America and adapted their methods to the circumstances that pertained to any particular area. Indians made similar calculations of self-interest and employed a similarly wide range of strategies. For both, survival and the enhancement of their own culture were the paramount objectives.

6

THE COASTAL SOCIETIES: RESISTANCE, ACCOMMODATION, AND DEFEAT

The Indian was rarely a passive agent in the first century of contact with European culture, as was dramatically apparent in the last quarter of the seventeenth century in Massachusetts and in the first quarter of the eighteenth century in South Carolina. During this period Indian tribes in both regions rose up in determined attempts to prevent becoming a colonized people. In other areas, such as Virginia and Pennsylvania, small tribes resisted encroachment by Europeans but, bereft of Indian allies and weakened by population decline, moved out of the path of colonial expansion or succumbed to confinement on reserved parcels of land. Rather than conceiving of these coastal native societies as brittle and static, and thus unable to adapt to the arrival of dynamic European culture, we might better perceive them as malleable societies with which the colonists rarely wished to mix.

Faced with the growing power of the Europeans, Indian societies improvised a variety of responses, ranging from resistance to accommodation to withdrawal. Each of these can be seen as an attempt to preserve corporate unity and cultural integrity. The period from 1675 to 1725 was one of great stress for the coastal tribes, but those who have argued that it caused wholesale cultural disintegration have offered little proof to substantiate their claim. What seems most remarkable is that so many of the coastal societies that were experiencing the brunt of European population buildup "continued to view the changing world from the frame of logic of their own cultures" and fought with a determination that far exceeded their numbers. We can see this—and simultaneously explore the variety of responses to the swelling power of the colonizers—by looking at this time of troubles for Indian peoples of the coastal plain in New England, the Chesapeake, and the Carolinas.

METACOM'S WAR

Following the Pequot War of 1637 in New England, the Narragansetts, who had joined the English against the Pequots, attempted to maintain their autonomy by keeping their distance from the English colonists. But the Narragansetts occupied precisely the territory toward which Puritan expansion into the Connecticut River Valley was destined to go. In 1643 the colonies of Massachusetts, Connecticut, and Plymouth, eager to forge an offensive league against the powerful Narragansetts (and also against the pestiferously deviant colony of Rhode Island), formed the New England Confederation. Military preparedness was the purported goal of the Confederation; military conquest was its true goal. Strength was added to this Puritan front by alliances with the Mohegans, enemies of the Narragansetts. In 1643, when the Narragansett sachem Miantonomo sold a large tract of valuable land on Narragansett Bay to the arch-heretic Samuel Gorton, who was cordially hated throughout Puritan New England for his outspoken criticism of Massachusetts policy, the New England Confederation arranged the murder of Miantonomo by his Mohegan enemies. Two years later they mobilized for war against the Narragansetts. Calculating the odds, the Narragansetts submitted to a treaty that saddled them with the cost of the mobilization and required a large cession of land. By such tactics the Puritans were gradually able to erode the land base of the Narragansetts, who, along with the Wampanoags, were the chief obstacle to territorial expansion.

While Puritans were pushing southward and westward, their population growing to 25,000 by 1650 and 50,000 by 1675, a few men were attempting experiments in Christianization among the remaining fragments of the eastern New England tribes. Led by John Eliot, Thomas Mayhew, and Daniel Gookin, the missionaries concentrated their efforts among the tribes whose numbers had been deeply diminished by epidemics and war, who had already lost much of their land, and who had already become economically dependent upon the colonizers. "The Algonquians who converted," it has been observed, "were those whose communal integrity had been compromised step-by-step—from the plague of 1616 to the treaties of political submission—and whose sources of collective identity and individual social stature had been destroyed."[1] Several thousand "praying Indians" were es-

---

[1] Neal Salisbury, "Red Puritans: The 'Praying Indians' of Massachusetts Bay and John Eliot," *William and Mary Quarterly*, 31 (1974), 50.

tablished in fourteen villages where they attempted to become white men in red skins, following English methods of agriculture, praying to the English God, adopting English hairstyles, dress, and customs. The repudiation of their culture was the price of admission to "civilization." Yet, while the praying villages have appeared to be a halfway house on the road to full assimilation into white society, the Puritans never acted as if assimilation was a part of their overall plan. This must have been apparent to acculturated Indians like the Christianized John Neesnummin, who was denied lodging in Boston when he visited there in 1708.

Other New England tribes, where stronger leaders and greater numbers prevailed, resisted the missionary work of Eliot and Gookin. "Each of the great sachems of the mid-seventeenth century—Massasoit, Metacom, Ninigret, Uncas—resisted the missionaries as threats to his tribe's survival."[2] Metacom, sachem of the Wampanoags, is said to have told John Eliot "that he cared no more for the white man's gospel than he did for the button on Eliot's coat."[3] But even the more cohesive tribes, which had maintained a degree of independence from the expanding Puritan society, were aware by the early 1670s that their position was precarious and worsening steadily. Their options were limited. They could submit to the English colonies by selling their land, putting themselves under Puritan government, and performing day labor within the white man's settlements. Or they could sell their land for whatever they could get and migrate westward, attempting to place themselves under the protection of the stronger Iroquois tribes at their backs. Or they could attempt what had never been successfully undertaken before anywhere on the continent—a pan-Indian offensive against a people who greatly outnumbered them and who had at their disposal a far greater arsenal of weapons.

It was the third alternative that the Wampanoags chose. In part this can be explained by the leadership of Metacom, or King Philip as the English called him. Metacom was a son of Massasoit, the Wampanoag leader who had allied himself with the Plymouth settlers when they first arrived in 1620 and fought with them against other tribes throughout his life. Massasoit had died in 1661, and Metacom had watched his older brother, Wamsutta, preside over the deteriorating position of the Wampanoags. In 1662 Wamsutta died mysteriously after the Plymouth officials had interrogated him about rumors concerning an Indian conspiracy. For the next decade, Metacom, as sachem of the Wampanoags, brooded over the position of his people and was forced to accept one humiliating blow after another. The worst came in 1671 when he was compelled to surrender a large stock of guns and accept a treaty of submission in which he agreed not to sell any land without permission of the government of the Plymouth colony. From that time on he began building a league of Indian resistance, convinced that the steady loss of

[2]Salisbury, "Red Puritans," p. 38.

[3]G. E. Thomas, "Puritans, Indians, and the Concept of Race," *New England Quarterly*, 48 (1975), 6.

Wampanoag land and arms, combined with the corrosive effects of the Puritans' alcohol and the discriminatory character of the white man's government, could be reversed only by Indian initiative.

Metacom's ability to recruit support for his resistance movement is one indication that the Wampanoags, despite the setbacks of the previous decades, were far from a demoralized people. They lacked neither resources nor spirit to rebel. Still valuing their ancient cultural traditions, they sought new alliances with nearby tribes and embarked upon a war which in itself was a symbol of hope and a commitment to the advent of a revitalized culture.

The triggering incident of Metacom's War was the trial of three Wampanoags haled before the Puritan courts for an act of tribal vengeance against a Christianized, Harvard-educated Indian, John Sassamon, who had served for a time as Metacom's assistant. Sassamon was a man caught between two cultures. Though he had fled white society some time after his Harvard experience, he was moved to inform the government at Plymouth in the spring of 1675 that the Wampanoags were preparing for a general attack on the English settlements. When he was found murdered shortly afterwards, the Plymouth officials produced an Indian who claimed he had witnessed the murder and could identify the felons. Three Wampanoags swung at the end of English ropes in June 1675, and their execution carried with it the implication that the conspiracy allegedly being organized by Metacom was a reality.

War did not break out immediately. In fact the haphazard and sporadic burning and looting that occurred during the next few weeks conveys the impression that Metacom was attempting to restrain the more fiery young men of his tribe who were pushing hard for a war that would renew their sense of integrity and bring back to their culture the honor that had been compromised by their fathers over the years. But the war came in full force by the end of the summer. The execution of the three Wampanoags had been the catalyst, but the underlying cause was the rising anger of the young Wampanoag males, who refused to accept the inheritance of their fathers. Unwilling to face a lifetime of submission to an alien culture and with the rankling thought that so much had been sacrificed in order to accommodate the white invader, they girded themselves for battle. Revitalization of their culture through war was probably as important a goal as the defeat of the white encroacher.

The roots of the war, however, lay not only in the discontent of the younger Wampanoags. This was also a war of Puritan aggression, "the Second Puritan Conquest," as it has been called. Though Puritan military actions in the first stages of the conflict have been presented as "anticipatory defense," all the parties to the New England Confederation—Massachusetts, Connecticut, and Plymouth—had long been awaiting the opportune moment to subjugate the last remaining powerful tribes of southern New England and to seize their lands. That moment arrived in 1675.

In the first months of the war, Metacom's followers conducted daring hit-

and-run attacks on villages in the Plymouth colony. These were accomplished without the assistance of the other tribes in New England—the Narragansetts, Nipmucs, and Mohegans. But the failure of the English colonists to unify militarily for an immediate assault on the Wampanoags brought new allies to Metacom's side. When they found that his warriors were easily evading their pursuers, attacking the Puritan flanks and conducting guerrilla operations, many Indians decided that this was the opportunity they had long awaited. Tribe after tribe joined Metacom and by late summer in 1675 towns all along the New England frontier felt the sting of Indian raids. Although the English retained the allegiance of the Niantics and Mohegans, the Pocomtucks, and Pocassets, the latter inspired by the female leader Weetamoo, the widow of Wamsutta, joined Metacom's cause. Most important, the Narragansetts, who had attempted to stay officially neutral while apparently offering clandestine aid to the Wampanoags, were driven into the war by Puritan attacks on them. Even the Nipmucs, a tribe of local Indians near Springfield, who had silently nursed grievances for years but were thought by the colonists to be faithful allies, joined the offensive by late summer. A few months later the River Indians of the upper Hudson were mobilizing for an attack on the New Englanders. Their plans were aborted only when the governor of New York incited the Mohawks to attack them.

By the time of the first November snowfall the entire upper Connecticut Valley had been laid waste by Indian forays and the New England frontier was reeling under the attacks of the highly mobile Indian warriors. By March 1676, Metacom's forces were attacking Medfield and Weymouth, less than twenty miles from Boston and Providence. "At various points the line of English settlement had been pushed back toward the coast, and people in all but the largest and best-defended seaports were in a state of almost constant apprehension."[4] Thoughts of English superiority began to fade as ambush after ambush punished the colonial forces. Draft resistance became epidemic by the spring of 1676 and eastern communities grumbled at the influx of refugees from the frontier towns. Food scarcities in the towns produced opportunities for profiteering among those who controlled supplies. Even in times of military crisis, it seemed, the centrifugal forces that had been compromising the Puritan concept of community for a generation were difficult to overcome.

In the spring of 1676 the Indian offensive began to wane, not as the result of colonial military victories but because of food shortages and disease among the Indians. In what had become a war of attrition, they had more and more difficulty obtaining food supplies and weapons to replenish their depleted stores. Attempts to obtain guns and ammunition from the Mohawks near Albany met with some success, but when the New York authorities succeeded in cutting this vital supply line, they dealt Metacom's forces a mortal

[4]Douglas E. Leach, *Flintlock and Tomahawk: New England in King Philip's War* (New York: W. W. Norton & Company, Inc., 1966), p. 170.

blow. Slowly, in the summer of 1676, groups of Indians began to surrender, while others headed westward to seek shelter among tribes there. Most of the leaders who surrendered or were captured were executed. But to pay for the costs of the war the New Englanders sold many others, including Metacom's wife and son, into slavery, and shipped them to West Indian and Mediterranean slave markets. Metacom was killed in a battle near the Wampanoag village where the war had begun. Regarded by the Puritans as an agent of Satan—"a hellhound, fiend, serpent, caitiff and dog," as one leader put it—his head was carried triumphantly back to the English settlements.[5] By the end of the summer the war was over, although "hunting redskins became for the time being a popular sport in New England, especially since prisoners were worth good money, and the personal danger to the hunters was now very slight."[6]

At the end of the war several thousand English and perhaps twice as many Indians lay dead, a casualty rate probably unexceeded in any American war since then. Of some ninety Puritan towns, fifty-two had been attacked and twelve destroyed by the "tawney serpents," as Cotton Mather called them. Not for forty years would the white frontier advance again to the point where it had been on the eve of the war. The Indian villages were devastated even more completely. For the Indians of coastal New England it was the last gasp. Had they been able to secure the aid of the Abenakis, a powerful tribe on the northern frontier that had strong connections with the French, or with the Mohawks, the easternmost Iroquois nation, the outcome might have been different. But ancient intertribal hostilities still prevailed. Perhaps more important, the stronger interior tribes valued their trading partnership with the English far more than the fate of the coastal Indians. For the survivors there remained only the bitter fact that the English had prevailed and must now be recognized as their "protectors." In the aftermath of the war the New England Confederation subjected even the tribes that had remained neutral or rendered military assistance to the colonies to far more rigorous regulation. By a law passed in 1677 most remaining Indians, regardless of their religious preferences, were confined in one of the four surviving praying villages controlled by English supervisors. A few hundred others became tenant farmers and hired servants in the English communities.

In spite of the finality of the English victory, which was accomplished by the exhaustion of the Indian effort rather than through English military superiority, Metacom's War demonstrated that some of the coastal tribes were prepared to risk extinction rather than become a colonized and culturally imperialized people. A truly assimilationist policy was never attempted by the Puritans because they were not prepared to accept the Indians except as

[5]Quoted in Alvin M. Josephy, Jr., *The Patriot Chiefs: A Chronicle of American Indian Resistance* (New York: The Viking Press, Inc., 1958), p. 35.

[6]Leach, *Flintlock and Tomahawk*, p. 237.

unresisting subjects controlled by, but not included within, English society. The weakest of the coastal tribes succumbed to this policy, but the stronger chose to resist, even at the risk of annihilation, a society that outnumbered them in men and material resources.

BACON'S REBELLION

While New Englanders fought for their lives during 1675–76, the Chesapeake colonies were also locked in a struggle that involved not only war between the red and white communities but war within the white community. By the time Metacom's War was over in New England, several hundred whites and a larger number of Indians lay dead in Virginia and Maryland, the capital city of Jamestown was smoldering in ashes, and a thousand English troops were on their way across the Atlantic to suppress what the king took to be an outright rejection of his authority in Virginia. This deeply tangled conflict, called Bacon's Rebellion, took its name from the 29-year-old planter Nathaniel Bacon, who had come to the Chesapeake only two years before.

Bacon's Rebellion seemed to come almost without warning. Virginia had grown rapidly since mid-century, achieving a population of about 40,000 by 1670. Sir William Berkeley presided over the colony's fortunes as royal governor, an office he had held intermittently for more than twenty years. Pitted against both the Indians and the royal governor was Bacon, who had been educated at Cambridge in England, enjoyed status as the governor's second cousin and a member of his council, and had arrived in Virginia with sufficient wealth to purchase an already established tobacco plantation, complete with a number of slaves.

Bacon and many others who were seeking economic gain in Virginia were deeply troubled by declining social opportunity which they associated with the Indian policy fashioned over the years by Berkeley. In 1646, at the end of the second Indian uprising against the Virginians, the Powhatan tribes were guaranteed by treaty the territory north of the York River, which ran northwest from the Chesapeake Bay into the interior of Virginia. Red and white leaders had agreed that the price of peace was granting each society exclusive land rights in specified regions. For almost three decades after 1646 conflict had been avoided. In fact, a profitable trade for furs with several tribes developed, although some in Virginia grumbled that it was monopolized by the governor and his circle of favorites. This stabilization of Indian relations, however, became increasingly odious to the wave of new settlers who arrived in Virginia in the 1650s and 1660s, and especially to the mass of white indentured servants who had served their time only to find that in an era of depressed tobacco prices they could not compete with established planters. As their numbers grew they put more and more pressure on the government to open up for settlement the lands north of the York River. Why should this area be reserved forever for a handful of Indians, they argued, when the Virginia charter ran all the way to the "South Sea," leaving plenty of room to the west for the local tribes? Governor Berkeley wrote home on several occasions that one of every three or four men was landless or impoverished and that all of them "we may reasonably expect, upon any Small advantage the Enemy may gaine upon us, would revolt . . . in hopes of bettering their Condicion by Shareing the Plunder of the Country with them."[7]

This land hunger and constriction of opportunity turned to violence in July 1675 when a group of Doeg Indians, affronted by the failure of a planter to pay them for goods they had traded, attempted to steal his hogs. The settlers thwarted their plans and killed several of them. When the Doegs took revenge, killing several of the offending whites, thirty of the neighboring planters launched a retaliatory assault. Ten Doegs and fourteen Susquehannocks, who had been allied to the Virginians for many years, lay dead at the end of the foray. When the Virginia government did nothing to make reparations for the deaths of the friendly Susquehannocks, the Indians sought revenge through attacks on outlying settlements along the Maryland and Virginia frontier.

The incident, as white Virginians later admitted, came as the result of the land fever and hatred of Indians that led to "takeing up the very Townes or Lands they [the Indians] are seated upon, turning their Cattell and hoggs on them, and if by vermin or otherwise any be lost, then they exclaime against the Indians, beate & abuse them (notwithstanding the Governors endeavour to the contrary)."[8] Even more at the root of the indiscriminate English attacks was the fact that the Virginia Indians had been reduced in number and power so drastically in the previous decades as to offer only weak resistance to the "land lopers," as they were later dubbed. Such men saw the opportunity to open up all land still remaining in Indian hands through the out-and-out annihilation of the remnants of the Chesapeake tribe. Less than one thousand Indian males remained in the Virginia region by this time and these, as Berkeley had written in 1671, "are absolutely subjected, so that there is no fear of them."[9] Such weakness proved an invitation to white violence. Marylanders and Virginians could easily put a thousand armed men in the field and it was just this that occurred in September 1675. One thousand Chesapeake planters and militiamen marched against an abandoned stockade on the Potomac River, which had been assigned to the Susquehannocks by the Maryland government. Surrounding a village con-

[7]Edmund S. Morgan, "Slavery and Freedom: The American Paradox," *Journal of American History*, 59 (1972–73): pp. 21–22.

[8]"Virginia's Deploured Condition" (1676), Massachusetts Historical Society *Collections*, 4th Ser., 9 (Boston, 1869): 164.

[9]Quoted in Wilcomb E. Washburn, *The Governor and the Rebel: A History of Bacon's Rebellion in Virginia* (Chapel Hill: University of North Carolina Press, 1957), p. 20.

taining about one hundred braves with their families, they demanded that the chiefs come out to parley. When the Susquehannocks denied any responsibility for the frontier attacks, their chiefs were led away from the village and murdered.

Though the militia officers involved in this crime were tried, they were given only small fines or cleared of the charges by local courts. Appalled by this English "savagery," Berkeley denounced the attack and the legal proceedings. But he found scanty support in the colony. The Indians were heavily outmatched and served only as an obstacle to further expansion; hence few Virginians would speak in their behalf or act against those who precipitated hostilities with them. With the Susquehannocks now fully committed to war, despite overwhelming odds against them, Virginia prepared for their version of what they had already heard was happening to the north under the leadership of Metacom. Rumors swept through the colony that the Susquehannocks were offering vast sums to western Indian nations to join in attacking the Europeans and even that a confederacy linking Metacom's followers and the southern Indians had been formed.

Bent on revenge, the Susquehannocks attacked during the winter of 1675–76. The assault took the lives of thirty-six colonists. Angered and apprehensive, the frontiersmen turned on the Indians closest at hand, the settled Appomattox and Pamunkeys who lived within the white area of settlement on reservations which a postwar writer admitted "had long been coveted by neighboring Virginians."[10] In what has been labeled a "blood sacrifice" Nathaniel Bacon assumed the leadership of a frontier movement and began annihilating friendly Indians in the region.[11] Arguing that the subject Indians "have been soe cunningly mixt among the severall Nations or familyes of Indians that it hath been very difficult for us, to distinguish how, or from which of those said nations, the said wrongs did proceed," Bacon asked Governor Berkeley for a commission to lead his volunteers against any Indians that could be found.[12] When Berkeley refused to sanction indiscriminate attacks, the fiery Bacon announced his intention to proceed with or without the governor's approval. Berkeley declared Bacon a rebel, stripped him of his councilor's seat, and led an expedition of three hundred Virginia planters to capture Bacon. The frontier leader in turn gathered his forces around him and headed for the wilderness and "a more agreeable destiny then you are pleased to designe mee," as he defiantly informed the governor.[13]

Berkeley attempted to salvage the deteriorating situation by dispatching punitive expeditions to chastise any Indians who had attacked the white settlers while also attempting peace negotiations. Meanwhile, he intended to

---

[10]"Virginia's Deploured Condition," p. 166.

[11]Washburn, The Governor and the Rebel, p. 35.

[12]Quoted in ibid., p. 37.

[13]Ibid., p. 41.

build a string of forts along the frontier to keep peace between the two peoples. It was a defensive—and an expensive—policy. The money to build and garrison the forts could come from only one place—the pocketbooks of the planters, who would have to pay increased taxes over the next few years.

Berkeley misjudged both the white settlers and the Indians. The Susquehannok sachems could not control their own warriors, who were launching attacks even as their chiefs negotiated with the governor. As for the white Virginians, they wanted no part of the governor's expensive containment policy. The tobacco market had slipped badly in recent years, an epidemic had carried off half the colony's cattle in the previous summer, a drought had cut deeply into the 1675 harvest, and now, they argued, the governor was suggesting a weak and expensive solution to the biggest Indian crisis in three decades. In their minds the problem could be more easily and less expensively solved.

By May 1676 Bacon had declared himself the leader of the rebellious frontiersmen, who were determined to pursue their own Indian policy. Their first objective was a fortified settlement of Occaneechee Indians, who had been regarded as friendly and had recently destroyed a band of Susquehanncks encamped near them as evidence of their fidelity to the Virginians. Attacking the unsuspecting Occaneechees at midnight, Bacon's men annihilated the band. Later critics claimed that £1000 in beaver skins inside the Occaneechee fort had whetted the appetites of Bacon's men. With his supporters growing at every new attack on the Indians, Bacon then marched to Jamestown to confront the governor, who had charged him with treason against the government. Bacon demanded a commission to legitimize his attacks on the Indians; under great pressure the governor acceded. But when Bacon left with his Indian fighters, Berkeley again declared him in rebellion, gathered his own supporters, and pursued Bacon's force. For the rest of the summer Bacon's and Berkeley's forces maneuvered around each other, recruiting additional support, sniping at each other's heels in quasi-military forays, and puzzling over how to stop the chain of events that had started with a disagreement over Indian policy. Time was on the side of Berkeley because once the Indians had been crushed, the Virginia rebels were anxious to return to their homes. Moreover, Berkeley's reports of the rebellion in England had brought the dispatch of a thousand royal troops. By the time they arrived with a royal investigating commission in January 1677 Nathaniel Bacon was dead of swamp fever and his followers had melted back into the frontier region.

Although the Virginians who followed Bacon were disaffected by high taxes, favoritism in government, and the tight grip on power and profit exercised by Berkeley and his friends, it was the governor's protective Indian policy before the first bloodshed and his unaggressive policy thereafter that provided the strongest impetus for insurrection. A war of extermination was demanded by men who in the 1670s no longer feared an Indian population shrunken by disease and sporadic fighting in the previous decades. Peace had been useful for many years because the Treaty of 1646 left plenty of room for expansion. But the population had quadrupled in the intervening thirty years while the Indians had only grown weaker. It was not peace that frontier Virginians now wanted but war.

The royal investigators perceived this genocidal mentality shortly after arriving in Virginia in 1677. In a message to the House of Burgesses, which was debating a peace treaty with the remaining Indians, the commissioners denounced the "inconsiderate sort of men who soe rashly and causelessly cry up a warr, and seem to wish and aime at an utter extirpation of the Indians." When a peace treaty was signed in May 1677, one of its articles referred specifically to the "violent intrusions of divers English into their [the Indians'] lands, forcing the Indians by way of Revenge, to kill the Cattle and hoggs of the English."[14] Thus Virginians recognized that settlers had purposely goaded Indians into retaliatory attacks, which were then used as a reason for a war of extermination.

The significance of Bacon's Rebellion for interracial relations is that it proved that even the highest authorities in an English colony, dedicated though they might be to preserving peace between the two societies, could not prevent genocidal attacks by white settlers. Though he represented the authority of the king in Virginia, Berkeley could not control those who saw the Indians as an impediment to the aggrandizement of land on the frontier. After 1675 the House of Burgesses, reflecting the interests of local planters, withdrew the governor's power to disallow individual land grants, an authority that the governor had exercised since 1666 to prevent settlers from taking up land too close to Indian settlements. Thereafter it was a simple matter to intimidate Indians into selling their land in areas adjacent to white settlement. As the Secretary of Virginia wrote in 1678, "the english would ordinaryly either frighten or delude them into a bargaine and for a trifle get away the grownd . . . , then he comes and settles himselfe there and with his cattle and hoggs destroyes all the corne of the other Indians of the towne. . . . This was a great cause of this last warr, and most of those who had thus intruded and were consequently the principall cause of it were notwithstanding amongst the forwardest in the rebellion and complained most of grievances."[15] Against this kind of tactic even a royal governor was helpless. Power in the colonies tended to devolve to the local level, making it impossible for even the most fair-minded colonial governor to stabilize intercultural relations. Probably nobody vested with authority tried more consistently than William Berkeley to hold back the aggressive genocidal

[14]*Ibid.*, p. 161.
[15]Quoted in Washburn, *The Governor and the Rebel*, p. 161.

tendencies of the land-hungry Englishmen on the seventeenth-century Chesapeake frontier. For his troubles, Berkeley saw his colony plunged into civil war, the capital city burnt to the ground, and a personal estate valued at £8000 evaporate under the attacks of those who were prepared to fight against both their fellow Englishmen and the Indians.

For the Susquehannocks and other tribes of the coastal region the lesson must have been unmistakably clear. Even when they recognized the authority of the Europeans, declared themselves subject to English law, abided by that law, and even when they fought against the Indian enemies of the white government, they could not expect to live in peace. The same authority that bound them to treaties of amity and mutual defense with the colony of Virginia was the authority that was unable to control its own white subjects. They also learned that even when European society was divided against itself, as in Virginia in 1676, they could be outmatched by the more populous and better armed whites. Scattered in small towns, each representing a fragment of a tribe that had once been larger and more powerful, the coastal Indians were doomed whether they chose war or peace. The price of survival in Virginia, as in New England, was the sacrifice of an independent tribal identity and submission to white civilization as tenant farmers, day laborers, and domestic servants.

THE COLONIZATION OF SOUTH CAROLINA

As some Englishmen were spilling blood in Bacon's Rebellion, others were mounting a colonizing effort to the south of the Chesapeake in what was to be called "South Carolina." This vast fertile region was later to become the center of the plantation slave system in North America; but in the 1660s, when English settlement began, it was in the eyes of the colonizers no more than another wilderness frontier.

South Carolina was one of the Restoration colonies, founded in the aftermath of a long period of English civil war and the reinstallation of the English monarchy in 1660. Strategic considerations dictated that England cement her claims on the North American coast by removing the Dutch in the Middle Atlantic area and establishing a presence between the Chesapeake and Spanish Florida. With this in mind, Charles II issued charters for a cluster of colonies in the mid-Atlantic region—New York, New Jersey, Pennsylvania, and Delaware—and for the colony of Carolina on the lower Atlantic coast. All of these charters, specifying title to vast tracts of land and conferring rights of government, were granted to favorites and creditors of the king, men who had stood by Charles II when he was in exile during the republican regime of Oliver Cromwell in the 1650s. In the case of Carolina, the recipients of the king's favor were the Duke of Albemarle, who had been a leading officer in the royalist army; the Earl of Clarendon, the king's chief minister; the Earl of Craven, a prominent royalist during the years of the English civil war; Sir William Berkeley, the governor of Virginia; and Sir John Colleton, a prominent Barbados planter and supporter of the monarchy during its years of eclipse. All of these men had claims on the king; all had political power which the restored king was eager to keep on his side; and all saw the opportunity to extend their wealth and power by planting a colony in Carolina.

When Charles II granted a proprietary charter to these men in 1663, they set about devising a framework of government that would avoid the instability which had beset earlier English colonies and that would entice a large number of settlers to Carolina.

The main work of devising a blueprint for the Carolinas fell to Anthony Ashley Cooper, an expert in colonial affairs who had served Cromwell while still maintaining friendly connections with the exiled king. In 1669 Ashley drafted a constitution for Carolina with the assistance of his friend and protégé John Locke, the tutor of Ashley's children and secretary to the Council for Trade and Plantations.

Ashley and Locke devised a bizarre combination of the modern and feudal. In order to attract colonists land was offered not at a bargain price but for nothing. At first each adult male immigrant could claim eighty acres; later the ante was increased to 150 acres. But this liberal land system was grafted onto a semi-medieval system of government, which provided the eight Carolina proprietors, their deputies, and a limited number of quasi-noblemen with a monopoly of legislative, administrative, and judicial power. They would hold undisputed reign through an elaborate system of courts, committees, and councils—all tied to the wisdom and authority of eight proprietors in London.

The reality of settlement in Carolina bore little correspondence to what had been planned. Nobody who came to the colony took the distant London proprietors very seriously, least of all the tough, unsentimental planters who streamed in from Barbados and Virginia where depressed economic conditions had made a new start in the Carolina wilderness seem attractive. They came to take up 150 acres of free land and quickly laid claim to the best land they could find without respect for proprietary plans for settling in compact, rectangular patterns. The land they occupied first lay along the rivers, the arteries of transportation by which they could transport their crops to market.

In government, as in land affairs, they did what they pleased. The London proprietors appointed a governor to take command, but he quickly found out that without the cooperation of the local planters he could do nothing. Viewing the London proprietors as self-interested aristocrats who knew nothing about the rigors and problems of frontier life, they set about shaping their own institutions of government.

CAROLINA-INDIAN RELATIONS

For the scattered and politically separate tribes of the Carolina country—Guales, Yamasees, Apalachees, Tuskegees, Hitchitis, Westos, Creeks, Cusabos, and many others—the arrival of the English provided both opportunities and dangers, depending on their previous position. For the missionized Indians of Spanish Florida the English probably appeared as a threat, for they would now be subject to English attacks and the onslaught of other tribes drawn into the English orbit. For the coastal Indians of the region around the mouth of the Ashley River, site of the maritime center of Charleston, the English may have appeared as saviors, for these tribes had been under heavy attack from their western neighbors for a number of years. "We have them in a pound," exclaimed one of the first English colonists in a letter to London, "for to the Southward they will not goe, fearing the Yamases, Spanish Comeraro as the Indians terms it. The Westoes are behind them a mortall enemie of theires, whom they say are ye man eaters. Of them they are more afraid then the little children are of the Bull beggers in England. To ye Northward they will not goe for their they cry that is Hiddeskeh, that is to say sickly, soe that they reckon themselves safe when they have us amongst them."[16] To the west of the Westos, the Creeks may also have looked favorably upon the English arrival because an alliance with the newcomers promised an opportunity to gain indisputable control of the Carolina interior.

Prior to English arrival the inland Westos had gained an edge in the regional internecine hostility largely because they had been able to build a trade connection with traders in Virginia, who provided them with guns. Now the Westos found they would have to use their English weapons against incoming Englishmen who had allied with their coastal enemies. Within months of their arrival the English had secured the firm friendship of the local tribes along the coast. Not long thereafter the Creeks, several hundred miles to the west, sent emissaries to the coast, professing their friendship and suggesting a military alliance.

For the English colonists, the intricacies of intertribal rivalry, once unraveled, offered unsuspected opportunities. Most of the original settlers came from the sugar island of Barbados. They had anticipated using African slave labor to carve out sugar plantations, just as they had done in the Caribbean. But soon after their arrival it became apparent that a faster way to wealth was beckoning. The southeastern part of the continent, it was apparent, was more densely populated than the northeast. If the major tribes—Cherokees, Creeks, and Choctaws—could be drawn into trade, they might reap vast wealth from contact with the native peoples. The Spanish had done little to exploit this potential, for their main goal had been to stake

[16]Quoted in *ibid.*, p. 67.

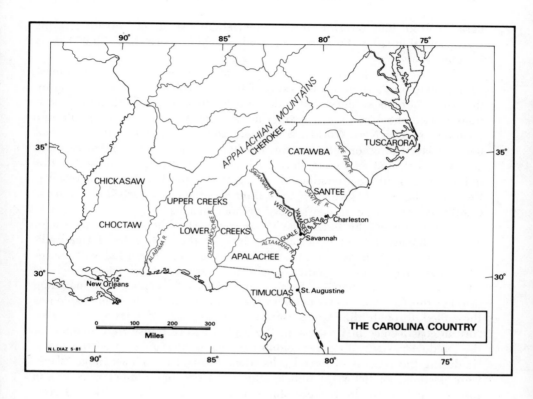

THE CAROLINA COUNTRY

N.L.DIAZ 5-81

out a claim to the territory and protect it by establishing missions that gathered local Indians into a sedentary agricultural mission life.

One of the first Englishmen in Carolina, Henry Woodward, quickly perceived the trade potential of the area. He had come to Carolina on a scouting expedition in 1666, remained for two years with the coastal Cusabos, and became the first Englishman to penetrate the Carolina interior—"a Country soe delitious, pleasant and fruitful," he reported, "that were it cultivated doubtless it would prove a second Paradize."[17] Woodward and the other leaders also knew that Virginians had already opened a profitable trade with the Catawbas and Westos to the west and northwest.

It was not beaver that beckoned in the Carolina Indian trade, for this valuable animal that had enriched so many traders to the north was available only in small numbers in the warmer climate of Carolina. Instead it was deerskin, also highly marketable in Europe and available in the Carolina country in great profusion. "There is such infinite Herds," wrote one of the Carolina leaders in 1682, "that the whole Country seems but one continued

[17]Verner W. Crane, *The Southern Frontier, 1670–1732* (Ann Arbor: University of Michigan Press, 1956), p. 13.

Park."[18] From 1699 to 1715 Carolina exported an average of 54,000 deerskins a year and thereafter the trade increased, reaching more than 150,000 skins in some years.

What began as a trade for the skins of deer was transformed almost immediately into a trade for the skins of Indians. This was not anticipated by the early Carolina settlers, and in fact the rapid growth of the Indian slave trade caused shock and consternation in London. African slavery was already a familiar part of New World colonization, and Indians defeated in war had been enslaved in other colonies. But nowhere in English North America had colonists instigated an Indian slave trade based on predatory raids. Yet this quickly became the cornerstone of commerce for the Charleston merchants. Inured to the use of slave labor from their experience in Barbados, the early Carolinians embraced Indian slavery without qualms.

In most respects the Indian slave trade resembled the African slave trade. The Carolinians did not penetrate the interior themselves but formed alliances with coastal native groups, whom they armed, rewarded with European trade goods, and encouraged to make war on weaker tribes, some of whom were ancient enemies. By the early 1670s slave coffles were marching through the Carolina backcountry to the coast in much the same fashion as they filed through the African interior to the trading forts on the west African coast. Once in Charleston, the captives were transferred to ships for the "middle passage" to other colonies, much as Africans crossed the Atlantic during the process of forced relocation. Most of Carolina's Indian slaves were destined for the West Indies, although a sizeable number remained in the colony and hundreds were shipped northward to New York and New England. In 1708 the population of the white settlements in Carolina included about 5,300 whites, 2,900 African slaves, and 1,400 Indian slaves.[19]

As the Carolina proprietors suspected it would, the Indian slave trade plunged the colony into a series of Indian wars. Through their agents in the colony, the proprietors forged a trade agreement with the inland Westos. But independent planters, resentful at the Indian trade monopoly claimed by the proprietors in London, contrived to thwart this policy by eliminating the Westo tribe. The Carolina planters had no desire to risk their own lives against the Westos and in fact lacked sufficient strength to defeat the powerful tribe. But they solved their problem by arming a migrating group of Shawnees, who had migrated across the Appalachian Mountains, and offering them lavish gifts to defeat and enslave the proprietary-linked Westos. In early 1680 the subcontracted war against the Westos began. Three years later the Carolina proprietors in London learned that not more than fifty of their former allies and trading partners were still alive. The rest had been killed or sold into slavery. Destroyed with the Westos was the proprietary Indian trade monopoly.

[18]Quoted in *ibid.*, p. 111.
[19]*Ibid.*, p. 113.

For the next few decades the private traders, who had now grasped control of the provincial government, armed the Shawnees, or Savannahs as they became known, and engaged in "an orgy of slavedealing."[20] The search for more and more slaves took the Savannahs farther and farther afield until by the end of the seventeenth century they were conducting slave operations deep into the interior and far down the coast into Spanish Florida. Indian slave trading reached its peak in the first decade of the eighteenth century. In 1704, a Carolina Indian trader, Thomas Moore, led about 1,000 Creek warriors and fifty of his countrymen into Apalachee territory. Other raids in the next six years left the Spanish mission system, initiated in 1573, in a shambles. Some 10,000 to 12,000 Timucas, Guales, and Apalachees were caught in the net of English slavery. Marched to Charleston, they were sold to the slave dealers and shipped out to all points in England's growing colonial empire.

The London proprietors were helpless to stop these perversions of their Indian policy. When they denounced the Indian slave trade as immoral and reckless, the colonists replied that the public safety required the elimination of some of the lesser tribes and maintained that transporting them out of the colonies or using them as slaves kept them "from being put to Cruell deaths" by the Savannahs. The proprietors were not fooled by this twisted logic. They understood perfectly, as they informed the local government, that the colonists were exploiting the Savannahs'

covetousness of your gunns Powder and Shott and other European Comodities . . . to ravish the wife from the Husband, Kill the father to get the Child and to burne and Destroy the habitations of these poore people into whose Country wee were Ch[e]arefully received by them, cherished and supplyed when wee are weake, or at least never have done us hurt.[21]

For several decades after the Westo War the Carolina traders conducted a slave trade with their Savannah allies while also developing a profitable trade in deerskins with the interior Creeks. The Indian trade was filled with abuses, but regulation of the trade was "hopelessly entangled in the bitter factionalism of Carolina politics."[22] As some had predicted, abuses of the trade and encroachments on Indian land finally led the Savannahs to end their alliance with the Carolinians, which was suicidal in its implications. Understanding that attempts to obtain fair treatment stood little chance of success and that war against those who exploited them might be too costly, most of the Savannahs decided in 1707 to migrate northward into the backcountry of Maryland and Pennsylvania. But rather than let the Savannahs extricate themselves from the trade dependency, the Carolinians offered huge bounties to a tribe of about 450 Catawba Indians to attack and

---

[20]*Ibid.*, p. 139.
[21]Quoted in *ibid.*, pp. 139–40.
[22]*Ibid.*, p. 145.

extirpate the Savannahs. Twice in 1707 and 1708 small numbers of Carolinians joined the Catawbas in attacks on the Savannahs. Governor John Archdale justified the policy by writing that "thining the barbarous Indian natives" had seemed necessary. The "thinning" was so thorough that by the end of the first decade of the eighteenth century the two principal tribes of the coastal plain, the Westos and the Savannahs, were virtually extinct.[23]

For the Indian tribes of the Carolina region the arrival of the English had disastrous effects. Many of the coastal tribes had been incorporated previously in the Spanish mission system. Though this had rendered them dependent and altered their way of life, it had not destroyed them. But the settlement of South Carolina had catastrophic effects, for it introduced a trade in European cloth, guns, and other goods that pitted one tribe against another, and greatly intensified Indian warfare. Even the stronger tribes of the area with whom the English forged trade alliances found that after they had used English guns to enslave weaker tribes, they themselves were scheduled for elimination.

Yet, in spite of the attritional effects of trading with the English, the Indian desire for trade goods was so strong that nothing could deter new tribes from forging alliances with the colonizers while others were being destroyed. The Creeks, the strongest of the interior tribes, were abandoning their ancient villages on the Chattahoochie River in the late seventeenth century and migrating eastward to the Altamaha in order to be close to the English. Even a terrible smallpox epidemic that spread through their villages in 1697 did not convince the Creeks that the European connection might better be spurned. Vast quantities of deerskins, carried on the backs of native burdeners, moved eastward along the Indian trail that led from more than five hundred miles deep in the interior to the coastal trading center of Savannah. Supplied with English weapons, the Creeks also served the English by making war on the Spanish and their client tribes and on the Choctaws of the Alabama and Mississippi region. "Through the media of intensified warfare, hunting and trading," a historian of the Creeks has written, "the Creeks became, comparatively speaking, a fiercely acquisitive and affluent Indian society," and yet "abjectly dependent upon the English trading system."[24]

THE TUSCARORA AND YAMASEE WARS

In the early eighteenth century the depopulation of the region south of Virginia continued. The Tuscaroras were the first to be drawn into the ghastly cycle of trade, war, and elimination that the South Carolina colo-

[23]John Archdale, "A New Description of . . . Carolina" (1707), in Alexander A. Salley, *Narratives of Early Carolina, 1650–1708* (New York: Charles Scribner's Sons, 1911), p. 285.

[24]David H. Corkran, *The Creek Frontier, 1540–1783* (Norman: University of Oklahoma Press, 1967), p. 53.

nizers coordinated from the small beachheads they had established along the coast.

The Tuscaroras were a numerous people living in North Carolina in large villages and "castles" where they gathered hemp, grew crops, and tended orchards on tidewater plantations which they had cultivated for generations. For years neighboring tribes, allied with Virginia and South Carolina traders, had raided their villages, stealing their children and selling them to the white slave traders. In 1709 they had watched a swarm of Germans and Swiss, led by a displaced count, Baron de Graffenried, invade their lands with the tacit consent of the provincial government. In local trade they also found that they could expect little from the Europeans' system of justice. They recognized, however, the difficulties of forging a pan-Indian alliance and were aware of what had happened to those who resorted to force against the colonial settlers. Better than this, they decided, was to migrate northward to Pennsylvania where they might obtain refuge in the Quaker colony. In 1710 their leaders met with representatives of the Pennsylvania government and the Iroquois League under whose protection they wished to place themselves. Their hopes were shattered, however, for the Pennsylvania government backed away from promising refuge.

Finding withdrawal impossible, the Tuscaroras gathered as many local tribes with similar grievances as possible—Corees, Pamlicos, Matamuskeets, and others—and fell on the European encroachers. About 130 English and Germans were killed in the initial attack. Boiling with internal dissension and as yet thinly populated, North Carolina turned to neighboring colonies for help since she had only a ragtag militia to send against the Indians. Virginia's government promised clothing and money but no men, for the Virginians were not ready to sacrifice their lives to defend the North Carolinians with whom they were engaged in a bitter boundary dispute. But in South Carolina the embattled North Carolinians found the assistance they needed. Historians have traditionally sung the praises of the South Carolina government for altruistically coming to the rescue of her northern neighbors and for assuming "the financial and military burdens" of the war.[25] The truth of the matter is that the Indian slave traders of South Carolina gladly entered the fray because they sniffed profit in the breeze. Colonel John Barnwell, an important South Carolina Indian trader, led an army of 500 men into Tuscarora country. But the army included only thirty whites, for the South Carolinians intended their Indian allies, especially the Yamasees, to do most of the fighting for them. Behind the offer of assistance to the beleaguered North Carolinians stood the chance to defeat the Tuscaroras and enslave large numbers of them for sale on the West Indian market. Before Barnwell reached the Tuscarora forts in January 1712 many of the Indians in his army had deserted. But the remainder of the force defeated one group of

[25]M. Eugene Sirmans, *Colonial South Carolina; A Political History* (Chapel Hill: University of North Carolina Press, 1966), p. 111.

Tuscaroras and took thirty slaves. To Barnwell's dismay, however, his Yamasee allies deserted with their prizes.

Barnwell moved on to destroy hundreds of Tuscarora houses and take several prisoners whom, as recorded in his journal, he "ordered immediately to be burned alive."[26] He then attempted to storm another Tuscarora fort; but finding his own forces weak and badly supplied, he arranged a truce. Faced with returning to South Carolina with only a handful of slaves, Barnwell broke the truce and scoured the countryside for additional prisoners on his way back to South Carolina. In response to this violation of the truce the Tuscaroras renewed their attacks and the South Carolinians were again invited to enrich themselves by helping their neighbors. A special representative of the North Carolina government, urging a second expedition, advertised the "great advantage [that] may be made of Slaves there," with three or four thousand Tuscaroras ready for plucking.[27]

The second expedition was led by another Indian slave merchant, James Moore, a veteran of slaving expeditions in Spanish Florida. Moore recruited an army composed of 33 white colonists and nearly 900 Cherokees, Yamasees, Creeks, and Catawbas. Storming the Tuscarora fort at Nooherooka in March 1713, they soundly defeated the North Carolina tribe. Several hundred of the enemy were burned alive in the fort; 166 male captives regarded as unsuitable for slavery were slaughtered; and 392 Tuscaroras, mostly women and children, were led back to the Charleston slave market. The South Carolina attackers suffered 57 casualties—22 whites and 35 Indians. In the course of the war the loss of Tuscarora life was estimated at nearly one thousand and as many as 700 may have been enslaved.[28] The scattered remnants of the tribe drifted northward in the aftermath of the war, seeking shelter under the wing of the Iroquois.

Two years after the Yamasees had participated in the defeat and enlavement of the white man's enemies in North Carolina, they were themselves providing the leadership for the largest and most successful anti-European resistance movement in the eighteenth-century history of the southern colonies. Their ability to spearhead a pan-Indian uprising that encompassed not only many of the fragmented remains of the coastal societies but also the powerful and populous interior tribes—Creeks, Choctaws, and Cherokees— brought them as close to wiping out the European colonists as ever Native Americans came in the colonial period. Only the last-minute success of the Carolinians in winning the Cherokees to their side saved the colony from an Indian resistance movement that according to the South Carolina Assembly included fifteen Indian nations with a total population of more than 30,000.

The Yamasees, like almost every other southern tribe, had eagerly sought

[26]Quoted in Chapman J. Milling, *Red Carolinians* (Chapel Hill: University of North Carolina Press, 1940), p. 120.

[27]*Ibid.*, p. 128.

[28]Crane, *Southern Frontier*, p. 161.

trade connections with the English and then lived to regret the dependency fostered by the trade. Even while the Yamasees were attacking weaker tribes in order to supply the Charleston slave traders and were helping the Carolinians subdue the Tuscaroras, they were reaching the desperation point in their relations with the English settlers. Cattle raisers in the coastal area south of Charleston expanded so rapidly in the first decade of the eighteenth century that the Carolina government was obliged to pass an act in 1707 "to Limit the Bounds of the Yamasee Settlement, to prevent Persons from Disturbing them with their Stocks." Despite the argument that the act was designed to help the Yamasees, the real intention, as its title indicated, was to restrict the Indians to reservations in order to open up the rest of the land to white settlers. Three years later the Carolina authorities were struggling with encroachers who were taking up land within the territory reserved for the Yamasees.

Even more oppressive were the Indian traders upon whom the Yamasee people had come to depend. The Indian commissioners listened to report after report "of the callous brutality of some of the traders, of petty thieving, of illegal enslavement of free Indians, of the abuse of rum to facilitate sharp dealing, of the use of cheating weights," and, as a Virginia Indian trader informed his London agent in 1715, of the debauching of Indian women when their men were on deer-hunting and slave-raiding expeditions.[29] The Yamasees were being reduced to peonage, as was indicated by a report to the Indian commissioners in 1711 that they were in debt to the amount of 100,000 skins—the equivalent of four or five years of hunting. When Charleston traders began seizing Yamasee women and children to be sold as slaves in partial payment of these debts, the Yamasees revolted.

The Yamasee attack on Good Friday, April 15, 1715, was carefully coordinated with the inland Creeks who had been equally exploited in the trade. One of the three most populous interior tribes, the Creeks were spurred on by the French, who had been building forts and trading posts in the lower Mississippi valley since 1701 and trying to woo the Creeks away from the English. It may have been the emerging Creek leader, Brims of Coweta, who planned the attacks in a general strategy to drive the Europeans out of the Southeast. All along the border settlements and wherever traders resided, the Creeks and Yamasees struck, aided by lesser tribes of the coastal plain such as the Saraws, Catawbas, Congarees, Caccamaws, Apalachees, and Santees. Refugees poured into Charleston during the summer of 1715, as the Carolina government tried desperately to patch together a military force from planters, indentured servants, slaves, and mercenaries from Virginia and North Carolina. Supplies arrived even from far-off New England, as the authorities in Charleston issued gloomy predictions that if the Carolinians succumbed, Indian tribes all over the continent would be inspired to hurl themselves at white settlements.

[29]*Ibid.*, pp. 165–66.

The Carolinians mounted effective counterattacks on the Yamasees in the fall of 1715, but the more numerous Creeks were still carrying the torch to every settlement they could reach. More dangerous, it was learned that they were negotiating with the Cherokees, the largest Indian nation neighboring the southern colonies. Residing in the mountainous southern Appalachia area, the Cherokees, according to an estimate in 1715, could muster nearly 4,000 warriors and boasted a total population four times as large. During the first half-year of the war the Cherokees had remained neutral, but the chances of the hard-pressed Carolinians seemed to rest on obtaining their support or at least preventing a Creek-Cherokee alliance. In an evenly matched struggle, the Cherokees occupied a pivotal position, as was apparent by the frantic attempts of both sides to secure their pledge of allegiance.

The Cherokees recognized the momentous importance of their decision and wavered back and forth, first agreeing to an alliance with the English in August 1715, but then failing to appear for a scheduled November offensive against the Creeks. Realizing that decisive action was necessary, the Carolina government sent a military expedition of 300 men, including one company of black slaves, deep into the mountainous Cherokee country in order to galvanize the vacillating Indian nation. While the expedition leaders pressed the Cherokees for a commitment, a dozen Creek headmen were also haranguing the Cherokee chiefs and arguing for a joint attack on the white army encamped in the woods near by. The Cherokees were split between a war party and a peace party. When the war party prevailed, they fell on the Creek emissaries and killed them. It was the Cherokees' dependency on the English trade goods that finally swung them against the Creeks. As they told the Carolinians, unless they were at war with the Creeks "they should have no way in geting of Slaves to buy ammunition and Clothing" from the white traders.[30]

With the Cherokees arrayed against them, the Creeks abandoned the towns they had settled in eastern Carolina in order to be nearer the source of English trade goods and migrated back to their old townsites on the Chattahoochee River. To replace their trading and military connections with the English they sought new links to the French on the Alabama River and the Spanish in Florida. The remaining Yamasees fled south to join the Spanish in Florida.

For white Carolinians, the flight of the Creeks and Yamasees left new lands open for the taking. But their thirst for revenge in a war that had cost them more than 400 lives and £400,000 was nearly unquenchable. "Many of the Yammonses [Yamasees] and Creek Indians," wrote an Anglican clergyman in the colony, "were against the war all along; But our Military Men are so bent upon Revenge, and so desirous to enrich themselves, by making all the Indians Slaves that fall into their hands, but such as they kill (without

[30]*Ibid.*, p. 182.

making the least distinction between the guilty and the innocent, and without considering the Barbarous usage these poor Savages met with from our vilainous Traders) that it is in vain to represent to them the Cruelty and injustice of Such a procedure."[31]

The Yamasee War defined both the limits of white economic exploitation and the limitations of Indian resistance. Nowhere in colonial America was naked exploitation of the indigenous people less restrained by church, government, or the attitudes of the people, than in South Carolina. By 1717 a white population of only about 1,500 males had succeeded in employing the larger tribes to enslave and shatter nearly a dozen coastal tribes and then had driven a wedge between the Creeks and Cherokees at the moment when an alliance between them might have ended English presence in the region. Throughout this process, covering almost a half century, the primary weapon of the English had been trade goods. For despite the extraordinary abuses in the Indian trade and the devastating toll that slave raiding took on tribes as far west as the Mississippi, it was only with great reluctance, usually accompanied by internal division, that tribes of the Carolina region turned on those who supplied them with European goods.

As in other parts of the continent, the key to English success in an area where they were greatly outnumbered was the promotion of intertribal hostility. This was not only instrumental in the procurement of slaves who could be profitably sold in New England and the West Indies but also was a major factor in depopulating tribes whose land then became accessible to the settlers. This doubly disastrous effect of the English connection became the basis of French attempts to win the Creeks to their side. Since the closing years of the seventeenth century the French had been building forts and establishing contacts with the interior tribes. As early as 1702, Pierre Le Moyne Iberville, the architect of the French empire in Louisiana, parleyed with chiefs from the warring Choctaw and Chickasaw nations and attempted to convince them of the destructive nature of the English connection. For almost a decade, he pointed out, the Chickasaws had allied themselves with the Charleston traders, using English guns to raid the Choctaws and selling the captives they took in order to procure still more guns and ammunition. In the course of taking about five hundred slaves, the Chickasaws had killed more than 1,800 Choctaws and lost some 800 of their own warriors. Englishmen delighted in this arrangement, he explained, for they built their fortunes on the trade in slaves and guns while watching the Choctaws and Chickasaws decimate each other. When the two tribes had sufficiently weakened each other they would no longer be able to protect their land from the English settlers, whose strength grew with the death of every Indian, whether friend or enemy. Iberville offered peaceful trade with both nations, not for slaves but for deerskins.

[31] *Ibid.*, p. 179n.

For the land-hungry English cattle raisers and rice growers of eastern Carolina, who were importing slaves from Africa in ever-growing numbers by the early eighteenth century, the Indian slave trade had no direct benefits since the profits accumulated in the hands of the Charleston merchants. But the secondary advantages were invaluable, for the Indian population of the lower South followed a downward trajectory as a result of the slave trade and thus facilitated southward and westward expansion from the initial settlements around Charleston. The extent of the Indian slave trade has never been determined, but it is certain that the number enslaved reached the tens of thousands in the half century after Carolina was settled by Europeans. A conservative estimate might place the loss in the Indian population due to disease, war, and enslavement during the first half century of English settlement at about 60 percent.

When the Creeks, Yamasees, and other tribes revolted against the Charleston traders and their agents in the interior, they came as close as Indian tribes were ever to come in the colonial period to overwhelming the Europeans who had entrapped them through cultivating a dependency upon European weapons and other trade goods. Using English guns purchased with Indian slaves, they turned on those who had supplied them. Out of a white population of about six thousand the Indians were able to inflict casualties of about 7 percent in the Yamasee War, as high as in New England during Metacom's War. But neither Creeks nor Yamasees nor any other tribe was willing to storm the Europeans at Charleston once the outlying settlements and isolated Indian traders had been destroyed. This called for siege or a massive assault—European forms of warfare that the Indians never adopted. When the Cherokees refused to join the Creeks, the English policy of divide and rule, practiced so extensively in the New World, prevailed. When the English promised them a shower of trade goods for their help, the Cherokees accepted the payoff rather than risk a prolonged war with the Europeans. Even with the best opportunity at hand since the arrival of the English, the Cherokees chose to assist rather than to assault the white colonists. But in the aftermath of war, consistent with the calculation of their own interests, they turned their backs on the Carolina trade, opening a trade with Virginia and haughtily telling their former partners, as a Carolina trader wrote, that "they valued us of Carolina no more than dirt."[32]

The process of decimation, dispossession, and decline among the Indian societies of the coastal areas was thus accomplished in different ways during the first century of English colonization. In New England and on the Chesapeake, the demise was almost complete by the time English settle-

[32]Quoted in W. Stitt Robinson, "Virginia and the Cherokees: Indian Policy from Spotswood to Dinwiddie," in *The Old Dominion: Essays for Thomas Perkins Abernethy*, ed. Darrett B. Rutman (Charlottesville: University Press of Virginia, 1964), p. 30.

ment was beginning in Pennsylvania and South Carolina. It had come in the north after steady resistance from the stronger tribes, who finally succumbed in pitched battle to an enemy that sought no genuine accommodation with them and was able to keep enough tribes out of the fray to prevail in a war of attrition. In Virginia and Maryland another course of events defeated the tidewater tribes. Here the Indians genuinely strove for accommodation following the unsuccessful resistance movements of 1622 and 1644. But, as in New England, their inability to function in any way that served European society finally led to conflict initiated by whites. Even as a friendly colonized people they were obstacles in the path of an acquisitive and expanding plantation society.

In South Carolina still another variation in the process of decline occurred. It was not dead Indians but Indians alive and in chains that benefited the white settlers. The buildup of the white population was slow enough and the desire among the Indians for trade goods intense enough that the white Carolinians could watch the coastal tribes obliterate each other in the wars for slaves, and then, when they were exhausted, attempt to employ the same strategy with the more powerful interior tribes.

The result was roughly the same in all the colonies along the seaboard. By the 1680s in the older colonies and by the 1720s in the newer ones, the coastal tribes were shattered. Devastated by disease and warfare, the surviving members of these tribes either incorporated themselves as subjects of stronger inland groups or entered the white man's world as detribalized servile dependents. The Indian's failure to survive cannot be attributed to an unwillingness or inability to intermix with the European newcomers—learning their languages, intermingling with them, adapting to their methods of trade and negotiation—as some historians have argued. The failure, rather, was to adapt too well to the material culture of the colonizers. It was the attachment to European trade goods and the persistence of ancient intertribal hostilities that thwarted pan-tribal resistance, which alone could have ensured the survival of the coastal cultures once it became apparent that their value as trading partners was incidental in comparison with the value of the land which their destruction would convert to European ownership.

Too much can be made of the inability of the coastal tribes to unite in order to ensure their survival. Indian "factionalism" is the common explanation for their eventual defeat, and it carries with it the implication that Indians were incapable of political unification because of their backwardness. This is to forget, however, that "Indian" is a term invented by Europeans to describe a great variety of peoples who did not think of themselves as united in any racial, political, or even cultural sense. "European" is a similar term, used to embrace a number of people who would have shuddered at the idea that they were politically, culturally, or religiously the same. They had been fighting each other furiously in Europe for centuries to prove that this was not so. As colonizers in America, they continued their antagonisms. Moreover, specific European groups, such as the English, were divided badly among themselves, which was a true case of factionalism. In Metacom's War these divisions among English colonizers were so great that they were only barely able to defeat an enemy whom they greatly outmatched in men and supplies. The picture of Metacom's difficulties in obtaining the aid of neighboring tribes is real; but it must be considered alongside the picture of Governor Andros of New York invading Connecticut as the war was in progress and the picture of Bostonians expelling from their town the Massachusetts refugees who streamed in from burned-out frontier villages.

Although they were defeated, the coastal cultures performed a major service for tribes farther inland. Their prolonged resistance gave the interior societies time to adapt to the European presence and to devise strategies of survival as the westward-moving frontier approached them. "People like the Iroquois," it has been pointed out, "owed a great deal to the resistance of the coastal Algonkians, and both peoples were well aware of this."[33] The coastal tribes provided a buffer between the Indians of the interior and the Europeans, and when the coastal tribes lost their political autonomy, their remnants were often incorporated into the larger inland tribes. These were important factors in the far stronger opposition that the Iroquois, Cherokees, and Creeks offered to European encroachment—a resistance so effective that for the first century and a half of European colonization, the white newcomers were restricted to the coastal plain, unable to penetrate the Appalachians where the interior tribes, often allied with the French, held sway.

[33]T. J. C. Brasser, "The Coastal Algonkians: People of the First Frontiers," in Eleanor B. Leacock and Nancy O. Lurie, eds., *North American Indians in Historical Perspective* (New York: Random House, 1971), p. 73.

7

EUROPE, AFRICA, AND THE NEW WORLD

The African slave trade, which began in the late fifteenth century and continued for the next four hundred years, is one of the most important phenomena in the history of the modern world. Involving the largest forced migration in history, the slave trade and slavery were crucially important in building the colonial empires of European nations and in generating the wealth that later produced the Industrial Revolution. But often overlooked in the attention given to the economic importance of the slave trade and slavery is the cultural diffusion that took place when ten million Africans were brought to the western hemisphere. Six out of every seven persons who crossed the Atlantic to take up life in the New World in the 300 years before the American Revolution were African slaves. As a result, in most parts of the colonized territories slavery "defined the context within which transferred European traditions would grow and change."[1] As slaves, Africans were Europeanized; but at the same time they Africanized the culture of Europeans in the Americas. This was an inevitable part of the convergence of these two broad groups of people, who met each other an ocean away from their original homelands. In addition, the slave trade created the lines of communication for the movement of crops, agricultural techniques,

[1]Sidney W. Mintz, "History and Anthropology," in *Race and Slavery in the Western Hemisphere*, Stanley L. Engerman and Eugene D. Genovese, eds. (Princeton: Princeton University Press, 1975), p. 483.

diseases, and medical knowledge between Africa, Europe, and the Americas.

Just as they were late in colonizing the New World, the English lagged far behind their Spanish and Portuguese competitors in making contact with the west coast of Africa, in entering the Atlantic slave trade, and in establishing African slaves as the backbone of the labor force in their overseas plantations. And among the English colonists in the New World, those on the mainland of North America were a half century or more behind those in the Caribbean in converting their plantation economies to slave labor. By 1670, for example, some 200,000 slaves labored in Portuguese Brazil and about 30,000 cultivated sugar in English Barbados; but in Virginia only 2,000 worked in the tobacco fields. Cultural interaction of Europeans and Africans did not begin in North America on a large scale until more than a century after it had begun in the southerly parts of the hemisphere. Much that occurred as the two cultures met in the Iberian colonies was later repeated in the Anglo-African interaction; and yet the patterns of acculturation were markedly different in North and South America in the seventeenth and eighteenth centuries.

THE ATLANTIC SLAVE TRADE

A half century before Columbus crossed the Atlantic, a Portuguese sea captain, Antam Gonçalvez, made the first European landing on the west African coast south of the Sahara. What he might have seen, had he been able to travel the length and breadth of Africa, was a continent of extraordinary variation in geography and culture. Little he might have seen would have caused him to believe that a natural inferiority characterized African peoples or that they had failed to develop over time as had the peoples of Europe. This notion of "backwardness" and cultural impoverishment was the myth perpetuated after the slave trade had transported millions of Africans to the western hemisphere. It was a myth which served to justify the cruelties of the slave trade and to assuage the guilt of Europeans involved in the largest forced dislocation of people in history.

The peoples of Africa may have numbered more than 50 million in the late fifteenth century when Europeans began making extensive contact with the continent. They lived in widely varied ecological zones—in vast deserts, in grasslands, and in great forests and woodlands. As in Europe, most people lived as agriculturalists and struggled to subdue the forces of nature so as to sustain life. That the African population had increased so rapidly in the two thousand years before European arrival suggests the sophistication of the African agricultural methods. Part of this skill in farming derived from skill in iron production, which had begun in present-day Nigeria about 500 B.C. It was this ability to fashion iron implements that triggered the new farming techniques necessary to sustain larger populations. With large populations came greater specialization of tasks and thus additional technical improvements. Small groups of related families made contact with other kinship groups and over time evolved into larger and more complicated societies. The pattern was similar to what had occurred in other parts of the world—in North America, Europe, the Middle East, and elsewhere—when the "agricultural revolution" occurred.

Recent studies of "pre-contact" African history have showed that the "culture gap" between European and African societies was not as large as previously imagined when the two peoples met. By the time Europeans reached the coast of West Africa a number of extraordinary empires had been forged in the area. The first, apparently, was the Kingdom of Ghana, which embraced the immense territory between the Sahara Desert and the Gulf of Guinea and from the Niger River to the Atlantic Ocean between the sixth and tenth centuries. Extensive urban settlement, advanced architecture, elaborate art, and a highly complex political organization evolved during this time. From the eighth to the sixteenth centuries, it was the western Sudan that supplied most of the gold for the western world. Invasion from the north by the Moors weakened the Kingdom of Ghana, which in time gave way to the Empire of Mali. At the center of the Mali Empire was the city of Timbuktu, noted for its extensive wealth and its Islamic university where a faculty as distinguished as any in Europe was gathered.

Lesser kingdoms such as the kingdoms of Kongo and Benin had also been in the process of growth and cultural change for centuries before Europeans reached Africa. Their inhabitants were skilled in metal working, weaving, ceramics, architecture, and aesthetic expression. Many of their towns rivaled European cities in size. Many communities of West Africa had highly complex religious rites, well-organized regional trade, codes of law, and complex political organization.

Of course, cultural development in Africa, as elsewhere in the world, proceeded at varying rates. Ecological conditions had a large effect on this. Where good soil, adequate rainfall, and abundance of minerals were present, as in coastal West Africa, population growth and cultural elaboration was relatively rapid. Where inhospitable desert or nearly impenetrable forest held forth, social systems remained small and changed at a crawl. Contact with other cultures also brought rapid change, whereas isolation impeded cultural evolution. The Kingdom of Ghana bloomed in western Sudan partly because of the trading contacts with Arabs who had conquered the area in the ninth century. Cultural change began to accelerate in Swahili societies facing the Indian Ocean after trading contacts were initiated with the Eastern world in the ninth century. Thus, as a leading African historian has put it, "the cultural history of Africa is . . . one of greatly unequal development among peoples who, for definable reasons such as these, entered recognizably similar stages of institutional change at different times."[2]

―――――――――――――

[2] Basil Davidson, *The African Genius* (Boston: Little, Brown and Company, 1969), p. 187.

The slave trade seems to have begun officially in 1472 when a Portuguese captain, Ruy do Sequeira, reached the coast of Benin and was conducted to the king's court, where he received royal permission to trade for gold, ivory, and slaves. So far as the Africans were concerned, the trade represented no strikingly new economic activity since they had been long involved in regional and long-distance trade across their continent. This was simply the opening of contacts with a new and more distant commercial partner. This is important to note because often it has been maintained that European powers raided the African coasts for slaves, marching into the interior and kidnapping hundreds of thousands of helpless and hapless victims. In actuality, the early slave trade was a reciprocal relationship between European purchasers and African sellers, with the Portuguese monopolizing trade along the coastlands of tropical Africa for the first century after contact was made. Trading itself was confined to coastal strongholds where slaves, most of them captured in the interior by other Africans, were sold on terms set by the African sellers. In return for gold, ivory, and slaves, African slave merchants received European guns, bars of iron and copper, brass pots and tankards, beads, rum and textiles. They occupied an economic role not unlike that of the Iroquois middlemen in the fur trade with Europeans.

Slavery was not a new social phenomenon for either Europeans or Africans. For centuries African societies had been involved in an overland slave trade that transported black slaves from West Africa across the Sahara Desert to Roman Europe and the Middle East. But this was an occasional rather than a systematic trade and it was designed to provide the trading nations of the Mediterranean with soldiers, household servants, and artisans rather than mass agricultural labor. Within Africa itself, a variety of unfree statuses had also existed for centuries but they involved personal service, often for a limited period of time, rather than lifelong, degraded, agricultural labor. Slavery of a similar sort had long existed in Europe, mostly as the result of Christians enslaving Moslems and Moslems enslaving Christians during centuries of religious wars. One became a slave by being an "outsider" or an "infidel," by being captured in war, by voluntarily selling oneself into slavery to obtain money for one's family, or by committing certain heinous crimes. The rights of slaves were restricted and their opportunities for upward movement severely circumscribed, but they were regarded nevertheless as members of society, enjoying protection under the law and entitled to certain rights, including education, marriage, and parenthood. Most important, the status of slave was not irrevocable and was not automatically passed on to his or her children.

Thus we find that slavery flourished in ancient Greece and Rome, in the Aztec and Inca empires, in African societies, in early modern Russia and eastern Europe, in the Middle East, and in the Mediterranean world. It had gradually died out in Western Europe by the fourteenth century, although the status of serf was not too different in social reality from that of the slave.

It is important to note that in all these regions slavery and serfdom had nothing to do with racial characteristics.

When the African slave trade began in the second half of the fifteenth century, it served to fill labor shortages in the economies of its European initiators and their commercial partners. Between 1450 and 1505 Portugal brought about 40,000 African slaves to Europe and the Atlantic islands—the Madeiras and Canaries. But the need for slave labor lessened in Europe as European populations themselves experienced great growth beginning late in the fifteenth century. It is possible, therefore, that were it not for the colonization of the New World the early slave trade might have ceased after a century or more and be remembered simply as a short-lived incident stemming from early European contacts with Africa.

With the discovery of the New World by Europeans the course of history changed momentously. Once Europeans found the gold and silver mines of Mexico and Peru, and later, when they discovered a new form of gold in the production of sugar, coffee, and tobacco, their demand for human labor grew astonishingly. At first Indians seemed to be the obvious source of manpower and in some areas Spaniards and Portuguese were able to coerce native populations into agricultural and mining labor. But European diseases ravaged native populations and often it was found that the Indian, far more at home in his environment than the white colonizer, was a difficult person to subjugate. Indentured white labor from the mother country was another way of meeting the demand for labor, but this source, it soon became apparent, was far too limited. It was to Africa that colonizing Europeans ultimately resorted. Formerly a new source of trade, the continent now became transformed in the European view into the repository of vast supplies of human labor—"black gold."

From the late fifteenth to the mid-nineteenth centuries, almost four hundred years, Europeans transported Africans out of their ancestral homelands to fill the labor needs in their colonies of North and South America and the Caribbean. The most recent estimates place the numbers who reached the shores of the New World at about ten to twelve million people, although several million more lost their lives while being marched from the interior to the coastal trading forts or during the "middle passage" across the Atlantic. Even before the English arrived on the Chesapeake in 1607 several hundred thousand slaves had been transported to the Caribbean and South American colonies of Spain and Portugal. Before the slave trade was outlawed in the nineteenth century far more Africans than Europeans had crossed the Atlantic Ocean and taken up life in the New World. Black slaves, as one eighteenth-century Englishman put it, became "the strength and the sinews of this western world."[3]

[3]Eric Williams, *Capitalism and Slavery* (Chapel Hill: University of North Carolina Press, 1966), p. 30.

Once established on a large scale, the Atlantic slave trade dramatically altered the pattern of slave recruitment in Africa. For about a century after Gonçalvez brought back the first kidnapped Africans to Portugal in 1441, the slave trade was relatively slight. The slaves whom other Africans sold to Europeans were drawn from a small minority of the population and for the most part were individuals captured in war or whose criminal acts had cost them their rights of citizenship. For Europeans the African slave trade provided for modest labor needs, just as the Black Sea slave trade had done before it was shut off by the fall of Constantinople to the Turks in 1453. Even in the New World plantations, slaves were not in great demand for many decades after "discovery."

More than anything else it was sugar that transformed the African slave trade. Produced in the Mediterranean world since the eighth century, sugar was for centuries a costly item confined to sweetening the diet of the rich. By the mid-fifteenth century its popularity was growing and the center of production had shifted to the Portuguese Madeira Islands, off the northwest coast of Africa. Here for the first time an expanding European nation established an overseas plantation society based on slave labor. From the Madeiras the cultivation of sugar spread to Portuguese Brazil in the late sixteenth century and then to the tiny specks of land dotting the Caribbean in the first half of the seventeenth century. By this time Europeans were developing an almost insatiable taste for sweetness. Sugar—regarded by nutritionists today as a "drug food"—became one of the first luxuries that was transformed into a necessary item in the diets of the masses of Europe. "Together with other plantation products such as coffee, rum, and tobacco," writes Sidney Mintz, "sugar formed part of a complex of 'proletarian hunger-killers,' and played a crucial role in the linked contribution that Caribbean slaves, Indian peasants, and European urban proletarians were able to make to the growth of western civilization."[4]

The regularization of the slave trade brought about by the vast new demand for a New World labor supply and by a reciprocally higher demand in Africa for European trade goods changed the problem of obtaining slaves. Criminals and "outsiders" in sufficient number to satisfy the growing European demand in the seventeenth century could not be found. Therefore African kings resorted to raids and warfare against their neighbors as a way of obtaining "black gold" with which to trade. European guns abetted the process. Thus, the spread of kidnapping and organized violence in Africa became intricately connected with the maintenance of commercial relations with European powers.

In the forcible recruitment of slaves, adult males were consistently preferred over women and children. Primarily this represented the preference of New World plantation owners for male field laborers. But it also reflected the decision of vanquished African villagers to yield up primarily their men to raiding parties because women were the chief agriculturalists in their

[4]Mintz, "Time, Sugar, & Sweetness," *Marxist Perspectives*, No. 8 (1979), p. 60.

society and, in matrilineal and matrilocal kinship systems, were too valuable to be spared.

For the Europeans the slave trade itself became an immensely profitable enterprise. In the several centuries of intensive slave trading that followed the establishment of New World sugar plantations, European nations warred constantly for trading advantages on the west African coast. The coastal forts, the focal points of the trade, became key strategic targets in the wars of empire. The great Portuguese slaving fort at Elmina on the Gold Coast, begun in 1481, was captured a century and a half later by the Dutch. The primary fort on the Guinea coast, started by the Swedes, passed through the hands of the Danes, the English, and the Dutch between 1652 and 1664. As the demand for slaves in the Americas rose sharply in the second half of the seventeenth century, European competition for trading rights on the west African coast grew intense. By the end of the century monopolies for supplying European plantations in the New World with their annual quotas of slaves became a major issue of European diplomacy. The Dutch were the primary victors in the battle for the west African slave coast. Hence, for most of the century a majority of slaves who were fed into the expanding New World markets found themselves crossing the Atlantic in Dutch ships.

Not until the last third of the seventeenth century were the English of any importance in the slave trade or in the demand for slaves in their North American colonies. Major English attempts to break into the profitable trade began only in 1663, when Charles II, recently restored to the English throne, granted a charter to the Royal Adventurers to Africa, a joint-stock company headed by the king's brother, the Duke of York. Superseded by the Royal African Company in 1672, these companies enjoyed the exclusive right to carry slaves to England's overseas plantations. For thirty-four years after 1663 each of the slaves they brought across the Atlantic bore the brand "DY" for the Duke of York, who himself became king in 1685. In 1698 the Royal African Company's monopoly was broken due to the pressure on Parliament by individual merchants who demanded their rights as English-men to participate in the lucrative trade. Thrown open to individual entre-preneurs, the English slave trade grew enormously. In the 1680s the Royal African Company had transported about five to six thousand slaves annually (though interlopers brought in thousands more). In the first decade of free trade the annual average rose above twenty thousand. English involvement in the trade increased for the remainder of the eighteenth century until by the 1790s England had become the foremost slave trading nation in Europe.

THE DEVELOPMENT OF SLAVERY
IN THE ENGLISH COLONIES

Even though they were long familiar with Spanish, Dutch, and Portuguese use of African slave labor, English colonists did not turn immediately to Africa to solve the problem of cultivating labor-intensive crops. When they

British North America
10,000

Old World
25,100

Spanish America
292,500

British Caribbean
263,700
French Caribbean
155,800

Dutch
Caribbean
40,000

Brazil
560,000

Scale on Equator

0   1000   2000
MILES

**ATLANTIC SLAVE TRADE
1601–1700**

Source: P.D. CURTIN, *The Atlantic Slave
Trade: A Census*, p. 119.

N. L. DIAZ

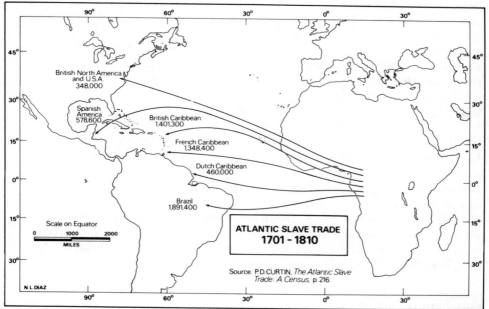

British North America
and U.S.A.
348,000

Spanish
America
578,600

British Caribbean
1,401,300

French Caribbean
1,348,400

Dutch Caribbean
460,000

Brazil
1,891,400

Scale on Equator

0   1000   2000
MILES

**ATLANTIC SLAVE TRADE
1701–1810**

Source: P.D. CURTIN, *The Atlantic Slave
Trade: A Census*, p. 216.

N. L. DIAZ

did, it could have caused little surprise, for in enslaving Africans Englishmen were merely copying their European rivals in attempting to fill the colonial labor gap. No doubt the stereotype of Africans as uncivilized creatures made it easier for the English to fasten chains upon them. But the central fact remains that the English were in the New World, like the Spanish, Portuguese, Dutch, and French, to make a fortune as well as to build religious and political havens. Given the long hostility they had borne toward Indians and their experience in enslaving them, any scruples the English might have had about enslaving Africans were quickly dissipated.

Making it all the more natural to employ Africans as a slave labor force in the mainland colonies was the precedent that English planters had set on their Caribbean sugar islands. In Barbados, Jamaica, and the Leeward Islands (Antigua, Montserrat, Nevis, and St. Christopher) Englishmen in the second and third quarters of the seventeenth century learned to copy their European rivals in employing Africans in the sugar fields and, through extraordinary repression, in molding them into a slave labor force. By 1680, when there were not more than 7,000 slaves in mainland America and the institution of slavery was not yet unalterably fixed, upwards of 65,000 Africans toiled on sugar plantations in the English West Indies. Trade and communication were extensive between the Caribbean and mainland colonists, so settlers in America had intimate knowledge concerning the potentiality of slave labor.

It is not surprising, then, that the American colonists turned to the international slave trade to fill their labor needs. Africans were simply the most available people in the world for those seeking a bound labor force and possessed of the power to obtain it. What is surprising, in fact, is that the American colonists did not turn to slavery more quickly than they did. For more than a half century in Virginia and Maryland it was primarily the white indentured servant and not the African slave who labored in the tobacco fields. Moreover, those blacks who were imported before about 1660 were held in various degrees of servitude, most for limited periods and a few for life.

The transformation of the labor force in the Southern colonies, from one in which many white and a relatively small number of black indentured servants labored together to one in which black slaves served for a lifetime and composed the bulk of unfree labor, came only in the last third of the seventeenth century in Virginia and Maryland and in the first third of the eighteenth century in North Carolina and South Carolina. The reasons for this shift to a slave-based agricultural economy in the South are twofold. First, English entry into the African slave trade gave the Southern planter an opportunity to purchase slaves more readily and more cheaply than before. Cheap labor was what every tobacco or rice planter sought, and when the price of slave labor dipped below that of indentured labor, the demand for black slaves increased. Also, the supply of white servants from England began to dry up in the late seventeenth century, and those who did cross the Atlantic were spread among a growing number of colonies. Thus, in the late seventeenth century the number of Africans imported into the Chesapeake colonies began to grow and the flow of white indentured servants diminished to a trickle. As late as 1671 slaves made up less than 5 percent of Virginia's population and were outnumbered at least three to one by white indentured servants. In Maryland the situation was much the same. But within a generation, by about 1700, they represented one-fifth of the population and probably a majority of the labor force. A Maryland census of 1707 tabulated 3,003 white bound laborers and 4,657 black slaves. Five years later the slave population had almost doubled. Within another generation white indentured servants were insignificant in number and in all the Southern colonies African slaves made up the backbone of the agricultural work force.

To the north, in Pennsylvania, New Jersey, and Delaware, where English colonists had settled only in the last third of the seventeenth century, slavery existed on a more occasional basis, since labor-intensive crops were not as extensively grown in these areas and the cold winters brought farming to a halt for a considerable part of the year. New York was an exception. During the period before 1664 when the colony was Dutch, slaveholding had been extensively practiced, encouraged in part by the Dutch West India Company, one of the chief international suppliers of slaves. The population of New York remained largely Dutch for the remainder of the century, and the English who slowly filtered in saw no reason not to imitate Dutch slave owners. Thus New York became the largest importer of slaves north of Maryland. In the mid-eighteenth century, the areas of original settlement around New York and Albany remained slaveholding societies with about 20 percent of the population composed of slaves and 30 to 40 percent of the white householders owning human property.

As the number of slaves increased, legal codes for strictly controlling their activities were fashioned in each of the colonies. To a large extent these "black codes" were borrowed from the law books of the English West Indies. Bit by bit they deprived the African immigrant of rights enjoyed by others in the society, including indentured servants. And gradually they reduced the slave, in the eyes of society and the law, from a human being to a piece of chattel property. In this process of dehumanization nothing was more important than the practice of hereditary lifetime service. Once servitude became perpetual, relieved only by death, then the stripping away of all other rights followed as a matter of course. When the condition of the slave parent was passed on to the child, then slavery had been extended to the womb. At that point the institution became totally fixed so far as the slave was concerned.

Thus, with the passage of time, Afro-Americans had to adapt to a more and more circumscribed world. Earlier in the seventeenth century they had been treated much as indentured servants, bound to labor for a specified period of years but thereafter free to work for themselves, hire out their labor, buy land, move as they pleased, and, if they wished, hold slaves themselves. But, by the 1640s, Virginia was forbidding blacks the use of firearms. In the 1660s marriages between white women and black slaves were being described as "shameful Matches" and "the Disgrace of our Nation"; during the next few decades interracial fornication became subject to unusually severe punishment and interracial marriage was banned.

These discriminatory steps were slight, however, in comparison with the stripping away of rights that began toward the end of the century. In rapid succession Afro-Americans lost their right to testify before a court; to engage in any kind of commercial activity, either as buyer or seller; to hold property; to participate in the political process; to congregate in public places with more than two or three of their fellows; to travel without permission; and to engage in legal marriage or parenthood. In some colonies legislatures even prohibited the right to education and religion, for they thought these might encourage the germ of freedom in slaves. From human status, slaves descended to property status. More and more steps were taken to contain them tightly in a legal system that made no allowance for their education, welfare, or future advancement. The restraints on the slave owner's freedom to deal with his slaves in any way he saw fit were gradually cast away. Early in the eighteenth century many colonies passed laws forbidding the manumission of slaves by individual owners. This was a step designed to squelch the strivings of slaves for freedom and to discourage those who had been freed from abetting attempts by their black brothers and sisters to gain their liberty.

The movement to annul all the slave's rights had both pragmatic and psychological dimensions. The greater the proportion of slaves in the population, the greater the danger to white society, for every colonist knew that when he purchased a man or woman in chains he had bought a potential insurrectionist. The larger the specter of black revolt, the greater the effort of white society to neutralize it by further restricting the rights and activities of slaves. Thus, following a black revolt in 1712 that took the lives of nine whites and wounded others, the New York legislature passed a slave code that rivaled those of the Southern colonies. Throughout the Southern colonies the obsessive fear of slave insurrection ushered in the institutionalization of violence as the means of ensuring social stability. Allied to this need for greater and greater control was the psychological compulsion to dehumanize slaves by taking from them the rights that connoted their humanity. It was far easier to rationalize the merciless exploitation of those who had been defined by law as something less than human. "The planters," wrote an Englishman in eighteenth-century Jamaica, "do not want to be told that their Negroes are human creatures. If they believe them to be of human kind, they cannot regard them . . . as no better than dogs or horses."[5]

Thus occurred one of the great paradoxes in our history—the building of what some thought was to be a utopia in the wilderness upon the backs of black men and women wrenched from their African homeland and forced

[5]Edward Long, *The History of Jamaica* . . . (London, 1774), II, Book 2, p. 270.

into a system of abject slavery. America was imagined as a liberating and regenerating force, it has been pointed out, but became the scene of a "grotesque inconsistency." In the land heralded for freedom and individual opportunity, the practice of slavery, unknown for centuries in the mother country, was reinstituted. Following other parts of the New World, America became the scene of "a disturbing retrogression from the course of historical progress."[6]

The mass enslavement of Africans profoundly affected white racial prejudice. Once institutionalized, slavery cast Africans into such lowly roles that the initial bias against them could only be confirmed and vastly strengthened. Initially unfavorable impressions of Africans had coincided with labor needs to bring about their mass enslavement. But it required slavery itself to harden the negative racial feelings into a deep and almost unshakable prejudice that continued to grow for centuries. The colonizers had devised a labor system that kept the African in America at the bottom of the social and economic pyramid. Irrevocably caught in the web of perpetual servitude, the slave was allowed no further opportunity to prove the white stereotype wrong. Socially and legally defined as less than a person, kept in a degraded and debased position, virtually without power in their relationships with white society, Afro-Americans became a truly servile, ignoble, degraded people in the eyes of the Europeans. This was used as further reason to keep them in slavery, for it was argued that they were worth nothing better and were incapable of occupying any higher role. In this long evolution of racial attitudes in America, nothing was of greater importance than the enslavement of Africans.

SLAVERY IN NORTH AND SOUTH AMERICA

Because slavery existed in virtually every part of the New World we can best discover what was unique about the system of bondage that evolved in the North American colonies by comparing it with the institution of slavery in other areas of the New World. We know that only about 4.5 percent of the slaves brought to the New World came to British North America. The 350,000 Africans who arrived there between 1619 and 1780 were dwarfed by the two million transported to Portuguese Brazil, the three million taken to British, French, and Dutch plantations in the West Indies, and the 700,000 imported into Spanish America. How did slaves fare in different parts of the New World, and how can we explain the differences in their treatment, their opportunities for emancipation, and their chances, once free, to carve out a worthwhile niche for themselves in society?

[6]David Brion Davis, *The Problem of Slavery in Western Culture* (Ithaca, N.Y.: Cornell University Press, 1966), p. 25.

The first comparativists to study slavery in the Americas argued that crucial differences evolved between the status of slaves in the Spanish or Portuguese colonies and the English colonies. These differences, they maintained, largely account for the fact that racial mixture is much more extensive today in Latin America than in North America, that formal policies of segregation and discrimination were never embodied in Latin American law, and that the racial tension and conflict that has characterized twentieth-century American life has been largely absent in Latin American countries such as Brazil. Miscegenation can be taken as one poignant example of these differences. Interracial marriage has never been prohibited in Brazil and would be thought a senseless and artificial separation of people. But in the American colonies legal prohibitions against interracial mixing began in the mid-seventeenth century. Virtually every American colony prohibited mixed marriages by the early eighteenth century. Modified from time to time, these laws remained in force throughout the period of slavery and in many states continued after the abolition of slavery. As late as 1949 mixed marriages were prohibited by law in twenty-nine states, including seventeen outside the South.

Such differences as these, it has been argued, are indicative of the fact that slavery in Spanish and Portuguese America was never as harsh as in Anglo-America nor were the doors to eventual freedom so tightly closed. In Latin America, it is said, Africans mixed sexually with the white population from the beginning; they were never completely stripped of political, economic, social, and religious rights; they were frequently encouraged to work for their freedom; and, when the gate to freedom was opened, they found it possible to carve a place of dignity for themselves in the community. In the North American colonies, on the contrary, slaves lost all of their rights by the early eighteenth century and were thereafter treated as mere chattel property. Emancipation was rare and in fact several colonies prohibited it in the eighteenth century. Those Afro-Americans who did obtain their freedom, especially after the American Revolution, found themselves permanently consigned to the lowliest positions in society, where social and political rights initially granted them as citizens were gradually withdrawn. In entitling his book *Slave and Citizen*, Frank Tannenbaum, a pioneer in the comparative study of slavery, signified his view of the differing fates of the African migrant in the two continents of the New World.[7]

By what series of events or historical accidents had the Africans in the Latin American colonies been placed on the road to freedom while in English North America the roal traveled by blacks was always a dead end, even after freedom was granted? Tannenbaum and those who followed him suggested that the answer lay in the different ideological and cultural climates in which the Africans struggled in the New World. Those who were

[7]Frank Tannenbaum, *Slave and Citizen: The Negro in the Americas* (New York: Alfred A. Knopf, 1946).

enslaved in the Spanish and Portuguese colonies entered a culture that was Catholic in religion, semimedieval and authoritarian in its political institutions, conservative and paternalistic in its social relations, and Roman in its system of law. Africans brought to America, by contrast, confronted a culture that was Protestant in religion, libertarian and "modern" in its political institutions, individualistic in its social relations, and Anglo-Saxon in its system of law. Ironically it was the "premodern" Spanish and Portuguese culture that protected slaves and eventually prepared them for something better than slavery. The Catholic church not only sent its representatives to the New World in far greater number than did the Protestant churches, but wholeheartedly devoted itself to preserving the human rights of Negroes. Affirming that no individual, no matter how lowly his position or corrupt his behavior, was unworthy in the sight of God, the Catholic clergy toiled to convert people of every color and condition, wherever and whenever they found them. Indians and Africans in the Latin American colonies were therefore fit subjects for the zeal of the Jesuit, Dominican, and Franciscan priests, and the church, in viewing masses of enslaved Indians and Africans as future Christians, had a tempering effect on what slave masters might do with their slaves or what legislators, reflecting planter opinion, might legislate into law.

In a similar way the transference of Roman law to the Iberian colonies served to protect the slave from becoming mere chattel property, for Roman law recognized the rights of slaves and the obligations of masters to them. The slave undeniably occupied the lowest rung on the social ladder but he or she remained a member of the community, entitled to legal protection from a rapacious or sadistic master.

Still a third institution mediated between master and slave—the government itself. Highly centralized, the Spanish and Portuguese political systems revolved around the power of the monarch and the aristocracy, and this power was expected to radiate out from its metropolitan centers in Europe to the New World colonies. Colonies existed under strict royal governance, and since the Crown, closely tied to the Catholic church, was dedicated to protecting the rights of slaves, slave owners in the colonies had to answer to a social policy formulated at home. In sum, a set of interconnecting institutions, derived from a conservative, paternalistic culture, worked to the advantage of African slaves by standing between them and their masters. Iberian institutions, transplanted to the New World, prohibited slave owners from exercising unbridled rein over their slaves and ensured that the slave, though exploited, was also protected and eventually prepared for full membership in the society.

In the English colonies of North America and the Caribbean, it is argued, these intermediating institutions were notably absent. Slave masters were far freer to follow their impulses in their treatment of slaves and in formulating social and legal policy that undergirded slavery. In North America, government was more localized and democratic, church and state more separate, and individuals less fettered by tradition and authority. Hence slaves were at the mercy of their masters to an unusual degree. The Protestant church had little interest in proselytizing slaves. When it did, its authority was far more locally based than in the Spanish and Portuguese colonies and therefore subject to the influence of the leading slave owners of the area.

Government too was less centralized; England allowed the colonists to formulate much of their own law and exercised only a weak regulatory power over the plantations. Anglo-Saxon law, transferred to the New World, was silent on the subject of slavery since slavery had not existed in England for centuries. This left colonists free to devise new law, as harsh and exploitive as they wished, to cope with the labor system they were erecting. In America, it is maintained, slave owners molded a highly individualistic, libertarian, and acquisitive culture that would brook few checks on the right of slave owners to exploit their human property exactly as they saw fit. It was property rights that the Anglo-American culture regarded as transcendently important. With relatively few institutional restraints to inhibit slave owners, nothing stood between new African immigrants and a system of total subjugation. Consequently, Tannenbaum and others have argued, a far more closed and dehumanizing system of slavery evolved in the more "enlightened" and "modern" environment of the English colonies than in the more feudalistic and authoritarian milieu of the Spanish and Portuguese colonies.

In the last few decades historians, sociologists, and anthropologists have raised many objections to this analysis of slavery and race relations in the New World. By looking too intently at Spanish and Portuguese laws, traditions, and institutions in the mother countries, they have said, we may have ignored the gap that often separates legal pronouncements from social reality. Is it possible that in the Spanish and Portuguese law books slaves were carefully protected, but in actuality their lives were as bad or worse than in the English plantations? Laws do not always reflect actual social conditions. If we had only the post-Civil War legal statutes as a guide to the status of the American Negroes in the nineteenth and twentieth centuries, we might conclude that Afro-Americans enjoyed equality with white Americans in the modern era. The laws guarantee nothing less. But what the law specifies and what actually occurs are two different things.

As historians have looked more closely at local conditions in various New World colonies, they have found that the alleged differences between North and South American slavery do not loom so large. Where the Catholic church and royal authority were well established, such as in urban areas, the treatment of slaves was indeed more humane than in areas of the American colonial South, such as South Carolina, where the Protestant churches took only shallow root. But in rural areas of the Spanish and Portuguese colonies, where slavery was most extensively practiced, the church's sway was not so strong and the authority of the Spanish colonial officials was more tenuous. In these areas individual slave masters were left to deal with their slaves as they saw fit, much as in the English colonies.

Moreover, recent studies have shown that wide variations in the treatment of slaves occurred within the colonies of each European nation. In Puritan New England and Quaker Pennsylvania conditions were never so inhumane as in the South, partly because the Puritan and Quaker churches acted as a restraint on the behavior of slave owners and partly because slaves, always a small percentage of the population, were more frequently employed as artisans and household servants than in the South, where mass agricultural labor was the primary concern of slave masters. Likewise, conditions were far better for slaves in the Brazilian urban center of Recife than on the frontier plantations of the remote southern province of Rio Grande do Sul.

Other factors, quite separate from the ideological or cultural climate of a given area, have claimed the attention of historians more forcefully in recent attempts to delineate differences in slave systems and to isolate the unique facets of English slavery in North America. The most important factor shaping a slave society was its economic base. Where blacks worked in the plantation system, producing cash crops such as sugar, coffee, tobacco, and rice, they suffered thralldom at its brutal worst. In these areas the conditions of human life could be appalling. This included the English rice plantations in the eighteenth century, the Portuguese coffee plantations in the nineteenth century, and the sugar plantations of all European colonizers from the seventeenth to the nineteenth centuries. Maximization of profit was the overriding goal on such plantations, and it was best achieved by literally working slaves to death and then replacing them with newly imported Africans.

When agricultural areas were enjoying boom times and rapid expansion, as in the cases of eighteenth-century South Carolina and nineteenth-century Cuba, the exploitation of slaves was usually found at its extreme limits because special incentives existed for driving bondsmen and bondswomen to the limit of human endurance. Also of great significance in the lives of slaves was the kind of crop they were employed at growing. Sugar was particularly labor intensive, its cultivation requiring the most strenuous, debilitating labor, as opposed, for example, to wheat or corn. Perhaps nowhere was the treatment of slaves so callously regarded as on the sugar plantations of the Caribbean where the combination of absentee ownership, the work regimen, and the highly capitalized nature of the economic system made life a living hell for slaves, regardless of whether they toiled on English Barbados, Dutch Surinam, French Martinique, or Spanish Cuba. Slaves were regarded "as so many cattle" who would "perform their dreadful tasks and then expire" after seven or eight years, as one Englishman wrote in 1788.[8]

In fringe areas, by contrast, where slaves were used for occasional labor or as domestic servants and artisans, conditions were much better. In northerly areas only one crop a year was possible and winter brought slack times. In cities the work rhythms were not so intense and the social climate existed for religious and humanitarian ideology to temper the brutality inherent in the master-slave relationship. In Anglo-Dutch New York City and Portuguese Recife, as well as in rural New England and New France, slaves were often badly used by their masters, but their chances for survival were far greater than on the expanding cash crop plantations.

A second factor affecting the dynamics of particular slave societies was the simple ratio of blacks to whites. Where slaves represented a small fraction of the total population, such as in New England and the mid-Atlantic English colonies, slave codes did not strip Afro-Americans of all their rights. Religion and education were commonly believed to be beneficial to slaves, and no protests were heard when Quakers and Anglicans set up schools for Negroes in places such as Boston and Philadelphia. Marriage was customary and black parents often baptized their children in the Protestant churches, even though death brought burial in a separate "strangers" graveyard. Slaves were freer to congregate in public places and were recognized before courts of law in these areas.

From Maryland to Georgia, however, conditions were markedly different. In the Chesapeake colonies, slaves represented about 40 percent of the population by mid-eighteenth century and in South Carolina they outnumbered whites at all times after 1710. In these areas far more repressive slave codes were legislated. The same was true in the English Caribbean islands where whites were vastly outnumbered in the eighteenth century. Surrounded by those whom they had enslaved, control became a crucial factor for white slave owners, who lived in perpetual fear of black insurrections. Numerically inferior, they took every precaution to ensure that their slaves would have no opportunity to organize and plot against them. Living in a kind of garrison state amidst constantly circulating rumors of black revolt, white planters heaped punishment on black offenders and retaliated with ferocity against black aggression in the hope that other slaves would be cowed into submissiveness. Castration for sexual offenses against whites and burning at the stake for plotting or participating in insurrection were common punishments in colonies with a high proportion of black slaves. But where slaves represented only a small fraction of the population no such elaborate attempts were made to define their inferior status in precise detail or to leave them so completely at the mercy of their owners.

Two other factors affecting the lives of slaves operated independently of

---

[8]Quoted in C. Vann Woodward, *American Counterpoint: Slavery and Racism in the North-South Dialogue* (Boston: Little, Brown and Company, 1971), p. 101.

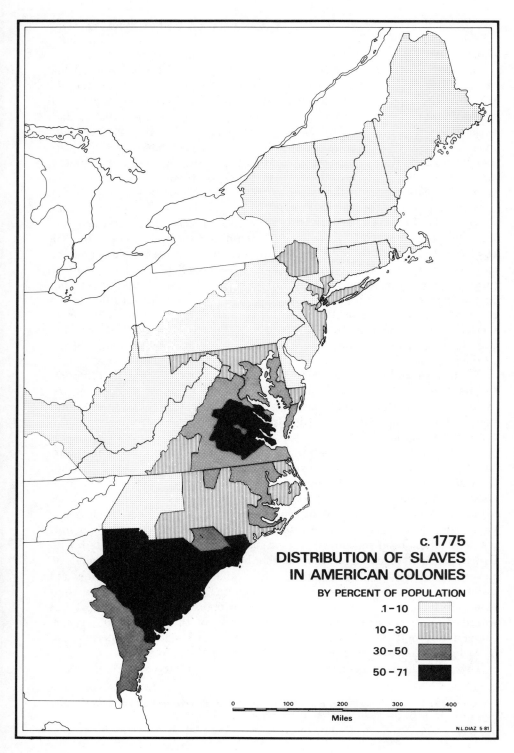

c. 1775
**DISTRIBUTION OF SLAVES
IN AMERICAN COLONIES**

BY PERCENT OF POPULATION

.1 – 10

10 – 30

30 – 50

50 – 71

0   100   200   300   400
Miles

N.L.DIAZ 5-81

the national backgrounds of their owners. The first was whether or not the slave trade was still open in a particular area. When this was so, new supplies of Africans were continuously available and the treatment of slaves was usually harsh. To work a slave to death created no problem of replacement. Where the slave trade was closed, however, greater precautions were taken to safeguard the capital investment that had been made in human property, for replacement could be obtained only through reproduction—a long and uncertain process. The sugar island of Barbados, for example, was a death trap for Africans in the eighteenth century. From one-third to one-half of all slaves died within three years of their arrival. But with fresh supplies of African slaves readily available and with virtually no intermediary institutions to restrain them in the treatment of their human property, sugar planters were free to build their fortunes through an exploitation of slave labor that was limited only by calculations of cost efficiency. This, along with ravaging epidemics, resulted in a phenomenally high mortality. Between 1712 and 1762 deaths outnumbered births by 120,000 among a slave population that averaged about 50,000. This meant little to the English planters, for they could view this carnage as an inevitable if regrettable part of the process by which wealth was created and sugar produced for household consumption in every village in Great Britain.

A final factor affecting slave life was the prevalence of tropical diseases. In the temperate zones, including most of North America, slaves were far less subject to the ravaging fevers that swept away both Europeans and Africans in the tropical zone. This is of the utmost importance in explaining why mortality rates were lower and fertility rates higher in the English colonies of North America than in the Caribbean and South American colonies of various European powers. The startling fact is that less than 5 percent of the slaves brought to the New World came to British North America and yet by 1825 American Negroes represented 36 percent of all peoples of African descent in the hemisphere. By contrast, Brazil, which imported about 38 percent of all slaves brought to the Americas, had only 31 percent of the African descendents alive in the hemisphere in 1825. The British West Indies imported about 850,000 slaves between 1700 and 1787 but the black population of the islands in the latter year was only about 350,000. In contrast, the American colonies imported less than 250,000 in the same period, but counted about 575,000 Negroes in the population in 1780. These starkly different demographic histories reflect several variables—differences in male-female ratios during the slave period, treatment of slaves, and fertility rates among free Negroes, for example. But however these factors may ultimately sort out, it seems clear that Africans brought to the North American colonies had a far better chance for survival than their counterparts in the tropical colonies.

Alongside the treatment of slaves on the plantations of the different European colonizers we need to consider the access to freedom which slaves found in one colony as opposed to another. While historians are still arguing vigorously about the question of comparative treatment, they largely agree that slaves in the Spanish and Portuguese colonies had far greater opportunities to work themselves free of the shackles of bondage than did slaves in the English colonies. Census figures for the eighteenth century are fragmentary, but we know that by 1820 the ratio of free Negroes to slaves was about one to six in the United States, one to three in Brazil, one to four in Mexico, and one to two in Cuba. In Spanish Cuba alone, free blacks outnumbered by 30,000 the number of manumitted slaves in all the Southern states in 1800, although the black population of the American South exceeded that of Cuba by about three to one.

Some historians have interpreted this greater opportunity for freedom in the Spanish and Portuguese colonies as evidence of the relatively flexible and humane nature of the system there and as proof of the Iberian commitment to preparing the slave for citizenship. But others, who argue that demographic and economic factors were preeminently important, are more persuasive. They point out that the white *need* for free blacks, not humanitarian concern for black freedom, motivated most Spanish and Portuguese slave owners to emancipate their human property. Because the English had emigrated to the American colonies in far larger numbers than the Spanish or Portuguese they were numerous enough to fill most of the positions of artisan, overseer, cattle tender and militiaman—the "interstitial work of the economy."[9] But the relatively light European emigration to the Spanish and Portuguese colonies left them desperately short of people who could function above the level of manual labor. Therefore it became necessary to create a class of free blacks, working for whites as wage laborers; otherwise the economy would not have functioned smoothly for the benefit of white landowners, merchants, and investors. Where Afro-Americans were functional as freedmen in the white man's society, they were freed; where they were not, they remained slaves. To be sure, masters were seldom limited by law in manumitting their slaves in Spanish and Portuguese colonies, as they were in English colonies; but this testifies more to the fact that the law followed the social and economic needs of society than to any benevolent concern for the slave derived from ancient precedent. If free blacks had not been needed in Latin American society or if it had been more profitable to close the door to freedom than to keep it ajar, it is unlikely that slaves would have been manumitted in such large numbers. Conversely, Portuguese and Spanish slave owners often emancipated their infirm or aged slaves in order to be free of the costs of maintaining unproductive laborers, a practice also well-known in the English colonies.

A second way in which free blacks were vital to the interests of white colonizers in Latin America and the Caribbean was as a part of the system of

[9]Carl N. Degler, *Neither Black Nor White: Slavery and Race Relations in Brazil and the United States* (New York: The Macmillan Company, 1971), p. 44.

military defense and internal security. North American and Brazilian slave systems, for example, diverged strikingly in their attitudes toward arming slaves and in creating a community of free blacks. Brazilian colonists could not have repelled French attacks in the late sixteenth century, the Dutch invasion in the second quarter of the seventeenth century, and the French assaults in the early eighteenth century without arming their slaves. "Because the mother country . . . was too weak or unconcerned to offer much assistance," writes Carl Degler, "all the resources of the sparsely settled colony had to be mobilized for defense, which included every scrap of manpower, including black slaves."[10] In the American colonies, by contrast, the need to arm slaves was comparatively slight. Colonial shipping was intermittently endangered by naval raiders of other European powers, but the colonies were only rarely subjected to external attack. Where they were, principally in South Carolina, then the Portuguese pattern was duplicated. Precariously situated with regard to the Spanish in Florida, the Carolinians passed a law in 1707 requiring every militia captain "to enlist, traine up and bring into the field for each white, one able Slave armed with a gun or lance."[11] In the Yamasee War, South Carolina gladly used slaves to stave off the attacks of their Indian enemies. But this was the exception rather than the rule.

For the internal security of plantation society armed slaves would have been a contradiction, but free blacks were not. They could be used to suppress rebellion, to repel marauding escaped slaves living beyond the plantations, or to invade and defeat maroon communities. But rebellion and marronage occurred primarily in plantation societies where blacks massively outnumbered whites and where the geography was conducive to the establishment of communities of escaped slaves. Such was the situation in the English West Indies where the mountainous island interiors provided ideal refuges for maroons. By freeing slaves, the Caribbean planters secured the loyalty and the military service of a corps of islanders who kept the slave-based sugar economy going. In North America the security problem was not so severe. The ratio of white to black was more even and geography did not favor marronage since the interior was occupied by powerful Indian tribes who were only occasionally receptive to runaway slaves. Far from being regarded as loyal adjuncts of white society, the small number of free Negroes in the American colonies were usually seen as a threat to the security of the slave system and were therefore often compelled to leave the colony where they had been manumitted within a specific period of time.

A third, crucially important way in which the African was more valuable as a freed person than as a slave in the Caribbean and Latin American

[10]*Ibid.*, p. 79.

[11]Verner W. Crane, *The Southern Frontier, 1670–1732* (Ann Arbor: University of Michigan Press, 1956), p. 187n.

colonies was as a sexual partner. "No part of the world," writes one historian, "has ever witnessed such a gigantic mixing of races as the one that has been taking place in Latin America and the Caribbean since 1492."[12] In explaining this racial mixing, it is relevant that the Spanish and Portuguese had been interacting with people from Mediterranean, Middle Eastern, and North African cultures through centuries of war and economic relations. This developed in their societies a certain plasticity in race relations. The English, by comparison, had remained relatively isolated in their island fortress prior to the late sixteenth century, intermingling hardly at all with people of other cultures.

But the inherited Iberian attitudes, transported to the New World, would probably have faded had it not been for compelling circumstances that encouraged miscegenation in such places as Mexico, Peru, and Brazil. Spanish and Portuguese males emigrated without women to a greater extent than Englishmen, who came predominantly with their families. In the Spanish and Portuguese cases the colonizers carried with them a racial ideology that, while it favored white skin and European blood, was still malleable enough to justify mixing with Indian and African women. In the Latin American colonies interracial sexual relations were common, as the colonizers took Indian and African women as mistresses, concubines, and wives. Such partnerships were accepted with little embarrassment or social strain, for it was regarded as natural to have sexual relations with or even to marry a woman of dark skin.

Such was not the case in most of the English colonies. English women had come with English men to Puritan New England so that parity between the sexes was established relatively early. This obviated the need for Indian and African women. In the Southern colonies, where white women were in short supply for four or five generations, African women were also absent because the importation of slaves remained insignificant until the last decade of the seventeenth century. By the time black women were available in large numbers, the numerical disparity between white men and women had been redressed. It was not so much extreme ethnocentrism as it was the presence of white women that made miscegenation officially disreputable and often illegal, through practiced privately to a considerable extent. If white men had continued to lack English women at the time when African women began flooding into the Southern colonies, then the alleged English distaste for dark-skinned partners would doubtlessly have broken down. Womanless men are not easily restrained by ethnocentrism in finding release for their sexual urges as was demonstrated by the English experience in the West Indian sugar islands. In Barbados, Jamaica, and the Leeward Islands, English women were not as plentiful as in the mainland colonies. But surrounded by a sea of black women, Englishmen eagerly followed the

[12]Magnus Mörner, *Race Mixture in the History of Latin America* (Boston: Little, Brown and Company, 1967), p. 1.

practice of the Spanish and Portuguese, consorting with and occasionally marrying their slaves. "Not one in twenty can be persuaded that there is either sin or shame in cohabiting with his slave," wrote a Jamaica planter.[13] To outlaw sexual relations with Negro women, as was being done in the English mainland colonies in the eighteenth century, Winthrop Jordan has suggested, would have been more difficult than abolishing the sugar cane.[14] Where white women were absent, black women were needed; where they were needed, they were accepted and laws prohibiting interracial sex and marriage never entered the statute books.

Slavery in the Americas was characterized by a considerable degree of variation, both in the treatment of slaves, the degree of openness in the system, and the willingness of the dominant society to mix intimately with the Africans in their midst. The cultural heritage brought to the New World by the various European settler groups played some role in the formation of attitudes, policies, and laws. But the exigencies of life in the New World, including economic, sexual, and military needs, did far more to shape racial attitudes and the system of slavery.

[13]Long, *History of Jamaica*, II, Book 2, p. 328.

[14]Winthrop D. Jordan, *White Over Black: American Attitudes Toward the Negro, 1550–1812* (Chapel Hill: University of North Carolina Press, 1968), p. 140.

8

THE AFRICAN RESPONSE TO SLAVERY

It is easy to assume that Africans, once sold into slavery and brought to the New World, were simply fitted into a closed system of forced labor where they lived out their lives, abject and de-Africanized, as best they could. So much attention is lavished on the kind of slave system fashioned by slave owners—the black codes they legislated, their treatment of slaves, the economic development they directed—that the slaves themselves are often forgotten as active participants in a cultural process. How did they respond to the loss of their freedom and the separation from all that was familiar in their native culture? How did they live day by day in a vastly different culture? To what degree were they acculturated into white European society? To what degree did they mold a new Afro-American culture, distinct from the European culture surrounding them? Until we adopt the approach of studying the interior lives of slaves, replacing the question "What was done to the slaves?" with the question, "What did slaves do for themselves and how did they do it?", we will continue to view slaves only as the object but not the subject of our historical inquiries.[1]

[1] Eugene D. Genovese, *In Red and Black: Marxian Explorations in Southern and Afro-American History* (New York: Random House, Inc., 1971), p. 106.

CAPTURE AND TRANSPORT OF SLAVES

No accounts of the initial enslavement of Africans, no matter how vivid, can quite convey the pain and demoralization that must have accompanied the forced march to the west coast of Africa and the subsequent loading aboard ships of those who had fallen captive to the African suppliers of the European slave traders. As the demand for African slaves doubled and redoubled in the eighteenth century, the hinterlands of western and central Sudan were invaded again and again by the armies and agents of both coastal and interior kings. Perhaps 75 percent of the slaves transported to English North America came from the part of western Africa that lies between the Senegal and Niger rivers and the Gulf of Benin, and most of the others were enslaved in Angola on the west coast of Central Africa. Slaving activities in these areas were responsible for considerable depopulation of the region in the eighteenth and nineteenth centuries.

Once captured, slaves were marched to the sea in "coffles," or trains. A Scotsman, Mungo Park, described the coffle he marched with for 550 miles through Gambia at the end of the eighteenth century. It consisted of 73 men, women, and children tied together by the neck with leather thongs. Several captives attempted to commit suicide by eating clay, another was abandoned after being badly stung by bees; still others died of exhaustion and hunger. After two months the coffle reached the coast, many of its members physically depleted by thirst, hunger, and exposure, where they were herded into fortified enclosures called barracoons.[2]

The anger, bewilderment, and desolation that accompanied the forced march, the first leg of the 5,000-mile journey to the New World, was only increased by the actual transfer of slaves to European ship captains, who carried their human cargo in small wooden ships to the Americas. "As the slaves come down to Fida from the inland country," wrote one European trader in the late seventeenth century, "they are put into a booth or prison, built for that purpose, near the beach . . . and when the Europeans are to receive them, they are brought out into a large plain, where the [ships'] surgeons examine every part of every one of them, to the smallest member, men and women being all stark naked. Such as are allowed good and sound, are set on one side, and the others by themselves; which slaves so rejected are called Mackrons, being above 35 years of age, or defective in their lips, eyes, or teeth, or grown grey; or that have the venereal disease, or any other imperfection."[3] Such dehumanizing treatment was part of the commercial process by which "merchandise" was selected and bargained for. But it

[2]Daniel P. Mannix and Malcolm Cowley, *Black Cargoes: A History of the Atlantic Slave Trade, 1518–1856* (New York: The Viking Press, Inc., 1962), pp. 101–02.

[3]Quoted in Basil Davidson, *The African Slave Trade: Precolonial History, 1450–1850* (Boston: Little, Brown and Company, 1961), p. 92.

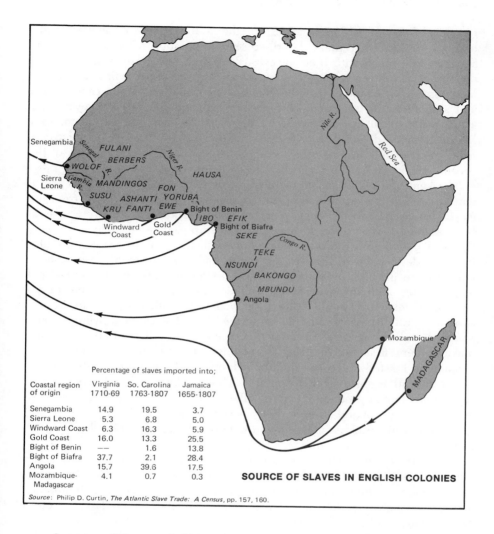

	Percentage of slaves imported into;		
Coastal region of origin	Virginia 1710-69	So. Carolina 1763-1807	Jamaica 1655-1807
Senegambia	14.9	19.5	3.7
Sierra Leone	5.3	6.8	5.0
Windward Coast	6.3	16.3	5.9
Gold Coast	16.0	13.3	25.5
Bight of Benin	——	1.6	13.8
Bight of Biafra	37.7	2.1	28.4
Angola	15.7	39.6	17.5
Mozambique-Madagascar	4.1	0.7	0.3

SOURCE OF SLAVES IN ENGLISH COLONIES

Source: Philip D. Curtin, *The Atlantic Slave Trade: A Census,* pp. 157, 160.

was also part of the psychological process that attempted to strip away self-respect and self-identity from the Africans.

Cruelty followed cruelty. After purchase, each slave was branded with a hot iron signifying the company, whether Spanish, Portuguese, English, French, or Dutch, that had purchased him or her. Thus were members of "preliterate" societies first introduced to the alphabetic symbols of "advanced" cultures. "The branded slaves," one account related, "are returned to their former booths" where they were imprisoned until a full human cargo could be assembled.[4] The next psychological wrench came with the

[4]*Ibid.*

ferrying of slaves, in large canoes, to the waiting ships at anchor in the harbor. An English captain described the desperation of slaves who were about to lose touch with their ancestral land and embark upon a vast ocean that many had never previously seen. "The Negroes are so wilful and loth to leave their own country, that they have often leap'd out of the canoes, boat and ship, into the sea, and kept under water till they were drowned, to avoid being taken up and saved by our boats, which pursued them; they having a more dreadful apprehension of Barbadoes than we can have of hell."[5] Part of this fear was the common belief that on the other side of the ocean Africans would be eaten by the white savages.

The kind of fear that inspired suicide while still on African soil was prevalent as well on the second leg of the voyage—the "middle passage" from the west African coast to the New World. Conditions aboard ship were miserable, although it was to the advantage of the ship captains to deliver as many slaves as possible on the other side of the Atlantic. The preservation rather than the destruction of life was the main object, but brutality was systematic, both in pitching overboard any slaves who fell sick on the voyage and in punishing offenders with almost sadistic intensity as a way of creating a climate of fear that would stifle insurrectionist tendencies.[6] John Atkins, aboard an English slaver in 1721, described how the captain "whipped and scarified" several plotters of rebellion and sentenced others "to cruel deaths, making them first eat the Heart and Liver of one of them killed. The Woman he hoisted up by the thumbs, whipp'd and slashed her with Knives, before the other slaves, till she died."[7] Though the naval architects of Europe competed to produce the most efficient ships for carrying human cargoes to the New World, the mortality on board, for both black slaves below decks and white sailors above, was extremely high, averaging between 10 and 20 percent on each voyage.

That Africans frequently attempted suicide and mutiny during the ocean crossing provides evidence that even the extraordinary force used in capturing, branding, selling, and transporting them from one continent to another was not enough to make the captives submit tamely to their fate. An eighteenth-century historian of slavery, attempting to justify the terroristic devices employed by slavers, argued that "the many acts of violence they [the slaves] have committed by murdering whole crews and destroying ships when they had it in their power to do so have made these rigors wholly chargeable on their own bloody and malicious disposition which calls for the same confinement as if they were wolves or wild boars."[8] The modern

[5]Quoted in Mannix and Cowley, *Black Cargoes*, p. 48.

[6]Equiano, *The Interesting Narrative of the Life of Olaudah Equiano, or Gustavus Vassa, the African* (London, 1789), rpr. in *Africa Remembered: Narratives by West Africans from the Era of the Slave Trade*, ed. Philip Curtin (Madison: University of Wisconsin Press, 1967), p. 92.

[7]Davidson, *African Slave Trade*, pp. 94–95.

[8]Edward Long, *The History of Jamaica* (London, 1774), quoted in Mannix and Cowley, *Black Cargoes*, p. 111.

reader can detect in this characterization of enslaved Africans clear proof that submissiveness was not a trait of those who were forcibly carried to the New World. So great was this resistance that special techniques of torture had to be devised to cope with the thousands of slaves who were determined to starve themselves to death on the middle passage rather than reach the New World in chains. Brutal whippings and hot coals applied to the lips were frequently used to open the mouths of recalcitrant slaves. When this did not suffice, a special instrument, the *speculum oris*, or mouth opener, was employed to wrench apart the jaws of a resistant slave.

Taking into consideration the mortality involved in the capture, the forced march to the coast, and the middle passage, probably not more than one in two captured Africans lived to see the New World. Many of those who did must have been psychologically numbed as well as physically depleted by the experience. But one further step remained in the process of enslavement—the auctioning to a New World master and transportation to his place

For slaves, the most traumatic part of acculturating to European colonial life was the dreaded "middle passage." (Courtesy the New York Public Library.)

European naval architects competed in designing ships which would most efficiently and profitably deliver their human cargoes to the New World. (Courtesy the Library Company of Philadelphia.)

of residence. All in all, the relocation of any African brought westward across the Atlantic may have averaged about six months from the time of capture to the time of arrival at the plantation of a European slave master. During this protracted personal crisis, the slave was completely cut off from all that was familiar—language, family, wider kinship relationships, tribal religion, and other forms of social and psychological security. Still facing these victims of the European demand for cheap labor was adaptation to a new physical environment, a new language, new work routines, and, most important, a life in which bondage for themselves and their offspring was unending.

ADJUSTMENT TO SLAVE LIFE

The central problem for Africans who found themselves in the possession of a white master 5,000 miles from their homeland was to create institutions and lifeways that would allow them to live as satisfactorily as possible under the oppressive slave regimen imposed upon them by the Euroamerican master class. This problem was not one of merging a West African culture with a European culture because the human cargoes aboard slave ships were not a single collective African culture. Slaves arriving in North America were culturally heterogeneous, having come from many different tribes with distinct characteristics. In the matter of language, for example, the slaves had no common medium of communication, for they spoke a diversity of tongues. Similarly, they had been taken from regions in Africa where kinship systems, social organization, and political structures differed markedly. Hence, arriving slaves did not form "communities" of people at the outset but could only become communities through forging a new culture out of the elements of many old cultures combined with elements of the dominant European culture that now bounded their existence. "What the slaves undeniably shared at the outset," it has been written, "was their enslavement; all—or nearly all—else had to be *created by them*."[9]

In the encounter between the diverse cultural heritages of the African slaves and the relatively homogeneous culture of the European slaveocracy the preponderance of power exercised by the colonizers must always be kept in mind. Slaves to be sure drew upon their various cultural heritages to make life bearable in the New World. White slave owners were aware of these attempts of their slaves to maintain inherited cultural practices, and they undoubtedly allowed this insofar as it did not interfere with the "seasoning" of new slaves. When it impeded adaptation to the new system of life and work, however, attempts were made to obliterate such Africanisms. But this involved a continuous struggle between slave and master. The master's ideal was to convert the slave into a mindless drudge who obeyed every command and worked efficiently for the master's profit. But never in the long history of slavery could the memory, habit, and belief of slaves be entirely wiped away. And never could slavery, however brutal and dehumanizing the behavior of the masters, completely overawe and cow its victims. Black men and women in the English colonies, as elsewhere, "were able to find the means to sustain a far greater degree of self-pride and group cohesion than the system they lived under ever intended for them to be able to do," not because "the system was more benign than it has been pictured, but rather that human beings are more resilient, less malleable, and less able to live without some sense of cultural cohesion, individual autonomy, and self-worth than a number of recent scholars have maintained."[10]

The status difference between slave and free, in other words, was immense, and power was very unequally divided. Yet the interaction of African and Euroamerican was continuous under slavery because both groups were tied together in a state of intimate interdependence. Masters could set the boundaries of the slave's existence, defining physical location, work roles, diet, and shelter; but the master had far less control on how slaves established friendships, fell in love, formed kin groups, raised their children, worshipped their gods, buried their dead, organized their leisure time, and

[9]Sidney W. Mintz and Richard Price, *An Anthropological Approach to the Afro-American Past: A Caribbean Perspective* (Philadelphia: Institute for the Study of Human Issues, 1976), p. 10.

[10]Lawrence W. Levine, *Black Culture and Black Consciousness: Afro-American Folk Thought From Slavery to Freedom* (New York: Oxford University Press, 1977), xi.

so forth. At this "much deeper and more fundamental level of interpersonal relationships and expressive behavior" Africans in America exercised a considerable degree of autonomy and were thus able to draw on their cultural backgrounds in shaping an Afro-American character.[11]

In all this process of adaptation there was a built-in premium on cultural innovation and creativity. This was both because slaves had to adjust rapidly to the power of the master class, which bore so heavily on them, and because of the initial cultural heterogeneity of the Africans brought to the colonies. Unlike the European colonizers, African slaves were immediately obliged "to shift their primary cultural and social commitment from the Old World to the New." Thrown together with slaves from other tribes and thrust into a system of bondage, "all slaves must have found themselves accepting, albeit out of necessity, countless 'foreign' cultural practices."[12] The nostalgia for the homeland no doubt endured, but the overriding instinct was to survive. This required rapid adaptation, learning new ways of doing things that would ensure survival. It was imperative, therefore, that Africans rapidly develop local slave cultures; and in doing this they adopted "a general openness to ideas and usages from other cultural traditions, a special tolerance (within the West African context) of cultural differences."[13] It can be said that of all the peoples converging in seventeenth- and eighteenth-century North America, the Africans, by the very conditions of their arrival, developed the greatest cultural dynamism, the greatest capacity for individual creativity and cultural change.

Masters, it can be readily imagined, were frequently insensitive to the cultural creativity of their slaves and to the local Afro-American cultures that were being formed from the time Africans first landed. They preferred to think of their slaves as animals or, in legal terms, as property. Property cannot think and create; animals cannot learn new languages, cultivate crops, create music and dance. This was the central contradiction in the New World system of chattel slavery—that while treating their human property inhumanely and defining their slaves as less than human, the master class implicitly had to recognize the humanity of their slaves, for the slaves' ability to work, think, and express emotion (and to revolt against, resist, and ridicule their oppressors) was in itself dramatic proof of this.

REGIONAL VARIATIONS OF AMERICAN SLAVERY

"Saltwater" Africans, as colonists called slaves brought directly from Africa, and their creole offspring, slaves born in America, did not all face the same conditions in the English colonies. Afro-American culture was shaped differ-

[11]David Dalby, "The African Element in American English," in Rappin' and Stylin' Out: Communication in Urban Black America, T. Kochman, ed. (Urbana: University of Illinois Press, 1972), p. 173.

[12]Mintz and Price, Anthropological Approach to the Afro-American Past, p. 24.

[13]Ibid., p. 26.

ently in three distinct regions because slavery itself varied markedly in the plantation systems of the Chesapeake Bay and the Carolina-Georgia low country and in the nonplantation North. The complexity of black culture in America cannot be understood without considering the evolution of these distinct, regional black societies, as they developed over a period of more than a century.

The Chesapeake

Slavery in Virginia and Maryland evolved through three different periods. For nearly the first half century after Africans first arrived in Virginia they were treated by the tobacco planters much as were white indentured servants. Life was brutal and often short, for the planters were intent upon wringing every bit of profit they could from the tobacco frontier. The Africans were predominantly male, and many of those who did not succumb to disease and the work regimen became landowners themselves once they gained their freedom. In this period before the 1660s, when slavery was legalized, they adapted rapidly to white society, for without many of their homelanders in the region—in 1675 there were only about 2,500 slaves in Virginia and half that number in Maryland—racial cohesiveness was difficult to maintain. Black and white bond laborers "ran away together, slept together, and, upon occasion, stood shoulder to shoulder against the weighty champions of authority."[14]

Beginning in the 1670s, Chesapeake planters began to import slaves in much larger numbers. By the early eighteenth century the agricultural labor force was overwhelmingly black. Probably 75,000 slaves, almost all of them coming directly from Africa, entered the Chesapeake colonies between 1700 and 1750. This had a profoundly Africanizing effect on black plantation society. In a period of rapid westward expansion, Virginia planters used most of these new immigrants to develop new upland plantations. They were disproportionately male, worked in small groups to clear the land and plant tobacco, and lived on a frontier that was remote from the older tidewater settlements that represented the mainstream of Chesapeake existence. Planters used creole slaves far more frequently in the tidewater area, where sex ratios were becoming better balanced and black family life was developing.

The convergence of African and creole slave societies in Virginia and Maryland began in the 1740s. By this time natural reproduction was supplying most of the additional slaves that Chesapeake planters needed. By the eve of the American Revolution only 10 percent of the annual increase in Virginia's slave population could be attributed to imports from Africa. An increasingly creole black population was reproducing itself, and with this reproduction came a rapid balancing of the sex ratio, which in turn created

[14]Ira Berlin, "Time, Space, and the Evolution of Afro-American Society in British Mainland North America," *American Historical Review*, 85 (1980): 69.

greater possibilities for family life. The growth of black kinship networks was further facilitated by the greater density of slave settlement, by the growth of larger plantations where hundreds of slaves labored together, and by the development of a network of roads and market towns that allowed for greater mobility between plantations. In addition, as the Chesapeake economy began to shift in the 1740s from tobacco monoculture to a mixed economy of tobacco, wheat, and iron production, the nature of black labor began to change. More slaves learned artisan skills, required in a more diversified and urbanized economy. This expanded their universe, drawing many away from the dull, backbreaking labor of tending tobacco plants and giving them many points of contact with the larger society beyond the single plantation.

By the late colonial period in the Chesapeake Afro-Americans had achieved considerable "social space" in which to maneuver. They continued to live in close proximity to whites, for almost all Virginia and Maryland planters resided on their plantations and "prided themselves on regulating all aspects of their far-flung estates through a combination of direct personal supervision and plantation-based overseers."[15] But while slaves might work from sunup to sundown under the overseer's whip and the master's shadow, from sundown to sunup and during the Sabbath and holidays they were largely out of sight and sound of their owners. Black culture grew in the unintended but inevitable interstices of an institution designed to extract labor from its victims. Because a growing proportion of them were American-born, had successfully established a family life, and labored within an increasingly diversified economy, they were becoming part of a unified Afro-American culture. At the same time, this culture was far more connected to Anglo-American culture and far more shaped by it than in the lowland colonies to the south.

The Carolina and Georgia Low Country

Africans first came to the marshy waterways of the Carolina coast with their West Indian masters who settled the country, so they had already made an adjustment to life in the English-speaking parts of the New World. The Carolina frontier was a rugged, dangerous place in the late seventeenth century, as the colonizers engaged in Indian wars, Indian slave trading, and periodic skirmishes with the Spanish and French. This vulnerability to external enemies made slaves vital to colonial defense, and thus South Carolina became the one colony that offered freedom to any slave "who in Time of an Invasion kills an Enemey."[16] This relative flexibility in the slave system was magnified by the familiarity of West Africans with the subtropi-

---

[15]*Ibid.*, p. 76.
[16][Thomas Nairne], *A Letter from South Carolina* . . . (London, 1710).

cal environment of the lowlands. White settlers depended upon their slaves in adapting African techniques of rice cultivation and cattle herding to a geography and climate that was foreign to them. "Transplanted Englishmen," it has been written, "learned as much or more from transplanted Africans as did the former Africans from them. . . . White domination made itself felt, but both whites and blacks incorporated much of West African culture into their new way of life."[17] Far more than on the Chesapeake, Africans defined the culture in which they labored in the early years of settlement.

In the early eighteenth century, after the agricultural skills of West Africans had made rice the keystone of the lowlands economy, slavery entered a new phase. Only about 4,000 slaves toiled in South Carolina in 1708 but that number tripled in the next twelve years and then tripled again by 1740, when nearly 40,000 slaves inhabited the rice coast, outnumbering whites by two to one. This demographic revolution brought the end of the relatively open, flexible system of slavery known in the early years. Large rice and indigo plantations emerged; slaves lived in larger units and worked under brutal conditions in field gangs; increasingly prosperous planters retreated to the coastal cities, especially Charleston; and field labor was left to the supervision of overseers and black drivers. By 1737 a Swiss newcomer opined that Carolina "looks more like a negro country than like a country settled by white people."[18]

A notable fracture appeared in the ranks of slaves as the coastal lowlands experienced the "rice and indigo revolution." In the capital city of Charleston, a creole population of Afro-Americans, representing more than half the city's population, lived in close proximity to white society. As house servants, boatmen, dockworkers, and artisans, they became relatively mobile, skilled, and privileged. Some mixed sexually with slave masters, producing a considerable mulatto population that formed the basis of a small free black population. Hewing close to white culture, these urban Afro-Americans mastered the English language and the intricate interracial personal relationships required in the cities to obtain privileges from the ruling whites.

But on the large plantations, black culture moved in the opposite direction. Slaves represented a large proportion of the population and lived in relative isolation from white culture. They had truck gardens to supply much of their own food needs and labored in the task system, where the daily work routine was defined by quotas—feet of irrigation ditch to be dug or rows of rice to be harvested. Both of these developments conferred upon them a degree of independence from close white management. Combined with the fact that so many of them were recently arrived from Africa, this led to the creation of a culture that more than anywhere else in British

[17]Berlin, "Afro-American Society in British Mainland North America," p. 56.

[18]Quoted in Peter Wood, *Black Majority: Negroes in Colonial South Carolina from 1670 through the Stono Rebellion* (New York: Alfred A. Knopf, 1974), p. 132.

An eighteenth-century painting from South Carolina reveals the preservation of African cultural forms in North America. The non-secular dance is believed to be of Yoruba origin, as were the stringed instrument and drum. (Abby Aldrich Rockefeller Folk Art Collection, Colonial Williamsburg Foundation.)

North America was West African in its characteristics. This was reflected in their distinctive language patterns, burial ceremonies, religion, and child-naming preferences. For example, Gullah became the primary tongue on the rice coast among slaves. A "pidgin," or mixture of several languages, it combined elements of English and a variety of West African dialects. Gullah emerged as the slaves' "central mode of communication and expression, linking together people of widely disparate backgrounds" who, because of their numerical superiority and relative isolation from white society, did not have to assimilate so thoroughly to white culture as did slaves in the Chesapeake colonies.[19] This greater degree of West African cultural persistence can also be seen in naming patterns. African day names (given for the day of the week on which the child was born) such as Quaco, Juba, Quashee, and Cuba can frequently be found in the plantation records of South Carolina and Georgia but are far less common in plantation records of

[19]*Ibid.*, p. 191.

Virginia and Maryland. On the rice and indigo plantations of the Carolina lowlands Afro-Americans remained more culturally distant from the world of their captors than in other colonies, and thus culturally closer to Africa.

The North

Slaves in the North made up only 3 percent of the population in most of New England and perhaps 10 to 15 percent in Rhode Island, New Jersey, New York, and Pennsylvania. Besides representing a small minority in the population, the nature of the slave's work differed in the Northern regions. Infrequently employed in field gangs, Northern slaves typically worked as artisans, farm hands, or personal servants. Whereas a majority of Southern slaves worked on plantations with many other slaves, the typical Northern slave labored alone or with only one or two of his or her countrymen. Moreover, the plantation slave quarters, where blacks could maintain a considerable degree of cultural autonomy and privacy away from the watchful eye of the owner, had no equivalent in Northern slave life. Virtually every Northern slave ate, slept, and lived in the house of the master. All of these factors—their low proportion of the population, wide dispersion, and unrelieved contact with whites—made attempts to retain a link to the African past extremely difficult, while ensuring that acculturation proceeded at a relatively rapid pace.

In the Northern cities slavery was far more deeply rooted than in the countryside. In New York City, where the Dutch had begun a tradition of relying on slave labor during the half century they controlled the town, almost 20 percent of the population was Afro-American in 1750 and two of every five householders owned at least one slave. In Philadelphia and Boston in the mid-eighteenth century, slaves made up about a tenth of the population and could be found in the homes of nearly every fifth family. In all three cities more than a thousand black slaves labored for their masters in the decade before the Revolution. These urban blacks were always rubbing elbows with lower-class whites—on the docks, at the markets, in the workplace of the master craftsman, in taverns, and at street entertainments such as cockfights. Slavery in the North was onerous to be sure, but its harshest features were mitigated by the absence of death-dealing gang labor in the fields, by the closer living relationship between masters and bond persons, and, in the cities, by the large degree of mobility and privileges that Afro-Americans gradually wrung from the master class.

The assimilationist tendency in the North was somewhat reoriented by the large influx of slaves directly from Africa beginning in the 1740s. As the Northern colonies grew rapidly in the eighteenth century, the call for bond labor increased. More and more large shipments of slaves arrived, reaching a peak during the late 1750s when the Seven Years War cut off the supply of white indentured servants from Ireland and Germany. Urban white officials noticed the introduction of African ways—burial ceremonies, dances, song, and other entertainments. Perhaps the most vivid evidence of the infusion of an African strain in Northern Afro-American culture was the mid-century introduction in many Northern towns of "Negro Election Day," an annual festival that drew blacks from the surrounding countryside to the cities for feasting, parading, dancing, and the election of black kings, judges, and other officials. "All the various languages of Africa, mixed with broken and ludicrous English filled the air," reported a white observer in Newport, Rhode Island, "accompanied with the music of the fiddle, tambourine, the banjo [and] drum."[20] In a ritual of role reversal, blacks in the towns dressed in the clothes of their masters, rode their masters' horses, feasted and drank on tributes exacted from their owners, and symbolically ruled the town for a day. Negro Election Day gave Northern slaves an opportunity to express momentarily the travail of thralldom, but it also provided a mechanism for blacks to choose and recognize their own leaders, who acted throughout the year in a semiofficial capacity as adjudicators of disputes and counselors to the black community.

Despite the infusion of African culture that accompanied the importation from Africa of thousands of slaves between 1740 and 1765, the over-all tendency in the North, far more than in either area of the plantation South, was for speedy assimilation with Anglo-American culture. Slavery was more benign in the North, slaves were more widely dispersed, and black-white contact was far too extensive to allow for a long-lasting retention of African culture.

SLAVE RESISTANCE AND REBELLION

While African-born and creole slaves struggled to adapt to bondage in various geographical, topological, and economic regions of North America, they also rankled, resisted, and rebelled in ways that kept their captors constantly aware of the costs of building and maintaining the edifice of slavery. The forms of resistance, like the forms of slavery itself, varied depending upon the circumstances of enslavement and the makeup of the slaves.

The spirit of resistance among "saltwater" Africans fresh from their home-lands was often immediate and open and was rarely easy to break, if eighteenth-century accounts can be believed. A North Carolinian was sure that newly imported slaves in his colony, most of them from Guinea, were far less industrious and more active in resisting slavery than "country-born"

[20]Quoted in Berlin, "Afro-American Society in British Mainland North America," p. 54.

blacks.[21] "If he must be broke," warned another observer of the African newcomer, "either from Obstinacy, or, which I am more apt to suppose, from Greatness of Soul, [it] will require . . . hard Discipline. . . . You would really be surpriz'd at their Perseverance . . . they often die before they can be conquer'd."[22] A study of fugitive slaves in eighteenth-century Virginia and South Carolina makes clear that newly imported Africans often ran away and did so in ways that reflected the communal folk ethos which they had known on the other side of the ocean. When they took flight, they did so in groups, particularly in company with slaves from their own country. In 1773, for example, fourteen freshly imported slaves fled as a group from a Virginia slave merchant, plunging into an unknown countryside in search of refuge.[23] Newspaper advertisements in South Carolina in the eighteenth century also reveal this kind of cooperative effort that brought slaves from the same region of Africa together in attempts at escape. The newspapers frequently advertised for groups of runaway "Gambia men" or slaves from the "Fullah Country." The Carolina backcountry as well as the Spanish-Indian Florida frontier acted as a magnet to those who were bent on escape, especially after 1733 when a Spanish decree promised escaped English slaves freedom in Florida.

This kind of overt rebelliousness often changed as Africans began assimilating the culture of the English-speaking plantation. Living on plantations with other slaves, many of them American-born, new arrivals learned the routine of planting, transplanting, weeding, worming, harvesting, and transporting crops. They also learned ways of reducing the tediousness of their tasks and minimizing the exertion which slave masters attempted to maximize. Dragging out the job, feigning illness, pretending ignorance, breaking tools, and other forms of "gold-bricking" were ways of avoiding physical depletion and also subtle forms of resistance against slavery itself. Planters like Landon Carter of Virginia complained endlessly that "my people seem to be quite dead hearted and either cannot or will not work."[24] An English observer of American slavery noted that the slave "does not appear to perform half as much, as a labourer in England" and added a comment about "the slovenly carelessness with which all business is performed by the slave."[25] More direct forms of resistance were truancy, which usually took the form of hiding out in the woods; arson by which the runaway slave struck against the white man's fields, barns, and houses; crop destruction;

[21]John Brickell, *The Natural History of North-Carolina* (Dublin, 1737; repub. Raleigh, N.C.: [n.p.] 1911), pp. 272–73.

[22]Quoted in Darold D. Wax, "Negro Resistance to the Early American Slave Trade," *Journal of Negro History,* 51 (1966): 11.

[23]Gerald W. Mullin, *Flight and Rebellion: Slave Resistance in Eighteenth-Century Virginia* (New York: Oxford University Press, Inc., 1972), pp. 39–47.

[24]Quoted in Mullin, *Flight and Rebellion,* p. 53.

[25]Quoted in *ibid.,* p. 54.

poisoning; murder; and organized pilfering in which groups of slaves requisitioned chickens, livestock, crops, liquor, tools, and household items by moonlight and sold them in black-market systems that spread over considerable distances.

When creole slaves moved from the field to the house and changed their role from gang laborers to household servants, they underwent further transformations which affected resistance. From the slaveholder's point of view the slaves could congratulate themselves on this advance in position, for it brought them closer to "civilized" life, conferred status upon them in the plantation hierarchy, and lightened the burden of their work. Although not many slaves resisted this chance for "advancement," accompanied by opportunities for better food, clothes, and shelter, many were aware that the role of domestic servant carried a heavy price, for it brought them into a far more intimate relationship with their captors and thus inhibited their ability to preserve some of the ancient ways that could be practiced in the relative privacy of the slave quarters. The household slave lost full membership in the black community and the chance to be out of sight of the white people of the plantation. New demands to acculturate more thoroughly were placed on these slaves, as every aspect of their behavior was now scrutinized by the master and mistress. Involved in a close, daily relationship with those who dominated their lives, many slaves developed speech problems such as stuttering—an outward sign of an inward difficulty in attempting to act in ways that satisfied the master and mistress but conflicted with real impulses and feelings. Rebelliousness could not take the same forms as in the field, and so in the "big house" drunkenness, malingering, and elaborate verbal and emotional contests of will with those whose authority hung over them became the slaves' means of resisting.

Because the plantation was a small world in itself, relatively self-sufficient and encompassing a wide variety of tasks, it required artisans skilled in carpentry, blacksmithing, milling, bricklaying, weaving, coopering, plastering, leatherworking, and butchering. Slaves were trained in these tasks. As skilled workers, they became more fully assimilated into white society, moving more freely between house, field, and workshop, and between the plantation and the town, the warehouse and the wharf. Other skilled labor, such as piloting tobacco- and rice-laden rafts and ferries through the maze-like inland waterways of the South, took the slave away from the plantation and out into a larger world. Slaves living in this wider world became skilled and imaginative in their manner of resistance. They ran away more frequently, sometimes trying to pass for free Negroes in other colonies, hiring themselves out as sailors, trading from carts, and living in towns with other free blacks and poor whites. They learned to cope with the white world. When they ran away, it was not in groups but individually, and they used their new skills and their new resourcefulness—a measure of how fully they had become acculturated—to maneuver their way into situations that would improve their lot. Their status at the top of the slave hierarchy gave them skills and privileges which they were often able to convert into attempts to subvert the slave system. A study of slavery in the eighteenth-century capital of Virginia notes the high incidence of run-aways among slave artisans—the most fully acculturated Afro-Americans in the colony.[26]

Even in the North, where slavery was more benign, there were few misapprehensions about the contentedness or submissiveness of slaves. Magistrates continually faced cases of black resistance to slavery in Boston, and Puritan clergymen such as Cotton Mather often felt compelled to lecture slaves about the glory in God's eyes earned by those who willingly submitted to their masters. But the "fondness for freedom" that led slaves to defy their masters, run away, destroy property, and express their discontent in drunkenness and rowdyism never stopped trying the patience of Bostonians. Puritan clergymen and magistrates attempted to convince slaves that "Your Servitude is Gentle . . . you are treated, with more than meer Humanity, and fed and clothed and lodged, as well as you can wish for." They warned that "if you were Free, many of you would not Live near so well as you do." But still, wrote a Boston judge early in the eighteenth century, slaves engaged in "continual aspiring" after "forbidden Liberty."[27]

In Philadelphia, where the efforts of Quakers to abolish slavery may have produced the most humane type of slavery in North America, slaves also malingered, balked, and struggled for their freedom. Benjamin Franklin, himself a slave owner, wrote in 1770 to a European friend: "Perhaps you may imagine the Negroes to be a mild-tempered, tractable Kind of People. Some of them indeed are so. But the Majority are of a plotting Disposition, dark, sullen, malicious, revengeful and cruel in the highest Degree."[28] The opinion of another slave owner, Joseph Galloway, that the slaves of Philadelphia were intent on obtaining their freedom was borne out in 1777 when the British army entered Philadelphia. A large proportion of the city's slaves, including some belonging to Philadelphians known for their kindly treatment of black servants, made their personal declaration of independence by joining the British troops.

Viewing the enslavement of Africans in America as an encounter or interaction of two cultures, we can see that slaves not only adapted to the death-dealing daily toil of the plantation but also educated themselves in strategies of survival, resistance, and rebellion. Slave owners wanted to socialize their slaves as quickly as possible, but ironically "assimilation into

[26]Thad W. Tate, *The Negro in Eighteenth-Century Williamsburg* (Williamsburg, Va.: Colonial Williamsburg, 1965), pp. 198–99.

[27]Lawrence W. Towner, " 'A Fondness for Freedom': Servant Protest in Puritan Society," *William and Mary Quarterly*, 3d Ser., 19 (1962): 202.

[28]"A Conversation between an Englishman, a Scotchman, and an American," in Verner W. Crane, "Benjamin Franklin on Slavery and American Liberties," *Pennsylvania Magazine of History and Biography*, 62 (1938): 8.

colonial society made a few Africans and many of their descendants outwardly rebellious and so, more difficult to control."[29] Slave masters extracted labor and obedience from their slaves in an overall sense—if they had not, slavery would have collapsed as an economic and social institution—but they did so only with great difficulty and never with the degree of success they wished for.

Rebellion, of course, was the supreme expression of rebelliousness. A number of historians have contrasted the relatively small number of American slave rebellions with the frequent revolts of Brazilian and West Indian slaves and have concluded that Africans in America were far less rebellious than slaves elsewhere in the hemisphere. It is true that there is no American parallel for the massive slave uprisings that occurred in Jamaica in the eighteenth century or the wave of insurrections that kept the city of Bahia in northern Brazil in a state of disruption in the first few decades of the nineteenth century. The largest uprising in colonial America took place in South Carolina in 1739 when about one hundred slaves obtained a cache of arms, killed several whites, and fled toward the Florida frontier where they hoped to take refuge with the Spanish, as handfuls of slaves had done for years. The plan was squashed by the white militia, which intercepted the slave band and, with Indian assistance, defeated them in a pitched battle. While there were a few other revolts that were nipped in the bud, such as the plot to capture Annapolis, Maryland, in 1740, large-scale rebellions of this kind were rare in the history of American slavery. Nor is there an American parallel to the semi-states created by escaped slaves in Dutch Surinam, French Guiana, Spanish Cuba, and Portuguese Brazil. In these hideaways thousands of runaway slaves built their own communities and held out for decades against periodic assaults of colonial troops. Only Spanish Florida, to which hundreds, but not thousands, of slaves fled in the eighteenth century, offers an American parallel.

Examples such as these do not really prove the greater rebelliousness of Latin American slaves. What they do indicate is that the chances for slaves to mount a successful rebellion increased in inverse proportion to the power of the white community. "The greater number of blacks, which a frontier has," warned one observer in 1741, "and the greater the disproportion is between them and her white people, the more danger she is liable to; for those [blacks] are all secret enemies, and ready to join with her open ones on the first occasion."[30] When slaves outnumbered whites six or eight to one, they could be counted on to rebel more frequently than when they were a minority or only a slight majority in the population. By the same token, the incidence of flight from slavery was related to the chances for successful escape. In Brazil, where Africans and Indians had mixed for

[29]Mullin, *Flight and Rebellion*, p. 38.

[30][Benjamin Martyn], *An Impartial Inquiry into the State and Utility of the Colony of Georgia* (London, 1741), quoted in Peter Wood, *Black Majority;* p. 166.

generations, there were far more opportunities to hide out or join an Indian community beyond the frontier than in colonial America, where the slave plantations were rarely situated more than one hundred miles from the Atlantic coast and where African-Indian mixing was slight by comparison. Fewer open rebellions in the English mainland colonies do not prove the greater servility of the American slave but serve only to indicate roughly the greater problems which any potential insurrectionist faced in rising against his oppressors. Under different conditions, rebelliousness became channeled into other forms—more subtle, less dangerous, and more effective.

Almost all the colonies passed special laws against arson and poisoning in the first decades of the eighteenth century and then reorganized these laws a generation later, increasing the severity to punishment. This is only one indication of the persistent resistance of enslavement and the enduring hostility manifested by slaves against their masters. In fact, "the sharpest evidence of slave resistance," it has been observed, "is not the historical record of armed revolts . . . so much as the codes that legalized branding, flogging, burning, the amputation of limbs, hamstringing and murder to keep the slaves 'non-violent.' "[31] A similar kind of evidence that blacks did not lapse into passive dependency and abject obedience can be found in the ever-present fear of black rebellion that coursed through white communities. A vivid example of this can be found in the reaction of the Southern colonies to the onset of the Seven Years War in 1755. William Shirley, commander of the British forces in North America, complained that nothing could be expected of the Southern militias because if they left their local communities the slaves would flee *en masse* to the French, who were promising "liberty & Lands to settle upon." Lewis Evans, a Pennsylvania strategist, also conceded that the Southern militia could not make a move: "The Thing is impossible," he wrote, "they have . . . scarce Whites enough to prevent the Defection of their Slaves; and if any considerable Party should happen to be defeated, when abroad, it could be scarce possible to prevent their total Revolt."[32] The governor of Virginia hoped to spare a few militia units for the intercolonial war effort but greatly feared "the Combinations of the Negro Slaves, who have been very audacious on the Defeat on the Ohio [of Braddock's army]" and prayed that "we shall be able to defeat the Designs of our Enemies and keep these Slaves in proper Subjection."[33]

Even in the North it proved impossible to shape slaves into mild-tempered, compliant workers. In New York City in 1712, a group of more than twenty slaves set fire to a building and then lay in wait for the white men who came to extinguish the flames. Wielding knives, axes, and guns, they

[31]Sidney Mintz, "Toward an Afro-American History," *Journal of World History*, 13 (1971): 321.

[32]Quoted in Lawrence H. Gipson, *The Great War for Empire: The Years of Defeat, 1754–1757* (New York: Alfred A. Knopf, Inc., 1946), pp. 14–15.

[33]*Ibid.*, p. 15.

killed nine whites and injured others before making their escape. It was later reported that "had it not been for the Garrison [of English soldiers] there, that city would have been reduced to ashes, and the greatest part of the inhabitants murdered."[34] After the rebels were suppressed, officials investigated the plot and took about seventy slaves into custody. Forty-three were brought to trial and twenty-five, including several women and Indian slaves, were convicted. The terror of black insurrection, which ran like a fever through the white community, was evident in the sentences imposed: thirteen slaves died on the gallows, one was starved to death in chains, three were burned at the stake, and one was broken on the wheel. Six others killed themselves rather than endure retribution at the hands of the white community. The New York Assembly quickly passed a new slave code, which strictly regulated the slaves' freedom of movement and stripped away most of the rights that until this time distinguished their lot from that of their Southern counterparts. In neighboring colonies, legislators scurried to impose new restrictions on blacks or, as in Pennsylvania, to pass import duties so high as to make further importations of Africans unprofitable.

Even the medieval torture imposed upon the black conspirators of 1712 did not achieve the desired results of cowing Northern Negroes into submissiveness. A generation later, within the memory of many living slaves, a wave of slave unrest swept the Northern seaboard. It began in New Jersey in 1740 with a few incidents of barn burning. Two slaves paid with their lives for this act of rebellion. A few months later a rash of thefts and fires struck New York City. Among the buildings ignited was Fort George, which housed the English garrison. Indicted in these incidents were a white tavern keeper, his wife, and an indentured servant girl who served as a prostitute in the tavern. Helped along by some low-grade torture, the servant girl confessed that her master was involved with several slaves in a conspiracy to burn the town to the ground and kill all its white inhabitants. Two slaves were brought to trial for theft and possible conspiracy. When the conspiracy charge against them could not be substantiated, they were hanged for theft, dying "very stubbornly" on the gallows without confessing to anything more. A month later the tavern keeper and his wife were hanged for treason, though they too went to their deaths with closed lips concerning a slave plot. When the servant-prostitute went to the gallows for conspiracy, she died renouncing the statements she had made concerning black insurrectionists. But fear and a desire to cow the city's blacks had overtaken the town, and the dragnet began pulling in slaves, who were threatened with torture and execution if they did not reveal the identity of the slave conspirators. In the following months 67 confessions were extracted from terrified slaves. Before the trial was over, 150 slaves and 25 whites had been im-

[34]Quoted in Kenneth Scott, "The Slave Insurrection in New York in 1712," *New-York Historical Society Quarterly*, 45 (1961): 51.

prisoned, 18 slaves and 4 whites had been tortured and hanged, 13 slaves had been burned at the stake, and 70 others transported to the West Indies.

Many of those arrested, tortured, deported, or killed were probably innocent victims of the fear and anger that overtook New York in 1740 and 1741. Yet the ferocious white response, which might be compared to the Salem witch trials of the 1690s, reflected the pervasive fear in the city that slaves at their core were indeed insurrectionists and could be counted on to repeat acts of aggression and rebellion against the white community unless the most draconic measures were taken. Had New Yorkers regarded their slaves as docile and childish "Sambos," no such conspiracy would have been believable and no such brutal punishment would have been meted out. New Yorkers were not eager to destroy human property in which they had invested. But they lived with a gnawing fear that their slaves would revolt, for they knew from everyday slave behavior that the African captive was a truculent, resistant worker whose desire for freedom seldom flagged. Incidents such as the one in New York show that even in the Northern colonies slaves awaited opportunities to cast off their chains or to inflict upon white society some of the pain that had been apportioned to them.

BLACK CULTURE IN COLONIAL AMERICA

Resistance and rebellion were forms of attacking the system of slavery, of attempting in piecemeal fashion to bring the instituition to an end. The balance of power was always massively stacked against the slave in this quest and therefore it is not surprising that the incidence of organized group resistance was low. More important than counting slave rebellions is understanding how slaves, living within the confining limits of a degrading, brutal system, struggled to carve out areas of cultural and personal autonomy in order to make life bearable. Viewing the plantation or the city as "a battlefield where slaves fought masters for physical and psychological survival"[35] enables us to turn our gaze to the existential side of black life and culture in colonial America.

In this quest for the essence of slave culture several things must be kept in mind about the acculturation process. First, slaves came from a diversity of cultures in West Africa and therefore did not bring to the New World a single collective culture. This tribal heterogeneity did not mean that they did not share a number of important characteristics; but it does mean that upon arriving in America slaves could only forge communities and fashion a subculture by a process of blending their various cultural heritages within the limiting framework imposed by the slave system itself. This process of

[35]John W. Blassingame, *The Slave Community: Plantation Life in the Antebellum South* (New York: Oxford University Press, 1972), p. 184.

amalgamating specific cultural backgrounds within the context of the European slave masters' culture began with language aboard the slave ships, where on the long middle passage a variety of pidgins were devised to allow communication. The process continued from that moment forward.

Second, in drawing upon their varous cultural backgrounds while adapting to slavery in the Americas, slaves found it far easier to perpetuate or adapt religious values, expressive forms, craft skills, and modes of socializing and forming male-female bonds than they did to recreate formal institutions. A Dahomean priesthood could not survive the transition to the slave South but voudou and burial rituals could. Yoruban regal ceremonies had no opportunity to transit the Atlantic but the ceremonial use of the drum did. With these two strictures in mind, we can examine the creation by slaves of a new culture in colonial America, focusing particularly on religion, the family, and work.

Religion

Slaves brought with them to the New World a complex religious heritage, and no amount of desolation or physical abuse could wipe out these deeply rooted beliefs. In fact people enduring the kind of daily stress inherent in the master-slave relationship typically turned to their deepest emotive sources for relief. Coming from cultures where the division between sacred and secular activities was much narrower than in European society, where life and afterlife were not regarded as so separate, African slaves made religious activities "areas of considerable potential creativity and social strength."[36] In fact, religion was at the heart of Afro-American slave culture, and the development of Black Christianity in the eighteenth century reflected both the proximity of slaves to the religion of their masters and the endurance of the religion they carried from their homelands.

Most of the slaves coming to the American colonies, though they were born in a variety of societies with many religious differences, shared certain religious principles and ritual patterns. Widespread among the societies from Senegambia to Angola on the west coast of Africa was belief in a Supreme Creator of the cosmos and a pantheon of lesser gods who were associated with forces in nature such as rain, animals, and the fertility of the earth. These gods had the power to intervene in the affairs of humankind and therefore had to be propitiated. Ancestors, in the West African belief system, also had the power to affect the welfare of village life, for they mediated between the living and the higher gods. It was therefore important to ensure their entrance into the spiritual world with elaborate funeral rites that honored them properly for the role they would play after death.

[36]George Rawick, *From Sundown to Sunup: The Making of the Black Community* (Westport, Conn.: Greenwood Publishing Co., 1972), p. 32.

Finally, West Africans believed in spirit possession, where the gods spoke to men and women through priests and other religious "experts."

African religious customs, funeral rites, sacred images, and charms for protection against evil spirits were no doubt attenuated on New World plantations or melded with elements of Christianity. How fast this happened is not yet known, but clearly it varied from place to place. In New England slaves were few in number and the attempts to indoctrinate them in Christian belief were relatively strenuous. Both private religious instruction and public churchgoing were common among slaves, and by the mid-eighteenth century many black children were attending schools opened by Anglicans and Quakers. In the Northern towns Protestant ministers performed slave marriages and baptized their children. Also because slaves usually lived within white households in small numbers rather than in slave quarters amidst a black community, Africanisms were probably obliterated much more rapidly than in the South.

On Southern plantations, slave masters were not so eager to see their slaves instructed in Christianity. But the missionary wing of the Anglican church, acting on Morgan Godwyn's broad plan of 1680 to Christianize the Africans and Indians of the English colonies, sent its agents into many areas in the eighteenth century, and other churches also engaged in the instruction of slaves. Moreover, African beliefs and rituals probably persisted far longer than in the North because on the plantation the slave could maintain a greater sense of a collective experience and was constantly in touch with Mother Africa through freshly arriving slaves. Realizing this, slave masters were caught in a dilemma. If the perpetuation of African religion fostered a collective identity and fed the spirit of resistance, then it was imperative to replace it with Christian belief. But at the same time the owner was not eager to have his human property subjected to a new religion that would make him or her a less willing worker. So, when masters permitted their slaves to attend church, it was with the hope that they would learn the Christian ideals of meekness, humility, and obedience, as the missionaries promised, and not the ideals of the brotherhood of man or the story of the Hebrew flight from oppression.

The problem of Christian instruction was that it was extremely difficult to expose slaves to the elements of religious thought which would make them submissive while quarantining them from the elements that fed the desire for freedom. Protestant clergymen were careful to impress upon slaves that acceptance of Christ was not to be confused with obtaining freedom, and most colonies passed laws to make crystal clear that baptism did not place the master under the slightest obligation to manumit his slaves. But try as they might to suppress it, the idea spread among slaves in the eighteenth-century South that baptism, though not intended to release them from chains, was a first step in this direction. Whether this reflected slave familiarity with the Western tradition that no Christian could enslave another Christian or sprang from another source is uncertain. But the equation of baptism and eventual freedom spread. In 1730, following a period of unusual missionary activity in Virginia, a number of baptized slaves began circulating the word that their acceptance of Christ entitled them to freedom. Several hundred slaves gathered in Norfolk and Princess Anne counties in Virginia to foment a rebellion, but the plan was discovered and four black leaders were hanged. Thereafter the resistance to catechising slaves grew.

Another obstacle to Christianization was the opinion of many slave owners that exposure to the tenets of the carpenter of Nazareth made slaves "proud and saucy," as Thomas Bacon, a Chesapeake clergyman, told slaves. "You must not be eye servants, that is such as will be very busy [only] in your master's presence," warned Bacon.[37] But it was widely believed, as a Swedish traveler in America noted, that if slaves were Christianized, their masters "would not be able to keep their Negroes so subjected afterwards" because of the pride which Africans would develop "on seeing themselves upon a level with their masters in religious matters."[38]

The Great Awakening in the 1740s ushered in a new era of activity among those eager to Christianize slaves and a new era of receptivity among slaves to the precepts of Christianity. In the Anglican parish of Williamsburg, the capital of Virginia, nearly a thousand slaves were baptized in a single generation from 1746 to 1768. Presbyterians were also active in the Southern colonies beginning about 1740. Samuel Davies, a leading Presbyterian, boasted that he had one hundred slaves in his congregation in Hanover County, Virginia in 1750 and a few years later claimed that some three hundred blacks received instruction from him. The Anglican Jonathan Boucher recorded that he baptized 315 slaves on a single day in 1767. By this time a sizable portion of Virginia's slaves, especially those living in the vicinity of small towns such as Williamsburg and Norfolk, had been indoctrinated in Christian religion by Anglicans, Presbyterians, and Methodists.

What gave these efforts special force was the appeal that the Awakeners' style and message had to slaves. For a people whose ancestral religion was grounded primarily in an understanding of nature as indwelling and whose eschatological vision allowed for no sharp differences between the secular and the sacred, religion and daily life being conjoined, Protestantism always had a limited appeal. Highly literate and rational, sanitized of its mystical elements, guarded over by professional clergymen who stressed passivity among worshippers, the Protestant service had little power to render intelligible or tolerable the strange and repressive world in which slaves found

---

[37]Bacon, *Sermons Addressed to Masters and Servants. . .* (Williamsburg, Va., 1743), in *Bases of the Plantation Society*, ed. Aubrey C. Land (New York: Harper & Row, Publishers, 1969), p. 232.

[38]*Peter Kalm's Travels in North America*, ed. Adolph B. Benson (New York: Dover Publications, Inc., 1966), I: 209.

themselves. But the revivalists of the 1740s and 1750s, preaching a personal rebirth, using music and body motion, and asking for the dynamic participation of each individual in an intense emotional experience, had a tremendous appeal to Africans. Here was a religious outlook which shared enough with ancestral styles and beliefs such as spirit possession, and which had meaning for the daily experience of slave life, to allow for the creation of a unique Black Christianity. Especially in the ecstatic expression associated with evangelical religion, in the dancing, shouting, rhythmic clapping, and singing, the merging of West African spirit possession and European Christianity took place.

It was the hope of slave masters that Christian doctrine, whether of the ascetic, rational variety or the emotional, revivalistic type, would be the opiate of their slaves. Even if their chattels shared nothing of what their labor produced, even if they lost all their rights in a life of perpetual servitude, they could at least comfort themselves with the knowledge that Christianity sanctified the weak, the poor, and the humble. It is with this formulation in mind that those who have studied black religion have traditionally explained that the most important effect of Protestantism on the slave community was to deflect the minds of slaves "from sufferings and privations of this world to a world after death where the weary would find rest and the victims of injustice would be compensated."[39] But slaves did not passively accept what the Anglican or Presbyterian minister chose to inculcate in them. They drew selectively from white Christianity and shaped their own religious experience in a fashion that not only gave them an area of life which was semi-independent from the control of the master but also provided an important psychological mechanism for channeling anger and projecting aggression in ways that would not bring physical retribution from the white community.

Black spirituals reveal a great deal about this two-edged nature of religion. Many of the slave spirituals were adaptations of white spirituals or a unique blend of African rhythm patterns, Anglo-American melodies, and adapted words, which reflected the pain of the slave experience. Some of the spirituals were called "sorrow songs" and the musical expression of this pain was no doubt cathartic for those who sang them communally. Another theme of the spirituals, however, was that of worth and strength. We cannot know whether such songs as "We Are the People of God," or "I Really Do Believe I'm a Child of God," or "I'm Born of God, I Know I Am" were sung by slaves in the eighteenth century since it is extremely difficult to date their origins. But there is little reason to believe that if slaves found them sustaining in the nineteenth century, they would not have created songs and spirituals with similar themes in the pre-Revolutionary period. What is impressive about these songs is that they portray feelings of worthiness and

[39]E. Franklin Frazier, *The Negro Church in America* (New York: Schocken Books, 1964), p. 45.

even a belief that slaves will ultimately prevail because they are superior to the masters. In the midst of a society that worked to convince slaves of their lack of worth, the poverty of their African culture, and their barbarism, the songs show a strong black self-esteem, an abiding feeling of communal fellowship, and a sense of purpose to life. Black religious music demonstrates how difficult it was for white society to remake the black consciousness and to coerce the black slave into internalizing white values.[40]

The theme of resistance and rebellion was also woven into many of the slave songs. The spiritual celebrating Samson, who sang, "If I had my way, I'd tear this building down," may have had only Biblical meaning for the whites who sang it on Sunday mornings in the parish churches of the South. But for black workers in the field the building was the edifice of slavery and tearing it down meant nothing less than the destruction of the slave system. Similarly, the spiritual "Didn't My Lord Deliver Daniel," which referred to the deliverance of the Hebrews from their enemies, had a more modern meaning for the black slaves who adopted the song as one of their own.

Almost all the symbolic figures of the black spirituals—Daniel, David, Joshua, Jonah, Moses, and Noah—were children of the Hebrews, figures from the Old Testament who struggled against their persecutors in this world and not in the afterlife. Some of them were delivered from oppression in ways that had special meaning for slaves. The Red Sea opened to allow the Hebrew slaves to pass through and then closed to engulf Pharaoh's armies; the blind and vulnerable Samson brought the mansion of his conquerors crashing down. In these spirituals slaves sang about far more than deliverance in the next world. As Lawrence Levine has pointed out, their religious music was not sacred in the narrow sense of being strictly attached to religious ceremony and the Sunday service. It was sacred in a distinctly African way, in the larger context of uniting one's present condition with the ritual and mythical past and linking it also to the possibility of rebirth in the future. Slaves trapped in the grasp of lifelong servitude created a measure of cultural autonomy "by transcending the narrow confines of the world in which they were forced to live. They extended the boundaries of their restrictive universe backward until it fused with the world of the Old Testament, and upward until it became one with the world beyond. The spirituals are the record of a people who found the status, the harmony, the values, the order they needed to survive by internally creating an expanded universe. . . ."[41] Through religious music and through plantation conjurers, voudou men, and witch doctors, Afro-Americans struggled to adjust to white culture while still maintaining a separateness from the world of their masters.

[40]Lawrence W. Levine, "Slave Songs and Slave Consciousness: An Exploration in Neglected Sources," in *Anonymous Americans: Explorations in Nineteenth-Century Social History*, ed. Tamara K. Hareven (Englewood Cliffs, N.J.: Prentice-Hall, Inc., 1971), pp. 99–130.

[41]*Ibid.*, p. 115.

Work

American slaves also turned daily labor—the very core of their existence and the entire reason for the investment of capital in chattel property—into a contested area and adapted African work habits to New World conditions in a way that made life more bearable. Slaves were only too well aware that the labor they did benefited only the master. But in their daily work they behaved in a number of ways—shamming sickness, breaking hoes, uprooting freshly planted seedlings, and harvesting carelessly—that signaled their defiance of the exhortations and floggings of the masters, overseers, and drivers. From these responses masters learned that there were limits beyond which they could not go, for to push too hard was only to prove the law of diminishing returns. To deny the slaves the traditional Sunday holiday or the usual Christmas respite, for example, only guaranteed that less rather than more work would be done in the future. Similarly, to set work standards too high only encouraged slaves to accomplish less or to retaliate against their masters. The lesson was clearly stated in 1732 by the South Carolina *Gazette*, which reported that a master who had driven his slaves late into the night, cleaning and barreling a rice crop, found his barn "and all that was in it" burned to ashes by morning.[42]

Masters, of course, wanted to wring from their slaves the maximum amount of work. To do this they employed a gamut of devices, running from the whip at one end of the spectrum to positive incentives at the other. Many of them concluded that nothing could turn the slave into a willing worker. "I find it almost impossible," complained Landon Carter, one of Virginia's largest slave owners, "to make a negro do his work well. No orders can engage it, no encouragement persuade it, nor no Punishment oblige it."[43] In the end, Southern planters learned that, though the white work ethic could never be instilled in those who labored only to produce profits for others, they could get the most from their slaves by delegating authority and creating a hierarchy of black workers. The tasking system, used especially along the rice coast of South Carolina and Georgia, was another method of maximizing output and, from the slaves' point of view, ensuring work boundaries that left them time to cultivate their own plots and engage in leisure activities. In nearly every plantation situation, then, "the work rhythm of the slaves had to be hammered out as a compromise between themselves and their masters."[44]

Slaves also reacted in positive ways to work, developing a "black work ethic." Since most slaves had been taken from agrarian societies, they were

[42] South Carolina *Gazette*, Oct. 14, 1732, quoted in Wood, *Black Majority*, p. 293.
[43] Jack P. Greene, ed. *The Diary of Colonel London Carter of Sabine Hall, 1752–1776* (2 vols.; Charlottesville, University of Virginia Press, 1965), II, 733.
[44] Eugene D. Genovese, *Roll, Jordan, Roll: The World Slaves Made* (New York: Vintage Books, 1976), p. 303.

already partially prepared for agricultural field work. This part of the adjustment to slavery was probably easier than most of the others, the more so for women because they had been primarily responsible for crop cultivation in their homelands. Reflecting work patterns that were traditional, slaves proved that they would work harder and longer at tasks that required collective labor, but offered resistance to working by themselves. In this preference for collective labor they demonstrated an attitude toward work that was in sharp contrast with the European norm of the individual following his "calling" and laboring independently. Their African background had inured them to collective agricultural labor; they strove to maintain this pattern of work in their lives as slaves. "The black ethic represented at once a defense against an enforced system of economic exploitation and an autonomous assertion of values generally associated with preindustrial people."[45]

The Family

It was at the level of the family—the close intimate connections between man and woman, parent and child, and brother and sister—that slaves developed the most important bastion of defense against the hardships of slavery. In West Africa all social relations were centered in kinship, and kinship lines, stretching backward to include the dead, were vitally important to the individual in locating himself or herself in the local society. Hence, in developing new lifeways under the ordeal of slavery, Africans had to surmount the horror of being torn from their kinship networks and deprived of their prior status in ancestral societies. For this reason the task of rebuilding kin groups, within which the most intimate aspects of life were carried out—love, sexuality, birth, child rearing, and death—must have been regarded as of the utmost importance.

From the master's point of view slave family life was theoretically impossible. Allegiance and the flow of authority was to run in only one direction—from bond servant to owner and never between slaves themselves. In most English colonies, unlike Spanish and Portuguese America, law prohibited contractual marriage, for chattels could not make contracts. But in reality, domestic life was another area in which slaves and masters struck a bargain between the autonomy and submission of slaves. For their part, slave owners found that it was hardly conducive to the profitable management of the plantation or farm to prohibit family life. For the slaves, defining their own social and interpersonal relations within the confines of slave quarters became so important that they were willing to risk the master's ultimate power of life and death over them to secure the right to play an active role in shaping familial relationships.

To be sure, slave masters placed obstacles in the way of slaves as they

[45]*Ibid.*, p. 286.

or father often made only weekly visits. Under such circumstances a maternal group took form and the tradition of the Negro woman's responsibility for her family took root."[49] Following this formulation, it is assumed that the slave emerged after emancipation with only a faint tradition of normal family life. Buffeted by the problems of trying to adapt as a freeman to an increasingly urban and industrial world, ex-slaves were never able to knit together the same nuclear, two-parent family that served as the norm in the white community.

Although the black matriarchal family structure no doubt existed to some extent in the eighteenth-century Southern colonies, doubt remains that it was characteristic of the slave family. Slave men were undoubtedly emasculated in important ways since they could not occupy the dominant role in family and community relationships as they had in the tribal villages of Africa. But the black male did assert his authority by supplementing the food supply through trapping and fishing; by organizing the garden plot behind the slave cabin; by disciplining his children; and most of all by being the principal figure in the active resistance to slavery. Slave men did marry slave women and together they established a relatively stable family life, considering the deterrents inherent in the situation. In some cases slaves were able to preserve these relationships by threatening rebellion. For example, the government of South Carolina, reeling under the blows of the Yamasees in 1715, negotiated a promise of 130 militiamen from Virginia in exchange for an equal number of slave women. But threats of a full-scale insurrection if the women were sent northward forced the Carolinians to renege on their part of the bargain.[50]

While slave men struggled to preserve their familial role, black women came to occupy a position in the family and in the black community that was strikingly different from that of white women. By custom and law in the Anglo-American world women were regarded as inferior to men and subservient to them in almost all matters. Moreover, on Southern plantations, the ideology of domesticity kept white women confined in the home where they were expected to be the guardians of white virtue and culture. Black women, by contrast, remained indispensably important to both the work of the plantation and the stablity of the slave community. They worked in the fields and they worked in the slave cabin. It was ironic, Angela Davis has written, that the slave woman "had to be released from the chains of the myth of femininity. . . . In order to function as slave, the black woman had to be annulled as woman—that is, as woman in her historical stance of wardship under the entire male hierarchy. The sheer force of things ren-

[49]The Negro Family in America, quoted in Black Matriarchy: Myth or Reality? ed. John H. Bracey, August Meier, and Elliott Rudwick (Belmont, Cal.: Wadsworth Publishing Co., 1971), p. 8.

[50]David D. Wallace, South Carolina: A Short History, 1520–1948 (Chapel Hill: University of North Carolina Press, 1951), p. 91.

dered her equal to her man. . . . Male supremacist structures could not become deeply embedded in the internal workings of the slave system."[51]

Female passivity and the retreat to the "cult of domesticity," which was beginning to characterize the life of white women on large plantations and in upper-class homes of the Northern towns was thus no part of the black woman's life. Caught in the net of slavery, the black woman, paradoxically, maintained a position of strength and autonomy within the black community that made her far more equal to the male than was the case of women in white society. The black family was a partnership of equals in the tasks performed and responsibilities shouldered. In this respect it bore closer resemblance to Algonkian and Siouian family structure than to European family organization, for in Indian cultures women were also vitally important in agricultural work, child-rearing responsibilities were shared, and the woman in general maintained a degree of power and autonomy that was unallowable in Euroamerican society.

Because slavery was above all else a system for extracting the maximum amount of labor from its victims, it all too often involved cruelties that made family life almost impossible to maintain. But, in general, American slaves were better clothed, fed, and treated than those in the West Indies, Brazil, or other parts of the New World where settled white society took only shallow root and plantation owners found it more profitable literally to work their slaves to death and then purchase fresh replacements from Africa. When conditions were at least conducive to sustaining life, slaves were effective in defining a culture of their own. As one black scholar has recently written: "Slaves were able to fashion a life style and a set of values—an ethos—which prevented them from being imprisoned altogether by the definitions which the larger society sought to impose. This ethos was an amalgam of Africanisms and New World elements which helped slaves . . . 'feel their way along the course of American slavery, enabling them to endure.'. . . "[52]

How much of African culture survived under eighteenth-century slavery can never be determined quantitatively. Nor is it especially important to do so. It is enough to understand that Africans in the English plantations adapted elements of African culture to the demands of a new life and a new environment. There can be little doubt that slave masters were intent on obliterating all Africanisms that reduced the effectiveness of slaves as laborers and that they had some success in this. It is also true that slavery eliminated many of the cultural differences among slaves, who came from a wide variety of African cultural groups—Fulanis, Ibos, Yorubas, Malagasies, Ashantis, Mandingos, and others. At the same time, it must be remembered that throughout the eighteenth century, unlike in the nineteenth, large

[51]Davis, "The Black Woman's Role," p. 7.
[52]Sterling Stuckey, "Through the Prism of Folklore: The Black Ethos in Slavery," *The Massachusetts Review*, 9 (1968): 418.

numbers of new Africans were arriving each year. Slave importations grew rapidly in the eighteenth century so that probably never more than half the adult slaves were American-born. This continuous infusion of African culture kept alive many of the elements that would later be transmuted almost beyond recognition. Through fashioning their own distinct culture, within the limits established by the rigors of the slave system, blacks were able to forge their own religious forms, their own music and dance, their own family life, and their own beliefs and values. All of these proved indispensable to survival in a system of forced labor. Though slaves might feign deference or submissiveness and were severely constrained in many respects, they drew upon important elements of traditional culture and learned to carve out important areas of activity that gave meaning and importance to life.

9

THE TRANSFORMATION
OF EUROPEAN SOCIETY

In 1650 the European population of the colonies clinging to the eastern edge of the continent was about the same as the daytime population of a large university campus today—roughly 50,000. A half century later this number had increased fivefold to a quarter million. By 1750 the number had again increased fivefold, including about 240,000 Africans. Such a rate of population growth was unknown in other parts of the world. By the middle of the eighteenth century the inhabitants of the English colonies in America were one third as numerous as the English themselves and the rate at which the gap between the two populations was closing led early demographers such as Benjamin Franklin to estimate that before another four generations passed the colonizers would outnumber those in England itself.

THE EIGHTEENTH-CENTURY
EUROPEAN IMMIGRANTS

These rapidly multiplying proto-Americans were not simply Englishmen. The seventeenth-century immigrants had come primarily from England, mixing with a small number of Dutch, Swedes, and Finns already settled along the seaboard and with a relatively insignificant number of Germans,

POPULATION GROWTH: 1690-1770

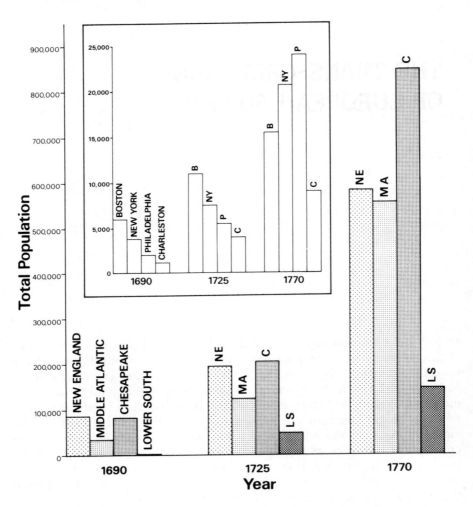

Scots-Irish, French, and Africans who arrived late in the seventeenth century. But the eighteenth century belonged to the non-English so far as immigration was concerned. Beginning in the second decade of the century thousands of Germans, Swiss, Ulster Scots-Irish, and Africans began pouring into the colonies. Some came voluntarily and some involuntarily, but whether they arrived as slaves, indentured servants, or free persons, they drastically altered the gene pool of the existing population. By the end of the colonial period, as the Revolution loomed on the horizon, roughly half the inhabitants of the Thirteen Colonies had no English blood in their veins.

This proportion of non-English was greater than at any time in American history, even after the tremendous influx of Europeans in the late nineteenth and early twentieth centuries.

History has told us primarily about the lives of only an infinitesimally small segment of this population. We know a great deal about the political and military leaders, the men who amassed fortunes, and those who because of their high positions in society left their names and opinions in the official and private records of the time. But the cultural change occurring in the century prior to the Revolution bore far more relation to the roughly congruent behavior of thousands of "historically voiceless" individuals than to the actions of leaders whose words and deeds form the basis of most of our written history. After the Revolution John Adams would write that "the poor man's conscience is clear; yet he is ashamed . . . he feels himself out of the sight of others groping in the dark. Mankind takes no notice of him. He rambles and wanders unheeded. In the midst of a crowd, at church, in the market . . . he is in as much obscurity as he would be in a garret or a cellar. He is not disapproved, censured, or reproached; he is only not seen."[1] Similarly, historians have "not seen" the largest part of colonial society whose footprints are only now being discerned in the sands of time.

It was the work, the wanderings, the attitudes, and the hopes and fears of the masses of inconspicuous individuals that led to cultural change so distinct in America in the eighteenth century that Europeans never tired of touring the colonies and setting down the characteristics of the people they saw—so different from what they knew in Europe. What they described, though they did it in an entirely untheoretical way, was a set of economic activities, forms of social and political organization, and a constellation of values and beliefs that were fused together in what we call a culture. During the first three quarters of the eighteenth century this culture was transformed so extensively that a John Smith or John Winthrop, had he still lived, would have been amazed at what he saw.

The social origins of those who flocked to the colonies in the eighteenth century played a part in the social transformation. From the top layers of European society came almost nobody. In the seventeenth century a number of Englishmen at the apex of the social pyramid had taken an active role in colonizing the New World—men such as Walter Raleigh and Richard Grenville in Virginia; the Calverts, who founded Maryland; the insiders of the court of Charles II who became the proprietors of Carolina and New Jersey; and a handful of others. But for the most part they contributed money and organizational ability rather than their lives. Only a few tore free of their moorings in England and emigrated permanently to America. In the

---

[1] Quoted in James A. Henretta, *The Evolution of American Society, 1700–1815* (Lexington, Mass.: D. C. Heath and Company, 1973), pp. 3–4.

eighteenth century upper-class immigrants were even rarer. Only an occasional Baron de Graffenried or Count von Zinzendorf, usually leaders of groups of Germans, Swiss, or Scots-Irish immigrants, represented the upper stratum of European society.

Below the nobility were the country gentry, and grouped with them on the social scale were officeholders, members of the professions, and the wealthier merchants. These men ran the joint-stock companies which had been so important in launching the early seventeenth-century settlements, and they continued to provide a major portion of the investment capital necessary for the economic development of overseas territories. In the seventeenth century they contributed substantially to the Atlantic migration, either by coming themselves or by sending their younger sons. The Oxford- and Cambridge-trained Puritan ministers, many of the early merchants of Boston and Philadelphia, and some of the large planters of Virginia, Maryland, and the Carolinas were included in this category. But in the eighteenth century they came in smaller numbers.

A rung below the gentry were the yeoman farmers of the countryside and the artisan-shopkeepers of the cities. In the social hierarchy of European communities these were respected men who bulked large in the membership of the church and were entitled to participate in the political life of the community. Through hard work, good fortune, or a judicious marriage they often propelled themselves upward a rung on the social ladder or at least lived to see a son enter one of the professions or embark on a career as a merchant. They may have composed as much as one-third of the immigrants to the colonies. Once there, they provided the backbone of the middle class and often moved rapidly upward in a society that had plenty of room at the top. As a group, they were skilled, industrious and ambitious; their fortunes advanced much faster than if they had remained at home.

Taken together, these recruits from the nobility, gentry, and middle class of European society accounted for roughly one half of all those Europeans who traveled the water highway to the west side of the Atlantic in the seventeenth century and probably less than a third of the eighteenth-century immigrants. The remaining colonizers consisted of indentured servants—men, women, and children who lacked sufficient resources to pay their way to the New World and therefore contracted out their labor for a number of years in return for passage. Their backgrounds were mixed. Some were obscure shopkeepers, artisans, schoolteachers, and farmers who were down on their luck or sorely pressed by a downturn in economic conditions. Many more had never risen above the subsistence level and could not expect to do so. These were the best of them. The worst were paupers and petty criminals—people who sometimes left England, Scotland, Ireland, and Germany voluntarily and sometimes at the request of the authorities. Local officials could rid themselves of the community's undesirables and reduce the poor taxes by banishing the disinherited to what they promised would be a new life—or a quick death—in the New World. The Scottish Privy Council, for example, in attempting to organize a colonizing expedition to New York in 1669, sent out warrants to local authorities urging that they recruit "strong and idle beggars, vagabonds, egyptians, comon and notorious whoores, theeves and other dissolute and lousy persons banished or stigmatized for gross crymes."[2]

Indentured Servants

Since the indentured servant came to represent a high proportion of the eighteenth-century immigrants, it is important to understand the mechanics of the profitable business of transporting bound laborers to the colonies. Like African and Indian slaves, white indentured servants were invaluable in a society that was rich in land but poor in labor. Labor in the colonies, Benjamin Franklin wrote in 1759, "is performed chiefly by indentured servants brought from Great Britain, Ireland, and Germany, because the high price it bears cannot be performed in any other way."[3] Franklin was forgetting that black slaves were as numerous as white servants in 1759, even in his hometown of Philadelphia, and that in the Southern colonies they comprised the bulk of the labor force. But his general point is valid: colonial America was being developed by unfree laborers. No matter whether he was a small tobacco planter in Virginia, a shopkeeper in New York, a farmer in Connecticut, or a shipwright in Boston, nearly every free member of colonial society wanted a bound laborer by his side as soon as he had accumulated the £20 to £40 required to purchase one. Additional labor meant the ability to produce more goods or services, which in turn meant greater profits. In an age before machines, commanding the labor of others became preeminently important, and human labor became an European-exported commodity which the colonists eagerly sought.

The terms of indentured servitude were simple. A servant bound himself or herself by contract to a ship captain for a specified length of time, usually four to seven years. In return the captain agreed to transport the servant across the Atlantic and place him or her on the auction block in one of the colonial seaports. The ship captain signed the work contract over to the highest bidder at the time of the auction. By the terms of the indenture the servant agreed to serve faithfully in return for food, clothes, shelter, and, at the end of the contract, a small sum of money, occasionally some tools, and sometimes the right to a few acres of land.

The traffic in bound labor became a regular part of the commerce linking

---

[2]Quoted in Peter Gouldesbrough, "An Attempted Scottish Voyage to New York in 1669," *Scottish Historical Review*, 40 (1961): 56.

[3]Quoted in Marcus W. Jernegan, *Laboring and Dependent Classes in Colonial America, 1607–1783* (New York: Frederick Ungar Publishing Co., 1965), p. 55.

Europe and America. A combination of merchants, ship captains, immigrant brokers, and recruiting agents kept thousands of Europeans on the road to the colonies throughout the pre-Revolutionary period. Like any other cargo, servants were loaded onto boats, carried across the ocean, and sold on the other side. It was a system that provided labor for the established members of colonial society, eventual freedom and the chance for a better life for those caught in the net of European poverty, and profits for the middlemen involved. There were, to be sure, chronic abuses in the system. Just as the trade in Indian and African slaves was ridden with callous disregard for human life, so also the trade in contract white labor was often a dirty business. Kidnapping and shanghaiing of drifters and drunks was endemic. Many unfortunate seaport dwellers waked one morning with a head-splitting hangover to find themselves in the hold of a ship headed westward across the Atlantic. Once on the ship, they found appalling conditions. The description of Gottlieb Mittelberger, who accompanied a boatload of German servants sailing from Rotterdam to Philadelphia in 1750, conveys some feeling for what those seeking a better life in the American colonies endured for the opportunity to sell their labor for some of the prime years of their life:

> During the journey the ship is full of pitiful signs of distress—smells, fumes, horrors, vomiting, various kinds of sea sickness, fever, dysentery, headaches, heat, constipation, boils, scurvy, cancer, mouth-rot, and similar afflictions, all of them caused by the age and the highly-salted state of the food, especially the meat, as well as by the very bad and filthy water, which brings about the miserable destruction and death of many. Add to all that shortage of food, hunger, thirst, frost, heat, dampness, fear, misery, vexation, and lamentation, as well as other troubles. Thus, for example, there are so many lice, especially on the sick people, that they have to be scraped off the bodies. All this misery reaches its climax when in addition to everything else one must suffer through two to three days and nights of storm, with everyone convinced that the ship will go to the bottom with all human beings on board. . . . Children between the ages of one and seven seldom survive the sea voyage; and parents must often watch their offspring suffer miserably, die, and be thrown into the ocean, from want, hunger, thirst, and the like. I myself, alas, saw such a pitiful fate overtake thirty-two children on board our vessel, all of whom were finally thrown into the sea.[4]

Mittelberger described how the limits of endurance were reached on the high seas and then the inmates of the ship turned on each other. But mostly they recalled the villages from which they had come: "Oh! If only I were back at home, even lying in my pig-sty!" Probably one-quarter of those embarking from European ports never lived to see the forests of the New World or, in their weakened condition, died shortly after arrival—a mortality rate approximating that of the Atlantic slave trade. For those who did survive the ordeal, the dangers of "seasoning" in North America—the ac-

---

[4]Gottlieb Mittelberger, *Journey to Pennsylvania*, ed. and trans. Oscar Handlin and John Clive (Cambridge: Harvard University Press, 1960), pp. 12–15.

climatization to new conditions—lay ahead. In addition there was the physical and psychological adjustment to an environment and a master that were completely unknown. Especially in the Southern colonies, agricultural labor took a deadly toll among those whose masters were determined to extract as much labor as possible during the years of the work contract. Adding to the difficulty of the servant's life was the right of the master to forbid marriage. Because it invariably led to pregnancy among female servants, and thus a loss of time, most masters denied their servants a family life.

Given the harshness of the indentured labor system, it is not surprising that colonial newspapers were filled with advertisements for runaway servants, interspersed with notices for runaway slaves. Servants knew the penalties for this: whipping and additional service, usually reckoned at twice the time lost to the master, but sometimes, as in Pennsylvania, calculated at a five-to-one ratio and in Maryland at ten-to-one. Even so, servants fled their masters by the hundreds and occasionally staged minor insurrections. When war came, they flocked to enlist in the British army. Many masters were willing to take the compensation paid by the army and let a balky servant go.

The great goal of every servant was to obtain a place on the ladder of opportunity—or what *seemed* to be such a ladder from a vantage point in the villages of Scotland, Ireland, and Germany. But as one historian has reminded us, "it will not do simply to assume that freed servants, especially those from the tobacco fields, were in any mental or physical condition to start vigorous new lives, or that long and ripe years of productivity lay ahead of them."[5] Although it is extremely difficult to follow the lives of freed servants, the most informed study of white servitude indicates that out of every ten indentured servants only one attained a position as a farmer in comfortable circumstances and one more achieved the status of artisan. The other eight died before they obtained their freedom or became propertyless day laborers, vagrants, or denizens of the local almshouse after completing their indentures.[6] The life chances of a servant were better than this in the seventeenth century but worsened thereafter, as some of the early fluidity of society disappeared. Though our attention has been claimed by the handful of servants who prospered or achieved fame—revolutionary leaders such as Daniel Dulany, Charles Thomson, and John Lamb—the statistical probability for rising even to middle-class position was slight. Among the large mass of those who sought opportunity in the American colonies it is the story of relentless labor and ultimate failure that stands out. The chief beneficiaries of the system of bound white labor were not the laborers themselves but those for whom they labored.

[5]Richard Hofstadter, *America at 1750: A Social Portrait* (New York: Alfred A. Knopf, Inc., 1972), p. 61.

[6]Abbot E. Smith, *Colonists in Bondage: White Servitude and Convict Labor in America, 1607–1776* (Chapel Hill: University of North Carolina Press, 1947), pp. 297–300.

LAND, GROWTH, AND CHANGING VALUES

Out of the combination of fertile land; a pool of bound laborers, white, black, and red; and the ambition of thousands of small farmers and artisans who labored independently two variants of agricultural society emerged in eighteenth-century America. In the North, small communities made up of farmers and artisans dotted the landscape. New Englanders engaged in mixed farming, which included farming the forests for timber used in barrels and ships, and farming the offshore waters for fish that provided one of the staples in the diet of the fast-growing slave population of the West Indies. The Middle Colonies specialized in producing corn, wheat, beef, and pork. By mid-eighteenth century they were provisioning not only the West Indies but also parts of Spain, Portugal, and England. Slaves were few in number in most of the Northern communities, rarely representing more than 5 percent of the population. A large percentage of free men owned land; and, though differences in ability and circumstances led gradually to greater social and economic stratification, the truly rich and abjectly poor were few in number and the gap between them was small in comparison to European society. Most men lived to acquire a farm of at least fifty acres. They extracted from the soil a modest income that allowed for security from want and provided a small inheritance for their children.

In the Southern colonies, where tobacco, rice, indigo, and timber products predominated, many yeomen farmers also struggled independently although they were more frequently dispersed across the land than clustered in villages. These men have been far less noticed by historians than the plantation owners with slaves and indentured servants who lived along the rivers and streams that flowed from the Piedmont through the coastal plain to the ocean. But the usual picture of a Southern plantation society made up of immensely wealthy men exploiting the labor of huge gangs of black slaves is badly overdrawn. Perhaps as much as 40 percent of the Southern white males worked as tenant farmers or agricultural laborers, and of the remaining men who owned land about two out of every three in the Chesapeake region worked farms of two hunded acres or less. In North Carolina farms were even smaller and men of real wealth rarer. In South Carolina the opposite was true; slaveholding was more widespread, plantations tended to be larger, and planters of substantial wealth represented a larger proportion of the population. As early as 1726 in St. George's Parish 87 of 108 families held slaves. A generation later in St. Bartholomew Parish about 250 white families owned more than 5,000 slaves.[7]

On the whole, probably not more than 5 percent of the white landowners

---

[7]Frank J. Klingberg, *An Appraisal of the Negro in Colonial South Carolina: A Study in Americanization* (Washington, D.C. The Asociated Publishers, 1941), pp. 58–60; William Langhorne, "An Account of the Spiritual State of St. Bartholomew's Parish," (1752), *South Carolina Magazine of History*, 50 (1949): 200.

were wealthy enough by mid-eighteenth century to possess a plantation worth £1000—not too different from the North. Similarly, those owning large numbers of slaves were not as numerous as we commonly think. The number of Southern slaves increased rapidly in the eighteenth century, rising from about 20,000 in 1700 to 240,000 in 1750. But a majority of white adult males held no slaves at all at mid-century and those who operated plantations with more than twenty slaves probably did not exceed 10 percent of the white taxables. South Carolina excepted, the South throughout the pre-Revolutionary period was dominated numerically by small landowners whose holdings, if perhaps twice the size of the average New England farm, were not more than half again as large as the typical farm in Pennsylvania, New Jersey, or New York.

Nonetheless, the ideal in the South, if not the reality, was the large plantation where black slaves would make the earth yield up profits sufficient to support the leisured life. Statistically speaking, not many white colonists in the South achieved the dream. But that is what people worked for, and they came to identify the quest for material comfort with the exploitation of African slave labor in an era when the Northern colonists were phasing out white bound labor and turning to a market economy where both goods and labor were freely exchanged.

The Protestant work ethic, which purportedly propelled people upward by inculcating a life of frugality, industriousness, and highly rationalized economic activity, perhaps operated less compellingly in the psyches of Southern colonists than in their Northern counterparts. But the abundant, fertile land of the South and the wider availability of slaves after 1690 provided all the incentive necessary for an aggressive, competitive society to develop. Much folklore about Southern cavaliers reposing under magnolia trees had been handed down in the history books, but in the eighteenth century European colonizers in the South were as avid in the pursuit of wealth and material comfort as European colonizers in the North. If the warm climate of the South bred languor, it was also true that farmers in the South had no long frozen winters when there was little to do but mend harness and chop wood. The typical New England farm produced just one crop each year; but a South Carolina rice or indigo plantation produced two. Moreover, the restraints of a New England community orientation and the Puritan bias against the accumulation of wealth which was not disposed of in socially useful ways never hindered entrepreneurial activity in the South. Organized religion was only shallowly rooted in most of the Southern colonies and the community orientation never took hold because communities themselves were few and far between.

Paradoxically, one of the effects of the growth and success of the colonies in eighteenth-century British America was to shatter the utopian dream of the first generation that communities could be built where men and women worked for the commonweal, not only for themselves. The Puritan work ethic and an atmosphere of seemingly limitless opportunity encouraged men to work arduously at their callings. That was to the good. And their labors had generally been rewarded with success. So was that. But living where the ratio of people to land was so favorable compared to the societies from which they came, many colonists developed an aggressive outlook that patterned their behavior. What was to hold a man back in these uncharted expanses of land and unclaimed river valleys, as soon as the Indians were gone? In Europe, the absence of uncultivated lands ripe for exploitation and the grinding poverty that enshrouded the lives of the great mass of people produced in the peasant consciousness a very low level of expectations. "The frontier zone between possibility and impossibility barely moved in any significant direction, from the fifteenth to the eighteenth century," writes Fernand Braudel.[8] But it moved in America. The new concept was of a society where anything was possible. A competitive, entrepreneurial spirit began to take hold.

Religion and commitment to community, which acted as brakes on competitive, individualistic behavior, were by no means dead in the eighteenth century. But in general, piety, in terms of defining one's life as a preparation for the afterlife, declined greatly. Even in the seventeenth century Roger Williams had deplored the "depraved appetite after the great vanities, dreams, and shadows of this vanishing life, great portions of land, land in this wilderness, as if men were in as great necessity and danger for want of great portions of land, as poor, hungry seamen have, after a sick and stormy, a long and starving passage."[9] In the eighteenth century land became ever more regarded not simply as a source of livelihood but a commodity to be bought and sold speculatively as a means of building a fortune. It was Franklin's little how-to-do-it best-seller, *The Way to Wealth*, that caught the spirit of the aggressive entrepreneurial eighteenth century. The brakes on economic ambition had been suddenly removed and with the decline of fervid Puritanism in the eighteenth century there was little left to restrain predatory instincts in those who were eager to pit themselves against their fellows in the pursuit of material gain. "Every man is for himself," lamented a prominent Philadelphian in 1706, only a generation after Penn had planted the seed of his "holy experiment."[10] Two generations later the lieutenant-governor of New York, who had grown up in the colony, put it more explicitly: "The only principle of life propagated among the young people," wrote Cadwallader Colden, "is to get money and men are only esteemed

[8]Braudel, *Capitalism and Material Life, 1400–1800*, George Weidenfeld, trans. (New York: Harper Torchbooks, 1973), p. ix.

[9]Quoted in Francis Jennings, *The Invasion of America: Indians, Colonialism, and the Cant of Conquest* (Chapel Hill: University of North Carolina Press, 1975), p. 181.

[10]Quoted in Gary B. Nash, *Quakers and Politics; Pennsylvania, 1681–1726* (Princeton: Princeton University Press, 1968), p. 303.

according to what they are worth—that is the money they are possessed of."[11] A contemporary in Rhode Island echoed the thought when he wrote "A Man who has Money here, no matter how he came by it, he is Everything, and wanting [lacking] that he's a meer Nothing, let his Conduct be ever so ereproachable."[12]

As these acquisitive values took hold, the individual replaced the community as the conceptual unit of thought. The advice of the ancestors, such as the Puritan minister John Cotton, to "goe forth, every man that goeth, with a public spirit, looking not on your owne things only," or Winthrop's maxim that "the care of the publick must oversway all private respects," carried less and less weight in eighteenth-century society. The conquest of the wilderness and its inhabitants had proceeded far enough, men had shown enough adaptability and endurance for a hundred years, and the future possibilities seemed so great that a mental set developed in which colonial Americans appeared bent upon proving wrong the Elizabethan poet, John Donne, who counseled that no man could survive as an island unto himself. Having gained something, the typical colonist wanted more. A French visitor, who took up residence in New York, described this psychological reorientation:

> An European, when he first arrives, seems limited in his intentions, as well as in his views; but he very suddenly alters his scale. . . . He no sooner breathes our air than he forms schemes, and embarks in designs he never would have thought of in his own country. . . . He begins to feel the effects of a sort of resurrection; hitherto he had not lived, but simply vegetated; he now feels himself a man, because he is treated as such; . . . he begins to forget his former servitude and dependence. . . .[13]

Paradoxically, this transformation of attitudes, while it helped promote phenomenal growth and unleashed economic energies, led toward material success that contained within it the seeds of social strain. The demand for land east of the Appalachian Mountain barrier grew rapidly after 1740, as the population rose rapidly through immigration and natural increase. Especially in New England, ungranted land in the coastal region was a thing of the past and the division and redivision of original land grants among sons and grandsons had progressed as far as it could go without splitting farms into unviably small economic units. New land—on the Maine frontier, in western Massachusetts and Connecticut, across the Appalachians in Pennsylvania, Virginia, Maryland, and the Carolinas—was the obvious solution to the problem of overcrowding. With the saturation of the Eastern coastal plain making the lands of the interior more attractive, land companies were

[11]Quoted in Henretta, *Evolution of American Society*, p. 99.

[12]Quoted in Carl Bridenbaugh, *Cities in Revolt; Urban Life in America, 1743–1776* (New York: Capricorn Books, 1964), p. 140.

[13]J. Hector St. John Crèvecoeur, *Letters from an American Farmer* (New York: E. P. Dutton & Co., Inc., 1957), pp. 54–56.

formed in the mid-eighteenth century. They laid claim, however flimsy, to the valuable Western lands, their investors understanding the enormous appreciation in value that would occur as the next generation came of age and sought *lebensraum* to the west. But before a westward movement could begin, interior Indian peoples, as well as the French and Spanish, had to be overcome.

THE CITIES

Even though only about 5 percent of the eighteenth-century colonists lived in cities (and none of these cities exceeded 16,000 in 1750) the commercial capitals of coastal North America were the cutting edge of economic, social, and political change. Almost all the alterations that we associate with the advent of capitalist society occurred first in the seaport towns and then radiated outward to the villages and farms of the hinterland. In the maritime centers of colonial life the transition first occurred from a barter to a commercial economy; where a competitive social order replaced one based on ascribed status; where a hierarchical and deferential polity gave way to participatory and contentious civic life; where factory production began to replace small-scale artisanal production.

In the seaport towns of Boston, Newport, New York, Philadelphia, and Charleston the competitive and acquisitive ethos took hold to an even greater degree than in the rural areas. This did not mean that artisans and laborers always worked feverishly to ascend the ladder of success. Craftsmen who commanded five shillings a day knew that weather, sickness, and the inconstancy of supplies made it difficult to work more than 250 days a year, which brought an income of £35 to £60. Hence, laboring people were far from the day when the failure to acquire property or accumulate a minor fortune produced guilt or aroused their anger against those above them. Their desire was not to reach the top but to get off the bottom. Yet they came to expect a "decent competency," as it was called, and did not anticipate the miserable hand-to-mouth existence of the laboring poor everywhere in Europe. Many of those who started as blacksmiths, carpenters, coopers, and shipwrights rose to the level of shopkeeper or even merchant. A handful did even better, such as William Phips, a sheep farmer and ship's carpenter from Maine who rose to the governorship of Massachusetts, or Benjamin Franklin, a poor printer who came to stand for the opportunities for upward mobility that many thought differentiated the American colonies from Europe.

In the half century between 1690 and 1740 Boston, New York, and Philadelphia blossomed into commercial centers that rivaled such British provincial ports as Hull, Bristol, and Glasgow. This urban growth reflected the development of the hinterlands to which they were commercially linked.

More and more, these seaports were drawn into the international market-place of the Atlantic basin. More and more, economic decisions were made in consonance with an emerging commercial ethic that rubbed abrasively against traditional restraints on entrepreneurial activity. The older economic ethic, medieval in origins, rested on the assumption of a world made up of many semiclosed economies, each operating in a nearly self-sufficient way. A city, according to this model, was connected to the immediately surrounding area, but the area itself remained semiautonomous. But the American seaports, by the early eighteenth century, had become a part of a far wider commercial network that linked them not only to their hinterlands but also to Newfoundland, the West Indies, Portugal and Spain, England and Ireland, and even Africa. Economic decisions were made under the new order of things not with reference to local and public needs but according to laws of supply and demand that operated internationally. This wider market was indifferent to individuals and local communities; the flow and price of commodities, as well as labor and land, were dictated by the invisible laws of the international marketplace. If grain fetched eight shillings a bushel in the West Indies, for example, and only five in Boston, then a New England merchant was entitled to send all the wheat he could purchase from local farmers to the more distant buyer.

It was not until a genuine crisis occurred that the full extent of the tension between the new entrepreneurial freedom and the older concern for the public weal became manifest. Such a moment occurred in Boston during Queen Anne's War (1702–1713) when Andrew Belcher, one of the town's largest grain merchants, decided to ship large quantities of wheat to the West Indies, where prices were far higher than in Massachusetts. Threatened with a bread shortage and appalled that a leading townsman would put profits ahead of the welfare of the community, ordinary Bostonians descended on one of Belcher's ships, which was about to sail with 6,000 bushels of grain, and sawed through the rudder. They then tried to run the disabled ship aground in order to liberate the grain from its holds. Such food shortages rarely occurred in the American colonies, usually only during wartime when unusual amounts of grain were needed for military provisioning. But when they did, urban people demanded to be fed at prices they could afford, regardless of the modern economic notions invoked by merchants that the laws of supply and demand must rule.

The urban social strain that grew with the spread of the individualistic and entrepreneurial ethic become more evident in the European wars of 1739 to 1747 into which the colonies were drawn. New England was drained of manpower and resources in King George's War, as its inhabitants engaged in costly attempts to overcome the French enemy to the north. But the war also offered opportunities for merchants and others to run up profits through war contracts and privateering. "A covetous selfish Spirit" ran through the people, lamented one Massachusetts spokesman, and "every Man looks at his own Things, and not at the Things of others." Gone was a "publick Spirit" and in its place stood a "Greedy desire of Gain."[14] Another commentator noted that food prices had escalated sharply during the war and that all around Boston men were turning from their professions to become buyers and butchers of livestock. They understood that by intercepting Boston's meat supplies and holding them for a time, they could drive up prices and take over the function of the town's butchers and hucksters. Known as "forestalling," this amounted to a sort of economic warfare between rural and urban society. The war against the French had not unified Massachusetts but instead had set one element against another in the pursuit of private gain.

The breakdown of an interdependent economic community was equally visible in the action of merchants in other colonies during King George's War. Foodstuffs exporters in New York and Philadelphia piled up profits by trading illegally with the French and Spanish enemy in the West Indies. Diverting food supplies from New England to the Caribbean, where the enemy paid high prices in order to feed their slave populations, they smuggled their way to fortune. "How surprizing it is that for the Sake of Private Gain, his Majesty's declared Enemies should be thus openly assisted to destroy his Subjects," cried the Boston *Post*.[15] Here was the ultimate betrayal of the public good by private economic interest, a betrayal reflected in the food bill of every Bostonian. War had spurred the growing tendency of the free market, with everyone from the lowliest tar aboard a privateer to the largest war contractor and merchant smuggler seeking to capitalize on the new opportunities for gain.

In many ways the throwing off of governmental and ideological restraints, the enthronement of the concept of self-interest, was the perfect rationalization for rapidly developing a vast area of land blessed with abundant natural resources and peopled by ambitious, tough-minded, innovating Europeans. The new system of values legitimated private profit-seeking, promoted the abandonment of economic regulation, and projected a future in which men's energies were cut loose from age-old mercantilist controls instituted to promote the good of all. This, it was argued, would produce a common good far better.

Thus two conceptions of economic life and social relations were contending for ascendancy in the Euroamerican mind. It was in the cities that merchants, shopkeepers, land speculators, and some ambitious artisans hewed more and more to the new economic dictates that provided a philosophical rationale for the integration of the seaport economies into a more international and more volatile network of commercial transactions.

Such thinking paralleled social thought in England and Europe. There too

[14]Nathaniel Appleton, *The Cry of Oppression* (Boston, 1748), pp. 36–37.
[15]*Boston Evening Post*, Feb. 1, 1748.

a new model of economic and social life had emerged, predicated on the notion that the market mentality was preferable to the older corporate society of persons finely attuned to the public good because that idealistic model refused to take men as they really were. Self-denial, moral rectitude, and the subordination of private to public interests were theoretically good, but they lay as dead weights on the economic order. National prosperity required something different—encouragement of acquisitive appetites and acceptance of the notion that "the self-seeking drive appeared more powerful than institutional efforts to mold people's actions."[16] In England the new formula for national prosperity assumed that if each individual sought his or her own improvement, all these separate efforts would produce, through a mysterious process later described by Adam Smith as the "invisible hand," a natural harmony and a prosperous, free society. Men could not be compelled to work for the good of the whole. But left to sort out their wants and to pursue their own material desires in open competition, they would collectively form an impersonal market that would regulate human affairs to everyone's advantage.

CHANGING SOCIAL STRUCTURE

Population growth and economic development, carried on for a century and a half by aggressive and opportunistic individuals, changed both the structure of colonial society and the attitudes of the people toward social structure—but changed them in opposite directions. Seventeenth-century Europeans on both sides of the Atlantic accepted the naturalness of hierarchy in human affairs, the inevitability of poverty, and the right of those in the upper stratum of society to rule those below them. The belief was general that social gradations and internal subordination were not only sanctioned by God but were also essential to the maintenance of social stability and cohesion. Therefore care was taken to differentiate individuals by dress, by titles, in social etiquette, and even in penalties imposed in criminal proceedings. Puritans, for example, did not simply file into church on Sunday mornings and occupy the pews in random fashion. Instead, each seat was assigned according to the social rank of the person in the community. "Dooming the seats," as the assignment process was aptly called, was the responsibility of a church committee, which used every available yardstick of social respectability—age, parentage, social position, service to the community, and wealth—in drawing up a seating plan for the congregation. Puritans never entered their church without being reminded where they stood in the ranks of the community.

[16]Joyce Appleby, "The Social Origins of American Revolutionary Ideology," *Journal of American History*, 64 (1978): 944.

In spite of the philosophical commitment to hierarchy, the early European immigrants in America were notably undifferentiated in their social makeup. Emigrant society was strongly lower-middle class in its composition, and the wide availability of land, combined with the lack of opportunities to amass great fortunes (when one had only his own labor and that of his wife, children, and a servant or two) kept the spectrum of wealth relatively narrow throughout most of the seventeenth century. Even in the cities, where the redistribution of wealth proceeded the fastest, the dawn of the eighteenth century witnessed a colonial society that was overwhelmingly middle class in character. In the Hudson River Valley and in the Southern colonies a handful of large plantation owners had made their mark, but the largest slave owners in Virginia at the beginning of the eighteenth century still owned fewer than one hundred slaves and not more than a handful of men had as much as £2000 to leave to their heirs. As late as 1722 one of Philadelphia's richest merchants died with personal possessions worth just over £1000—a sizeable estate but unimpressive by European standards.

In the eighteenth century, and especially in the half century before the Revolution, the customary commitment to hierarchy and deference waned at the same time that stratification in society was increasing. Social attitudes and social structure were moving in opposite directions. Below the elite free whites developed the ideal of egalitarianism. The middling sort of people, wrote a Philadelphian in 1756, "enjoy and are fond of freedom, and the meanest among them thinks he has a right to civility from the greatest."[17] Such comments were common. The Frenchman, Crèvecoeur, was surprised to see hired workers who "must be at your table and feed . . . on the best you have," and the schoolteacher Philip Fithian wrote of "labourers at the tables and in the parlours of their betters enjoying the advantage, and honour of their society and conversation."[18]

Europeans judged what they saw against what they had known at home and thus sometimes exaggerated the degree of egalitarianism that they thought they saw. But it was true that most American colonists believed they were creating a society where a wealthy aristocracy did not dominate and no masses of poor whites were ground into the dust. The ideal was a rough economic equality where each person would have enough and a social equality "in which invidious discriminations would be abolished."[19] When Benjamin Franklin toured the English countryside in 1772 he was appalled at what he saw and raised thanks that America was different. He described "landlords, great noblemen, and gentlemen, extremely opulent, living in the highest affluence and magnificence" alongside "the bulk of the people, tenants, extremely poor, living in the most sordid wretchedness, in dirty

[17]Quoted in Hofstadter, *America at 1750*, p. 131.
[18]*Ibid.*, p. 141.
[19]Jackson T. Main, *The Social Structure of Revolutionary America* (Princeton: Princeton University Press, 1965), p. 236.

hovels of mud and straw, and clothed only in rags." Franklin could only shake his head and take solace in the knowledge that America was different. Ignoring Indians and Africans, he wrote: "I thought often of the Happiness of New England, where every Man is a Freeholder, has a Vote in publick Affairs, lives in a tidy, warm House, has plenty of good Food and fewel, with whole cloaths from Head to Foot, the Manufacture perhaps of his own Family."[20] The German Mittelberger summed up the twin ideals of economic equality and democratic scorn for authorities and authoritarian institutions. Pennsylvania, he said, was "heaven for farmers, paradise for artisans, and hell for officials and preachers."[21]

All these commentators occupied favorable positions in society, which may account for the fact that they were describing not the reality but the ideal of colonial life. The reality, in fact, was that eighteenth-century society, even for white colonists, was moving away from the ideal. As the old deferential attitudes gave way to brash, assertive, individualistic modes of thought and behavior—what would become known as "the democratic personality"—society became more stratified, wealth became less evenly distributed, and impressively rich and truly impoverished classes emerged. Population growth and economic development in the eighteenth century made rich men of those with capital to speculate in land, buy slaves and servants, or participate in trade. The aggrandizement of wealth became clearly apparent in all sections of the country—North and South, rural and urban. In Boston, Newport, New York, Philadelphia, and Charleston stately town houses rose as testimony to the fortunes being acquired in trade, shipbuilding, and land speculation. Probably the last of these was the most profitable of all. "It is almost a proverb," wrote a Philadelphian in 1767, "that Every great fortune made here within these 50 years has been by land."[22] By the late colonial period it was not unusual to find merchant-land speculators with estates valued at £10,000–£20,000. Even in the rural areas of the North wealthy farmers amassed estates worth £4,000–£5,000. In the South, plantation magnates built even larger fortunes, for the rapid importation of African slaves after 1720 accelerated the rate at which profits could be extracted from the cultivation of tobacco or rice. By the eve of the Revolution the great planters of the Chesapeake region, men such as Charles Carroll, Robert "King" Carter, and William Byrd, had achieved spectacular affluence. Their estates, valued at £100,000 or more, were equivalent in purchasing power to a fortune of five million dollars in 1980. It was not unusual to see 300 to 400 slaves toiling on such plantations, whereas in the late seventeenth century the largest slaveholder on the continent had no more than 50 bound laborers.

[20]*The Writings of Benjamin Franklin*, 10 vols., ed. Albert H. Smyth (New York: The Macmillan Co., 1907), 5: 362–63.

[21]Mittelberger, *Journey to Pennsylvania*, p. 48.

[22]*Pennsylvania Magazine of History and Biography*, 1 (1877): 277.

While the rapid increase in population and large-scale capital investment in land and slaves enabled a small number of men to accumulate fortunes that would have been noteworthy even in English society, the development of colonial society also created conditions in which a growing number of persons were finding it difficult to keep bread on the table and wood in the fireplace. This was especially true in the cities, where the differentiation of wealth proceeded most rapidly. All the major cities built almshouses and workhouses in the second quarter of the century to provide for those who could not care for themselves—the aged, indigent, sick, insane, and orphaned. Between 1725 and 1760, however, the poor in the cities increased more rapidly than the urban population as a whole, and after about 1750 poverty was no longer confined to the old or physically depleted.

Boston, the first utopian settlement in Anglo-America, was the first to feel the pinch of economic hardship. The city had grown to about 12,000 in 1720 and increased to some 16,000 in the next two decades. But from 1740 until after the Revolution the city's population stagnated, as other coastal towns such as Salem, Marblehead, and Newbury captured some of the shipbuilding industry and the New England economy in general entered a period of declining productivity. Expenditures for poor relief edged upward in the 1730s and grew faster than the population in the 1740s. In 1753 the Overseers of the Poor reported to the Massachusetts legislature that poor relief expenditures in Boston were double that of any town of comparable size "upon the face of the whole Earth" by the reckoning of those acquainted with such matters. Though this may or may not have been true, it was certain that a large number of people in the town were in real distress. In 1757 the Overseers reported that "the Poor supported either wholly or in part by the Town in the Alms-house and out of it will amount to the Number of about 1000," and those receiving private charity from churches and philanthropic organizations swelled the total.[23]

Inevitably the expanding economy and the individualistic values incorporated in the society tended to favor the aggressive and able in their drive toward material success. The greater the opportunities—a primary characteristic of a democratic society—the greater the gulf became between the rich and the poor. The growth of cultural and political egalitarianism was accompanied by, and indirectly sanctioned, the decline of economic equality. An open society with ample opportunities in the eighteenth century for entrepreneurship, and with relatively few restraints imposed by government, led, paradoxically, to a concentration of economic power in the hands of a thin upper layer of society. Becoming a society in which the individual and not the common weal was the central concern, the white population of colonial America was transforming what they thought to be uniquely Ameri-

[23]*Records Relating to the Early History of Boston*, 39 vols. (Boston: Rockwell and Churchill, 1881–1909), 14: 240, 302.

can into what resembled more and more the European conditions they had fled.

The differing abilities of men to manipulate their economic environment, capitalize on the freedom to exploit white and black labor, and obtain title to Indian land were eventually recorded on the tax lists of the community where each man's wealth was set alongside that of his neighbors. Colonial historians have scrutinized those tax lists that have survived and have found that population growth and economic development led toward a less even distribution of wealth and an increase in the proportion of those without property in virtually every community. The change occurred slowly in rural areas and proceeded more rapidly in the seaboard centers of commercial activity.

In the rural town of Northampton, Massachusetts, for example, the upper 10 percent of property owners controlled 25 percent of the taxable wealth in 1676 and slowly increased their control of the community's assets to 34 percent in 1759. At the same time the proportion of the community's taxable property owned by the bottom third of the society remained steady at about 10 percent. In Chester County, Pennsylvania, a fertile wheat-growing region southwest of Philadelphia, the wealthiest tenth of the farmers commanded about 24 percent of the wealth in 1693 and almost 30 percent by 1760. During the same period the lowest 30 percent of the landowners saw their economic leverage decline from 17.4 to 6.3 percent of the taxable assets of the county. In three counties of Maryland the percentage of white freemen who owned land dropped from 44 to 37 between 1756 and 1771.

In the cities the rate of change was far greater. Boston's upper tenth in 1687 held 46 percent of the taxable property while the lowest 30 percent had a meager 2.6 percent of the wealth. Four generations later, in 1771, the top tenth had 63 percent of the wealth; the lowest three-tenths had virtually nothing—a mere tenth of one percent of the community's taxable resources. Economic polarization in Boston, where the population was static after 1735 and economic recession hit hard at many elements of the community, was duplicated in vigorously expanding Philadelphia. In 1693, little more than a decade after settlement, the wealthiest tenth laid claim to 46 percent of the city's wealth. Three quarters of a century later, in 1772, they possessed 71 percent of the taxable wealth. As in Boston, these gains were not made at the expense of those in the bottom third of society, who possessed only a meager 2.2 percent of the wealth in 1693, but were accomplished at the expense of those in the middling elements of society.

If poverty touched the lives of a growing part of the urban laboring class, it was the usual condition on the frontier. Here the gap between rich and poor hardly existed because the rich were nowhere to be found. In its social order the frontier of the mid-eighteenth century was even cruder than rural society on the edge of the continent a century before. Whether in the towns of western Massachusetts and Connecticut, founded in the second and third quarters of the eighteenth century by the sons of Yankee farmers; or the lands along the Mohawk River in New York and the Susquehannah River in Pennsylvania, which represented the hopes of the German and Scots-Irish immigrants; or the backcountry of Maryland, Virginia, and the Carolinas, which sponged up some 250,000 souls in the late colonial period, frontier society was composed of small farmers and rural artisans who all stood roughly on the same plane. They purchased land cheaply, often for as little as four shillings an acre and struggled to carve farms from the wilderness. Many hoped to get enough land under cultivation within a few years to produce surplus crops for market. But with only the help of one's sons and a few farm animals this often took most of a man's life. Others struggled only to make enough improvements on a piece of land so that other settlers pushing westward on the next wave of settlement would find it attractive enough to pay a price that rewarded one's laborers.

On the New England frontier, where people pushed westward in groups, they founded new towns and churches as they went, quickly reproducing the institutions of eastern society. While poor, these simple villagers and farmers lived a life where institutional ligaments had not been altogether severed. But southward from New York on the east side of the Appalachian slopes frontier society existed in what many observers took to be a semibar-barous state. William Byrd described one of the largest plantations on the Virginia frontier in 1733 as "a poor dirty hovel, with hardly anything in it but children that wallowed about like so many pigs."[24] Charles Woodmason, an itinerant Anglican minister who spent three years tramping from settle-ment to settlement in the Carolina backcountry in the 1760s, was appalled at what he found. "For thro' want of Ministers to marry and thro' the licen-tiousness of the People, many hundreds live in Concubinage—swopping their Wives as Cattel, and living in a State of Nature, more irregularly and unchastely than the Indians."[25] As an English Anglican, Woodmason carried with him all the prejudices that were usually harbored against the Presbyte-rian Scots-Irish, the main inhabitants of the region. But there is little reason to doubt that the crudeness of life he described actually existed. After preaching at Flat Creek to "a vast Body of People . . . Such a Medley! such a mixed Multitude of all Classes and Complexions," he paled at their after-service "Revelling Drinking Singing Dancing and Whoring" and threw up his hands that "most of the Company were drunk before I quitted the Spot—They were as rude in their Manners as the Common Savages, and hardly a degree removed from them." Some of what he saw made him close his eyes in horror, but he kept them open long enough to observe the young women who "have a most uncommon Practise. . . . They draw their Shift as

[24]Quoted in Richard R. Beeman, "Social Change and Cultural Conflict in Virginia: Lunen-burg County, 1746 to 1774," William and Mary Quarterly, 35 (1978): 455.

[25]Charles Woodmason, The Carolina Backcountry on the Eve of the Revolution, ed. Richard J. Hooker (Chapel Hill: University of North Carolina Press, 1953), pp. 15, 33.

tight as possible to the Body, and pin it close, to shew the roundness of their Breasts, and . . . their Petticoat close to their Hips to shew the fineness of their Limbs—so that they might as well be in Puri Naturalibus—Indeed Nakedness is not censurable or indecent here, and they expose themselves often quite Naked, without Ceremony—Rubbing themselves and their Hair with Bears Oil and tying it up behind in a Bunch like the Indians—being hardly one degree removed from them."[26]

THE GREAT AWAKENING

Nowhere did the line between social and economic change on the one hand and religion on the other crumble more swiftly than in the experiential and ideological upheaval called the Great Awakening. More than a solely religious movement, this period of sustained religious enthusiasm must be seen as a profound cultural crisis that had been building for several generations.

At its core the Great Awakening was "a search for new sources of authority, new principles of action, new foundations of hope" among people who had come to believe that the colonial churches "no longer met the spiritual needs of the people."[27] The Awakeners preached that the old sources of authority were too effete to solve the problems of the day, too encrusted with tradition, hypocrisy, and intellectualism to bring hope and faith to a generation that was witnessing the rapid transformation of the world of their fathers. A new wellspring of authority was needed, and that source, the evangelists preached, was the individual himself. Like the Quaker "inner light," which dwelled in every man and woman, the "new light" within the awakened would enable them to achieve grace through the conversion experience. When enough people were "born again," as the evangelists of the Great Awakening phrased it, a new sense of community would be forged, a new brotherhood of man achieved, and the city on the hill restored. The Awakening, in its way, was a "revitalization movement," similar to those that would occur periodically in Indian societies, as attempts were made to reject corrosive new ways and return to the traditions of the past.

The Awakening had its first stirrings in the colonies in the 1720s in New Jersey and Pennsylvania and then in the 1730s in Jonathan Edward's church in Northampton, Massachusetts. But it was not until 1739, with the arrival of George Whitefield from England, that it struck with full force. Whitefield was a master of open-air preaching and had trekked across the English countryside for several years preaching the word of God. A diminutive man with a magnificent voice, he began a barnstorming trip along the coast of

[26]*Ibid.*, pp. 56, 61.

[27]William G. McLoughlin, *New England Dissent, 1630–1833: The Baptists and the Separation of Church and State* (Cambridge: Harvard University Press, 1971), p. 335.

North America in 1739 that evoked a mass response of a sort never witnessed before in the colonies. Thousands turned out to see him, and with each success his fame grew. Especially in the cities, which were the crucibles of social change, his effect was extraordinary, as people fought for places in the churches to hear him or congregated by the thousands in open fields to receive his message.

Some of Whitefield's appeal can be attributed to his genius for dramatic performances, his perfection of the art of advanced publicity, and his ability to simplify theological doctrine and focus the attention of masses of people on one facet of religious life—the conversion experience. In his electrifying performances, where written sermons were cast away, where spastic body movements and magnificent voice control replaced dry, logical, rigidly structured sermons, thousands experienced the desire to "fly to Christ." But it was the message as well as the medium that explains why people flocked to hear Whitefield. He frontally assaulted traditional sources of authority, called upon people to become the instruments of their own salvation, and implicitly attacked the upper-class notion that the simple folk had no minds of their own.

When Whitefield began his American tour in 1739, the social dynamite buried deep in his message was not yet clearly perceived by the elite. After all, his preaching produced thousands of conversions and filled the churches that had been languishing for more than a generation. Whitefield magnified the importance of religion in almost everyone who heard him, so it is no wonder that he was welcomed as "an angel of God, or as Elias, or John the Baptist risen from the dead."[28] But Whitefield's popularity soon waned among the gentry because he was followed by itinerant Awakeners whose social radicalism was far less muted and because of the effects the evangelists' message had on the lower orders. Roaming preachers like Gilbert Tennant infused evangelical preaching with a radical egalitarianism that left many former supporters of Whitefield sputtering. Tennant attacked the established clergy as unregenerate and encouraged people to forsake their ministers. "The sapless Discourses of such dead Drones" were worthless, he proclaimed.[29] James Davenport, another itinerant preacher, told huge crowds that they should drink rat poison rather than listen to the corrupt clergy. Even more dangerous, Davenport indicted the rich and powerful, criticized the growing gap between rich and poor, and exhorted ordinary people to resist those who exploited and deceived them. Only then, he cried, would the Lamb Jesus return to earth.

Crowds followed Davenport through the towns, singing and clapping so that "they look'd more like a Company of *Bacchanalians* after a mad Frolick, than sober Christians who had been worshipping God," as one distressed

---

[28] Perry Miller, *Jonathan Edwards* (New York: World Publishing Co., 1949), pp. 166–67.
[29] *Ibid.*, p. 166.

Boston newspaper complained.[30] Respectable people were convinced that revivalism had gotten out of hand and that social control of the lowest layers of society was crumbling. Revivalism had started out as a return to religion among backsliding Christians but now was turning into a social experience that profoundly threatened the established culture, which stressed order, discipline, and submissiveness from laboring people. The fear of the Awakeners' attacks on genteel literate culture, on wealth and ostentatious living, was epitomized in New London, Connecticut in 1743 when Davenport scandalized the gentry by inducing a huge crowd

> to burn "sundry good and useful treatises, books of practical godliness, the works of able divines," as well as "hoop petticoats, silk gowns, short cloaks, cambrick caps, red heeled shoes, fans, necklaces, gloves, and other such apparell." While psalms and hymns were sung over the pile, the preacher added his own pants, "a pair of old, wore out, plush breaches." This, commented one critic, would have obliged him "to strutt about bare-arsed" had not the fire been extinguished.[31]

By 1742 New England and the middle colonies were being crisscrossed by a procession of itinerant gospelers and haranguers, all of them labeled social incendiaries by the established clergy. Of all the signs of social leveling that conservatives saw springing from evangelicalism, the one they feared the most was the practice of public lay exhorting. Within the established churches there was no place for lay persons to compete with the qualified ministry in preaching the word of God. Nor was there room for "self-initiated associations of the people meeting outside of regularly constituted religious or political meetings," for to do so was to relocate authority collectively in the mass of common people.[32] Lay exhorting shattered the monopoly of the educated clergy on religious discourse, put all people on a plane in the area of religion, gave new importance to the oral culture of common people, whose spontaneous outpourings contrasted sharply with the literary culture of the gentry, established among them the notion that their destinies and their souls were in their own hands instead of the hands of the elite clergy, and turned the world upside down in allowing those who had traditionally been consigned to the bottom of society to assume roles customarily reserved for educated, adult men. In lay exhorting, class lines were crossed and sexual and racial roles were defied, as ordinary men, women, and even children, servants, and slaves rose before throngs to testify emotionally to their own conversion and exhort others to a state of religious ecstasy by preaching extemporaneously the Lord's truth.

The Great Awakening thus represented far more than a religious earth-

---

[30]*Boston Evening Post*, Aug. 2, 1742.

[31]J. M. Bumsted and John E. Van de Wetering, *What Must I Do to Be Saved? The Great Awakening in Colonial America* (Hinsdale, Ill.: The Dryden Press, 1976), p. 90.

[32]Harry S. Stout, "Religion, Communications, and the Ideological Origins of the American Revolution," *William and Mary Quarterly*, 34 (1977): 527.

quake. Through it, ordinary people haltingly enunciated a distinctive popular ideology that challenged inherited cultural norms. To some extent, as many historians have noted, the Awakening represented a groundswell of individualism, a kind of protodemocratic spirit that anticipated the Revolution. This was true, especially among the middling people of colonial society for whom the revival years involved an expansion of political consciousness and a new feeling of self-importance, as they partook of spontaneous meetings, assumed new power in ecclesiastical affairs, and were encouraged by the evangelists to adopt a skeptical attitude toward dogma and authority. But among the lowliest members of society, including impoverished city dwellers, servants, slaves, and those who struggled to gain a foothold on the treacherous slopes of economic security, the Awakening experience implied not a movement forward toward democratic bourgeois revolution but backwards to an earlier age when it was conceived that individuals acted not for themselves, always striving to get ahead at the expense of their neighbors, but pulled together as a community. Hence the dispossessed harked to the anti-entrepreneurial, communalistic tone permeating the exhortations of the radical evangelists such as Tennant, who preached that in any truly Christian community "mutual *Love* is the *Band* and *Cement*. . . . For men, by the Neglect of its Exercise, and much more by its Contrary, will be tempted, against the *Law of Nature*, to seek a *single* and independent State, in order to secure their Ease and Safety."[33]

The radical Awakeners were not preaching class revolt or the end to wealth-producing commerce. What they urged was "a thorough reconsideration of the Christian ethic as it had come to be understood in the America of the 1730s."[34] Nor were those who harked to the Awakeners inspired to foment social revolution, for in fact the seeds of overt political radicalism were still in the germinative stage. But the multitudes who were moved by the message of the revivalists, in the North in the 1740s and in the South during the next decade, began to believe that it was justifiable in some circumstances to take matters into their own hands. This is why Jonathan Edwards, a highly intellectual, latter-day Puritan minister, was seen by the commercial elite and their clerical allies as "the grand leveler of Christian history,"[35] even though sedition and leveling were not what he had in mind. The Great Awakening produced the greatest flow of religious energy since the Puritan movement a century before, but this outpouring was intimately connected with the tensions in colonial society that had grown from generations of social and economic change.

---

[33]Gilbert Tennant, *Brotherly Love Recommended* (Philadelphia, 1748).

[34]Alan Heimert, *Religion and the American Mind from the Great Awakening to the Revolution* (Cambridge: Harvard University Press, 1966), p. 32.

[35]*Ibid.*, p. 93.

10

WARS FOR EMPIRE
AND INDIAN STRATEGIES
FOR SURVIVAL

Between 1675 and 1763 three European powers—France, Spain, and England—employed diplomacy and war in an ongoing struggle for trade and territory in the vast area between the Mississippi River and the Atlantic Ocean and in the waters of the Caribbean. Both the trade and the territory they coveted in North America required them to be in close and continual touch with the powerful tribes of interior North America. Our history books have largely forgotten what was patently obvious throughout this period—that much of the time and energy of the European governments, whether in New Spain, New France, New England, or elsewhere in the European colonies, was spent negotiating, trading, and fighting with and against Indians of various cultures, and filing reports, requests, and complaints to the home governments concerning the state of Indian affairs. Those in charge of colonial affairs in Madrid, Paris, and London knew almost as much about the Indian inhabitants of the territories they claimed as they did of their own colonists.

In this three-cornered fight for a continent, it has often been imagined that Indians were merely the objects of European power, manipulated like pawns on a continental chessboard before finally being swept from the board altogether. This view is part of the myth of the overwhelming cultural superiority and military force of the European colonizers and the Indians' acquiescence when confronted with it. But the power of the Europeans has been greatly exaggerated and that of native societies greatly underestimated. It is more accurate to say that Indian societies of the interior were not only reciprocally involved in the complicated maneuvers between contending European powers but played a dynamic role in the unfolding of events. They could not turn back the clock or drive the Europeans back into the sea. But the interior tribes were far stronger than the less populous and weaker coastal tribes that had succumbed to the invaders in the seventeenth century. They were therefore able to interact with the Europeans in a much different way. Throughout the eighteenth century Indians helped to shape their own history. Pitted against each other and sometimes divided among themselves, the European powers had too few resources to overpower the inland tribes and had to rely on Indian allies to maintain themselves even in the limited areas they occupied. Understanding the Europeans' weaknesses gave Indian nations an opportunity to exercise initiative and to gain much in exchange for their support. That they were eventually the losers should not obscure the fact that the interaction was truly a two-way process. Europeans used Indians to enhance their own power and Indians used Europeans in precisely the same way.

IROQUOIS DIPLOMACY

Only by also looking at European imperial rivalry from the Indian point of view can we understand the real nature of intercultural contact in North America. For example, while European governors and colonial bureaucrats were putting millions of words on paper, moving armies and navies across an ocean, and engaging thousands of people in the manufacture and shipment of Indian trade goods, all as a part of empire-building, the preliterate woodlands Iroquois, never numbering more than 2500 warriors and 12,000 people, were adroitly pursuing their own self-interest and shaping events in North America. The French historian La Potherie wrote in 1722: "It is a strange thing that three or four thousand souls can make tremble a whole new world. New England is very fortunate in being able to stay in their good graces. New France is often desolated by their wars, and they are feared through a space of more than fifteen hundred leagues of the country of our allies."[1] A generation later an Indian "expert" in New York warned the governor that "on whose ever side the [Iroquois] Indians fall, they will cast the balance."[2]

The strategy of France, in the period after Louis XIV took the throne in

[1]Quoted in Anthony F. C. Wallace, "The Origins of Iroquois Neutrality: The Grand Settlement of 1701," *Pennsylvania History*, 24 (1957): 235.

[2]Archibald Kennedy to George Clinton, 1746, Clinton Papers, vol. 3, Clements Library, University of Michigan.

1661, was to establish an inland empire in North America that would surround the English and keep them pinned to the coast. New France was placed under royal supervision in 1663, a thousand soldiers were dispatched to the colony two years later, and an aggressive policy of territorial expansion was set in motion. By the early 1680s France had not only consolidated her hold in the St. Lawrence River valley but had established a string of trading posts and forts along an arc that swung north and west of the English settlements like a long encircling arm. The French made exploratory trips all the way down the Illinois and Mississippi rivers to the Gulf of Mexico and within another two decades French forts and trading posts rose at Mobile and Biloxi. When that occurred the deerskin and slave traders of South Carolina found themselves faced with new competitors in the vast lower Mississippi area which they had previously called their own.

The dreams of continental hegemony that obsessed Louis XIV involved all the major European powers in a series of global wars that occupied most of his half-century reign. Between 1665 and 1675 the French king twice cooked up a European war in order to attack his Hapsburg rivals in Europe. In the first of these he succeeded in overwhelming the Spanish Netherlands. But in the second the Protestant forces of Europe united against him, aware that the balance of power in Europe, upon which everybody depended for the preservation of peace, was in grave danger. A decade later, beginning in 1688, Louis moved again, turning first on the weakest of his neighbors, the German Rhineland, and at the same time symbolizing his determination to crush Protestant Europe by expelling all the Protestants of his country. Many of these Huguenots emigrated to England or to her colonies in America. War in Europe brought war in North America. For the next quarter century, with brief interruptions, the armies and navies of England and France clashed around the world.

In the two wars from 1689 to 1697 and 1701 to 1713 the English and French in America discovered the incredible difficulties involved in merely bringing their military forces into contact. In a vast area, known primarily to its native inhabitants, the problems of weather, disease, transport, and supply were so great that only irregular warfare was possible. The English made three attempts to strike at the centers of French power—Port Royal, Nova Scotia, which commanded the mouth of the St. Lawrence River, and Quebec, at the center of New France. In 1690, during the War of the League of Augsburg, they captured Port Royal, but their assault on Quebec was a complete disaster. In the next war Massachusetts launched an expedition to storm Port Royal, but it bogged down and failed in 1707. Even when England sent a flotilla of sixty ships and an army of five thousand men in 1709, the expeditions floundered before reaching their destinations. Boston merchants with provisioning contracts were the only real winners in these inglorious attempts.

With European-style warfare abysmally unsuccessful, both England and

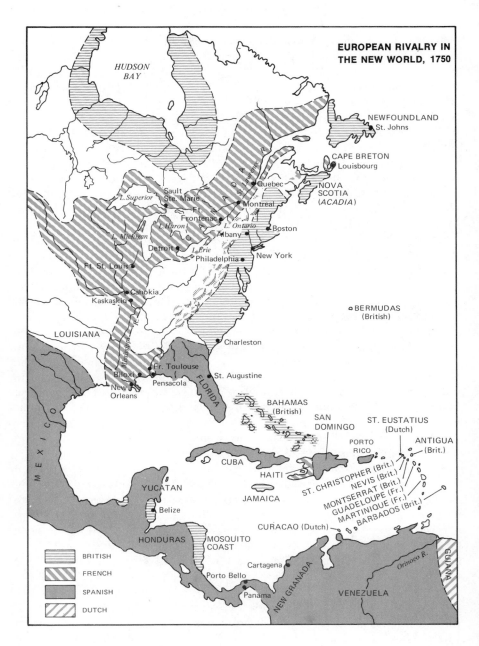

EUROPEAN RIVALRY IN THE NEW WORLD, 1750

HUDSON BAY

NEWFOUNDLAND
St. Johns

CAPE BRETON
Louisbourg

NOVA SCOTIA
(*ACADIA*)

Quebec
Sault Ste. Marie
L.Superior
Montreal
Ft. Frontenac
L. Huron
L. Michigan
L. Ontario
Albany
Boston
Detroit
L. Erie
Philadelphia
New York

Ft. St. Louis

Cahokia
Kaskaskia

BERMUDAS
(British)

LOUISIANA

Charleston

Fr. Toulouse
Biloxi
Pensacola
FLORIDA
St. Augustine
New Orleans

M E X I C O

BAHAMAS
(British)

SAN DOMINGO

ST. EUSTATIUS
(Dutch)

PORTO RICO

ANTIGUA
(Brit.)

CUBA

HAITI

ST. CHRISTOPHER (Brit.)
NEVIS (Brit.)
MONTSERRAT (Brit.)
GUADELOUPE (Fr.)
MARTINIQUE (Fr.)
BARBADOS (Brit.)

YUCATAN

JAMAICA

Belize

CURACAO (Dutch)

HONDURAS

MOSQUITO COAST

Cartagena

Porto Bello

Panama

NEW GRANADA

Orinoco R.

GUIANA

VENEZUELA

	BRITISH
	FRENCH
	SPANISH
	DUTCH

France attempted to subcontract military tasks to their Indian allies. This was occasionally successful, especially with the French, who were not reluctant to send their own troops into the fray with their Indian allies. Schenectady, New York was wiped out in February 1690; Wells, Maine and

Deerfield, Massachusetts were razed in 1704; and other towns along the New England frontier felt the force of the combined French-Indian attacks. But the English, though they pressured the Iroquois again and again to attack their enemies, went unrewarded for their efforts. The Iroquois were well aware of the internal divisions that rent the fabric of English colonial society. These were most visible in 1688–1689, at the outset of the War of the League of Augsburg, when internal rebellions in Massachusetts, New York, and Maryland set Englishman against Englishman. Even when differences within colonies were settled, animosities between colonies made intercolonial cooperation all but impossible, as a succession of royal governors and colonial administrators sent out from London discovered. All of this was no secret to the Iroquois. When they were urged to take up arms against the French in 1692, they were quick to reply: "You Sett us on dayly to fight & destroy your Enemies, & bidd us goe on with Courage, but wee See not that you doe anything to it yourSelfs, neither doe wee See any great Strength you have to oppose them if the Enemy should breake out upon you."[3]

The English were equally unsuccessful in attempts to squeeze a recognition of English sovereignty out of their supposed allies. A succession of royal governors in New York attempted to apply the terminology of "father" and "children" in their negotiations with the Iroquois. This linguistic device, which was a sure sign of the weakened state of an Indian nation, had been accepted by the Hudson River tribes after they had suffered devastation in wars with the Dutch and the English between 1640 and 1680. But the Iroquois had no need to accept the terminology of subordination. Adroit at the European game of twisting words so that appearance and reality became confused, the Iroquois frequently made statements such as in 1684 that "Wee have putt our selves under the great Sachim Charles that lives over the great lake" and then completed their speech with the reminder that "we are a free people uniting our selves to what sachem we please."[4] For the Iroquois, alliance with the English in the 1680s was only part of a game of diplomacy and no more than a temporary promise of support which could be reversed at any time.

This is not to suggest that the Iroquois were not enmeshed in the Anglo-French struggle for empire. They were. But their involvement was not directed by the English or the French or with the goals of either European power in mind. The Iroquois calculated their own interests and made their own decisions within the councils of the Five Nations, centered at Onondaga. It was here that the representatives of the Five Nations wrestled with a problem that called for all their diplomatic skill and military strength in

[3]Lawrence H. Leder, ed., *The Livingston Indian Records, 1666–1723* (Gettysburg, Pa.: Pennsylvania Historical Association, 1956), p. 165.

[4]Allen W. Trelease, *Indian Affairs in Colonial New York* (Ithaca, N.Y.: Cornell University Press, 1960), pp. 264, 267–68.

the last half of the seventeenth century—how to maintain Iroquois strength which was based on a major role in the fur trade and their conquest of the western tribes of the Great Lakes region. This could only be done by continuing to intercept the western furs from the west, while at the same time fending off enemies such as the Susquehannocks to the south and the Shawnees to the southwest. To that end, the Iroquois built an alliance between the Ottawa suppliers, themselves as middlemen, and the Albany buyers. The higher prices which the English offered for furs, the better quality of English woolen goods, and the higher alcoholic content of English rum made trade at Anglo-Dutch Albany far more desirable than trade at French Montreal.

Understanding that an Ottawa-Iroquois alliance spelled disaster for New France, the French spent the last third of the seventeenth century attempting to disrupt this trading partnership. The French and their Indian allies made periodic attacks into Iroquois country, killing their enemies and burning villages and food supplies. These forays were successful enough that some Iroquois villages sued for peace and invited French missionaries into their towns to guide them in "the true way." But when they calculated the time was right, such as after defeating the Susquehannocks in 1675 and incorporating them into their fighting forces, the Iroquois expelled the Jesuit missionaries and launched devastating blows at French settlements. In the 1680s the Five Nations invaded the Illinois country, destroying villages and French forts, and seizing canoes and furs on the river arteries leading east.

From time to time the French were able to enlist limited support from the Ottawas and remnants of the Hurons in their attacks on the Iroquois. But these western tribes understood clearly that their natural alliance was with those who offered the best price in trade goods. Accordingly, they gave the French enough support to keep them satisfied but never fully committed themselves to war with the Iroquois. In fact, for the most part, they gave only the appearance of hostility against the Iroquois, hewing to the policy that "we are all brothers, who ought to form only one body, and possess but one and the same spirit." The French, they reasoned, "invite us to go to war against the Iroquois; they wish to use us in order to make us their slaves. After we have aided in destroying the enemy, the French will do with us what they do with their cattle, which they put to the plow and make them cultivate the land. Let us leave them to act alone; they will not succeed in defeating the Iroquois; this is the means for being always our own masters."[5]

By the end of the seventeenth century, after years of exhausting warfare, it had become apparent to all parties involved that though the English vastly outnumbered the French, they could not defeat the Canadians because of disunity among the colonies and the unwillingness of the government at

---

[5]Wallace, "Origins of Iroquois Neutrality," p. 226.

home to supply military forces. Nor could the French either destroy or forge an alliance with the Iroquois because they lacked sufficient military strength for the former and suffered a competitive disadvantage in the fur trade that prohibited the latter. The Iroquois retained the strategic geographical position in the northern part of the continent. But in spite of their successes and the expansion of their influence over tribes to the south and west of them, they paid dearly in maintaining a pivotal role in the fur trade. By the end of the seventeenth century, hard hit by French attacks and war weary, they sought a formula for maintaining their security that did not necessitate attritional warfare.

The solution to their problem was sudden and bold. In the summer of 1701 the Iroquois entered negotiations with both the English and the French, signing treaties almost simultaneously at Montreal and Albany. To the French they promised neutrality in any future war between England and France—a great gain for the French who had often been stung by the Iroquois military forays. To the English, who now lost a military ally, the Iroquois ceded their western hunting lands, conquered a half century before from the Hurons. By this clever piece of diplomacy, the Iroquois implied that their primary allegiance was still to the English. But it was only a symbolic land cession, for the English had not the slightest ability to occupy or control this territory; in fact the lands in question had recently been reconquered by the French and their allies, the Wyandots. To complete their compromise negotiations the Iroquois made peace with the tribes to the west of them.

For almost half a century after the 1701 treaties the Iroquois policy of playing one European power against another worked well. The Five Nations (which became the Six Nations after the addition of the Tuscaroras) disengaged from the costly beaver wars, pursued their role as fur suppliers, and increased their population by absorbing remnants of coastal tribes decimated by Europeans and elements of western tribes which they had themselves conquered. Since the early seventeenth century, when they began struggling to assert themselves against other tribes of the Great Lakes region, the Iroquois had become the dominant power in the northeast and a force to be reckoned with by both the French and the English. Though hardly more numerous than the inhabitants of the province of New York at the beginning of the eighteenth century, their will to fight, their diplomatic skill, and their strategic position athwart the fur trading routes had raised them to a position of utmost importance. The governor of Quebec respectfully took note of this when he wrote home in 1711 that war with the Iroquois was to be avoided at all costs, for "the five Iroquois villages [nations] are more to be feared than the English colonies."[6] A decade later, after several Iroquis chiefs had

[6]Quoted in William J. Eccles, *The Canadian Frontier, 1534–1760* (New York: Holt, Rinehart and Winston, Inc., 1969), p. 133.

visited Boston, a New Englander wrote that "they are Courted and Caressed like the potentates of the Earth."[7]

Less than a year after the Iroquois had concluded their treaties at Albany and Montreal in 1701 another Anglo-French war broke out. But while the French and their local Indian allies put the torch to towns along the New England frontier, the Iroquois remained on the sidelines, content to see the English and French trade blows. They were confirmed in their opinion that the English were unreliable military allies by New York's refusal to come to New England's aid. Afraid of jeopardizing their profitable fur trade and the black-market traffic they were conducting with the French Canadian enemy, the New Yorkers kept their minds to commerce and, according to some Massachusetts authorities, even marketed in Albany plunder from devastated New England frontier towns. The Iroquois' one act of assistance was to send three Mohawks and one Mahican to London with two prominent New Yorkers to argue for English assistance in the war against Canada. Arriving in London in 1710, they paid their respects to Queen Anne, stopped the show when they attended the theatre, ran down a stag in the royal park, and were followed by throngs everywhere they went.

At the conclusion of Queen Anne's War in 1713, the English made substantial gains in North America. France ceded Nova Scotia, Newfoundland, and Hudson's Bay to England; recognized the sovereignty of the British over the Iroquois (the Iroquois made no such concession); and permitted English traders to open commerce with the western tribes that had previously been linked to the French. But these concessions on paper meant little, for the English could not implement them by occupying the areas they had gained or by establishing trading posts deep in the interior. Not for another generation would the English find the strength to concern themselves with these distant regions. For now they fixed their attention on the buildup of population between the coast and the Appalachian Mountains. Only in constructing a fort and trading post at Oswego on Lake Ontario did England take advantage of the French concessions. The final act of the imperial drama, and the fate of the Iroquois and more western tribes, was postponed for forty years.

CREEK DIPLOMACY

Just as the Iroquois were able to protect their trading interests and avoid warfare by playing one European power against another, the Creek confederation of the Southeast mastered the principles of *realpolitik* following the Yamasee War of 1715–1717. Like the Iroquois, the Creeks had been a

---

[7]Richard R. Johnson, "The Search for a Usable Indian: An Aspect of the Defense of New England," *Journal of American History*, 64 (1977): 648n.

defensive and loosely integrated confederacy before European settlement began. They too capitalized on the European trade to become the most formidable society in a vast region coveted by England, France, and Spain. And like the Iroquois, they not only enhanced their strength but suffered in the process through the intensification of warfare brought about by the introduction of the European trade. Less than two decades after the Iroquois perfected their "playoff system" between the English and French, the Creeks had made themselves "the custodians of the wilderness balance of power in the South."[9] Through a quarter century of adroit maneuvering they extended and withdrew promises to the English, French, and Spanish in order to extract trade and military concessions. At the same time they maintained their autonomy. Just as the English attempted to play Creeks and Cherokees against each other—"how to hold both as our friends, for some time, and assist them in Cutting one another's throats without offending either," as one Carolinian put it—the Creeks worked to keep French, English, and Spanish pitted against each other, with no one of the European powers gaining dominance over the other two. So skillful was the Creek leader Brims in this that one Englishman opined that he was "as great a Politician as any Governor in America."[10]

The new policy of aggressive neutrality was a logical course for the Creeks to follow after the trading alliance with the English earlier in the century had brought flagrant abuses by the Carolina traders. Greatly aroused, the Creeks had declared war against their exploiters, but their inability to persuade the Cherokees to join them in an all-out offensive against the English thwarted their efforts in the Yamasee War. Thereafter, they pursued a policy of limited cooperation. Despite their defeat in war, it was far from a passive strategy. Instead it was the active response of Indian leaders who were attempting to build the strength of their people while recognizing the advantages of interacting with the foreigners in their country.

The Creek politics of survival had to be devised within the context both of intra-Indian rivalries and of Anglo-French-Spanish rivalry. Ever since the English had arrived in Carolina and harassed the northern frontier of Spanish Florida, Spain had dreamed of mounting an expedition by land and sea that would wipe out English pretensions in the region. The Spanish made such an attempt in 1702, but it was an abysmal failure, producing only an English counterattack two years later that laid most of the Spanish missionary frontier in Florida in waste. English attacks on French trading posts on the lower Mississippi and along the Gulf of Mexico were planned in 1708. But a more profitable way of striking at nascent French power was found in 1711. Coordinating a military expedition primarily composed of Indian allies, the English attacked the Choctaws, the principal Indian allies of the French.

[9]Verner W. Crane, *The Southern Frontier, 1670–1732* (Ann Arbor: University of Michigan Press, 1956), p. 260.

[10]*Ibid.*, pp. 263, 260–261.

Yet none of these assaults on the frontier outposts of rival European nations succeeded in establishing English control in the lower South from the Atlantic to the Mississippi. It was this design of English hegemony that the Creeks hoped to prevent, while still maintaining trade connections with them.

In the aftermath of the Yamasee War the Creeks took measures to restore the balance of power by making overtures to the Spanish, whom they had fought at English instigation for many years. Chief Brims sent his son to St. Augustine in 1716 with instructions to allow the Spanish to build a fort at Coweta, the principal town of the Lower Creeks. Other Creek emissaries were sent to Mexico City to seal an alliance. During the next year Creek leaders also conferred with the Senecas, more than a thousand miles to the north, and with the English in Charleston. By 1717, they had fashioned a complicated arrangement by which some of their villages would remain within the Spanish orbit and some within the English. A treaty was signed with South Carolina which left the Creeks free to trade with whomever they pleased but set fixed rates in their trade with the English, guaranteed ammunition and arms for use against tribes not friendly to the English, and established a policy of mutual accountability for Creeks and Carolinians who committed crimes or injuries against each other.

Brims symbolized his balance of power strategy by commissioning one son as his principal emissary to the English and another son as principal emissary to the Spanish. Both English Carolinians and Spanish Floridians, struggling for the upper hand with the Creeks, attempted to persuade Brims to name "their" son his successor. The English attempted to gain a controlling hand in the Creek political process in 1722 by giving a commission to Ouletta, the son whom Brims sent to the English as an emissary of the Creek nation. This attempt to force a recognition of English sovereignty was shattered two years later when the Yamasees, inveterate enemies of the English and still allied with the Spanish, murdered Ouletta. Seepeycoffey, the Spanish client son of Brims, was now the only candidate as Brims's successor. When Seepeycoffey died in 1726, Brims's brother inherited the primary claim to headship of the Creeks.

Until he died in the early 1730s Brims maintained the policy of playing Spanish and English against each other. The Creeks continued to aid the Yamasees, with whom the English were intermittently at war, and they continued to attack the Cherokees with whom the English were closely allied. The English attempted various strategies to coerce the Creeks into an unqualified English connection—interference in Creek political affairs, trade embargoes, and the threat of a joint Cherokee-English war against them. These tactics succeeded in bringing the Creeks closer to the English and in convincing them to break off their traditional support of the Yamasees; but the Creeks still preserved their autonomous position and remained the pivotal force in the region. The Creeks, wrote the Assembly of South

Carolina in 1737, "have been treated with as Allies but not as Subjects of the Crown. . . . They have maintained their own Possessions, and preserved their Independency."[11] Numerically strong and diplomatically skilled, the Creeks were able to preserve their central position thoughout the decades after the Yamasee War. Their emissaries ranged for thousands of miles; between 1715 and 1733 they parleyed with the Spanish in St. Augustine, Vera Cruz, and Mexico City; with the English in Charleston and London; with the French at Fort Toulouse on the Alabama River; and with headmen of other Indian nations from the Florida border to the Great Lakes. At times they carried out simultaneous negotiations with two European powers that were at swords' points, just as the Iroquois had conducted dual negotiations at Montreal and Albany in 1701.

In the decades after Brims's death, the Creeks twice succeeded in preserving their policy of neutrality at critical junctures. In 1739, when England declared war on Spain, the Carolina government put enormous pressure on the Creeks to join General James Oglethorpe, who had founded the colony of Georgia between South Carolina and Florida only seven years before, in an assault on St. Augustine. Although warriors from a few villages joined the English expedition, which ended in disaster, most of the Creeks remained out of the fray, convinced that the policy of trading with whoever offered the best prices, but allying militarily with no single European power, was the keystone to Creek survival. The Creeks might well have congratulated themselves for adhering to their policy, for the Cherokees who joined the English brought back smallpox that spread disastrously in the Cherokee towns in 1740–1741. In the next year, a Creek headman gave new expression to the old strategy when he asserted that "The [Creek] land belonged to the English as well as the French and indeed to neither of them. But both had liberty to Come there to Trade."[12]

In the 1740s, when France joined Spain in war against England, the Creek policy of neutrality was again put to the test. The governor of South Carolina summoned headmen from the Upper Creek towns to Charleston in 1746 and confided the rewards he had in mind if the Creeks would join an English military assault on Fort Toulouse, the main French bastion on the Alabama River. Back in their own country, however, Creek headmen vetoed the project; the English were again thwarted in their efforts to obtain the Indian support they needed to drive the French from the lower South. South Carolina attempted again to mobilize the Creeks and Cherokees for attacks on the French in 1747. Failure was again the result when Malatchi, the youngest son of Brims and a pro-French chief, gained recognition as

[11]*The Colonial Records of South Carolina, Journal of the Commons House of Assembly, Nov. 10, 1736–June 7, 1739,* ed. J. H. Easterby (Columbia: Historical Commission of South Carolina, 1951), p. 75.

[12]Quoted in M. Eugene Sirmans, *Colonial South Carolina; A Political History* (Chapel Hill: University of North Carolina Press, 1966), p. 198.

emperor of the Lower Creeks. Malatchi had been at the Charleston conference in 1746 and had refused to let the Carolina governor browbeat him with threats of withdrawing the English trade. He had returned to the Lower Creek villages, spoken against the English plan, and then personally visited St. Augustine and Fort Toulouse to inform the Spanish and French of the English proposals. The English were summarily told that they were welcome to trade in Creek country but could not build forts and should expect no Creek support for military expeditions against the Spanish or French.

CHEROKEE DIPLOMACY

The Cherokees were even larger in number than the Iroquois and Creeks, probably totaling about 12,000 at mid-eighteenth century. The English regarded their allegiance, or at least their neutrality, as indispensable to security in the region from Virginia to Georgia. Settled in the Appalachian Mountains to the west of the Carolina and Georgia settlers, and known for the valor of their warriors, they had been allied to the English in trade and war since the late seventeenth century. Faced with other Indian enemies, the Carolinians came to regard Cherokee support as a cornerstone of their Indian policy. The Cherokees were not unaware of this. They understood that they had played the decisive role in the Yamasee War of 1715, maneuvering, as the Carolinians admitted, in the best tradition of European power politics. "The last time they were here [in Charleston] they insulted us to the last degree," complained Carolina leaders in 1717, "and indeed by their demands (with which we were forced to comply) made us their tributaries."[13]

The support of the Cherokees wavered at various points after the Yamasee War, especially in the 1730s. The abuses of English traders during that decade aroused their ire, and when an immigrant German mystic, Gottlieb Priber, reached them in 1736, he found them ripe for his peculiar message. Priber's genuine respect for Indian culture and his disaffection from European society, which he regarded as hopelessly corrupt, made him welcome in the Cherokee towns. Priber preached about the need to establish communal states in the English colonies based on Plato's Republic. Wherever he went he was regarded as a dangerous radical, for very few of the colonizers wanted to abandon the concept of private property and return to an arcadian past. But the Cherokees' values were much closer to Priber's, and they esteemed him for teaching them the use of weights and measures so they could protect themselves against dishonest traders. Priber also cautioned them to maintain their freedom by trusting no Europeans and encouraged them to cultivate trade connections with the French at New

---

[13]Quoted in David D. Wallace, *South Carolina: A Short History, 1520–1948* (Chapel Hill: University of North Carolina Press, 1951), p. 90.

Orleans as a way of diminishing the English influence. His plan for Indian survival in the South included a confederacy of all the major tribes of the region, a city of refuge for escaped slaves and debtors within Cherokee territory, and an iron resolve among the Indians to surrender no territory, make no concessions to any European power, and continue the balance-of-power strategy in relations with the French, English, and Spanish. The Cherokees regarded him as "a great beloved man," which indicates how vibrantly anti-European ideas could resonate in the Cherokee mind, even while they maintained close relations with the Carolinians.

When South Carolina authorities ordered Priber's arrest in 1739, the Cherokees refused to surrender him. But in 1743, while making his way to the French in New Orleans, he was captured by the Creeks and turned over to the English. He died after a few years of imprisonment in Frederica, Georgia, much to the regret of his Cherokee friends. In 1748 the South Carolina government further antagonized the Cherokees by refusing to honor a treaty of mutual support when the Cherokees were attacked by the Upper Creeks. In response the Cherokees attacked white Carolina traders, demonstrating that they did not regard themselves as English dependents and possessed enough power to control their own destiny. Overtures to the French were periodically made to keep the English off balance.

That the dependency of the English upon the Cherokee was at least as great as Cherokee dependence upon the English was plainly admitted in 1750 when the governor of South Carolina reminded the assembly that "it is absolutely necessary for us to be in friendship with the Cherokees," for "they are reckoned to be about three thousand gunmen, the greatest nation we know of in America except the Choctaws. . . ."[14] Because the Choctaws had long been tied to the French in the trans-Mississippi area the Cherokees provided an indispensable buffer between the English and their French enemies. Recognizing this, the Crown committed £6000 for presents to the Creeks and Cherokees in 1749 and 1750, sterling testimony to the English regard for maintaining the alliance. South Carolina expenditures for Indian presents doubled between 1750 and 1758, reaching £14,837 in the latter year—further proof of the ability of the Indians to play on the English colonizers' dependence on them.[15]

TRANSFORMATIONS IN INDIAN SOCIETY

During the first half of the eighteenth century, the interior Indian nations of North America demonstrated their capacity for adapting to the presence of Europeans and for turning their economic and political interaction with

[14]David H. Corkran, *The Cherokee Frontier: Conflict and Survival, 1740–1762* (Norman: University of Oklahoma Press, 1962), p. 15.

[15]Sirmans, *Colonial South Carolina*, p. 275; Wilbur R. Jacobs, ed., *Indians of the Southern Colonial Frontier: The Edmond Atkin Report and Plan of 1755*, (Columbia: University of South Carolina Press, 1954), pp. 27n, 31n.

them to their own advantage. For a century and a half the culture of the Europeans had been revealed to the Indians. From it they drew selectively, adopting through the medium of the fur, skin, and slave trade European articles of clothing, weapons, metal implements, and a variety of ornamental objects. To this degree their material culture was changed. To some extent this incorporation of material objects robbed the Indians of their native skills. But agriculture, fishing, and hunting, the mainstays of Indian subsistence before the Europeans came, remained so thereafter. European implements such as the hoe only made Indian agriculture more efficient. The knife and fishhook enabled the natives to fish and trap with greater intensity in order to obtain the commodities needed in the barter system. However, pottery making declined and the hunter became more dependent upon the gun.

Still, interaction with European societies over many generations transformed Indian culture in important ways that boded ill for the future. By looking at several aspects of life among the interior tribes—trade, warfare, political organization, and the use of distilled spirits—we can sort out the overall effects of Indian contact with Europeans while at the same time exploding some of the myths that have clouded Native American history for years.

The Fur Trade

The fur trade was "one among a cluster of interrelated cultural influences,"[16] but it is the proper place at which to begin a consideration of the transformation of Indian societies because from almost the first moment of contact it brought and kept Native Americans and Euroamericans together. Indian tribes had traded extensively with each other over long distances for centuries before Europeans arrived, so the concept of exchanging goods was not novel to them. The simple commodity exchange of the pre-contact period also served the purpose of maintaining social and territorial relations among neighboring tribes. Profit was not involved, and the trade tended to reinforce peaceful relations rather than inciting competition and conflict.

The introduction of European trade goods, especially iron and steel implements, textiles, firearms and ammunition, transformed several aspects of the Native Americans' culture. It is not necessary to turn Indians into acquisitive capitalists to explain their desire for trade goods. They did not seek the trade goods because they wished to become part of a bourgeois culture, accumulating material wealth from the fur trade, but because they recognized the advantages, within the matrix of their own culture, of goods fashioned by societies with a more complex technology. It was the utility of

[16]Calvin Martin, *Keepers of the Game: Indian-Animal Relationships and the Fur Trade* (Berkeley and Los Angeles: University of California Press, 1978), p. 2.

the Europeans' trade goods, not the opportunities for profit provided by the fur trade, that drew Native Americans into it. From the Indian point of view, trade was carried on within the context of a political and social alliance. Haggling over prices appalled them at first, for, according to their values, trade was an aspect of friendship.

Whatever the tensions created by the encounter of tribal and bourgeois values in the fur trade, it required an enormous reallocation of human resources and "metamorphosed the tribes' internal economies."[17] Subsistence hunting, limited by the food requirements of a tribe, turned into commercial hunting, limited only by the quantity of trade goods desired. Indian males spent far more time away from the villages trapping and hunting, and the importance of their activity to the life of the tribe, which soon became dependent on trade goods, undermined the relatively egalitarian matrilineal base of society. Women were also drawn into the new economic organization of villages, for the beaver, marten, or fox, once killed, had to be skinned and the skins scraped, dressed, trimmed, and sewn into robes. Among some tribes the trapping, preparation, and transporting of skins became such a time-consuming industry that food resources had to be procured in trade from other tribes. Ironically, the reorientation of tribal economies toward the fur trade dispersed villages and weakened the localized basis of clans and lineages. Breaking up in order to be nearer the widely spread trapping grounds, Indian villagers moved closer to the nomadic woodland existence that Europeans had charged them with at the beginning of contact.

Involvement in the fur trade also drastically altered the relationship of Native Americans to their ecosystem. In their pre-contact cosmology Indians regarded the destinies of man and animal as linked, for both inhabited a spiritual world governed by a Great Creator. This spiritual symbiosis between human and animal life imposed obligations on hunters and animals alike. "Man and Nature both had to adhere to a prescribed behavior toward one another."[18] The Indian hunter knew that he must never take more animals than he needed and must treat their bodies with respect; the animals in return must not resist capture but must "consciously surrender themselves to the needy hunter." In this sense, killing was ordained and the hunter was engaged in a "holy occupation."[19]

The tremendous destruction of animal life triggered by the advent of trade with Europeans corrupted the spiritual framework within which hunting had traditionally been carried out. Trappers declared all-out war on the beaver and other fur-bearing animals, which was, in effect, a repudiation of man's traditional role within the cosmos, "a corruption of the Indian-land

[17]Francis Jennings, *The Invasion of America: Indians, Colonialism, and the Cant of Conquest* (Chapel Hill: University of North Carolina Press, 1975), p. 86.

[18]Martin, *Keepers of the Game*, p. 73.

[19]*Ibid.*, p. 115.

relationship in which the native had merged himself sympathetically with his environment."[20]

A final effect of the trade was to broaden vastly the scale of intertribal tensions, which often led to war. Pre-contact trade had been based on intertribal cooperation. But Europeans of different nationalities competed for client tribes in the fur trade, and the tribes were therefore sucked into the rivalry of their patrons. In addition, as furs became depleted in the hunting grounds of one tribe, they could maintain their trade connection with the Europeans only by conquering more remote tribes whose hunting grounds had not yet been exhausted or by using armed force to intercept the furs of other tribes as they were being brought to trading posts near the coast. The Mohawks of the Hudson River Valley drove the Mahicans away from Dutch traders in 1624–1628 in order to ensure their preeminent position in the fur trade. Likewise, the Iroquois decimated and dispersed the Hurons of the eastern Great Lakes region in the mid-seventeenth century as a part of their drive for "beaver hegemony." By the end of the century the Iroquois themselves were exhausted and their population depleted by the incessant warfare they had engaged in while attempting to maintain the role of fur trade broker for the entire Northeast.

Warfare

"Myth contrasts civilized war and savage war," writes Francis Jennings, "by accepting the formal as a rational, honorable, and often progressive activity while attributing to the latter the qualities of irrationality, ferocity, and unredeemed retrogression."[21] The point is important because a primary component of the stereotype of the American Indian has always been the blood lust that supposedly inspired "warfare that was insane, unending, continuously attritional from our point of view [and] . . . so integrated into the whole fabric of Eastern [Indian] culture, so dominantly emphasized within it, that escape from it was well-nigh impossible."[22] In point of fact, the tribes of eastern North America were relatively free of warfare, especially if compared with European societies of this era.

Before the arrival of Europeans intermittent violence between tribes did occur. Europeans, in fact, were adept at playing on these intertribal hostilities as they sought Indian allies after the first settlements were planted. But the nature of pre-contact Indian war was far different than the wars known in Europe, both in duration and in scale of operations. Unlike the Europeans, Native Americans could not conceive of total war that was fought for months or even years, that did not spare noncombatants, and that

[20]*Ibid.*, p. 65.

[21]Jennings, *Invasion of America*, p. 146.

[22]*Ibid.*, p. 149, quoting Alfred L. Kroeber, *Cultural and Natural Areas of Native North America* (Berkeley and Los Angeles: University of California Press, 1939), p. 148.

involved the systematic destruction of towns and food supplies. Wars among Indians were conducted more in the manner of short forays, with small numbers of warriors engaging the enemy and one or the other side withdrawing after a few casualties had been inflicted. Roger Williams wrote that in New England the Indian wars "are farre lesse bloody and devouring than the cruell Warres of Europe" and related that "when they fight in a plaine, they fight with leaping and dancing, that seldom an Arrow hits, and when a man is wounded, unless he that shot follows upon the wounded, they soon retire and save the wounded."[23] John Underhill, hero of the Pequot War, thought that the intertribal hostilities were "more for pasttime than to conquer and subdue enemies." Even in hand-to-hand combat, the Indians "fell on pell mell after their feeble Manner: Indeed it hardly deserves the name of Fighting."[24] Warfare was a ritualistic encounter with the object not of shedding as much of the enemy's blood as possible or devastating his villages and crops but making a show of force that would convince him of one's strength.

Drawn into the fur trade and eventually dependent upon it, Indian societies found new motives for intertribal conflict. Added to this was the effect of European weaponry, which Indians mastered quickly. Incorporating the military technology of the Europeans, tribes inflicted far greater casualties in their conflicts than in the pre-contact period. The Iroquois, perhaps the most militaristic of the northern Indian societies, reduced the population of the Hurons by half in a series of attacks between 1647 and 1659, only to see their own ranks of warriors reduced by half in the beaver wars that scourged Iroquoia at the end of the seventeenth century. Disease was by all odds the greatest killer of Native Americans during the contact period, but the loss of life that accompanied the adoption of European weaponry and the intensification of intertribal conflict within the context of the fur trade competition was also great.

Political Organization

Another cultural change that resulted from contact with European societies was in the realm of political organization. This varied from society to society, but the examples of the Creeks and Cherokees are instructive. Though they belonged to different linguistic groups and frequently warred against each other, their pre-contact political structures were similar and they encountered the same historical forces in the seventeenth and eighteenth centuries—trade, war, and land encroachment. Though loosely confederated, a fundamental feature of their pre-contact political structures was the local autonomy of towns and clans. It was to the town, not to the

[23]Quoted in Jennings, *Invasion of America*, p. 150.

[24]John Underhill, *Newes from America; or, A New and Experimentall Discoverie of New England* (London, 1638).

"confederacy," that the Creeks and Cherokees gave their primary loyalty. Attempts were sometimes made to coordinate the policy of various towns, but no party in disagreement with a majority decision was compelled to act against its wishes. Thus, in the early years of contact towns or groups of towns often parleyed separately with Europeans, made particular agreements with traders, and acted semi-independently in military affairs.

Important changes in political structure occurred as the result of trade, war, and diplomatic contact with Europeans in the eighteenth century. Towns began to align depending on their proximity to French or English traders. A split between the Upper Creek and Lower Creek towns, for example, developed because the former lived within the French trading orbit, while the latter had easier access to the English. Similarly, the towns of the Overhill Cherokees gravitated toward the French and the Middle and Lower Cherokees traded with the English. The need to deal with English, French, and Spanish traders and governments also obliged the towns to move toward loose confederacies where coordinated action would give them greater strength in their dealings with outsiders. Another political change involved a gradual move toward centralized tribal leadership and the establishment of patrilineal dynasties among the headmen or "micos." This altered the traditional structure and criterion of leadership. Before contact with Europeans leadership was local and descended in the dominant matrilineal clan of the village. But in the eighteenth century the tendency was to create supra-town chiefs and to allow their power to pass on to their sons rather than to their sisters' sons. One cause of these shifts was that English, Spanish, and French authorities wanted to deal with one chief rather than many and tended to promote and support the candidacy of the chief's son, consistent with the European view of social and political organization. This European attempt to intrude on the internal politics of Indian societies was meant to further the colonizers' control in their dealings with Indian military allies and trading partners. A cultural climate favoring the development of patrilineal institutions was also created by the intensified hunting, trading, and warring of the eighteenth century, which generally elevated the importance of male roles in Indian society.

Another way of attempting to control the political dynamics of Creek and Cherokee societies was to support the candidacy of a particular headman's son or even to commission certain individuals in order to facilitate communication and cooperation. The English tried to establish Ouletta, the son of the Creek headman Brims, as their client. When he died, they transferred their recognition to the Spanish candidate, his brother Seepeycoffee. Annual gifts, which were an essential part of good relations, were distributed through commissioned headmen, thus enhancing their prestige within their own society. The English practice of picking particular headmen with whom to negotiate conferred power on those who had not earned their authority in the traditional way, according to matrilineage and honor, but simply through the intervention of an external authority. In time, a commission from colonial officials became an important factor in the degree of influence wielded by a particular chief.

Intermarriage with an Indian woman was another way of gaining influence in a tribe, particularly if the woman was from an influential clan. Mary Musgrove Bosomworth, a niece of Brims, married three Englishmen in succession, and, though she was fiercely anti-English on occasion, her husbands attained positions of great importance within the Creek confederation. Thus, through commissioning client headmen and intermarrying with Indian women, the Carolinians worked to strengthen the pro-English faction in the Creek confederacy and to wield some influence in their political decisions.

Although this kind of interventionism upset traditional lines of political authority and customs for recruiting headmen in a way that benefited the English, it can also be regarded as a purposeful adjustment of traditional political practices by Indian peoples who faced new and powerful invaders and desired a continuous flow of trade goods. By modifying the customary criteria of kinship the Creeks selected leaders better equipped to act in their interest. Access to the English or Spanish was gained by marrying one's sister to a European, by accepting a commission, or by having a European father. In none of these cases were the Creeks simply passive and helpless objects responding to white initiative. In a period of shifting power among the European groups present in the region, they were "coping creatively in a variety of ways with the different situations in which they found themselves."[25]

Like the Creeks, the Cherokees changed their political practices in the eighteenth century in response to new needs related to war and trade with Europeans. Before about 1730 the nearly autonomous village was the basic unit of Cherokee political authority. Little need existed for the political unification of towns. But tension with their Creek neighbors, encouraged by the English, and intermittent hostilities with the English created a need for political centralization. By mid-century the Cherokees had formed a supravillage political organization. Civil chiefs or "priests," under the leadership of Old Hop, gathered together the fragmented authority of the earlier period and formed a tribal "priest state" in which the Cherokee towns coordinated decision making.

When this proved inadequate to the tasks at hand in the difficult years after mid-century, warriors began to assume the dominant role in tribal councils. The warrior had been greatly respected before this but was outranked by the civil chiefs. By the 1760s, adapting to a new era of strife, the

[25]Robert F. Berkhofer, Jr., "The Political Context of a New Indian History," *Pacific Historical Review*, 40 (1971): 364.

Cherokees made "warring and warriors an unambiguous part of the good life" and gave the war chiefs new and coercive political authority over the nation.[26] By this process the Cherokees made political changes that enabled dozens of villages to unify and amalgamate their strength.

Alcohol

A final aspect of culture change, which was both cause and effect, was the use of distilled spirits. There is little doubt that rum became an important item in the Indian trade. It was pushed hard by traders because, once Indians had acquired a taste for it, it added to the total stock of trade items that they needed. Increasing the volume of the trade was almost always foremost in the minds of traders and coastal merchants; hence the economic function of the Indians' taste for rum mattered most to them. As for the Indians, alcohol became an important element in internal and intertribal Indian relations. The quality of English as opposed to French rum became a major consideration in diverting the northern fur trade from Montreal to Albany. The decision of the Georgia government to allow no traffic in alcohol—a part of their attempt to reform the Indian trade in the 1730s—brought only protests from the Creek headmen, who understood the debilitating effects of rum on Creek society but were unwilling to give up the power they enjoyed as distributors of it.

How were Indian societies affected by the use of alcohol? The modern tendency has been to see alcohol as a painkilling device used by a people caught between two cultures. Unable to maintain their traditional ways of life after becoming dependent on the material items of European culture, but equally unable to gain acceptance into white society, Indians, it is argued, turned in despair to rum. Historians, anthropologists, and psychologists have viewed drunkenness as a way of escaping internalized feelings of unworthiness that came from prolonged contact with a white society that called them "savages" and "barbarians." Drunkenness provided at least temporary flight back into a romanticized past before the white man came and gave momentary assistance in resolving a painful crisis of identity. The difficulty with this explanation is that whatever its value in revealing the causes of alcoholism in modern society, it does not satisfactorily explain drunkenness among either Indians or Europeans in the eighteenth century. Europeans were not known for identity crises in pre-Revolutionary society; yet their alcoholic consumption was staggering even by modern American standards and was far greater than among Indians in this period. If nothing else, mere availability assured this. The spigots in thousands of colonial taverns rarely ran dry, but distilled spirits were only intermittently available to Indians spread over thousands of square miles of the interior.

When it is understood that the consumption of alcohol has different

[26]Fred Gearing, "Priests and Warriors; Social Structures for Cherokee Politics in the 18th Century," American Anthropological Association *Memoir* 93 (1962): 102.

meanings in different cultures and that drunken behavior takes many forms according to varying cultural norms, the role of alcohol in Indian societies can be better understood. Anthropoligists have recently suggested that for Indians in the early period of European contact drinking was primarily "an institutionalized 'time-out' period from ordinary canons of etiquette." Only later, in the nineteenth and twentieth centuries, did it become a form of social protest and a means of release from despair. In the seventeenth and eighteenth centuries Indians imbibed rum for cultural reasons that made sense within the context of their own culture—"expansive conviviality, the letting down of customary decorum, and in some cases, serious dignified drinking into a comatose state."[27] The consumption of alcohol was incorporated into a value system that earlier had adopted the smoking of tobacco as a cultural habit associated not only with sociability and generosity—"passing the pipe"—but also as a custom invested with religious functions and meanings.

Alcohol became important in Euro-Indian relations in another way. It was commonly distributed as a prelude to negotiations for land or trade goods. If many eighteenth-century commentators are to be believed, this was all to the advantage of the colonizers because Indians became befuddled and were then easily swindled. This, however, was probably the exception rather than the rule. Indians did not relish being cheated any more than Europeans and according to the testimony of many traders they were as skillful at driving a bargain as their white trading partners. The distribution of alcohol at the beginning of negotiations was, in their terms, a ritual for ensuring a mutually beneficial contract. So long as Indians had more than one place to trade, it was hardly good business practice for traders to drive them into the arms of competitors by getting them drunk and stealing their furs. This is not to deny that sharp practices occurred. On occasion unauthorized traders brought casks of rum to an Indian village, watched it eagerly consumed, and left with a winter's catch of furs and skins. But Europeans complained about being "held up" by Indians as often as Indians complained about European trickery. And when the trading was done at frontier posts or in Indian villages, which was the practice throughout the Carolina region and in the hinterlands of Virginia and Pennsylvania in the eighteenth century, it was not to the trader's advantage, or even good for his health, to cheat Indians who had been robbed of their senses by the overconsumption of alcohol. Indians took their furs where they could obtain the best prices and the amplest supply of trade goods. Their extraordinary mobility over land and inland waterways, combined with the availability of more than one European supplier, made it imperative for colonial traders to maintain a relationship

[27]Nancy Oestreich Lurie, "The World's Oldest On-Going Protest Demonstration: North American Indian Drinking Patterns," *Pacific Historical Review*, 40 (1971): 321; Craig MacAndrew and Robert B. Edgerton, *Drunken Comportment, A Social Explanation* (Chicago: Aldine Publishing Co., 1969).

that was to the Indians' satisfaction. When they did not, as in the case of the Carolina traders, the Indians took their trade to the French, the Spanish, or to rival traders in Georgia and Virginia.

When tribes lost their land, their autonomy, and their confidence in their traditional belief system, drinking could change from a form of social relaxation to a solvent for internalized aggressive impulses against whites. This seems to have been the case among some of the remnants of coastal tribes, which by the eighteenth century had lost their land and their power. They existed only as clients of white society, and the chronic and debauched drinking that many observers attributed to them may be indicative of their precarious inner state. Almost powerless and unable to express their hostility toward whites, their frustrations accumulated and were turned inward. Only drinking, and in extreme cases suicide, provided release from this situation. But where power was still balanced between Indians and whites, which was still the case in most parts of eighteenth-century America, the drunken Indian was not so much a character as he was a real stereotype of the aggressive, violent "savage."

CULTURAL PERSISTENCE

While the interior tribes blended a wide variety of European trade goods into their material culture and adapted their internal economies and political structures to meet new situations, other aspects of their life were characterized by a high degree of cultural persistency. Iroquois, Creeks, Cherokees, and other tribes were singularly unimpressed with most of the institutions of European life and saw no reason to replace what they valued in their own culture with what they disdained in the culture of others. This applied to the newcomers' political institutions and practices, their systems of law and justice, religion, education, family organization, and their child-rearing practices. In all these areas Native Americans carefully observed European customs but saw little that they regarded as worthy of emulation. Indeed, so far as they could ascertain, these institutions often failed to work successfully in the Europeans' own cultural system.

The Anglican missionaries of the Society for the Propagation of the Gospel were continually plagued by this paradox in their efforts to convert Indians to Christianity. Why, asked Indians, should they convert to a system that, despite its claims of superiority, was ridden with crime, social disorder, and political factionalism? "[The Indians] are for the most part great lovers of Justice & Equity in their dealings," wrote Robert Maule, an Anglican missionary in South Carolina in 1709, "and I have asked some of them whether they would learn to be or had any desire to become of the white men's religion. They have plainly told me no: what's the matter sayd I, why so? Because, replys they, Backarara [the white man] no good; Backarara

Cheat; Backarara Lye, Backarara Drink Brandy, me no Love that."[28] Itinerant clergymen in the Carolinas repeated the same message over and over in their reports to superiors in London. Most of the settlers, wrote a plaintive Charles Woodmason at the end of the colonial period, lived "after a loose and lascivious manner. . . . The Manners of the North Carolinians in General, are Vile and Corrupt—the whole Country is a Stage of Debauchery Dissoluteness and Corruption. . . . Polygamy is very Common, . . . bastardly, no Disrepute—Concubinage General."[29] Could it be any wonder, then, that he was unable to convince the Indians of the superiority of the white way of life?

John Lawson, a proprietary official in the Carolinas in the early eighteenth century, captured the essence of the reason for the lack of cultural borrowing outside the realm of material objects. "They are really better to us," he wrote in 1708, "than we are to them; they always give us Victuals at their Quarters, and take care we are arm'd against Hunger and Thirst: We do not so by them (generally speaking) but let them walk by our Doors Hungry, and do not often relieve them. We look upon them with Scorn and Disdain, and think them little better than Beasts in Humane Shape, though if well examined, we shall find that, for all our Religion and Education, we possess more Moral Deformities, and Evils than these Savages do, or are acquainted withal."[30] Indians were not secretive in their disdain of white culture. When it was suggested to the Iroquois in 1744 that they send some of their young men to Virginia for a white education, they counterproposed that "if the English Gentlemen would send a Dozen or two of their children to Onondaga, the great Council would take care of their Education, bring them up in really what was the best Manner and make men of them."[31]

In marriage and social relations it was much the same. Although Europeans often disparaged Indian customs of companionate marriage or serial monogamy and accused them of "licentiousness," "debauchery," and "faithlessness" in their sexual practices, domestic relations among the Indians, as a few European observers admitted, were entirely satisfactory to them and seemed infinitely better than those of their European critics. Shortly after his arrival in the colonies, Thomas Paine reported the opinion of an "American savage" concerning Christian marriages. "Either the Christian's God was not so good and wise as he was represented," the Indian reportedly avowed,

[28]Robert Maule to Society for the Propagation of the Gospel, [June 3, 1710], SPG Mss, A5, No. 133 (microfilm of Library of Congress transcripts), UCLA Research Library.

[29]Charles Woodmason, *Carolina Backcountry on the Eve of the Revolution: The Journal and Other Writings of Charles Woodmason, Anglican Itinerant*, ed. Richard J. Hooker (Chapel Hill: University of North Carolina Press, 1969), pp. 80–81.

[30]Lawson, *A New Voyage of Carolina*, . . . ed. Hugh T. Lefler (Chapel Hill: University of North Carolina Press, 1967), p. 243.

[31]Quoted in A. Irving Hallowell, "The Backwash of the Frontier: The Impact of the Indian in American Culture," in Paul Bohannan and Fred Plog, eds., *Beyond the Frontier: Social Process and Cultural Change* (Garden City, N.Y.: The Natural History Press, 1967), p. 325.

or he never meddled with the marriages of his people; since not one in a hundred of them had anything to do either with happiness or common sense. Hence as soon as ever you meet, you long to part; and not having this relief in your power, by way of revenge, double each other's misery. Whereas in ours [Indian marriages] which have no other ceremony than mutual affection, and last no longer than they bestow mutual pleasures, we make it our business to oblige the heart we are afraid to lose; and being at liberty to separate, seldom or never feel the inclination. But if any should be found so wretched among us, as to hate where the only commerce ought to be love, we instantly dissolve the band. God made us all in pairs; each has his mate somewhere or other; and it is our duty to find each other out, since no creature was ever intended to be miserable.[32]

In sum, while the material aspects of Indian culture were modified and political structures were altered, many aspects of Indian life were marked by cultural persistency in the long period of interaction with Europeans. Indian societies were as selective as European societies in borrowing from the cultures they encountered. They incorporated what served them well and rejected what made no sense within the framework of their own values and modes of existence.

Despite many areas of cultural persistence, the involvement of Indian societies in the European trade network brought many changes that were to the Native Americans' disadvantage. Trade hastened the spread of epidemic diseases, raised the level of warfare, depleted ecozones of animal life, and drew Indians into a market economy in which "they eventually destroyed the basis for the very economy they were trying to practice."[33] Over a long period of time, the fur trade constricted the economic freedom of Indian societies, for they reorganized productive relations within their own communities to serve a trading partner who, through the side effects of the trade, became a trading master.

[32]*The Complete Writings of Thomas Paine*, 2 vols., Philip S. Foner, ed. (New York: Citadel Press, 1945), 2:119–20.

[33]Jennings, *Invasion of America*, p. 87.

11

THE SEVEN YEARS WAR
AND ITS AFTERMATH

For the first half of the eighteenth century interior tribes such as the Creeks, Cherokees, and Iroquois maintained a state of equipoise with European colonial societies by artfully playing one colonizing power against another and serving periodic reminders to the Europeans that Indian trade and military assistance were as valuable to them as the European trade goods were to Native American societies. "To preserve the Ballance between us & the French," wrote New York's Indian secretary, "is the great ruling Principle of Modern Indian Politics."[1] Indians were useful to Europeans, Europeans were useful to Indians, and power was roughly divided between them. But in the third quarter of the eighteenth century historical forces were at work, both in the sphere of international politics and in the more limited sphere of the colonizers' communities, that would end the equilibrium between Indian and European peoples and deeply divide colonial society itself.

POPULATION INCREASE

On the North American side of the ocean, a tremendous population buildup, especially in the English colonies, created a shortage of land on the coastal

[1]Peter Wraxall, *An Abridgement of the Indian Affairs . . .*, Charles H. McIlwain, ed. (Cambridge: Harvard University Press, 1915), p. 219.

plain and by the 1750s was propelling thousands of land-hungry settlers toward the mountain gaps in the Appalachians in search of new territory. From a population of a quarter million in 1700, the English colonies grew to 1.2 million in 1750 and increased another 400,000 in the next decade. Three quarters of this increase came in the colonies south of New York. The advance agents of this enormous westward rush were Eastern land speculators. They had only to watch the German and Scots-Irish immigrants disembarking daily at Baltimore, Philadelphia, and New York to understand that fortunes were to be made by those who could lay claim to land west of the existing settlements.

With capital provided by London investors, Virginia tobacco planters, and Northern merchants, land companies were formed in the 1740s and 1750s to capitalize on this demographic explosion. The Ohio Land Company, organized in 1747, laid claim to half a million acres in the Ohio Valley. The Susquehanna Land Company, organized five years later, declared rights to hundreds of thousands of acres in Pennsylvania. In the next decade the Delaware Company, Miami Company, Indiana Company, and other private syndicates all raced to establish claims. Though some, like the Susquehanna Company, advertised that their purpose was to "open the most effectual Door for carrying the Light of the glorious Gospel of Christ among the numerous tribes of Indians that inhabit those inland Parts," nobody was confused about the principal object in mind.[2] Inexorably, the agents of English society exerted pressure on Indian leaders to cede and sell their lands in order to pave the way for new white settlements. The farther west settlement moved, the closer it came to the western trading empire of the French and the Indian nations allied to them.

THE SEVEN YEARS WAR

On the opposite side of the Atlantic the revival of international rivalries hastened this showdown west of the Appalachian Mountains. In 1748 France and England had composed the differences that had led them to war in 1744, but even as the ink was drying on the articles of conciliation the way was being prepared for a renewal of hostilities. The powerful merchant element in England, supported by American clients, called for a destruction of French overseas trade. Even before events in Europe brought formal declarations of war, fighting began in the North American wilderness. By the time it was over, in the early 1760s, France would have surrendered her North Atlantic claims and thus the precious system of balancing off European powers, the key to Indian autonomy, would be shattered.

[2]Petition of Subscribers to the Susquehannah Company, 1755, in Julian P. Boyd, ed., *The Susquehanna Company Papers* (Wilkes-Barre, Pa.: Wyoming Historical & Genealogical Society, 1930), 1: 255.

During the 1740s English fur traders from Virginia and Pennsylvania pushed deep into the Ohio Valley, establishing outposts on the Ohio River and its tributaries. By 1749 the French commander at Fort Miami, south of Detroit, reported that about three hundred English traders were operating in the Ohio country and successfully luring the Indians into their trade orbit. Men with a sense of geopolitics had realized for decades that the struggle for the continent would hinge on control of the trans-Allegheny west. For more than a century the English had been content to populate the narrow coastal plain, leaving the continental heartlands to their rivals and obtaining their share of the Indian trade through connections centered at Albany and Charleston. Now they challenged the French where the French interest was vital.

France's choices were to resist or surrender the continent to the English and Spanish. The French chose the former, attempting to block further English expansion by establishing forts throughout the Ohio Valley and by prying the Indians loose from their English connections. Attempts were made to convince the Iroquois, Shawnees, and Delawares of the Ohio region that only an alliance with the French would guarantee their survival. "The English," warned one French emissary in the early 1750s, "are much less anxious to take away your peltries than to become masters of your lands . . . and your blindness is so great, that you do not perceive that the very hand that caresses you, will scourge you, like negroes and slaves, so soon as it will have got possession of those lands."[3]

Though the Indians were aware of the westward surging white population, they were unwilling to break the connections with English traders that brought them commodities which the French could not match in price and quality. Moreover, English strength in their region was a reality and French talk of trade south of the Great Lakes only a promise. In 1752 France began a campaign to alter this situation, attacking English trading posts and building forts of their own. By 1755, they had driven the English traders out of the Ohio Valley, established themselves as far east as the forks of the Ohio River, near the present Pittsburgh, Pennsylvania, and smartly rebuffed the ambitious young Colonel George Washington, who attempted to expel them from Fort Duquesne.

English attempts to respond to this bold French campaign were fatally crippled by internal division. This was starkly revealed at the Albany Congress of 1754, an attempt of the colonies to unify for military purposes and through united action to woo the all-important Iroquois out of their position of neutrality. One of the main purposes of the Congress was to demonstrate to the Iroquois that fighting resolve and cohesion prevailed in the English colonies. But while representatives of the colonies attempted to work out a plan of confederation, land agents from Connecticut and Pennsylvania were

[3]Quoted in William J. Eccles, *The Canadian Frontier, 1534–1760* (New York: Holt, Rinehart and Winston, Inc., 1969), p. 158.

deep in intrigue concerning the purchase of Iroquois lands west of the Susquehanna River. The attempt at intercolonial cooperation fell to pieces and the Iroquois left the conference convinced that the English were "like women: bare and open and without fortifications."[4]

It was decided in the capitals of Europe, not America, to force a showdown. What ensued is known as the Seven Years War or the French and Indian War. In London, two regiments under the command of General James Braddock were dispatched. In Paris, three thousand regulars were ordered to the French strongholds at Louisbourg on Cape Breton Island, guarding the St. Lawrence River, and at Quebec. The year which it took Braddock to make his way across the Atlantic and then lead his army, reinforced by American enlistees, across Virginia and into the western wilderness was the last of his life. Less than twenty miles from Fort Duquesne the French and their Indian allies ambushed the British-Americans in 1755 and Braddock's reputedly invincible army of 2,200 was routed by an attacking force one third as large. Two thirds of the English force were killed and wounded; the survivors fled, leaving artillery, horses, cattle, and supplies behind.

For the rest of the summer in 1755 the Virginia and Pennsylvania backcountry was terrorized by Indian raiders, who for years had silently nursed grudges against white land encroachers and ungenerous traders. Now was their opportunity to align themselves with the French and to even scores that went back decades. Among the first to strike at the English, Scots-Irish, and German communities were the Delawares, who a generation before had been cheated out of their tribal lands in eastern Pennsylvania. Just as they had streamed westward as refugees from colonial oppression, now they sent thousands of European refugees fleeing eastward as they burned, killed, and pillaged all along the Pennsylvania frontier. "Almost all the women & children over Sasquehannah have left their habitations, & the roads are full of starved, naked, indigent multitudes," cried one colonist.[5]

In 1756 and 1757 one French victory after another threw the English colonies into panic. The English post at Oswego, at the eastern end of Lake Ontario, fell in August 1756. Two thousand troops at Fort William Henry, at the foot of Lake George, surrendered in August 1757. So desperate was the English situation that the governor of Pennsylvania, terrified at Indian attacks that had carried within thirty miles of Philadelphia, considered allowing hostile Indians free passage through his colony if they promised to concentrate their attacks on the Virginia frontier. Other raids on the New England border, in the Mohawk Valley of New York, and along the entire frontier from New York to Georgia led to gloomy speculations in the English

---

[4]E. B. O'Callaghan, ed., *Documents Relative to the Colonial History of the State of New-York* (Albany: Weed, Parsons & Co., 1855), 6: 870.

[5]Quoted in Douglas E. Leach, *The Northern Colonial Frontier, 1607–1763* (New York: Holt, Rinehart and Winston, 1966), p. 200.

settlements that the continent would fall to the French and their Indian allies. Never was disunity within the English colonies so painfully felt. Seventy thousand French Canadians and their Indian allies had taken on a million and a half English colonists, supported by the British army, and whipped them hollow.

In these circumstances, English hopes rested on obtaining the support (or, at the very least, pledges of neutrality) from the four main Indian confederacies of the interior—the Iroquois, Cherokees, Creeks, and Choctaws. If the French drew them into their camp, even the massive reinforcements of British troops and supplies being mobilized under the direction of William Pitt might not be able to stem the Gallic tide. Perhaps at no time since the initial settlers had been obliged to rely upon the coastal Indians for food to see them through the "starving time" were the English colonists so dependent on the Indians' goodwill.

But it was not clear how Indian support or neutrality could be secured. A century of intermittent hostility and the frantic hungering after the Indians' western lands during the previous decade suggested that the allegiance of the populous interior tribes would be difficult to obtain. Edmond Atkin, Charleston Indian trader and soon to become English Superintendent of the Southern Indians, sounded a prophetic note: The Importance of Indians is now generally known and understood. A Doubt remains not, that the prosperity of our Colonies on the Continent, will stand or fall with our Interest and favour among them. While they are our Friends, they are the Cheapest and Strongest Barrier for the Protection of our Settlements; when Enemies, they are capable by ravaging in their method of War, in spite of all we can do, to render those Possessions almost useless."[6]

INDIAN STRATEGY IN THE SEVEN YEARS WAR

The case of the Iroquois is illustrative of the English vulnerability to which Atkin pointed. In negotiations with the French the English pretended that Iroquois support was a certainty and bluntly informed the governor of Canada that all members of the Iroquois tribes were indisputably subjects of the King of England.[7] But the English knew that the allegiance of the Iroquois and their dependents, the eastern Delawares, could be secured in only two ways: through purchase or through a demonstration of power so great that the Iroquois would be convinced that the English would prevail with or without their support and would accordingly find it politic to choose the winning side at the outset. The first stratagem failed in 1754 when representatives of the Six Nations left the Albany Congress with thirty

[6]Wilbur R. Jacobs, ed., *Indians of the Southern Colonial Frontier; The Edmond Atkin Report and Plan of 1755* (Columbia: University of South Carolina Press, 1954), pp. 3–4.

[7]Governor Clinton to Governor of Canada, Oct. 10, 1748, in O'Callaghan, ed., *Documents Relating to Hist. of New-York*, 6: 492.

wagonloads of gifts but gave in return only tantalizing half-promises of support against the French, who continued to score major victories in the next three years. Only when paid as mercenaries, such as in 1757 when about five hundred Mohawks collected £33,602 for services rendered to the English forces in New York, would the Iroquois support the Anglo-Americans.[8]

The English colonists made further attempts during the next two years to get the Iroquois to subdue the attacking Delawares, who had driven the settlement line in Pennsylvania back to the eastern counties. Pennsylvania itself was badly divided between pacifistic Quakers, who believed that Scots-Irish frontiersmen were only reaping what they had sowed through years of abusing and defrauding Indians, and militant Anglicans and Presbyterians, who wanted taxes passed for a stern counteroffensive against the attackers. "The Indians learned our Weakness, by being informed of our Divisions," wrote the colony's official interpreter in 1757 after a conference convened for the purpose of buying off the Delawares' wrath.[9]

Not until October 1758 could the English get a promise from the Iroquois to halt the Delaware attacks on the Pennsylvania settlements. Agreement was reached at Easton, Pennsylvania, where the Indians left the conference with a wagon train of "gifts." It is easy to suppose that these Indian concessions were simply a response to white stimuli. From the Indian point of view, however, the Easton Treaty had a different meaning. No military commitment was made to the English. The Iroquois, in exchange for their pledge of neutrality and their assurance that the hostile Delawares would be quieted, resecured a vast tract of land west of the Susquehanna River that they had ceded to Pennsylvania four years before at the Albany Congress. This restored their territorial security west of the Alleghenies.

Except for the halfhearted support of the Mohawks, the easternmost of the Six Nations, the Iroquois either maintained their neutrality or, as in the case of the Senecas, fought with the French in the campaigns of 1757 and 1758. As for the Mohawks, their allegiance to the English can be explained by their proximity to the English trading center at Albany, by the huge amounts they were paid for their services, and by the fact that William Johnson, appointed British Superintendent of the Northern Indians, had married a Mohawk woman and lived among them for years. As all the English who attempted to woo the Iroquois in the dark years from 1754 to 1758 found out, the Six Nations steadfastly pursued their traditional policy of disengagement from European wars.

In 1759, however, the Iroquois reversed their position. Feelers by Johnson in February led him to report optimistically that if the English mounted an expedition against the French stronghold at Fort Niagara "or elsewhere,

[8]Wilbur R. Jacobs, *Diplomacy and Indian Gifts: Anglo-French Rivalry Along the Ohio and Northwest Frontiers, 1748–1763* (Stanford: Stanford University Press, 1950), p. 178.

[9]Lawrence H. Gipson, *The British Empire Before the American Revolution*, 14 vols. (New York: Alfred A. Knopf, 1936–69), 7:58.

thro' the Country of the Six Nations, I shou'd be able to prevail upon the greater Part if not the whole of them, to join His Majesty's Arms."[10] It was not Johnson who was able to "prevail," however, but the Iroquois, who in their own councils assessed the Anglo-French military situation and then reformulated their own polity. After four years of French victories the tide had turned in the British favor in July 1758 when Louisbourg and Fort Frontenac, the strategic centers of French power at opposite ends of the St. Lawrence, fell before Anglo-American assaults. In November 1758 the French abandoned Fort Duquesne at the forks of the Ohio River. By the end of the year the upper Ohio Valley was in English hands for the first time in four years. William Pitt had mobilized the fighting power of the English nation, putting more men in the field than existed in all of New France, and the colonists had put aside their intramural squabbling long enough to stem the French tide.

These English victories helped to move the Iroquois away from their long-held position of neutrality. Another incentive to join cause with the English was the capture of French ships bringing trade goods to Montreal, a turn of fortune that vastly improved the English position in wooing the Six Nations. In April 1759, the Iroquois chiefs came to the Mohawk town of Canajoharie and promised eight hundred warriors for an attack on Fort Niagara, the strategic French fur trading depot on Lake Ontario. The Iroquois had calculated correctly: the French were going down to defeat in North America.

Throughout the war the Six Nations were able to assess accurately the shifting military balance between the rival European powers and formulate their own policy accordingly. Though they wrote no field memoranda and moved no troops or supplies through the field, their communication network extended across the entire region in which the French and English were fighting. In their councils they demonstrated a keen understanding of when the strategic balance was tipping in the British direction. Most histories of the Seven Years War applaud William Johnson's skill in "winning over" the Iroquois and "persuading" them to join the English side. But the evidence indicates that the Iroquois continually reassessed their own position and calculated how their self-interest could best be served. Despite English blandishments, presents, and even the return of previously acquired territory, the Iroquois refused to join the English through the first four years of war or even to allow Anglo-American passage through their territory. But when the military superiority of the English began to show itself in 1759, the Iroquois quickly adjusted their policy of neutrality and joined in reaping the benefits of victory. If their policy of *realpolitik* failed at all, it was in not perceiving that the maintenance of French power in North America was essential to their long-range interests.

The Cherokees also played power politics during the Seven Years War

[10]*Ibid.*, p. 342.

but less successfully than the Iroquois. In 1753–1754 the governor of Virginia worked hard to gain Cherokee support for Washington's attempt to dislodge the French at the forks of the Ohio, believing that only with Indian support could the larger French forces be overcome. The Cherokee chiefs responded by promising the Virginians a thousand warriors; but at the same time they pressed South Carolina for better trading prices and consulted with the French at Fort Toulouse on the Alabama River. They expressed interest in a revival of the old Virginia-Cherokee trade, which in the past had been employed by the Cherokees to remind the Carolinians that their trade was desirable but not irreplaceable. In the end their promise to send warriors to join Washington on his foray into the wilderness disappeared like smoke.

In 1755, when the Virginians came again to seek support for Braddock's campaign, the Cherokees used promises of hundreds of warriors in order to gain a trade with Virginia on more favorable terms than the Carolinians offered. They were well aware that South Carolina and Virginia were close to blows in their struggle for control of the Cherokee trade, and they used this intercolonial feud to their own advantage. When Braddock suffered his disastrous defeat, he had only eight Indians with his army.

In May 1755 South Carolina agents met the Cherokee headmen deep in the backcountry for treaty making. When the Cherokees agreed to recognize the English king as their sovereign and to cede some of their lands to the Crown, the Carolinians believed they had accomplished a major breakthrough in luring the Indians out of their neutrality. In exchange they pledged to supply more trade goods at lower prices and to build a fort in Cherokee country that would offer protection against French and Creek enemies.

How badly the English could misapprehend Indian uses of diplomacy was clearly revealed in the next five years. Although the governor of South Carolina boasted that the treaty of 1755 added "near 10,000 people to his Majesty's subjects and above 40,000,000 acres to his territories," the Cherokees regarded themselves as subject to British authority only so long as it served mutually satisfactory goals.[11] About 250 Cherokees fought with the Virginia militia on the western frontier in 1757, but they agreed to serve not as allies but as mercenaries. When they were not paid according to agreement, they promptly plundered Virginia frontier settlements in order to collect by force what the white government failed to give them. The process was repeated in the next year, but this time Virginia frontiersmen began ambushing Cherokees who were returning from battle and living off the land as they made their way home. Thirty Cherokees lost their lives at the hands of their allies in 1758. Spurring the Indian-hating Virginians was the colony's £50 scalp bounty, meant to apply to enemy Indians such as the Shawnees.

[11]Quoted in David H. Corkran, *The Cherokee Frontier: Conflict and Survival, 1740–1762* (Norman: University of Oklahoma Press, 1962), p. 61.

To avaricious Virginians scalps were scalps, whether Cherokee or Shawnee. Each earned its bearer the equivalent of a year's income as a frontier farmer.

Nothing more than a few such incidents were required to fan into a roaring blaze the anti-English embers that had been kept alive in the Cherokee towns by the pro-French factions. Messengers went out to the Creeks and Chickasaws and by the winter of 1758–1759 talk of an Indian uprising had spread across the southern frontier. English agents countered with the warning that an English blockade of French shipping in North America would make it impossible for the Indians to obtain guns, ammunition, and even normal trade goods from the French.

Nonetheless, backcountry skirmishing from Virginia to South Carolina could not be contained, and so the Southern colonies turned the Seven Years War into a war with the Cherokees. With 1,700 men Governor Lyttelton of South Carolina invaded Cherokee territory. The peace treaty that he extracted from the Cherokees blamed the Indians for all that had happened. The Cherokee chiefs signed it under duress, but it served only to inflame them more.

The war erupted again in 1760, and this time the Cherokees were far more united in opposition to the English. The new governor of South Carolina, William Bull, soon recognized that the united Cherokees were more than a match for the largest force of militiamen he could put in the field. Bowing to circumstances, he agreed to a treaty which made concessions to the Cherokees on "terms that perhaps may not be thought suitable, according to the Rules of Honour, observed among Europeans," as the governor delicately put it.[12] The arrival of 1,300 crack troops under Sir Jeffrey Amherst and the subsequent expedition against the Cherokees proved again the difficulties of fighting Indians in their own territory. Bogging down in the hilly terrain, ambushed at every turn, the expedition "accomplished little, except possibly to boost Cherokee morale."[13] Badly mauled, the British force returned to Charleston. Shortly thereafter the main English garrison in Cherokee country surrendered to a Cherokee siege. But 1,800 British regulars, joined by 700 provincial militiamen, tried again in the summer of 1761, and this time, by burning Cherokee villages and crops, they succeeded. With supplies from the French virtually cut off, the Cherokees submitted to a peace treaty that acknowledged English sovereignty and established the eastern boundary of the Cherokee territory.

Throughout the Rebellion of 1759–1761, the Cherokees made attempts to enlist the support of the Creeks. Two generations before, the refusal of the Cherokees to join the Creeks in the Yamasee War against the Carolinians had deprived the Creeks of their victory. Now the Creek decision to remain neutral cost the Cherokees decisively. Left to fight the English themselves,

[12]Quoted in M. Eugene Sirmans, *Colonial South Carolina; A Political History* (Chapel Hill: University of North Carolina Press, 1966), p. 335.

[13]*Ibid.*, p. 336.

the Cherokees struggled against food shortages, lack of ammunition, and a smallpox epidemic. The only trade goods reaching them from the French, ironically, were provided by New England ship captains, who brought contraband supplies to the French forts on the Gulf of Mexico. The desperate shortage of trade goods forced the Cherokees back to ancient customs—fashioning clothes from deer and bear skins and tipping their arrows with bone points instead of trader's brass. Cut off from an alternate supply of trade goods and unable to organize a pan-Indian offensive, they joined the French as losers in the Seven Years War.

Whereas the Iroquois made common cause with the English once French weaknesses were evident and the Cherokees alternately allied with and fought against the English during the Seven Years War, the Creeks held fast to the policy of neutrality that had been the hallmark of their diplomacy since the Yamasee War. Their major concerns were trade and the maintenance of political sovereignty. Throughout the 1750s and early 1760s the Creeks ranged from the Cherokee country to the French trading posts at Fort Toulouse and Mobile, accepting presents from both English and French and driving hard bargains for more favorable terms in the deerskin trade. Pro-French, pro-English, and neutralist factions argued bitterly in the Creek towns. But by 1757, British naval superiority had strangled French shipping. This undermined the arguments of the Creek headmen who were advocating a pan-Indian, anti-English rebellion of Shawnees, Cherokees, Creeks, Chickasaws, and Catawbas. The English solidified their position with the Creeks in 1758 and 1759 by showering them with presents. Sensitive to the possibility that the Cherokee insurgency might spread, Governor Ellis of Georgia spent the spring of 1760 trying to "set every Person of Influence upon endeavouring to create a Rupture between those two Nations"—the Creeks and Cherokees.[14]

While refusing to join the Cherokees, the Creeks used the rebellion of their neighbors for their own benefit. When English trade goods became scarce or when prices rose, they dropped the word to English traders that the arguments of the Cherokees and French had taken on a new persuasiveness. Actually the outbreak of the Cherokee rebellion had badly divided the Creeks. The pro-French faction continued to urge the Cherokees on to greater efforts against the English and even murdered eleven English settlers in an attempt to precipitate an English attack which would galvanize the Creek nation behind the Cherokees. The Carolina and Georgia governments failed to rise to the bait, however. The decision not to respond to the murder of the traders or even to demand that the Creeks put the murderers to death was dramatic evidence of the precarious position of the Southern colonists and their vital need to keep the Creeks neutral. Had the balance of

---

[14]Quoted in W. W. Abbot, *The Royal Governors of Georgia, 1754–1775* (Chapel Hill: University of North Carolina Press, 1959), p. 80.

power lay with the English, strenuous measures would have been taken to make the Creeks accountable for such killings.

In spite of Cherokee victories in 1760 and in spite of their desire to check English expansionism, the Creek strategic options were crucially limited by the inability of the French to supply an alternate flow of vital weapons and trade goods. At a grand meeting of the French, Cherokees, and Creeks at Fort Toulouse in March 1761 it became clear that the French had no munitions, presents, or trade goods to back up their talk of expelling the English from the continent. English victories in the North had nearly sealed the fate of the French on the continent. For a half century the Creeks had maintained their neutrality and kept open a profitable trade with both the French and English. But in the process they had become dependent on the European trade connection, which was shortly to be monopolized by the English.

Anglo-American victories in the North began in 1759 with the capture of Fort Niagara, continued with Wolfe's dramatic victory at Quebec, and culminated in the following year with the fall of Montreal. This marked the end of hostilities in North America. Almost two centuries of French presence on the continent was coming to an end.

For the Indian nations which had demonstrated such independence of action and impressive power during the Seven Years War the Peace of Paris was a severe blow. Unlike the coastal tribes, whose numbers and autonomy had ebbed through contact with European colonizers, the interior tribes had grown stronger, more militarily awesome, and more technologically developed as a result of their political and economic connections with the English, French, and Spanish. Although they had become dependent on the European trade, they had been able to turn this dependency to their own advantage so long as more than one source of trade goods existed. They had mastered the European style of diplomatic intrigue, used it to serve their own self-interests, and proved their ability to evade or defeat numerically superior European forces.

But while they played a powerful role on land, the Indian nations possessed not a shred of power to control the ocean separating Europe and North America or the trade goods that flowed across it. In the end it was this factor that undermined their strength. Control of the Atlantic by the British navy dealt a near-fatal blow to the playoff system, for the French in America without trade goods were hardly better than no French at all. The inability to obtain French trade goods diminished Native Americans' room for maneuver and rendered futile the nascent pan-Indian movements against the English which potentially extended from Seneca country on the shores of the eastern Great Lakes to Yamasee territory in Florida and included the Miamis, Shawnees, Delawares, Cherokees, Catawbas, Creeks, Choctaws, and Chickasaws, to name only the larger tribes. A mere fraction of these peoples had driven back the Anglo-American frontier to within one hundred miles of the coast in the early stages of the Seven Years War. Had they been unified under French arms and supplies, the designs of the French imperialists to rule the continent might have materialized.

By the terms of the Peace of Paris, signed by England, France, and Spain in 1763, Canada and all of North America east of the Mississippi River was recognized as English territory. France ceded the territory west of the Mississippi to Spain. Spain ceded Florida to England. From that year onward English sway in the eastern half of North America was unchallenged in the courts of Europe. No longer could the Creeks, Cherokees, or Iroquois employ the playoff system to gain advantages in trade, since only one source of trade goods remained. Also, hostilities subsided between the colonies, which Indian groups had often exploited, for the wartime effort had unified the thirteen English provinces to an unprecedented degree. Two centuries of European rivalry for possession and control of eastern North America had come to a dramatically swift end. To this reality Iroquois, Cherokees, Creeks, and other interior tribes were now forced to adjust.

INDIAN-WHITE RELATIONS AFTER 1763

At the conclusion of seven years of international war the English government attempted to coordinate a continental Indian policy in North America where for a century and a half each colony had been left to conduct its own Indian affairs. Stung by the fact that most of the North American tribes had given their allegiance to the French in the Seven Years War, the English government launched a new policy intended to separate Native Americans and colonizers, while guaranteeing the integrity of Indian territory. "It is just and reasonable, and essential to our Interest, and the Security of our Colonies," stated the King's proclamation in 1763, "that the several Nations or tribes of Indians with whom We are connected, and who live under our Protection, should not be molested or disturbed in the Possession of such Parts of our Dominions and Territories as, not having been ceded to or purchased by Us, are reserved to them, or any of them, as their Hunting Grounds."[15]

By the terms of the Proclamation of 1763, a racial boundary was created from Maine to Georgia, roughly following the crestline of the Appalachian Mountains. The various colonial governors were charged with forbidding "for the present and until our further Pleasure be known" any surveys or land grants beyond the Appalachian watershed. "All the Lands and Territories lying to the Westward of the Sources of the Rivers which fall into the Sea from the West and North West" were specifically reserved for Indian na-

[15]Quoted in Francis Paul Prucha, *American Indian Policy in the Formative Years; The Indian Trade and Intercourse Acts, 1790–1834* (Lincoln: University of Nebraska Press, 1970 rpr.), p. 5.

tions. All white settlers already beyond the Appalachian divide were charged to withdraw east of the line.

The Proclamation of 1763 is one of the most poignant documents in American history. Historians who subscribe to the "frontier thesis" of Frederick Jackson Turner have argued that this attempt to dam up the energy of restless westward-looking Americans alienated the colonists and provided a major impetus for throwing off the restraining yoke of the mother country. Other historians, while agreeing that the proclamation was an irritant that contributed to revolutionary sentiment, point out that those most alienated by it were the large land speculators of the Eastern seaboard, who boiled at seeing such a fabulous source of profit put beyond their grasp. What has rarely been noted is that for several years before the bureaucrats in London drew the 1763 boundary the Indian tribes of the interior, from the Senecas, Ottawas, Illinois, Miamis, and Sioux of the North to the Cherokees, Creeks, and Choctaws of the South, had themselves been attempting to fix a territorial line that would limit white expansion. Their attempts were inspired by their certainty that, contrary to the language of the Proclamation of 1763, they did not live under English "protection" but in fact could protect their own interests and ensure their survival only by throwing off English "protection" and fighting to preserve their land.

Though the Indian tribes of the interior had no way of counting the population increase in the Thirteen Colonies, they were keenly aware that settlers in unprecedented numbers were moving into their tribal hunting grounds almost on the heels of the Anglo-American armies that had pushed the French out of the Ohio Valley beginning in 1759. The population rise between 1750 and 1765, in fact, equaled that which occurred during the entire first half of the eighteenth century and more than half of the increase was concentrated in the colonies of New York, Pennsylvania, and Virginia. It was through the western parts of these colonies that land-hungry speculators and immigrants began pouring as soon as the French were expelled. Both before and after the Proclamation Line of 1763 had been set, land poachers were staking out claims to lands to which the English, by the terms of their own treaties with Indian tribes, had no claim. Creek lands, for example, were guaranteed by a treaty signed in 1733, and the limits of white settlement in Cherokee territory had been set at the end of the Cherokee War in 1761 in a treaty with the government of Virginia. But neither of these treaties stopped white land speculators and settlers, who swarmed into Indian territory, secure in the knowledge that their provincial governments had neither the desire nor the power to do much about it.

Even without the possibility of French aid the Indian response was to meet force with force. The Southern frontier was marked with bloody clashes in the early 1760s, as Indians and settlers fought over Indian lands which the provincial governments had guaranteed to the tribes. Some Indian leaders attempted to form another pan-Indian defensive league, even at the risk that the English would cut off their supply of trade goods. The colonists did their best at a series of conferences to wheedle land cessions from the Creeks and Cherokees, while privately they fanned enmity between the major tribes. It was obvious from the determination of the Southern tribes to resist English encroachments that the defeat of the Cherokees in 1761 "had not dampened the martial ardor of the southern Indians."[16] Even with the French removed from the continent, their power was still considerable. This was vividly indicated in 1763 by the refusal of the Creeks to surrender their tribesmen who had murdered fourteen white land poachers and by the decision of the English, who tried unsuccessfully to obtain the support of the Cherokees and Choctaws for a war against the Creeks, to let the murders go unavenged. The Creeks, on the other hand, were unable to forge a Southern Indian alliance in 1763 when such a unified Indian movement might have joined a major Indian uprising in the Northwest to give the native peoples their best advantage of the eighteenth century.

If the Indian reaction to the Anglo-American victory over France was not one of cowed submission in the South, it was even more aggressive in the North. In June 1761 the Senecas, always the most pro-French of the Six Nations, carried a red wampum belt (signifying an intention to go to war) to Detroit where the British army was garrisoned among the various tribes that had formally fought with the French—the Delawares, Shawnees, Ottawas, Hurons, Chippewas, and Potawatomies. The Senecas were taking the lead in resisting the new English Indian policy, which curtailed trade, required the Indians to bring their furs to the British forts, ended the system of annual "presents," prohibited trade in rum, and in general instituted trading terms far less satisfactory to the Indians than those existing before the war. The Senecas had an additional incentive for taking to the warpath. General Amherst, the commander-in-chief of the Anglo-American forces during the Seven Years War, had seen fit to reward some of his officers with Seneca lands near Niagara in violation of a treaty between the Iroquois and the New York government. Such generosity at the expense of the Senecas was not lightly regarded in the Indian towns.

To the northern tribes the Senecas proposed a coordinated attack on all the English outposts which ranged along the Great Lakes and as far south as Pittsburgh. Acting together, they would drive the English out of the Ohio Valley, out of Iroquois country, and back across the mountains to the piedmont. Whether this "nativistic" plan included a resolve to give up the English trade altogether is not certain, although it is possible that after many years of trade difficulties they considered no trade at all preferable to a restricted trade at pinched prices. Although the western tribes rejected the Seneca plan after long discussion, they were far from pleased by what they

[16]John R. Alden, *John Stuart and the Southern Colonial Frontier: A Study of Indian Relations, War, Trade, and Land Problems in the Southern Wilderness, 1754–1775* (Ann Arbor: University of Michigan Press, 1944), p. 177.

heard from Sir William Johnson, the Northern Indian superintendent, when he arrived at Detroit three months later. Johnson claimed he came to brighten "the chain of friendship," and spoke glowingly of the King's concern for the welfare "of all his subjects." But he had nothing to promise in regard to the high price of trade goods, the unavailability of rum, the stoppage of annual presents, and the inadequate supplies of ammunition that were now allotted to the tribes. These, he said, were matters of official policy beyond his control.

Although Johnson reported optimistically to General Amherst at the conclusion of the conference, averring that he left Detroit with matters "settled on so stable a foundation there that unless greatly irritated thereto, they will never break the peace," the fact was that the Indians, for all their show of amity, were deeply embittered.[17] The most experienced English trader in the Ohio Valley, George Croghan, accurately perceived the situation. The Indians "had great expectations of being very generally supplied by us, and from their poverty and mercenary disposition they can't bear such a disappointment. Undoubtedly the general [Amherst] has his own reason for not allowing any present or ammunition to be given them, and I wish it may have its desired effect, but I take this opportunity to acquaint you that I dread the event as I know Indians can't long persevere. . . . Their success at the beginning of this war on our frontiers is too recent in their memory to suffer them to consider their present inability to make war with us, and if the Senecas, Delawares and Shawnees should break with us, it will end in a general war with all western nations. . . ."[18]

Adding to the inflammatory state of affairs were the preachings of a charismatic Delaware prophet named Neolin. At the moment when the English were cutting off trade goods to which the Indians had become accustomed, Neolin began an odyssey through the Indian territories, preaching that Native Americans must return to "their original state that they were in before the white people found out their country" or face slow extinction at the hands of the swarming settlers crossing the mountains. Several traders described in detail the renaissance of traditional Indian culture that the Delaware Prophet preached. Neolin's vision, which he related had been conveyed to him in dreams by the Master of Life, was that the Indians' salvation lay not in adopting Christianity and European culture but in returning to ancient customs. Rum must be forsworn. The material objects of white culture must be abandoned. Population increase must be curbed through abstinence so that the difficult return to the old ways could be accomplished.

Neolin's message resonated with tremendous force not only in Delaware country but also among other western Indian nations. It called not only for

[17]Quoted in Howard H. Peckham, *Pontiac and the Indian Uprising* (Chicago: University of Chicago Press, 1961), p. 86.

[18]*Ibid.*, pp. 97–98.

cultural renaissance but also for revolutionary resistance. "Wherefore do you suffer the whites to dwell upon your lands?" he asked. "Drive them away; wage war against them. I love them not. They know me not. They are my enemies, they are your brothers' enemies. Send them back to the lands I have made for them. Let them remain there."[19] Throughout 1762 Neolin's admonitions were passed by word of mouth and on inscribed deerskin parchment from one Indian settlement to another.

Neolin's formula for cultural revitalization was not a complete return to the traditional elements of Indian culture. Instead, it represented a blend of native and European elements. Some of the old customs, such as war rituals and polygamy, were not to be revived and some Christian concepts, such as written prayers and a written "Bible" or "Great Book," were to be retained. But Neolin's appeal for the de-Europeanization of Indian culture demonstrated how autonomously and creatively the western tribes could respond to the new situation that confronted them after the defeat of the French. His disciples carried his message throughout the western territories; large numbers of Indians, acting on his advice to boycott European trade goods, hunted only to supply their own needs; and, most spectacularly, an Ottawa leader named Pontiac became a convert to Neolin's doctrine and made it the spiritual underpinning of the uprising he led against the English beginning in May 1763.[20]

According to a French account, Pontiac inspired his warriors with a speech that reflected Neolin's nativism. "It is important for us, my brothers," he exhorted, "that we exterminate from our lands this nation which seeks only to destroy us."[21] Under this banner Pontiac led an assault on Fort Detroit, the strongest of the British garrisons in the Great Lakes region. While the Ottawas lay siege to the fort, other tribes rubbed out the British outposts in the western Great Lakes region and as far east as Pittsburgh. In rapid succession the forts at Michilimachinac, St. Joseph, Sandusky, Presqu' Isle, Le Boeuf, and Venango fell as Shawnees, Delawares, Chippewas, Hurons, Miamis, Potawatomis, and Senecas joined the fray. But the Indians were unable to overwhelm the three major British forts at Detroit, Niagara, and Pittsburgh. The war dragged on through the summer. When news of it reached London, the government hurriedly issued the Proclamation Act. Military reinforcements were sent from the East and by summer's end a standoff had been reached. Pontiac went on fighting sporadically for another two years, and the English colonies hummed with rumors that he was conspiring with Creek and Choctaw chiefs to organize a grand alliance of eighteen Indian nations. But the tribes lacked vital supplies of powder, shot, and guns; in the end they were forced to sue for peace. Without the

---

[19]Anthony F. C. Wallace, *The Death and Rebirth of the Seneca* (New York: Alfred A. Knopf, Inc., 1970), p. 118.

[20]*Ibid.*, pp. 120–21.

[21]Quoted in Peckham, *Pontiac and the Indian Uprising*, p. 119.

presence in North America of another European power they could not overcome their supply problems.

Though Pontiac's resistance movement collapsed, the major interior tribes continued to preserve their political autonomy in the decade prior to the outbreak of the American Revolution. "The Six Nations, Western Indians, etc.," wrote William Johnson to London in 1764, "having never been conquered, either by the English or French, nor subject to the[ir] Laws, consider themselves as a free people."[22] But the preservation of political autonomy could not stem the tide of frontier land speculators and farmers. By itself this demographic pressure was enough to overcome all the efforts of the English government to fashion an Indian policy based on equitable trade relations and respect for land boundaries.

Two factors determined the fate of the trans-Appalachian Indian territories after 1763. First, the English government, staggering under an immense debt accumulated in fighting the Seven Years War, was unwilling to commit resources for maintaining garrisons in the interior to enforce the provisions of the Proclamation Act of 1763. Economizing in colonial government took precedence over the protection of Indian land. Consequently, the interior garrisons were abandoned after Pontiac's Revolt and the plan to coordinate and control the Indian trade and Indian affairs of the various colonies was scrapped. Reliance was placed on drawing lines on maps—lines that theoretically separated Indians and colonizers—and on issuing stern commands to royal governors to uphold what was printed on the maps.

The second controlling factor in the trans-Appalachian West was that English officials had hardly a shred of power to enforce regulations in the interior, particularly after 1764 when a whole cluster of issues concerned with imperial authority in the colonies threw the colonists into a quasi-revolutionary state. The Proclamation Line of 1763 existed only on paper, and nobody, neither colonists nor Indians, took it seriously. Colonial governors, often closely connected with land speculators, bombarded colonial administrators in London with reasons why exceptions should be made to the Proclamation Act. These included scores of false assertions that interior tribes had abandoned their claims to various parcels of land west of the Appalachians. When such requests were denied, the governors turned their heads and permitted land grants, surveys, and private purchases of land from Indian tribes such as the Creeks and Cherokees, who did not recognize the right of the English government to demarcate boundaries. When settlers moved onto land still claimed by the Indians, they were usually left to fight it out among themselves.

Colonial governors and officials spent most of their energy not in enforcing the Proclamation Act but assisting expansionist-minded speculators and settlers through a policy of promoting and perpetuating intertribal Indian hostility. The main points of English Indian policy—prevention of encroach-

[22]Quoted in Prucha, *American Indian Policy*, p. 19.

ment on Indian lands and equity in the Indian trade—were reduced to a shambles in the decade before the Revolution. Few colonists on the frontier abstained from exploiting the dynamic combination of a ballooning population and vast tracts of Western land occupied only by Indians bereft of a European ally and an alternate supply of trade goods. Nor could anybody in England discover a means of compelling the Americans in the West to obey Crown commands at a time when even along the Atlantic seaboard the King's authority was being challenged.

For the interior tribes, the beneficiaries of an unenforceable English policy designed to guarantee them the land between the Appalachians and the Mississippi, the alternatives were limited after Pontiac's Revolt. They could seek other Indian allies in another attempt to forge a pan-Indian uprising, as did one faction of the Creeks led by The Mortar, who had been staunchly anti-English for decades. They could seek private revenge for white depredations and land grabbing, as did Logan, a displaced Cayuga living on the Virginia frontier, whose family had been wiped out by outlaw frontiersmen and who led a party of warriors in retaliatory raids that set off the brief but bloody Lord Dunmore's War in 1774. They could continue to seek French support in New Orleans while hoping for a French renaissance on the continent, as did the Choctaws. Or they could bow to the white tidal wave and sell off their land, tract by tract at the best price possible, to private individuals and land companies who were confident that they could safely ignore both the Proclamation of 1763 and colonial statutes forbidding such purchases.

THE COLONIZERS' SOCIETY AFTER 1763

Although the Seven Years War is primarily remembered as the climactic military struggle in which Anglo-American arms finally overcame the hated French in North America, it was also a war with social and political effects of the utmost importance in white communities. It was a war that convinced the American colonies of their growing strength and maturity, yet ironically left them weakened in manpower and debt-ridden at its end. It brought the greatest infusion of English capital in their history, yet rendered them unusually sensitive to the disadvantages of the British mercantile connection. It drove forward the commercialization of life, especially in the seaport towns, yet exposed in stark detail the social costs of the transition to the market economy.

War contracts and the general quickening of the economy brought prosperity to most of colonial America during the war years. But after the series of triumphant victories over the French in 1759 and 1760 the war theatre moved to the Caribbean, and a commercial downturn struck hard. Especially along the seaboard, unemployment, high prices, and a great rise in war-widowed families caused a crumbling of economic security. The greatest hardships fell upon the laboring classes, which included many artisans who occupied positions on the middle rungs of the social ladder. It was they who had the smallest savings and the thinnest margin between profit and loss and who devoted the largest proportion of their budgets to food, rent, clothing,

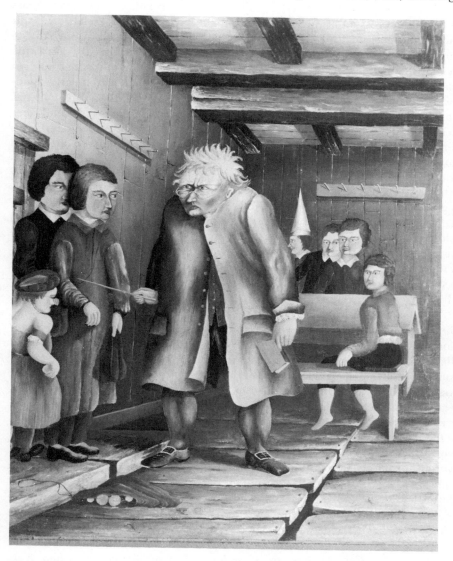

This eighteenth-century schoolmaster is iconographical testimony that fear and force were two key elements in European notions of child rearing and early education. (Courtesy of the Frick Art Reference Library.)

and fuel—expenses that could be little trimmed when times worsened. The war had created a class of wealthy merchants, but it had also left many communities strewn with crippled, widowed, and destitute persons. Pauperism spread in all the colonial cities and authorities struggled for ways of providing for the poor.

If all colonists had suffered equally in the aftermath of the Seven Years War, the depression of the early 1760s might have unified colonial society. It might have served to warn Americans that while growing more powerful in numbers, they were becoming less powerful in their ability to control the violent fluctuations in the Atlantic economy. This perception of the problem as externally caused did dominate thinking among merchants, large landowners, lawyers, and government officials. The drastic overhaul of imperial policy which Parliament instituted at the end of the war gave much credence to this point of view. It was apparent that an invigorated customs service, cracking down on colonial smugglers, dried up profits on the illegal importing of French tea and sugar. Clearly, the establishment of vice-admiralty courts placed violators of the Navigation Acts beyond the forgiving attitudes of local juries. It was plain that the Currency Act of 1764, restricting issuance of paper money in New York and Pennsylvania, put a further damp on trade already depressed. And the Stamp Act of 1765 obviously laid additional levies on communities still trying to pay off a heavy war debt. For many Americans the post-1763 parliamentary legislation and the contractionary actions of their British creditors were signals that a maturing American people must now expect their necks to be pinned to the ground by the paw of an insensitive British lion.

This feeling of alienation from the mother country was shared by many in the lower levels of the white communities. But interwoven with this perception was another strand of thought. War, it was understood, had required financial sacrifice from everyone in the form of higher taxes. Furthermore, war had spilt much blood, primarily the blood of the lower classes. That too was the usual way of things. But to many it was deeply disturbing that eight years of conflict had left many communities with social pyramids that had greatly broadened bases, swarming with the poor, and lofty pinnacles where a few men stood high above their neighbors. This social transformation, which had occurred most dramatically in the cities, was apparent to all who witnessed the urban mansions of the merchants rise in the 1760s at the same time that large almshouses were under construction to house the multiplying destitute. "Some individuals," charged a New Yorker in 1765, "by the Smiles of Providence, or some other Means, are enabled to roll in their four wheel'd Carriages, and can support the expense of good Houses, rich Furniture, and Luxurious Living. But is it equitable that 99, rather 999, should suffer for the Extravagance or Grandeur of one? Especially when it is considered that Men frequently owe their Wealth to the impoverishment of their Neighbors?"[23] This was the language of emerging class tension, bred

[23]*New-York Gazette*, July 11, 1765.

Boston in 1764 looks prosperous, but the city had just endured a devastating fire and was in the throes of economic depression. (Courtesy Bostonian Society, Old State House.)

out of ancient feelings of self-worth by those who labored with their hands, nurtured by periodic adversity, and extended and clarified by the depressing aftermath of the Seven Years War.

For many colonists who struggled for security in the aftermath of the Seven Years War a move to new lands on the frontier seemed a solution to their problems. By itself, the population buildup was a powerful incentive for such a move and the attraction of the frontier was increased by depressed conditions in many coastal communities. For those who exercised this western option the overall result was an increase in tension between themselves and the Native Americans into whose lands they pushed. For those who remained behind, economic problems had to be worked out within the boundaries of their own community or within communities to which they migrated in search of opportunity. Thus it was that the depression that enveloped coastal communities beginning in 1760 was accompanied by political turmoil.

It was not political power itself that those at the lower levels of these communities groped for after the Seven Years War but an equitable system in which they could pursue their modest goals. When their economic security was threatened, they responded by attempting to influence, not dominate politics and to redress grievances rather than dismantle the system of upper-class domination of politics inherited from their fathers. Yet they began to make excursions into "radical" politics in order either to conserve the corporate community of the past or to prize open the doors of opportunity in the new entrepreneurial age. Such forays into political activism, first nurtured during the Great Awakening, had a cumulative effect. A sense of their own power grew as their trust in those above them diminished and as their own experience expanded in making decisions, exercising leadership roles, and refuting those who were supposed to be wiser because they were wealthier. Hence factional politics intensified in the late colonial period. As never before, members of the lower ranks began to act for and of themselves, propelling forward their own leaders, making their muscle felt, and wreaking bitter violence, as occurred in the Stamp Act riots of 1765, against those they construed as their enemies. In this sense the Seven Years War that gave the Anglo-Americans supremacy in North America, the Seven Years War that placed the interior Indian tribes in an increasingly untenable position, was also the Seven Years War that initiated the rupture between colonists and mother country and led to political divisiveness within the colonizers' communities.

ABOLITIONISM

For Afro-Americans the period following the Seven Years War was one of both hope and despair. In the Northern colonies the banner of abolitionism was being raised sufficiently high to make the question of slavery a public issue for the first time since Africans had arrived in Jamestown in 1619. Quaker humanitarians such as John Woolman and Anthony Benezet led the way and were joined by a score of New England ministers, black spokesmen, and emerging revolutionary radicals. All of them argued that slavery was immoral and contradicted the principles of liberty and opportunity that demarcated the American experience from that of postfeudal Europe.

In developing a rationale for revolution in the decade after the Seven Years War and in mounting propaganda attacks on England, colonial leaders found themselves asking questions not only about the nature of English authority and its legitimate limits in the colonies, but also about the nature of the colonial society they had built. The revolutionary arguments about the natural rights of man, the consent of the governed, the nature of tyranny, and the naturalness of equality contained intellectual dynamite. These stirring phrases led toward regions where even the most radical patriot leaders had not intended to go. They were primarily concerned with the threatening actions of Parliament and the King's ministers. But when they spoke of inalienable rights or the dignity of all men or abuses of power they unconsciously pointed a finger at themselves. The more they used catchwords like "slavery" and "tyranny" to describe English imperial reforms, the more difficult it became to ignore domestic slavery, which by the 1760s embraced about 20 percent of the population in the colonies.

Men on both sides of the Atlantic and on both sides of the Anglo-American argument pointed out the contradiction. How could Americans treat Negroes "as a better kind of Cattle . . . while they are bawling about the Rights of human Nature?" asked one English official.[24] An American

[24]Quoted in Jordan, *White Over Black: American Attitudes Toward the Negro, 1550–1812* (Chapel Hill: University of North Carolina Press, 1968), p. 291.

patriot chided his countrymen: "Blush ye pretended votaries for freedom! ye trifling patriots! who are making a vain parade of being advocates for the liberties of mankind, who are thus making a mockery of your profession by trampling on the sacred natural rights and privileges of Africans; for while you are fasting, praying, nonimporting, nonexporting, remonstrating, resolving, and pleading for a restoration of your charter rights, you at the same time are continuing this lawless, cruel, inhuman, and abominable practice of enslaving your fellow creatures."[25]

The values invoked in defense of colonial freedom were thus used to indict the system of labor undergirding the colonial economy of the South and supporting economic enterprise in the North. Slavery was an insult to the principles for which the revolutionaries were preparing to fight. "Oh, the shocking, the intolerable inconsistence! . . . This gross, barefaced, practiced inconsistence,!" cried Samuel Hopkins, a Congregationalist minister of Rhode Island on the eve of war.[26]

Not only the degradation of blacks under slavery but also the accompanying degradation of whites concerned many of those who declared their opposition to slavery in the pre-Revolutionary decade. John Woolman, whose abolitionist efforts of the 1750s were widely ignored, was convinced that slave holding, even by the kindliest of masters, "depraved the mind in like manner and with as great certainty as prevailing cold congeals water." The absolute authority exercised by the master over the slave established "ideas of things and modes of conduct" that inexorably molded the attitudes of children, neighbors, and friends of slave holders.[27] As Woolman traveled through the colonies he became convinced that slavery was indelibly imbedding the notion of white superiority in the white mind. Such an idea was incompatible with both the Christian concept of the brotherhood of all men and rationalist thought of the eighteenth century, which stressed natural equality. Because slaves were always employed in servile labour and lived in abject conditions, most people grew to look upon them "as a contemptible, ignorant Part of Mankind."[28] The outward condition of the slave, the result of white exploitation and desire for material gain, was taken to correspond with the inward condition of the displaced African. But for Woolman, the slave's outer degradation was a function of the white man's "inner corruption." White men in the process of enslaving the African had enslaved themselves. The imprisonment of blacks was external and physical, while for the whites it was internal and spiritual. In either case the implications for the health of American society were fearful to contemplate.

[25][John Allen], *The Watchman's Alarm to Lord N____ h* (1774), in Bernard Bailyn, *The Ideological Origins of the American Revolution* (Cambridge: Harvard University Press, 1967), p. 240.

[26]Quoted in *ibid.*, p. 244.

[27]Quoted in Gary B. Nash, "Slaves and Slaveholders in Colonial Philadelphia," *William and Mary Quarterly*, 3d ser., 29 (1973): 243.

[28]Quoted in Jordan, *White Over Black*, p. 273.

Quakers, shown here in the meetinghouse, spoke out against slavery and the exploitation of Indians, and, unlike other Protestants, allowed women a nearly equal role in religious affairs. (Courtesy Museum of Fine Arts, Boston.)

These thoughts were raised not only in the North. Writing on the eve of the Revolution in Virginia, Jefferson warned his countrymen of the psychological and spiritual prison they had constructed for themselves by building their country on the backs of black slaves. "There must doubtless be an unhappy influence on the manners of our people produced by the existence of slavery among us," he wrote.

> The whole commerce between master and slave is a perpetual exercise of the most boisterous passions, the most unremitting despotism on the one part, and degrading submissions on the other. Our children see this, and learn to imitate it; for man is an imitative animal. . . . From his cradle to his grave he is learning to do what he sees others do. . . . The parent storms, the child looks on, catches the lineaments of wrath, puts on the same airs in the circle of smaller slaves, gives a loose to the worst of passions, and thus nursed, educated, and daily exercised in tyranny, cannot but be stamped by it with odious peculiarities. The man must be a prodigy who can retain his manners and morals undepraved by such circumstances.[29]

[29]Thomas Jefferson, *Notes on the State of Virginia*, ed. Thomas P. Abernethy (New York: Harper & Row, Publishers, 1964), p. 155.

From this increasing awareness of white racial prejudice and its effects came a movement to end slavery. For the first time the incompatability of enslaving Africans with the principles which white colonial society took to be the foundation of its uniqueness gained wide recognition. In response, a number of Northern colonies abolished the slave trade or taxed it out of existence before the Declaration of Independence was signed. Slavery, however, was not abolished, so while a small number of merchants were forced to reroute their ships, it cost other colonial whites little or nothing.

In the South the ideological war against slavery got nowhere. The 1760s, in fact, saw the largest slave importations of any decade in the colonial period. In South Carolina slaves imported between 1760 and 1770 exceeded those brought in during the previous quarter century and in the early 1770s the influx increased again. After the Seven Years War more than 85 percent of all American slaves were concentrated in the plantation colonies of Maryland, Virginia, North Carolina, and South Carolina, with the number in Virginia almost equaling those of the other Southern provinces. Virginians had never owned more than half as many slaves as the sugar planters of Jamaica between 1670 and 1730. But they overtook the Jamaicans by 1760 and a decade later counted almost 200,000 slaves in the colony.

The massive capital investment in black labor made the question of abolishing slavery almost academic in the parts of the country where it counted most. In Virginia, which had a white population equivalent to that of Sacramento, California, or Jersey City, New Jersey, today, the capital investment in slaves was about £5.5 million or, in terms of today's money, $300,000,000. Who would compensate slaveholders for this property? Thus, while Afro-Americans heard of pamphlets advocating abolition and even pondered reports that the legislatures of Virginia and other colonies were debating the issue, slaveholders with large sums invested in the institution were organizing to turn back the campaign which sought to eliminate what had become their primary source of wealth, power, and prestige. The abolitionist critique of American society resounded loudly where only one of every ten American slaves lived; it was barely heard, or listened to, where the other nine toiled.

As the colonial period drew to a close, Afro-American culture in the plantation South was in a state of flux. The importation of large numbers of Africans, at an all-time high in the South in the early 1770s, fanned the embers of militancy. In South Carolina, a wave of insurrectionary activity coursed through the province. Once before, following a period of heavy slave importations in the 1730s, Carolinians had been terrified by a series of uprisings that started at Stono. Even the execution of 44 blacks had not prevented another plot in Charleston and still another in the interior in the next year. So great was white fear that slave importations were forbidden for three years. Now in the 1760s the process was repeated. In 1761 a wave of poisoning swept over the colony. Four years later more than one hundred slaves made a concerted attempt to establish a colony in the interior. And in

1766 black men took literally the white rhetoric concerning liberty and equality by parading through the streets of Charleston chanting "Liberty, Liberty!" The words were so frightening that the city was put under arms for a week, as rumors of insurrection spread through the colony.[30] A nervous legislature quickly passed a three-year prohibitive tariff on slaves in order to reduce importations. More than seven thousand slaves had been imported in 1765 but in the next year the number dropped to 101.

Even in Virginia, where the burgeoning slave population primarily reflected natural increase rather than new importations, blacks were far from reconciled to plantation slavery. When opportunities arose to throw off the shackles of perpetual servitude, they moved with speed and determination. In 1775, when hostilities had already begun without a formal declaration of war, Governor Dunmore of Virginia issued a proclamation offering freedom to any Virginia slave who escaped his or her master and reached the British garrisons. The proclamation galvanized the South against England, for Dunmore hit a sensitive nerve by conjuring up the vision of a large body of free Negroes, armed by the British, abroad in the land. The proclamation, wrote one prominent Southerner, tended "more effectually to work an eternal separation between Great Britain and the Colonies—than any other expedient, which could possibly have been thought of." Another put it more graphically: "Hell itself could not have vomitted anything more black than this design of emancipating our slaves."[31]

Thousands of black Virginians made an attempt to reach the British garrisons in 1775 and in the war years that followed. Making personal declarations of independence, they achieved liberty by joining those whom white American patriots called enemies of freedom. In general, the appraisal of Joseph Galloway, a Philadelphia loyalist, would seem to characterize the Afro-American population on the eve of the Revolution. "The Negroes," wrote Galloway, "may all be deemed so many Intestine [internal] Enemies, being all slaves and desirous of Freedom, and would, was an opportunity offered them, Take up Arms against their masters."[32] This black war for independence in America occurred in every part of the country and was especially intense whenever slaves were within running distance of the British army or navy. Thus, while the Seven Years War and its aftermath militated against the continuing quest of Native Americans for cultural and political autonomy, it opened up new opportunities for Afro-Americans.

[30]Pauline Maier, "The Charleston Mob and the Evolution of Popular Politics in Revolutionary South Carolina, 1765–1784," *Perspectives in American History*, 4 (1970): 176–77.

[31]Quoted in Benjamin Quarles, *The Negro in the American Revolution* (Chapel Hill: University of North Carolina Press, 1961), p. 20n.

[32]Benjamin F. Stevens, ed., *Facsimiles of Manuscripts in European Archives Relating to America, 1773–1783* (London, 1889–1895), 24, No. 2079.

12

THE MIXING
OF PEOPLES

While Indians, Africans, and Europeans worked out their destinies in a complicated setting of tribal and imperial rivalry, economic growth, population change, and social and political transformation, they also interacted with each other at the most intimate and personal levels. This sexual and social mixing of individuals of different genetic stocks is usually called miscegenation. In itself it is of little interest unless one is concerned with pseudoscientific attempts to specify the relative size of various "racial" groups in a society, an exercise usually conducted with propagandistic and political purposes in mind. Miscegenation is, however, important in another way. By studying the extent of it we can develop insights into the process of acculturation and assimilation—the mixing of cultural elements and the absorption of one culture into another.

Most thinking on the subject of miscegenation in North America starts with the arresting notion that Europeans on this continent did not intermix with Africans and Indians with anywhere near the same frequency as in colonial Latin American societies. Nor did Africans and Indians mix to the same degree. Latin America is known as the area of the world where the most extensive intermingling of the races in human history has taken place. North America, where Europeans, Indians, and Africans also converged during roughly the same period of time, is noted for the general absence of any such intermixture. The census figures of modern North and South America seem to confirm this belief. They show, for example, that only 20 percent of the Venezuelans are classified as white, that only 11 percent of Panamanians are white, that mulattoes in Brazil make up a much larger portion of the population than in the United States, and so forth. Although the criteria for defining membership in a particular racial group vary greatly from place to place and are never exact, it is not necessary to be precise about the racial composition of any of the New World societies since the principal point is not in dispute—that widely practiced interracial sexual liaisons produced a dramatically larger proportion of mestizos (European-Indian), mulattoes (European-African), and mustees (African-Indian) in the southern half of the New World than in the northern half.

Two explanations are commonly advanced for this. First, before the European colonization of the New World the Spanish and Portuguese had a history of interacting with people of different cultures, particularly with darkskinned people, whereas the English did not. Through centuries of war and trade with the Berbers, Moors, and other peoples of the Middle East and North Africa, Iberian society had already absorbed new cultural and genetic elements and developed flexible attitudes about the sexual mixing of peoples. The English, by contrast, had remained within their island fortress, sheltered from other cultures and therefore predisposed toward viewing interracial contacts with suspicion and even alarm.

A corollary to this argument is that, once in the New World, the permissive attitudes of the Catholic church toward non-Christian people, the Roman system of law, which protected the slave, and the paternalistic attitudes of the Iberian governments combined to make racial intermixture acceptable and therefore common in the areas of the world where Spain and Portugal were confronting Indians and Africans in large numbers. By contrast, English Protestantism was unusually rigid in considering admittance of "savage" people to the church. English law had nothing to say on the subject of enslavement, leaving colonists free to create the most rigid institutions to contain their bound laborers. And the English government exercised much less authority in its colonies, especially in the matter of the treatment of subordinate non-English groups. Given these differences in prior experience, in institutions and attitudes, and in governmental policy, it was not surprising that the history of interracial mixing should be so different in the colonies of Spain and Portugal and the colonies of England.

Such arguments have lost much of their explanatory force in recent years as historians have analyzed the social and demographic conditions underlying the history of cultural interaction in various parts of the New World. The differences in the degree and nature of interracial mixing in North and South America now seem to be fundamentally related to conditions encountered in the New World rather than attitudes developed in the Old World. The availability of white women; the ratio of Europeans, Africans, and Native Americans in a given area; the extent to which Indians could be pressed into forced labor systems; and the need to employ non-Europeans in positions of importance—all of these had a role in shaping the pattern of intercultural mixing. Thus it made sense that in areas where European women were in short supply white men overcame the racial prejudices they had brought to the New World to consort with women of another race. Their alternatives were sexual abstinence, homosexuality, or bestiality. All three attracted some males; but the vast majority of men preferred heterosexual relations with women of a different cultural group. Similarly, where Indians or Africans were relatively numerous, intermixture was far more common than where they were relatively scarce. In New England, where Indians had been devastated by epidemics in the early years of European settlement, little red-white mixing occurred. In Mexico, where Spanish men were engulfed by the densely settled Indians, a great deal of mixing occurred throughout the colonial period.

INDIAN-EUROPEAN CONTACT

Contact between Indians and Europeans preceded all other contacts and influenced what later occurred, so it is best to begin with it. In New England, and later in the Mid-Atlantic colonies of New York, New Jersey, Pennsylvania, and Delaware, miscegenation between Europeans and Indians was extremely limited. Englishmen had emigrated to these regions with their families, or, if they were single men, found a sufficient number of single women to satisfy their needs for marriage partners. Parity between the sexes was established quickly and continued throughout the colonial period, except following periods of war when women sometimes outnumbered men by a small margin. Reinforcing this demographic situation was a strong cultural factor. Emigration by family ensured the rerooting of an entire cultural superstructure to which miscegenation was highly threatening, especially given the view, almost universal among whites, that their culture was far superior to that of Native Americans and Africans.

In the Northern colonies red-white mixing was also limited by the relatively small number of Indians and the inaccessiblity of those who escaped epidemics and war, which rapidly reduced the coastal Indian societies during the initial period of contact. Intercultural marriage was a rarity. A number of fur traders operating on the frontier took Indian wives, and almost all of them had frequent sexual contact with Indian women. But the one notable case of intermarriage in the settled regions involved William Johnson, the Northern Superintendent of Indian Affairs, who took a Mohawk wife. Later knighted for his military exploits, Johnson gained great influence with the Mohawk, who renamed him Warraghiyagey, meaning "man who undertakes great things." This high tribute was conferred in large part because

Johnson had deviated so radically from the white norm in accepting Mohawk customs and learning their language, as few white men cared to do. Johnson was not born or raised in the colonies and few cared to follow the example of even a high imperial official when it came to matrimony so long as there were European women to be found. It was said that Johnson's precedent-shattering marriage, noteworthy enough to attract the attention of the London newspapers, led to eighteen other red-white unions, but even so the number is insignificant.

In the Chesapeake colonies a different demographic pattern prevailed in the first few decades. With few exceptions, white women were unavailable in Virginia until about 1620. Yet white men had little recourse to Indian women. Several early eighteenth-century Virginia commentators believed that this was because the early colonizers found Indian women distasteful. William Byrd, no stranger to the pleasures of the flesh with women of different skin colors, claimed the English were imbued with a "false delicacy" in the early years and thus could not bring themselves to sleep with Indian women. Byrd believed that the Chesapeake tribes had been offended by this rejection and could never "perswade themselves that the English were heartily their Friends, so long as they disdained to intermarry with them." Robert Beverley, author of *The History and Present State of Virginia*, took a similar view, regretting that intermarriage had never occurred and convinced that the Indians had been eager for it.[1]

The limited evidence bearing on this question does not support such views, however. A large part of the predominantly male Virginia colony was composed of representatives of the English lower class, including many who had military experience in Ireland, the Spanish Netherlands, and other parts of the world. They were not known for squeamishness, and their later willingness to consort with African women suggests that the real cause of infrequent sexual contact with Indian women is to be found in Indian rather than European desires. The English did not establish themselves as conquerors in the early years, as had the Spanish and Portuguese, and therefore the Chesapeake tribes were under no compulsion to yield up their women. Indian women were not denied to Virginians who stole away from oppressive conditions in their own community to live among Powhatan's people, and their numbers became large enough to bring about laws imposing severe penalties on such renegade behavior. The one case of intermarriage within the white community involved John Rolfe and Pocahontas. Whatever love the two may have felt for each other, this was a political marriage. It is sometimes claimed that the King's council, by deliberating whether Rolfe had not committed high treason in marrying an Indian princess, discouraged

[1]William Byrd, *Histories of the Dividing Line Betwixt Virginia and North Carolina*, ed. William K. Boyd (Raleigh: North Carolina Historical Commission, 1929), p. 3; Robert Beverley, *History and Present State of Virginia*, ed. Louis B. Wright (Chapel Hill: University of North Carolina Press, 1960), pp. 38–39.

any further intermarriage. But the charge under consideration was high treason for marrying the daughter of a quasi-enemy, and Pocahontas and Rolfe were feted in London wherever they went, including the royal court. By the early eighteenth century the Board of Trade was pushing an official policy of intermarriage in the American colonies, indication enough that moral scruples were not offended in England by thoughts of the commingling of red and white blood.

By the end of the second Indian war in 1644 the native population in the tidewater area was only a small fraction of the white population; by the conclusion of Bacon's Rebellion in 1675, when white women were much more available, only a few Indians remained within the areas of white settlement. This puts in perspective Governor Spotswood's claim in 1717 that the "inclinations of our people are not the same with those of [the French] Nation" regarding intermarriage, as evidenced by the fact that not one such marriage was known in Virginia at that time.[2] Racial prejudice no doubt would have limited such partnerships. But neither the need nor the opportunity for Indian-white marriages remained. French "inclinations" in New France were different not so much because of variations in national character as because of different needs. Even along the St. Lawrence, where Frenchmen commonly took Indian wives and mistresses, European women were much preferred. But Indian women remained preferable to no women at all.

The only English area in which the demographic profile even roughly paralleled that in the Spanish and Portuguese colonies was the Southeast— the Carolinas and Georgia. In the early years white women were relatively unavailable but Indian women could easily be found. The result was a considerable contact between Englishmen and Indian women. Conspicuously absent from the records are indications of reticence when it came to intercultural sexual liaisons. Unembarrassed sexual relations between the two peoples seem to have been the rule. This was especially true of the fur traders who operated in the interior regions and would not give up the satisfactions of Indian "She-Bed-Fellows," as one eighteenth-century commentator called them. Women were specifically designated by the tribes as "Trading Girls" and were given special haircuts to denote that their role was to satisfy the traders while getting money "by their Natural Parts." Only these women were available to white men, however, for Indian males "are desirous (if possible) to keep their Wives to themselves, as well as those in other Parts of the World."[3]

While traders consorted with Indian women in the interior, white Carolinians confronted Indian women sold into slavery in the coastal settlements. After the Yamasee War of 1715, the enslavement of Indians in Carolina diminished. But during the first half century of the colony's history, the

[2]R. A. Brock, ed., *The Official Letters of Alexander Spotswood* . . . Virginia Historical Society *Collections*, N.S., (Richmond: Virginia Historical Society, 1885), 2: 227.

[3]Lawson, *Voyage to Carolina*, ed., Lefler, pp. 189–90.

large number of children of Indian mothers and white fathers in Charleston testified to the extensive miscegenation practiced there. White men outnumbered white women in South Carolina by more than 13 to 9 as late as 1708 and womanless men were not reluctant to avail themselves of Indian women. In Georgia no less a figure than Thomas Bosomworth, chaplain of Oglethorpe's utopian colony, found it respectable to marry a Creek women in the early years of settlement and many others followed his example, including John McDonald and Alexander Cameron, Deputy Indian Commissioners to the Cherokees in the late colonial period.

Interracial mixing between Indians and Europeans, then, was limited more by population ratios than by prior attitudes. It is also clear in the miscegenation laws passed by all the colonies during the colonial period that attitudes differed toward black-skinned Africans and tawny-skinned Indians. Miscegenation laws were aimed almost exclusively at white-black mating. Only North Carolina and Virginia forbade marriage between Indians and whites (though Massachusetts debated such a law), and no colonies applied special penalties for red-white fornication as they often did for cases involving blacks and whites. Many transplanted Europeans, applying their own standards of beauty, described Indian women as beautiful, whereas no such descriptions can be found of African women. Indian women, wrote Robert Beverley in 1705, were "generally Beautiful, possessing uncommon delicacy of shape and Features, and wanting no Charm but that of a fair complexion."[4]

The general lack of red-white sexual intermingling forecast the overall failure of the two cultures to merge. The amalgamation of Indians and whites never proceeded very far in eighteenth-century America because Indians were seldom eager to trade their culture for one which they found inferior and because the colonists found the Indians useful only as trappers of furs, consumers of European trade goods, and military allies. All these functions were best performed outside the white communities. This is a striking contrast to the Latin American colonies where the lack of white women and the subjugation of Indian laborers brought the two peoples into close contact, thus producing a large mestizo population. Even the most conservative estimates show that the mestizo population reached 25 percent of the whole in early nineteenth-century Spanish America. Many of these individuals rose to positions of artisan, foreman on the *encomiendas,* militiaman, and even collector of tithes and taxes. But in colonial America the half-Indian, half-white person, usually the product of a liaison between a white fur trader and an Indian woman, remained in almost all cases within Indian society. A number of the male offspring became fur traders themselves or intermediaries between English and Indian society. Others, such as Joseph Brant of the Mohawks and Alexander McGillivray of the Creeks, became noted leaders of Indian resistance in the second half of the eighteenth

[4]Beverley, *History and Present State of Virginia,* ed. Wright, p. 159.

century. Although historians have not yet systematically studied the American mestizo, who revealingly was called by the derogatory term "half-breed," there are indications that these persons, who white colonists recognized only as Indians, were the most alienated of all people from white society. One Virginian gave explicit expression to this in 1757 when he wrote that traders who consorted with Indian "squaws" left their offspring "like bulls or bears to be provided for at random by their mothers. . . . As might be expected," he pointed out, "some of these bastards have been the leading men or war captains that have done us so much mischief."[5]

The one case in which transculturation between Indians and Europeans did occur involved the Indianization of whites rather than the Europeanization of Indians. Throughout the colonial period, much to the horror of the leaders of white society, colonists ran away to Indian settlements, or, when they were captured in war and had lived with a tribe for a few years, often refused to return to white society. This "reversion to savagery," as those who insisted on the superiority of white culture regarded it, has attracted the attention of American novelists since the late eighteenth century. For white colonists the prospect of their own people preferring the Indian way of life was a disturbing anomaly. "None can imagine what it is to be captivated, and enslaved to such atheistical, proud, wild, cruel, barbarous, brutish (in one word) diabolical creatures as these, the worst of the heathen," wrote a seventeenth-century Puritan.[6]

In spite of such fantasy characterizations, the colonizers were obliged to live with the notion that many of their own kind found life in Indian communities preferable to life in Anglo-American culture. To make matters worse, virtually no Indians took the reverse route, choosing to remain in white society after exposure to it. "By what power does it come to pass," asked Crévecoeur, the famous Frenchman who lived in America for more than a decade in the late colonial period, in his celebrated *Letters from an American Farmer*,

> that children who have been adopted when young among these people, can never be prevailed on to readopt European manners? Many an anxious parent I have seen after the last war [Seven Years War], who at the return of peace, went to the Indian villages where they knew their children had been carried in captivity; when to their inexpressible sorrow, they found them so perfectly Indianised, that many knew them no longer, and those whose more advanced ages permitted them to recollect their fathers and mothers, absolutely refused to follow them, and ran to their adopted parents for protection against the effusions of love their unhappy real parents lavished on them! Incredible as this may appear, I have heard it asserted in a thousand instances, among persons of credit. . . . There must be in their social bond something singularly captivating, and far superior to anything to be boasted of among us; for

[5]Quoted in James Hugo Johnston, *Race Relations in Virginia and Miscegenation in the South, 1776–1860* (Amherst: University of Massachusetts Press, 1970), p. 169.

[6]Quoted in Roy Harvey Pearce, "The 'Ruines of Mankind': The Indian and the Puritan Mind," *Journal of the History of Ideas*, 13 (1952): 205.

thousands of Europeans are Indians, and we have no examples of even one of those Aborigines having from choice become Europeans.[7]

The phenomenon of the "white Indians" is partially explained by the Indian custom of adopting into their communities as full-fledged members any persons captured in war, a practice that became more important as disease and intensified warfare depleted the population of many tribes in the century after the Europeans arrived. In many instances a captive was even taken into a particular family to replace a lost child or other relative. This integration of newcomers into the kinship system and into the community at large, without judgmental comparisons of the superiority of the captor's culture, made it easy for the captured "outsider" to make a rapid personal adjustment. A white child taken into Indian society was treated on equal terms and prepared for any role open to others of his or her age. That a number of whites and Negroes who had fled to Indian communities or had been captured by them became chiefs is the most dramatic evidence of the receptiveness of Indian cultures to "outsiders."

White society differed sharply in this regard. Though a number of Indian children were adopted into white families, the general pattern was socially to isolate the newcomer. "It was not that the Indian could not be raised 'up' to the level of civilization," writes one student of the subject, "but rather the lack of an equivalent desire on the part of whites to welcome and assimilate the Indian, and the absence of any established cultural means that would mediate the transition from one culture to the other in a manner that was psychologically sound."[8] Even Christianized Indians trained in white schools, such as the Mohegan Samson Occum, were expected to return to Indian society rather than occupy a place of dignity among whites. Native Americans were always regarded as aliens and were rarely allowed to live within white society except as servants or dependents. Operating from their small communities and surrounded by a culture they regarded not only as inferior but as barbaric, the colonizers "erected a defensive wall of height-ened consciousness of superiority" in order to keep out those who seemed so threatening.[9] This inability to develop the mentality or social mechanisms for incorporating Indians into their midst betrayed a certain insecurity among a people who proclaimed the superiority of their way of life.

WHITE-BLACK INTERMIXTURE

White-black intermixture in colonial America is a more complicated phe-nomenon because whites and blacks were always in close proximity, both where white women were plentiful and where they were scarce. This physi-

[7] J. Hector St. John Crevecoeur, *Letters from an American Farmer* (New York: E. P. Dutton & Co., Inc. 1957), pp. 208–09.

[8] A. Irving Hallowell, "American Indians, White and Black: The Phenomenon of Trans-culturation," *Current Anthropology*, 4 (1963): 527.

[9] *Ibid.*, p. 528.

cal closeness led to widespread sexual contact, but it rarely involved inter-marriage. At first glance, one might imagine that the rarity of racial intermarriage stemmed from a deep-seated white aversion to blackness it-self, but if this was the case it would be difficult to explain what countless observers of eighteenth-century society claimed to see—that "the country swarms with mulatto bastards," in the words of one Virginian.[10] Such com-ments do nothing to define miscegenation with statistical precision, but eighteenth-century censuses help to clarify the point. In Maryland in 1755 a special census showed that 8 percent of the Negroes in the colony were mulatto. In Rhode Island the census of 1783 revealed that 16.5 percent of the Negroes were of mixed blood. A register of slaves for Chester County, Pennsylvania, in 1780 listed 20 percent of the Negroes as mulattoes.[11] In all three areas white females were almost as numerous as white men, indicating that even when white women were available, white men frequently had sexual relations with black women.

These contacts would probably have been even more extensive if black women had been available in the period when white women were in short supply. Slaves did not begin to enter the English colonies in significant numbers until the end of the seventeenth century and by that time the number of white women in all but the infant colony of South Carolina nearly equaled the number of white men. In the Southern plantations in 1720, the slave population was about 50,000; not more than about 10,000 of these could have been adult black females. At the same time some 70,000 adult white colonists inhabited the Southern colonies of whom almost half were women. This is in stark contrast to the situation in Portuguese Brazil, Spanish Peru, or even the English islands in the West Indies. In all of these zones of contact European women were relatively unavailable for much longer periods of time.

The example of the English Caribbean colonies provides further evidence for the case against prior attitudes determining the nature and degree of racial intermixture. English women were not present in roughly equal num-bers with white men until the second century of settlement, so African women were unhesitatingly exploited to fill the gap. Even married white plantation owners "keep a Mulatto or Black Girl in the house or at lodgings for certain purposes," reported one traveler, and a famous eighteenth-century historian of the English sugar islands colorfully pronounced that "He who should presume to shew any displeasure against such a thing as simple fornication, would for his pains be accounted a simple blockhead."[12]

In the mainland colonies, however, interracial sex brought private pleas-

[10]Quoted in Johnston, *Race Relations in Virginia*, p. 170.

[11]Edward B. Reuter, *The Mulatto in the United States* (rpr. New York: Negro Universities Press, 1969), pp. 112–14; Evarts B. Greene and Virginia D. Harrington, *American Population before the Federal Census of 1790* (New York: Columbia University Press, 1932), pp. 69–70.

[12]Jordan, *White Over Black: American Attitudes Toward the Negro, 1550–1812* (Chapel Hill: University of North Carolina Press, 1968), p. 140.

ure but public condemnation. The latter was mainly an eighteenth-century development. Africans in North America were being separated from whites shortly after their arrival in the second decade of the seventeenth century, but not until 1662, when Virginia passed a law imposing a fine for fornication between white and black partners that was twice the usual amount, did an unambiguous law appear on the books that expressed public distaste for racial intermixture. Interracial marriage was banned in Virginia in 1691, in Massachusetts in 1705, in Maryland in 1715, and thereafter in Delaware, Pennsylvania, North Carolina, South Carolina, and Georgia.

The key change in the eighteenth century was not a marked increase in miscegenation, reflecting changes in private urges, but a shifting of public attitudes toward racial mixing. "By the turn of the century," writes Winthrop Jordan, "it was clear in many continental colonies that the English settlers felt genuine revulsion for interracial sexual union, at least in principle."[13] The grand jury in Charleston, South Carolina, for example, inveighed against "The Too Common Practice of Criminal Conversation with Negro and other Slave Wenches in this Province" in 1743.[14] Similar comments can be found in other colonies. But with the black population growing rapidly and slavery becoming engrained in colonial society, lawmakers discovered that, while they could not manage biology, they could at least keep pure the blood lines of the dominant group by laws prohibiting interracial marriage. Under these laws mulattoes could never be legitimate and would always be classified as black.

In a society where slavery was touching the lives of a great proportion of the inhabitants, white colonists found it necessary to contain the black population in a tight web of authority and to assert repeatedly their dominance. One way of accomplishing this was to emphasize the heathen or "savage" condition of the slave, which justified slavery on the one hand and made sexual contact legally impermissible on the other. A variety of laws and public statements described the offspring of white-black copulation as "spurious" or "mongrel." Moreover, mulattoes were given no higher standing than pureblood blacks and in law were regarded as fully black. This contrasted sharply with the situation of the mulatto in almost every other part of the New World, where three-tiered racial systems had evolved. Black women were not needed by white males in a demographic sense. But sexual relations with them went on and on. Desire could not be legislated out of the white psyche, and if the laws and public pronouncements did not correspond with private urges, little harm was done so long as the domination of whites was preserved by disowning children of mixed racial inheritance.

By the early eighteenth century racial attitudes towards Indians and Afro-Americans had begun to diverge sharply. This divergence was closely tied to

[13]*Ibid.*, p. 139.
[14]Quoted in *ibid.*, p. 140.

striking differences in the nature and degree of sexual contact that characterized red-white and black-white relationships. White attitudes toward the black man cannot be dissociated from the fact that sexual relations, especially between white men and black women, were frequent and usually coercive throughout the eighteenth century. White men might ban interracial marriage as a way of stating with legal finality that the Negro, even when free, was not the equal of the white man. But white power was also served by sexually exploiting black women outside of marriage—a way of acting out the concept of white domination. Racial intermingling, so long as it involved free white men and slave black women, was a way of intimately and brutally proclaiming the superior rights and strength of white society.

Contact of this character had no parallel in the case of the Indian woman. When she was accessible, for example, to fur traders, she was not in the hapless position of a slave woman, nearly defenseless to resist the advances of a master with power of life and death over her. If an Indian woman chose to submit to a white man, it was usually on mutually agreeable terms. Furthermore, it was widely known that Indian men rarely molested female prisoners. In these differences we can find the source and meaning of a fear which has preoccupied white America for three hundred years—the fear of the black male lusting after the white woman. This vision of the "black rapist," so enduring in contemporary attitudes and literature, runs through the accounts of slave uprisings which occurred in the eighteenth and nineteenth centuries. This fear of black men, who are seen rising not in quest of their freedom but in pursuit of white women, seems to stem from feelings of guilt originating in the sexual exploitation of black women and an associated fear of the black avenger, presumably filled with anger and poised to retaliate against those who first enslaved him and then plundered his woman. This element of sexual fear is only rarely expressed in the literature concerning the Indian. Since little guilt could have been aroused by the occasional and noncoercive contacts with Indian women, white men, when they encountered hostile Indian males, rarely pictured them as sexual avengers. In the eighteenth century the Indian was almost never caricatured as the frenzied rapist, lurking in the bush or stalking white women. Indeed, the Indian was sometimes viewed as a peculiarly asexual creature. This in turn created a confused image in the white mind of a hostile, and yet sexually passive, "savage." His hostility was not doubted; but the hostile Indian was commonly regarded as a man with knife in hand, bent on obtaining the scalp of the white encroacher. It was imagined that hostile black men had focused on a different part of the anatomy in their quest for revenge.

The most striking fact about miscegenation in pre-Revolutionary America is that it did not result in widespread acculturation or assimilation, at least in comparison to other New World societies. In the Spanish and Portuguese colonies Indian women had been seized as a part of the general enslavement of the indigenous populations, and thereafter Spanish men lived surrounded by them. Through concubinage and intermarriage these women were incorporated into Spanish and Portuguese life and the mestizo offspring of such matches were recognized by their European fathers. Mestizos, in fact, were to play a large role in later stages of colonization and conquest. Though Spanish and Portuguese men would quickly reject their Indian women when Iberian women became available, the extent of intermixture was far greater than in North America and led to the assimilation of a sizable part of the Indian population.

The case of the African was similar. Slaves arrived earlier in the Spanish and Portuguese colonization process than in English North America; they came in larger numbers proportionate to their European masters; and their services as artisans and supervisors of Indian slaves gave many of them a status far above that of the common field laborer. As the Conquest period ended, the Iberian colonists evolved their own form of racism, with individuals classifed according to skin color—a "pigmentocratic system."[15] But because all the caste groups in the racial hierarchy were regarded as natural parts of a multiracial society, the prohibitions against interracial contact and racial intermarriage did not take root. As the degrees of intermixture between the three cultural groups became more elaborate, passage from one group to another became relatively easy until finally the system of trying to distinguish between *mestizo, castizo, mulatto, morisco, albino, torna atras, lobo, zambaigo, cambujo, albarazado, barcono, chamiso,* and so forth broke down.

In the North American colonies, however, assimilation was rejected by Englishmen, who had strong objections not to sexual relations with black-skinned women but to conferring status on blacks by accepting such intermingling as legitimate or by admitting its product to white society. Though skin color came to assume importance through generations of association with slavery, white colonists developed few qualms about intimate contact with black women. But raising the social status of those who labored at the bottom of society, those who were defined as abysmally inferior, was a matter of serious concern. It was resolved by ensuring that the mulatto would not occupy a position midway between white and black. The least portion of African blood classified a person as black; and to be black was almost always to be a slave. The "mulatto escape hatch" that Carl Degler has described in Latin American society did not exist in British North America, for there was little need to call upon Negores or mulattoes for important, status-conferring services, and the well-rooted institution of the white family, an outgrowth of a family pattern of settlement, gave special reasons for excluding the living evidence of a sexual congress that threatened the purity of white culture.

In the American colonies, then, the primary need was for plantation

---

[15]Magnus Mörner, *Race Mixture in the History of Latin America* (Boston: Little, Brown and Company, 1967), pp. 54–60.

labor. A secondary need was for occasional sex partners with whom one could act out sexual fantasies, heightened by the definition of black women as lascivious by nature. By prohibiting racial intermarriage, winking at interracial sex, and defining all mixed offspring as black, white society found the answer to its labor needs, its extracurricular and submerged sexual desires, its compulsion to maintain its culture purebred, and the problem of maintaining, at least in theory, absolute social control.

This system of sexual politics was linked not so much to the national prejudices of Englishmen as to the historical circumstances of English settlement in North America. This becomes clearer by looking at the status of the mulatto in English Jamaica. By the mid-eighteenth century more than 90 percent of the Jamaica population was black, and white men greatly outnumbered white women. Such a distorted demographic history called for a system in which black women would be available without scruple to white men and where mulatto offspring would rise to places of importance in the island society. This is precisely what happened. Miscegenation occurred on a massive scale, and by 1733 the practice of conferring privileges and property on mulattoes was written into law.

AFRICAN-INDIAN CONTACT

The convergence of African and Indian peoples is the least studied chapter in the history of race relations in early America. Naturally it is useless to look for this kind of acculturation in places where Indians and Africans did not meet in substantial numbers. Thus in New England, where the coastal tribes had been killed off before more than a trickle of Africans had arrived, little cross-fertilization was possible. It is notable, however, that in the few places such as Cape Cod where Indians did survive, their mixture with a small number of free Negroes was extensive by the late eighteenth century. This also occurred in a number of New England towns, especially along the coast, where many Indian slaves from South Carolina had been imported in the early eighteenth century. A census in South Kingston, Rhode Island, in 1730 showed 333 Negro slaves and 223 Indian slaves; the resulting intermixture of blood is not to be wondered at. A report in Massachusetts in 1795 stated that the blacks of Massachusetts "have generally . . . left the country and resorted to the maritime towns. Some are incorporated, and their breed is mixed with the Indians of Cape-Cod and Martha's Vineyard."[16] In New York, which contained the largest slave population north of the Chesapeake, intermixture of slaves and Indians, though unquantifiable, was far from unusual. Negro and Indian slaves had formed a blood bond in 1712 when they joined hands in an insurrection in New York City. Thereafter, provin-

[16]Quoted in Kenneth W. Porter, "Relations between Negroes and Indians within the Present Limits of the United States," *Journal of Negro History,* 17 (1932): 311.

cial officials knew that the best place to look for escaped slaves was among the small local tribes that remained on Long Island and in the Hudson River Valley. It was in the cities of the North, however, that black slaves were concentrated, and these were precisely the places where Indians in the second half of the eighteenth century were only occasionally to be found.

In the Chesapeake colonies, the possibility of African-Indian amalgamation was also reduced by the sheer force of circumstances. When Indians were relatively numerous in the tidewater region of Maryland and Virginia, slaves were present only in small numbers. In 1670, less than 2000 slaves inhabited the Chesapeake region and by the end of Bacon's Rebellion in 1676 the Indian population in the regions settled by whites was insignificant. Nonetheless, a considerable number of runaway slaves were given refuge by the coastal tribes. Their descendants, mixed with whites as well, exist today in isolated triethnic communities in Delaware, Maryland, Virginia, and North Carolina.

Only in South Carolina and Georgia did Indians and Africans in substantial numbers find themselves confronting Europeans simultaneously. Here was the one area in English America where the situation duplicated that prevailing in most regions of Portuguese and Spanish colonization.

The colonizers' position of numerical inferiority led to gnawing fears that Indians and slaves would combine forces and overpower them. Keeping Africans and Indians apart, therefore, became a necessity. Such fears were well grounded, for during the pre-Revolutionary period the Indians of the Southeast remained numerous in white areas of settlement and, combined with the black slaves, greatly exceeded the white population. White South Carolinians, for example, were outnumbered by their black and Indian slaves and by free Indians surrounding them by ratios of three or four to one throughout most of the early period of colonization. Even by the mid-eighteenth century, only about 25,000 whites inhabited the colony along with some 40,000 black slaves and 60,000 Indians gathered in the Creek, Cherokee, Choctaw, Chickasaw, and subsidiary tribes. Twenty years later, on the eve of the Revolution, the white population had increased to some 50,000 but the slave population had increased even faster—to about 75,000. South Carolinians lived surrounded by those who, if they could find a means for concerted action, might overwhelm them at any moment. Indian uprisings that punctuated the colonial period and a succession of slave uprisings and insurrectionary plots that were nipped in the bud kept South Carolinians sickeningly aware that only through the greatest vigilance and through policies designed to keep their enemies divided could they hope to remain in control of the situation.

That the white Carolinians were able to retain a hold on the situation testifies to their ability to play one Indian tribe against another and to their partial success in keeping Indians and Negro slaves divided. The policy, as one Carolinian put it, was "to make Indians & Negro's a checque upon each other least by their Vastly Superior Numbers we should be crushed by one or the other."[17] Various methods were devised to accomplish this. Laws were passed prohibiting Afro-Americans, whether slave or free, from traveling in Indian country as traders or traders' helpers. Indian tribes were repeatedly asked to return fugitive slaves, and treaties signed with Creeks, Cherokees, and other tribes almost always included a clause stipulating that escaped slaves must be turned over to the Carolina government. Bounties were offered to Indians for the capture and return of escaped slaves. Patrols were used in frontier areas to prevent slaves from reaching Indian country. And suspicion of blacks among the Indians was fostered as a way of keeping mutual aid between them to a minimum. "It has been allways the policy of this government," wrote Governor Lyttelton in 1738, "to create an aversion in them [Indians] to Negroes."[18]

A double purpose was served by incorporating black slaves into the South Carolina militia during Indian wars. Without them, the Carolinians would have been hard pressed to defeat their Tuscarora, Yamasee, or Cherokee enemies; secondly, the use of black soldiers helped to remind the Indians that Africans were not their friends. Half the Carolinian force which Governor Craven led against the Yamasee in 1715 was black, and another black company marched with Captain Pight in the same campaign. When these forces proved incapable of defeating the Yamasees, the Assembly called for a "standing army" of 1200 men, including "400 negroes or other slaves."[19] This was merely an implementation of the policy begun in 1708 to compose the militia of equal numbers of blacks and whites. In the 1740 expedition against St. Augustine seventy-three slaves were included. By 1747 the militia law was changed to allow for no more than one third of the soldiers to be black, a sign of a growing fear of black insurgency. In the campaigns against the Cherokee in 1760 a small number of black Carolinians again fought against Indian enemies of the white government. How precariously the Carolinians were suspended between red revolt and black insurrection was indicated in the Cherokee War. More blacks were needed to fight against the Indian enemy, but in an era of large slave importations the anxiety concerning black rebellion was also great. Thus a motion to equip 500 slaves "to serve against the savages" failed by a single vote in the South Carolina assembly.

Just as slaves were used to quash Indian uprisings, Indians were employed to put down black rebellions. In the most spectacular black insurrection in the South, the Stono revolt of 1739, the South Carolina government recruited "settlement" Indians to pursue the slaves, who had eluded white militiamen and were fleeing to Spanish Florida. The assembly equipped the

[17]Quoted in William S. Willis, Jr., "Divide and Rule: Red, White, and Black in the Southeast," *Journal of Negro History*, 48 (1963): 165.

[18]*Ibid.*

[19]David D. Wallace, *South Carolina: A Short History, 1520–1948* (Chapel Hill: University of North Carolina Press, 1951), p. 88.

Indians with clothes, guns, and ammunition and promised £50 for each slave brought back alive or £25 for each slave returned dead. Other attempts were made at warding off black rebellions by relocating Indian tribes in areas where large numbers of slaves were developing the rice and indigo plantations. This policy originated in the early eighteenth century and was pursued with special vigor in the 1730s when the buildup of the slave population kept Carolina vibrating with fears of black rebellion. In 1737 Cherokee warriors were requested "to come down to the settlements to be an awe to the negroes."[20]

In spite of these strenuous efforts at promoting hatred between Indians and Africans, a surprising number of slaves were harbored within the Indian communities throughout the colonial period. It is impossible to measure this phenomenon precisely, but the persistent inclusion in Indian treaties of a clause providing for the return of escaped slaves demonstrates that the bounties offered Indians for slave catching often evoked little response. The Tuscarora tribe, for example, gave refuge to a large number of slaves in the period before the outbreak of war in 1711. When war came, these Africans fought with the Tuscaroras and one of them, named Harry, was said to have designed the Tuscarora fortress on a tributary of the Neuse River. Four years later, during the Yamasee uprising, fugitive slaves were also active in the raids on white settlements. Even after the Yamasee had given up their struggle, they refused to return their black allies, which, according to one Carolina official, "has encouraged a great many more [slaves] lately to run away to that Place."[21]

Because the Yamasees were located along the coast between the English settlements and the Spanish outposts in Florida, slaves had additional reason to flee in this direction. As early as 1699 the Spanish issued a royal decree promising protection to all fugitive English slaves and this offer was repeated periodically during the first half of the eighteenth century. Even after the Yamasee War ended, the Indians not only encouraged Carolina slaves to join them but also engaged in slave-stealing raids on outlying plantations. In 1738, twenty-three slaves escaped from Port Royal and made thier way to St. Augustine. They joined an enclave of free Negroes where thirty-eight escaped slave men, many with families, were already settled. In a sense this was the advance guard of the fifty to a hundred slaves who rose at Stono in 1739 in a mass attempt to kill whites and flee to Spanish Florida. When Governor Oglethorpe of Georgia launched his attack on St. Augustine in 1740, he was met with the combined resistance of Spanish, Indians, and ex-Carolina slaves, who had no difficulty repulsing the expedition in which the Carolinians invested more than £7,000. Two years later the Spaniards retaliated with an attack on Georgia; among the invasion forces was a regiment

[20]Willis, "Divide and Rule," p. 175.

[21]Quoted in Chapman J. Milling, Red Carolinians (Chapel Hill: University of North Carolina Press, 1940), p. 153.

prohibiting miscegenation, and actual social practice, as visible in the large mixed-blood population, can only be explained in terms of the white desire to maintain social control while at the same time indulging in sexual gratification with partners of different skin color.

CULTURAL INTERACTION OF RED, WHITE, AND BLACK

At the end of the colonial period, American society, some 2.5 million strong, was far from a homogeneous culture. Almost two hundred years of European colonization and the continuous interaction of three large and internally diverse cultural groups had left a conglomeration of cultural entities. Each had its own goals and to a large extent its own values. Two of the groups, European and Indian, retained a considerable degree of autonomy, although both were limited in what they could do by the presence of the other and by the political and economic relationships that they had contracted during the colonial epoch. The third group, the Afro-Americans, was necessarily constrained by the fact that most of its members were enslaved. But Afro-Americans also retained a measure of autonomy, though it appeared in more subtle forms.

The complex interaction of the three cultural groups was filled with paradoxes. Europeans in America claimed that they wished to assimilate Indians and Africans, but they found that the most effective way to exploit the land of one and the labor of the other was to follow a nonassimilationist policy. Bringing Christianity to non-Christians was an expensive and time-consuming enterprise, useful only to the extent that it better enabled Europeans to employ the resources of those they sought to dominate. Since proselytizing often gave little promise of accomplishing that—and in fact frequently threatened to make the utilization of Indian land and African labor more difficult—it was given a low priority. Only minimal efforts were made to instruct Indian tribes in Christian doctrine, and most of the efforts were inspired by the expectation that conversion would go hand in hand with pacification and political control. To be sure, the Great Awakening produced a wave of missionizing attempts among Indian tribes, especially in the North, but it is worth noting that the Awakeners themselves were regarded by polite society as dangerous in their attempts to break down social, sexual, and racial lines. In the late colonial period Southern slaves were widely exposed to Christian doctrine in the upper South where the threat of slave revolt was not so keenly felt, but they were carefully shielded from the potentially radical message of Christianity in South Carolina and Georgia. Slaves in the North were broadly inculcated with Protestantism but this would probably not have happened if slaves had not been vastly outnumbered by whites. In education it was the same: Slaves were educated in those things that enabled them to function in their work more effectively; but education as a concept, as a process of inquiry, was shunned, for it promised only to cultivate aspirations that were inappropriate to those whose servitude was lifelong.

A handful of reformers and churchmen kept alive the humanitarian impulse, based on the theory that by uplifting Africans and Indians from heathenism they could be assimilated into Anglo-American society. But most colonists regarded the two cultural minorities in their midst as unassimilable, as was to be revealed when the emancipation of slaves in the Revolutionary era brought cries for their repatriation to Africa. So far as the assimilation of Indians was concerned, nothing could have been less desirable to European settlers, who coveted Indian land but not land with Indians on it.

Also working against assimilation was the inner need of white colonists to justify the exploitation of Africans and Indians by insisting on the wide gap that separated "savagery" from "civilization." By definition, assimilation would narrow this gap, making Africans and Indians more like Europeans. But when mighty master and lowly slave, or "rational" European and "unreasoning" savage were admitted to be alike, either in outward manners or inner capacity, then the entire rationale of domination and exploitation would crumble. This need to deny alikeness and to oppose any measures that would increase the similarity of peoples in colonial society was an important reason for resisting the Christianization of slaves. It also worked to convince white colonists that Indians were unassimilable. One of the mistaken notions about colonial Americans that endured in England was that the settlers would happily receive the missionaries of the Anglican Society for the Propagation of the Gospel, which hoped to convert both slaves and Indians to the word of Christ. The Bishop of London summed up this misconception of the colonial desire for assimilation when he "referred to Negroes as 'truly a Part of our own Nation'—which was just what the colonists were sure Negroes were not."[25] The same was true for Indians.

A second paradox was that white American culture developed the most pervasively negative attitudes toward the cultural minority in its midst that was indispensably valuable to it—the Afro-Americans—and held the more positive attitudes toward the cultural minority which stood only as an obstacle to white society once their military assistance was no longer needed—the Indians. Colonial society grew in size and strength in direct relationship to an increase in slaves and a decrease in "land-cluttering" Indians. Yet it was the black African upon whom the colonists fastened the most indelibly negative images. The key to this irony was that the colonist almost always encountered Africans as slaves and thus came to think of them as abject and less than human creatures. But the English settlers met Indians as adversar-

[25]Quoted in Jordan, *White Over Black*, p. 208.

ies or half-trusted allies. The Indian maintained the freedom to come and go, to attack and kill, to give and withhold support, and to retain political sovereignty. Though he was hated for many of these things, they earned him a grudging respect. The Anglo-Indian relationship in the eighteenth century was rarely that of master and slave with all rights and power concentrated on one side. Instead, when Indian and European colonizer met, they were involved in a set of power relationships in which each side, with something to offer the other, maneuvered for the superior position. The Indian was the ultimate loser in most of these interchanges but that cannot obscure the fact that for several hundred years Anglo-Americans confronted Indians as formidable adversaries rather than as chattels. Though they were exploited, excluded, and often decimated in their contacts with European civilization, Indians usually maneuvered from a position of strength.

Africans in America, by contrast, were rarely a part of any political or business equation. They had only their labor to offer and even that was not subject to contractual agreement. Slaves were not powerless in their dealings with white society, but they were powerless as compared with Indians. This uneven distribution of power in black-white relations could not help but affect attitudes. Unlike the Indians, the Africans were rarely able to win the respect of the white man because their situation was rarely one where respect was required or even possible. Tightly trapped in an authoritarian relationship where most of the power was on the other side, Africans, as they became more and more important to the white man's economy, sank lower and lower in the white man's estimation. Meanwhile the Indian, though hated, was respected for his fighting ability, his dignity, and even his oratorical skill. American colonists sometimes scoffed at the efforts of the Enlightenment philosophers to depict the American native as a "noble savage," the archetype of natural beauty and virtue, uncorrupted by materialistic Western civilization; but their image of the Indian came to have a positive side. The sociology of red-white and black-white relations had differed greatly over six generations. From these variations evolved distinct white attitudes, in both cases adverse, but in significantly different ways.

A third paradox in the convergence of cultures was that the group that was enslaved, degraded, and despised survived and flourished in America, while the group that maintained its freedom, much of its power, and a considerable amount of European respect suffered depopulation and gradual decline. It does not minimize the pain, humiliation, and brutality of slavery to point out that Africans in America were remarkably successful in a demographic sense, particularly in contrast to most other areas of the New World. The limited data available suggest that while black mortality was substantially higher than white mortality, black fertility may have been close to the white norm. It can be stated with certainty that slave mortality in eighteenth-century America was far lower than anywhere else in the New World. This is not necessarily explained by more humane treatment on

American plantations. More important was the more favorable epidemic environment of North America. The Caribbean islands were known as grave-yards for white and black alike, and in the Latin America countries tropical diseases swept away African slaves like leaves in a windstorm.

A comparison of Virginia and Jamaica slave imports and slave populations illustrates the point. The slave populations of the two colonies were almost equal in 1775, with Virginians owning about 200,000 slaves and the Jamaicans about 193,000. But between 1700 and 1775, Virginia had imported not more than 100,000 slaves by the most liberal estimates, while in Jamica net importations were more than three and a half times as great. Life for African slaves on eighteenth-century Southern plantations was healthier than in other parts of the New World and, because of a more favorable sex ratio than in other plantation areas, the chances of family life were much greater.

By contrast, the Indian tribes east of the Appalachian Mountains suffered disastrous population losses in the first two centuries of contact with Europeans. Although they were not struck down in the same catastrophic proportions as the indigenous people of Mexico and most parts of Latin America, their mortality rate and natural decline stood in stark contrast to the natural increase of enslaved Africans. In areas of white settlement along the coastal plain, only remnants of the Indian population remained on the eve of the Revolution. Connecticut, for example, counted only 930 Indians in a census in 1762; Massachusetts found 1,681 in 1764; Virginia listed only 130 in 1774; and Rhode Island tabulated 1,482 in the same year.

Several factors explain the different demographic histories of Africans and Native Americans. First, Africans were far more resistant to European epidemic diseases and by the mid-eighteenth century were being immunized, like whites, against smallpox, the biggest killer of all. Hardly an Indian tribe in the eastern part of the continent escaped the dread disease. The eastern Massachusetts tribes had been decimated even before the Puritans arrived and were again struck down in substantial numbers in the early years of white settlement. The Iroquois were scourged several times in the seventeenth and eighteenth centuries. The Catawba population of North Carolina was reduced by half during a single epidemic in 1759, and a raging smallpox epidemic hit the Cherokees so severely in 1738 that according to several estimates they lost nearly half their population. The disease swept the Creeks in the last years of the seventeenth century and continued to diminish their numbers in the following decades. Far less important as a killer were the wars which tribes fought with European settlers and with each other at the instigation of their trading partners. But these too took a toll on life that was not duplicated in the slave experience. Still another cause of depopulation was alcohol which, though it killed slowly in contrast to smallpox and other epidemic diseases, also counted many victims.

All the lethal factors that decimated Indian villages throughout eastern North America touched slaves only incidentally. This was not coincidental.

White colonists did not possess direct control over bacteriological and demographic factors, but they eagerly sought to increase the black slave population while reducing the Indian population. To this end they instituted policies which influenced, if they did not control, population curves. Blacks, for example, were inoculated against smallpox and given medical treatment in case of sickness. For a plantation owner to do this was only to preserve his property, just as he would attempt to maintain the health of his horses and farm animals. If Indians, however, contracted an epidemic disease, the colonist could only give thanks that God had seen fit to diminish their numbers in order to make more room for "civilized" persons. European colonists only occasionally waged bacteriological warfare in a conscious way, such as by spreading smallpox through infected trade goods, but they were uninterested in arresting epidemic disease among the Indians in contrast to their slaves. With alcohol it was the same. It was rationed out to slaves at holiday time and sometimes at week's end as a reward for work accomplished. But alcohol was distributed among Indian tribes in order to create not only dependency but addiction. Rum was a liquid form of control for white colonists in their dealings with both Africans and Indians. But it was intended to sustain life among blacks while destroying life among Indians.

War was the third killer and it was also controlled to some extent by whites. Black rebellion was, of course, quelled as quickly as possible, for it was a direct threat to the labor system and to social dominance by whites. But war with Indians and war among Indians was often artfully encouraged. As soon as they had determined that they could outmatch local tribes, colonists in the seventeenth century found reasons for making war on coastal tribes. For example, Emanuel Downing, John Winthrop's brother-in-law, thought a war with the Narragansett Indians would be of "verie considerable" advantage to the colony. Downing argued that it would be a sin in God's eyes for the Puritans, "having power in our hands, to suffer them to maynteyne the worship of the devill which their paw wawes often doe." He then predicted the history of the next century by pointing out that "If upon a Just warre the Lord should deliver them [the Narragansetts] into our hands, wee might easily have men, women, and children enough to exchange for Moores, which wilbe more gaynefull pilladge for us than wee conceive."[26]

Downing's willingness to please God while serving the colonists' material needs was a typical seventeenth-century mode of justifying war against local tribes. In the eighteenth century such arguments were couched in purely secular language and then applied to strong interior tribes rather than to small coastal societies. In this changed context, the policy became to create animosities between Indian groups. "If we cannot destroy one nation of

---

[26]Quoted in Almon W. Lauber, *Indian Slavery in Colonial Times Within the Present Limits of the United States* (New York: Columbia University Press, 1913), p. 311.

Indians by another," wrote South Carolina's governor in 1717, "our country must be lost."[27] This was not only the most effective deterrent to pan-Indian uprisings against the Europeans but also contributed to the general population decline of Indians.

Thus, while escaping slavery in most cases, Native Americans found themselves confronting a mushrooming European population that sought the land they occupied and found Indians useful only as auxiliaries in the destruction of other Indians. This had not been true for most of the colonial period, for so long as the European population was small, so long as it was divided among Spanish, French, and English contenders for continental supremacy, and so long as the fur and skin trade was a major factor in the colonial economy, the Indian had been indispensable to the colonizers. By the mid-eighteenth century, however, the Indian trade had become a minor part of the colonial economy. Fishing and shipbuilding in New England, grain and livestock production in the Middle Colonies, and tobacco, rice, and indigo production on Southern plantations had become the principal forms of economic activity. By 1763 the elimination of France as an imperial rival eliminated the need for Indian military support. Finally, the tremendous growth of population in the two generations before the Revolution made acquisition of the interior river valleys of the continent the preoccupation of both Eastern speculators, for whom population growth had created a new source of wealth far greater than the fur trade, and the swarming settlers who poured through the mountain gaps into the Trans-Appalachian region.

A final paradox was that Indian societies treasured many of the values that English settlers and other Europeans had braved the Atlantic to reestablish in the New World. Idealistic Europeans saw the "wilderness" of North America as a place where tired, corrupt, materialistic, self-seeking Europeans might begin a new life centered around the frayed but vital values of reciprocity, spirituality, and community. From John Winthrop to William Penn to John Woolman the notion of transplanted Europeans building a virtuous society in the New World coursed through the dreamlife of the newcomers. Yet as time passed and Europeans became more numerous, it became evident that the people in North America who best upheld these values were the people who were being driven from the land.

Even hard-bitten, unsentimental colonists often recognized that Indian society, though by no means without its problems and its own disreputable characters, put white society to shame. The English Commissioners investigating Bacon's Rebellion in 1676 wrote a scorching letter to the government of Virginia asking them to stop the land grabbing of settlers who already had title to all the land they could use but "still Covett & seek to deprive them [the Indians] of more, out of meer Itch of Luxurie rather than any reall lack of it, which shames us and makes us become a Reproach and a

[27]Quoted in Wallace, *South Carolina: A Short History, 1820–1948* pp. 91–92.

byword to those more Morall heathens."[28] Three quarters of a century later, Thomas Pownall, governor of Massachusetts, excoriated the colonists for violating their own principles and wrote that "the frauds, abuses, and deceits that these poor people have been treated with and suffered under have had no bounds."[29] Edmond Atkin, an Indian trader of South Carolina who knew Indians not from drawing-room accounts but from years of intimate contact, wrote in 1755 that

> No people in the World understand and pursue their true National Interest, better than the Indians. . . . Yet in their publick Treaties no People on earth are more open, explicit, and Direct. Nor are they excelled by any in the observance of them. . . . With respect to . . . all Ruptures of Consequence between the Indians & the white People, and the Massacres that ensued, . . . the latter were first the Aggressors; the Indians being driven thereto under Oppressions and Abuses, and to vindicate their Natural Rights.[30]

Throughout the colonial period European observers stood in admiration of the Indian traits of morality, generosity, bravery, and the spirit of mutual caring. Indians seemed to embody these Christian virtues almost without effort while colonizing Europeans, attempting to build a society with similar characteristics, were being pulled in the opposite direction by the natural abundance around them—toward individualism, disputatiousness, aggrandizement of wealth, and the exploitation of other humans. Many eighteenth-century colonial moralists made the point that Indians hewed closer to the precepts of Christianity than most of the settlers. "As a nation," John Brickell wrote of the Delawares, "they may be considered fit examples for many of us Christians to follow. They certainly follow what they are taught to believe more closely, and I might say more honestly, in general, than we Christians do the divine precepts of our Redeemer."[31]

This was a kind of innocence that beckoned destruction. By embodying some of the virtues around which Europeans had hoped to reorganize their cultural system, but could not, the Indian was a disturbing reminder of the retrogression of Europeans in their New World setting. English, Germans, Scots-Irish, Swedes, Finns, Dutch, French Huguenots, and others might congratulate themselves on the eve of the American Revolution for "taming the wilderness"; for building thriving seaports where none had previously existed; for raising towns, churches, schools, and governments along a thousand miles of coastal plain from Maine to Georgia. They had chosen productivity and acquisitiveness, but these had been pursued at the cost of

[28]*Virginia Magazine of History and Biography*, 14 (1906–07): 274.

[29]Quoted in Georgiana C. Nammack, *Fraud, Politics and the Dispossession of the Indians; The Iroquois Land Frontier in the Colonial Period* (Norman: University of Oklahoma Press, 1969), p. 31.

[30]Jacobs, ed., *Atkin Report and Plan*, p. 38.

[31]"John Brickell's Captivity," *American Pioneer*, 1 (1842), 47–48, quoted in James Axtell, "The White Indians of Colonial America," *William and Mary Quarterly*, 32 (1975): 86.

principles earlier regarded as central to the colonizers' dreams for life in the New World.

In the complex interaction of Native Americans, Europeans, and Africans the distribution of power between dominant and subordinate groups must always be kept in mind. It largely dictated the formal outcome of the cultural confrontation—the historical process at work. Laws, institutions, boundary lines, trade agreements, settlement patterns, and much else emerged as they did because white colonizers were ultimately stronger than native occupiers of the land or Africans brought to the New World in chains. All social, economic, and political relations had to be mediated, however, because the power available to Europeans was anything but absolute. Still, the colonizers' power grew in proportion to numbers and political cohesiveness, both of which rose sharply over the long period of pre-Revolutionary history.

Yet the pathways of power did not strictly dictate the history of cultural interchange—a point that is obscured if we mistakenly assume that under conditions of oppression and exploitation acculturation occurs in only one direction. The culture of Africans and Indians—their agricultural techniques, modes of behavior, styles of speech, dress, food preferences, music, dance, and other aspects of daily existence—became commingled with European culture in ways not automatically determined by the status differences of the three groups. For example, "the status of the master's child vis-a-vis his slave governess," write Mintz and Price, "would surely affect his learning of a style of command in dealing with slaves. But his speech, his food preferences, his imagery, his earliest ideas about men and women, and a good deal more of what would become in time his characteristic quality as an individual would be learned from someone far below him in status, but otherwise very much in control of him."[32] Most of this Africanization of European culture occurred within the intimate personal encounters of slaves and masters and their families—relationships that took place daily within the context of work, domestic service, and interracial sex. The Indianization of European culture occurred within a different context, for intimate encounters were occasional. Instead, the colonizers consciously borrowed Indian crops, pharmacopeia, trapping techniques, vocabulary, dress styles, and much else because they recognized the usefulness of these adaptations. "New World it is," we are reminded, "for those who became its peoples remade it, and in the process, they remade themselves,"[33] whether red, white, or black.

---

[32]Sidney W. Mintz and Richard Price, *An Anthropological Approach to the Afro-American Past: A Caribbean Perspective* (Philadelphia: Institute for the Study of Human Issues, 1976), p. 16.

[33]*Ibid.*, p. 44.

BIBLIOGRAPHICAL ESSAY

Students who wish to deepen their understanding of the interaction among ethnic and cultural groups in early America will soon learn that many of the books and journals they need to consult are not shelved in the American history section of their library but in the areas devoted to anthropology, ethnography, African history, and even music and folklore. In the bibliography that follows, particular attention is given to identifying these less familiar works of scholarship and relatively little attention is given to the immense historical literature concerning English colonists and other Europeans in North America during the colonial period. Comprehensive guides to this more traditional approach to the history of early America are Alden T. Vaughan, *The American Colonies in the Seventeenth Century* (New York, 1971) and Jack P. Greene, *The American Colonies in the Eighteenth Century, 1689–1763* (New York, 1969).

INDIAN CULTURE

A few general histories of Indian culture in North America are worth consulting by those who are making their first acquaintance with "the first Americans." Among the best are Harold E. Driver, *Indians of North Amer-*

ica (Chicago, 1961); Fred Eggan, *The American Indian: Perspectives for the Study of Social Change* (Chicago, 1967); Harold Fey and D'Arcy McNickle, *Indians and Other Americans: Two Ways of Life Meet* (New York, 1959); Frederick Hodge, ed., *Handbook of American Indians North of Mexico* (New York, 1960); Alvin M. Josephy, Jr., *The Indian Heritage of America* (New York, 1968); William Christie MacLeod, *The American Indian Frontier* (New York, 1928); D'Arcy McNickle, *They Came Here First: The Epic of the American Indians* (New York, 1949); Robert Spencer and Jesse Jennings, *The Native Americans: Prehistory and Ethnology of the North American Indians* (New York, 1965); W. W. Newcomb, Jr., *American Indian History: An Anthropological Perspective* (Pacific Palisades, Cal., 1974); Ruth M. Underhill, *Red Man's America: A History of Indians in the United States* (Chicago, 1953); Deward E. Walker, Jr., *The Emergent Native Americans: A Reader in Culture Contact* (Boston, 1972); Jennings C. Wise, *The Red Man in the New World Drama* (Washington, D.C., 1931); and Clark Wissler, *Indians of the United States: Four Centuries of Their History and Culture* (New York, 1940).

More detailed accounts of Indian life in North America before the arrival of Europeans are numerous, but students should be aware that new findings by archaeologists and new conceptual approaches by anthropologists are continually changing our understanding of how long human life has existed in North America, how societies changed, and how cultural diffusion took place. Some general works on the "prehistory" of North America are Jesse Jennings, *Prehistory of North America* (New York, 1968); Jesse Jennings and Edward Norbeck, eds., *Prehistoric Man in the New World* (Chicago, 1964); Paul S. Martin, George I. Quimby, and Donald Collier, *Indians Before Columbus: Twenty Thousand Years of North American History Revealed by Archaeology* (Chicago, 1947); Kenneth Macgowan and Joseph A. Hester, Jr., *Early Man in the New World* (Garden City, N.Y., 1962); William T. Sanders and Joseph Marino, *New World Prehistory: Archaeology of the American Indian* (Englewood Cliffs, N.J.: 1970); and Gordon Willey, ed., *Prehistoric Settlement Patterns in the New World* (New York, 1956). The volumes edited by Jennings and Norbeck and by Willey include references to almost all the important literature in this area.

Several special topics concerning Indian life before European colonization deserve special attention. The development of agriculture, which is of critical importance in the evolution of all societies, is discussed in Richard S. MacNeish, "The Origins of New World Agriculture," *Scientific American* 211 (1964), 29–37. As to the population of the Americas before European arrival—a question fraught with implications for the study of later European-Indian contacts—students should consult the long-standard work of James Mooney, *The Aboriginal Population of America North of Mexico* (Washington, D.C., 1928) and then read the revisionist literature: Henry F. Dobyns, "Estimating Aboriginal American Population: An Appraisal of Techniques with a New Hemispheric Estimate," *Current Anthropology* 7 (1966), 395–416; Wilbur R. Jacobs, "The Tip of the Iceberg: Pre-Columbian Indian Demography and Some Implications for Revisionism," *William and Mary Quarterly* 31 (1974), 23–32; and William M. Denevan, *The Native Population of the Americas in 1492* (Madison, Wis., 1976).

EUROPEAN-INDIAN CONTACT

After gaining some understanding of the peoples of North America before Europeans "discovered" the ancient "New World," students will be better able to comprehend the early stages of European-Indian contact. Books are legion on the early voyages of discovery, but a good place to start is with Carlo M. Cipolla, *Guns, Sails and Empires: Technological Innovations and the Early Phases of European Expansion, 1400–1700* (New York, 1966); John B. Brebner, *The Explorers of North America, 1492–1806* (New York, 1933); and Samuel E. Morison, *The European Discovery of America* (2 vols., New York, 1971–74)

For Europeans, the exploration of North America was not only geographical but psychic, for the native inhabitants had a profound impact on the European mind—an impact that was later to play an important role in the character of intercultural relations. Only an interdisciplinary approach will fully reveal what Europeans thought about these inhabitants of North America. Thus the following books represent the work of scholars in a half dozen disciplines: Henri Baudet, *Paradise on Earth: Thoughts on European Images of Non-European Man*, trans. Elizabeth Wentholt (New Haven, 1965); David Bidney, "The Idea of the Savage in North American Ethnohistory," *Journal of the History of Ideas* 15 (1954), 322–27; Edward Dudley and Maximillian E. Novak, eds., *The Wild Man Within: An Image in Western Thought from the Renaissance to Romanticism* (Pittsburgh, 1972); Leslie A. Fiedler, *The Return of the Vanishing American* (New York, 1968); Carolyn T. Foreman, *Indians Abroad, 1493–1938* (Norman, Okla., 1943); Lee E. Huddleston, *Origins of the American Indians: European Concepts, 1492–1729* (Austin, Texas, 1967); G. K. Hunter, "Elizabethans and Foreigners," in Allardyce Nicoll, ed., *Shakespeare in His Own Age* (Cambridge, 1964); Sidney Lee, "The American Indians in Elizabethan England," in Frederick S. Boas, ed., *Elizabethan and Other Essays* (Oxford, 1929); Fredi Chiapelli, ed., *First Images of America: The Impact of the New World on the Old* (Berkeley and Los Angeles, 1976); Robert F. Berkhofer, Jr., *The White Man's Indian: Images of the American Indian from Columbus to the Present* (New York, 1978); Karen Kupperman, *Settling with the Indians: The Meeting of English and Indian Cultures in America, 1580–1640* (Totowa, N.J., 1980); Gary B. Nash, "The Image of the Indian in the Southern Colonial Mind," *William and Mary Quarterly* 29 (1972), 197–230; Roy H. Pearce, *The Savages of America: A*

Study of the Indian and the Idea of Civilization (Baltimore, 1953); and "The Metaphysics of Indian-Hating," *Ethnohistory* 4 (1957), 27–40; Edmundo O'Gorman, *The Invention of America* (Bloomington, Ind., 1961); and Carl O. Sauer, *Sixteenth Century North America: The Land and the People as Seen by Europeans* (Berkeley, 1971).

The study of early European-Indian relations in North America begins not with English colonists and native peoples but with the arrival of the Spanish, Dutch, and the French on the continent. It is important to study this interaction of non-English people with Indian tribes because it allows for a comparative perspective on the later English experience. A general introduction to a comparative study of European-Indian relations is provided in Howard Peckham and Charles Gibson, eds., *Attitudes of Colonial Powers Toward the American Indian* (Salt Lake City, 1969). More detailed analyses of French-Indian relations in Canada by both historians and anthropologists are: Alfred G. Bailey, *The Conflict of European and Eastern Algonkian Cultures, 1504–1700* (St. John, New Brunswick, 1937); William J. Eccles, *The Canadian Frontier, 1534–1760* (New York, 1969); Robert Goldstein, *French-Iroquois Diplomatic and Military Relations, 1609–1701* (The Hague, 1969); John H. Kennedy, *Jesuit and Savage in New France* (New Haven, 1950); Conrad Heidenreich, *Huronia: A History and Geography of the Huron Indians, 1600–1650* (Toronto, 1971); Cornelius Jaenen, *Friend and Foe: Aspects of French-Amerindian Cultural Contact in the Sixteenth and Seventeenth Centuries* (Toronto, 1976); and Bruce G. Trigger, *The Children of Aataentsic* (Montreal, 1976). For French relations with Indian tribes on the Lower Mississippi, a case of culture contact that stands in vivid contrast to the Canadian experience, consult Andrew C. Albrecht, "Indian-French Relations at Natchez," *American Anthropologist* 48 (1946), 321–54; Jean Delanglez, "The Natchez Massacre and Governor Perier," *Louisiana Historical Quarterly* 17 (1934), 631–41; Jean Delanglez, *The French Jesuits in Lower Louisiana, 1700–63* (New Orleans, 1935); Charles E. O'Neill, *Church and State in French Colonial Louisiana: Policy and Politics to 1732* (New Haven, 1966); and Patricia D. Woods, "The French and the Natchez Indians in Louisiana, 1700–1731," *Louisiana History* 19 (1978), 413–36.

Spanish-Indian interaction in North America, which affected what followed in the English period of settlement, can be followed in Charles Gibson, *Spain in America* (New York, 1966); Woodbury Lowrey, *The Spanish Settlements within the Present Limits the United States*, vol. 1, *1513–1561*; vol. 2, *1562–1574* (New York, 1901–1905); William C. Sturtevant, "Spanish-Indian Relations in Southeastern North America," *Ethnohistory* 9 (1962), 41–94; and Edward Spicer, *Cycles of Conquest: The Impact of Spain, Mexico, and the United States on the Indians of the Southwest, 1533–1960* (Tucson, 1962). For the Dutch record in New Netherland the best studies are Allen W. Trelease, *Indian Affairs in Colonial New York: The Seventeenth Century* (Ithaca, N.Y., 1960) and Ted J. Brasser, *Riding on the Frontier's*

Crest: Mahican Indian Culture and Culture Change, National Museum of Man, Mercury Series, #13 (Ottawa, 1974).

Extending the scope of European-Indian relations to other parts of the New World is a valuable way of establishing the special character of cultural interaction in North America. Magnus Mörner's *Race Mixture in the History of Latin America* (Boston, 1967) is an excellent place to begin. Regarding Spanish colonization, see Lewis Hanke, *Aristotle and the American Indian: A Study in Race Prejudice in the Modern World* (London, 1959); Lewis Hanke, *The Spanish Struggle for Justice in the Conquest of America* (Philadelphia, 1949); Murdo J. MacLeod, *Spanish Central America: A Socio-economic History, 1420–1720* (Berkeley, 1973); and James M. Lockhart, *Spanish Peru, 1532–1560: A Colonial Society* (Madison, Wis., 1968). The Portuguese case is carefully examined in Charles R. Boxer, *Race Relations in the Portuguese Colonial Empire, 1415–1825* (Oxford, 1963); Mathias C. Kiemen, *The Indian Policy of Portugal in the Amazon Region, 1614–1693* (Washington, D.C., 1954); Alexander N. Marchant, *From Barter to Slavery: The Economic Relations of Portuguese and Indians in the Settlement of Brazil, 1500–1580* (Baltimore, 1942); and John Hemming, *Red Gold: The Conquest of the Brazilian Indians, 1500–1760* (Cambridge, Mass., 1978). Charles R. Boxer's *The Dutch Seaborne Empire, 1600–1800* (New York, 1965) includes material on Dutch relations with Indian peoples.

Before embarking on a more detailed investigation of English-Indian interaction in early America, students can profit by assaying the ideas of various historians on how this subject can—and ought to be—approached. In the order of their publication the most important of these are: William N. Fenton, *American Indian and White Relations to 1830: Needs and Opportunities for Study* (Chapel Hill, N.C., 1957); Stanley Pargellis, "The Problem of American Indian History," *Ethnohistory* 4 (1957–58), 113–24; Wilcomb E. Washburn, "A Moral History of Indian-White Relations: Needs and Opportunities for Study," *Ethnohistory* 4 (1957–58), 47–61; Bernard W. Sheehan, "Indian-White Relations in Early America: A Review Essay," *William and Mary Quarterly* 26 (1969), 267–86; Robert F. Berkhofer, Jr., "The Political Context of a New Indian History," *Pacific Historical Review* 40 (1971), 375–82; Wilcomb E. Washburn; "The Writing of American Indian History: A Status Report," *Pacific Historical Review* 40 (1971), 261–81; Robert M. Carmack, "Ethnohistory: A Review of Its Development, Definition, Methods, and Aims," *Annual Review of Anthropology* 1 (1972), 227–46; James Axtell, "The Ethnohistory of Early America," *William and Mary Quarterly* 35 (1978), 110–44; and Kenneth M. Morrison, "Native American History: The Issue of Values," *Journal of Ethnic Studies* 5 (1978), 80–89.

Another prerequisite for studying English-Indian relations is acquiring an understanding of tribal cultures at the time of contact. It is particularly important to comprehend how Native Americans differed from Europeans in their attitude toward land, their economies, their social and political organization, their values and religious beliefs, and their methods of diplomacy and warfare. On land, see A. Irving Hallowell, "The Nature and Function of Property as a Social Institution," in *Culture and Experience* (Philadelphia, 1955), 236–49; Ralph M. Linton, "Land Tenure in Aboriginal America," in Oliver La Farge, ed., *The Changing Indian* (Norman, Okla., 1942), 42–54; George S. Snyderman, "Concepts of Land Ownership among the Iroquois and Their Neighbors," in William N. Fenton, ed., *Symposium on Local Diversity in Iroquois Culture* (Washington, D.C., 1951), 13–34; A. L. Kroeber, "Nature of the Land-Holding Group," *Ethnohistory* 2 (1955), 303–14; and Anthony F. C. Wallace, "Political Organization and Land Tenure among the Northeastern Indians, 1600–1830," *Southwestern Journal of Anthropology* 13 (1957), 301–21.

The most comprehensive work on the economic organization of American Indian societies is Marshall Sahlins, *Stone Age Economics* (Chicago, 1972). Other useful essays are Merrill K. Bennett, "The Food Economy of the New England Indians, 1605–1675," *Journal of Political Economy* 63 (1955), 369–97; Judith Brown, "Economic Organization and the Position of Women Among the Iroquois," *Ethnohistory* 17 (1970), 151–67; and George S. Snyderman, "The Functions of Wampum," *Proceedings of the American Philosophical Society*, 98 (1954), 469–94.

On social organization it is especially important to study the role of women in Native American societies. Among the most important works are John R. Swanton, *Social Organization and Social Usages in the Southeast* (Washington, D.C., 1928); Anthony F. C. Wallace, "Women, Land, and Society: Three Aspects of Colonial Delaware Life," *Pennsylvania Archaeologist* 17 (1947), 1–35; Jon A. Schlenker, "An Historical Analysis of the Family Life of the Choctaw Indians," *Southern Quarterly* 13 (1975), 323–34; Judith K. Brown, "Iroquois Women: An Ethnohistoric Note," in Rayna R. Reiter, *Toward an Anthropology of Women* (New York, 1975); William S. Willis, Jr., "Patrilineal Institutions in Southeastern North America," *Ethnohistory* 10 (1963), 250–69; and Frank G. Speck, "The Family Hunting Band as the Basis of Algonkian Social Organization," *American Anthropologist* n.s. 17 (1915), 289–305.

Political organization, including the much misunderstood problem of factionalism among American Indians, is studied in: Elizabeth Tooker, "Clans and Moieties in North America," *Current Anthropology* 12 (1971), 357–76; William N. Fenton, "Factionalism in American Indian Society," *Tirage a part: Actes du IVᵉ Congres International des Sciences Anthropologiques et Ethnologiques*, II (Vienna, 1952), 330–40; P. Richard Metcalf, "Who Should Rule at Home: Native American Politics and Indian-White Relations," *Journal of American History* 61 (1974–75), 651–65; and Ralph W. Nicholas, "Factions: A Comparative Approach," in Michael Banton, ed., *Political Systems and the Distribution of Power* (London, 1965).

Very little of Indian-white relations can be understood without appreciation of the value system and religious beliefs of Native Americans. A good place to begin is with Ruth M. Underhill's *Red Man's Religion: Beliefs and Practices of the Indians North of Mexico* (Chicago, 1965). Also valuable are: Ake Hultkrantz, *The Religions of the American Indians*, trans. Monica Setterwall (Berkeley and Los Angeles, 1979); Claude Levi-Strauss, *The Savage Mind* (Chicago, 1966); Dennis Tedlock and Barbara Tedlock, eds., *Teachings From the American Earth: Indian Religion and Philosophy* (New York, 1975); and Walter H. Capps, ed., *Seeing With a Native Eye: Essays on Native American Religion* (New York, 1976).

On Indian diplomacy and warfare a number of essays are valuable. George S. Snyderman, "Behind the Tree of Peace: A Sociological Analysis of Iroquois Warfare," *Pennsylvania Archaeologist* 18 (1948), 2–93; Marian W. Smith, "American Indian Warfare," *New York Academy of Sciences, Transactions*, 2d Ser. 13 (1951), 348–65; Wendell S. Hadlock, "War among the Northeastern Woodland Indians," *American Anthropologist*, n. s. 49 (1947), 204–21; Nathaniel Knowles, "The Torture of Captives by the Indians of Eastern North America," American Philosophical Society *Proceedings* 82 (1940), 151–225; James Axtell and William C. Sturtevant, "The Unkindest Cut of All, or Who Invented Scalping?" *William and Mary Quarterly* 37 (1980), 451–72; Patrick M. Malone, "The Changing Military Technology Among the Indians of Southern New England, 1600–1677," *American Quarterly* 25 (1973), 48–63; and J. Frederick Fausz, "Fighting 'Fire' With Firearms: The Anglo-Powhatan Arms Race in Early Virginia," *American Indian Culture and Research Journal* 3 (1979), 33–50.

After studying the characteristics of broad cultural groups, one can turn to examining individual cases of European-Indian contact. These should be considered within a general understanding of "acculturation," a concept which has its own history. See, for example, Melville J. Herskovits, *Acculturation: The Study of Culture Contacts* (New York, 1938); Ralph Linton, ed., *Acculturation in Seven American Indian Tribes* (New York, 1940); Homer G. Barnett, et al., "Acculturation: An Exploratory Formulation," *American Anthropologist*, n.s. 56 (1954), 972–1002; Edward H. Spicer, ed., *Perspectives in American Indian Culture Change* (Chicago, 1961); and Frederik Barth, ed., *Ethnic Groups and Boundaries: The Social Organization of Culture Difference* (London, 1969).

In studying the first major Indian-English confrontation—in the Chesapeake area of Virginia—students must fathom a maze of articles written from a variety of approaches. From the historians have come important works, such as Wesley Frank Craven, *The Southern Colonies in the Seventeenth Century, 1607–1689* (Baton Rouge, 1949); "Indian Policy in Early Virginia," *William and Mary Quarterly* 1 (1944), 65–82; and *White, Red and Black: The Seventeenth-Century Virginian* (Charlottesville, Va., 1971); Bernard Sheehan, *Savagism and Civility: Indians and Englishmen in Colonial Virginia* (Cambridge, 1980); Keith Glenn, "Captain John Smith and the

Indians," *Virginia Magazine of History and Biography* 52 (1944), 228–48; W. Stitt Robinson, Jr., "The Legal Status of the Indian in Colonial Virginia," *Virginia Magazine of History and Biography* 61 (1953), 249–59; Alden T. Vaughan, "'Expulsion of the Salvages': English Policy and the Virginia Massacre of 1622," *William and Mary Quarterly* 35 (1978), 57–84; William S. Powell, "Aftermath of the Massacre: The First Indian War, 1622–1632," *Virginia Magazine of History and Biography* 66 (1958), 44–75; Carl Bridenbaugh, *Jamestown, 1544–1699* (New York, 1980); Wilcomb E. Washburn, *The Governor and the Rebel: A History of Bacon's Rebellion in Virginia* (Chapel Hill, N.C., 1957); and two biographies of Pocahontas, whose acceptance of the English colonists and marriage to one of them suggests why she, rather than her father Powhatan, has captured the American imagination: Philip L. Barbour, *Pocahontas and Her World* (Boston, 1970) and Grace Woodward, *Pocahontas* (Norman, Okla., 1969). From the anthropologists and ethnohistorians of early Virginia the following are particularly worthy of attention: Lewis R. Binford, "An Ethnohistory of the Nottoway, Meherran and Weanock Indians of Southeastern Virginia," *Ethnohistory* 14 (1967), 104–218; David I. Bushnell, Jr., "Virginia before Jamestown," in *Essays in Historical Anthropology of North America* (Washington, D.C., 1940); Christian F. Feest, "Powhatan: A Study in Political Organization," *Wiener Völkerkundliche Mitteilungen* (1966), 69–83; J. Frederick Fausz, "Opechancanough: Indian Resistance Leader," in David W. Sweet and Gary B. Nash, *Struggle and Survival in Colonial America* (Berkeley and Los Angeles, 1981); Nancy O. Lurie, "Indian Cultural Adjustment to European Civilization," in James M. Smith, ed., *Seventeenth-Century America: Essays in Colonial History* (Chapel Hill, N.C., 1959); Ben C. McCary, *Indians in Seventeenth-Century Virginia* (Williamsburg, Va., 1957); Maurice Mook, "The Anthropological Position of the Indian Tribes of Tidewater Virginia," *William and Mary Quarterly*, 2nd series 23 (1943), 27–40; and "Algonkian Ethnohistory of the Carolina Sound," *Washington Academy of Sciences Journal* 34 (1944), 181–97, 213–28; James Mooney, "The Powhatan Confederacy, Past and Present," *American Anthropologist*, n.s. 9 (1907), 129–152; Frank G. Speck, *Chapters on the Ethnology of the Powhatan Tribes in Virginia* (New York, 1928); *The Rappahonnock Indians of Virginia* (New York, 1925); and "The Ethnic Position of the Southeastern Algonkian," *American Anthropologist*, n.s. 26 (1924), 184–200; and Theodore Stern, "Chickahominy: The Changing Culture of a Virginia Indian Community," *Proceedings of the American Philosophical Society* 96 (1952), 152–225.

To the north and south of the Virginian-Powhatan encounter, the story of Anglo-Indian relations can be followed in Raphael Semmes, "Aboriginal Maryland, 1608–89," *Maryland Historical Magazine* 24 (1929), 157–72, 195–209; Francis Jennings, "Glory, Death, and Transfiguration: The Susquehannock Indians in the Seventeenth Century," *Proceedings of the American Philosophical Society* 112 (1968), 15–53; Jane Henry, "The Choptank

Indians of Maryland Under the Proprietary Government," *Maryland Historical Magazine* 65 (1970), 171–80; James H. Merrell, "Cultural Continuity among the Piscataway Indians of Colonial Maryland," *William and Mary Quarterly* 36 (1979), 548–70; and Douglas Rights, *The American Indian in North Carolina* (Durham, N.C., 1947).

The second major case of culture contact between Englishmen and native North Americans in the seventeenth century came in New England. Of special importance in understanding cultural interaction are recent works which probe the Puritan mind for characteristics that imparted a special quality to the Puritan approach to Indian affairs: James Axtell, "The Scholastic Philosophy of the Wilderness," *William and Mary Quarterly* 29 (1972), 335–66; Peter N. Carroll, *Puritanism and the Wilderness: The Intellectual Significance of the New England Frontier, 1629–1700* (New York, 1969); Roy H. Pearce, "The 'Ruines of Mankind': The Indian and the Puritan Mind," *Journal of the History of Ideas* 13 (1952), 200–217; Richard Slotkin, *Regeneration through Violence: The Mythology of the American Frontier, 1600–1860* (Middletown, Conn., 1973); and William S. Simmons, "Cultural Bias in the New England Puritans' Perception of Indians," *William and Mary Quarterly* 38 (1981), 56–72.

Widely divergent opinions are held by historians on how the Puritans intended to conduct their relations with people of a different culture. The labels "coexistence" and "coercion" can stand for the two approaches that historians have discerned. Both interpretations are well amplified in the following works: George F. Willison, *Saints and Strangers* (New York, 1945); Alden T. Vaughan, *New England Frontier: Puritans and Indians, 1620–1675* (Boston, 1965); Francis Jennings, *The Invasion of America: Indians, Colonialism, and the Cant of Conquest* (Chapel Hill, N.C., 1975); Neal E. Salisbury, *Manitou and Providence: Indians, Europeans, and the Beginnings of New England* (New York, 1982); and Douglas E. Leach, *Flintlock and Tomahawk: New England in King Philip's War* (New York, 1958). More specialized studies are Leonard A. Adolf, "Squanto's Role in Pilgrim Diplomacy," *Ethnohistory* 11 (1964), 247–61; David Bushnell, "The Treatment of the Indians in Plymouth Colony," *New England Quarterly* 26 (1953), 193–218; Jack L. Davis, "Roger Williams among the Narragansett Indians," *New England Quarterly* 43 (1970), 593–604; Gordon M. Day, "English-Indian Contacts in New England," *Ethnohistory* 9 (1962), 24–40; Chester E. Eisinger, "The Puritans' Justification for Taking the Land," *Essex Institute Historical Collections* 84 (1948), 131–43; Harry A. Wright, "The Technique of Seventeenth-Century Indian Land Purchases," *Essex Institute Historical Collections* 77 (1941), 185–97; M. K. Bennett, "The Food Economy of the New England Indians, 1605–75," *Journal of Political Economy* 63 (1955), 369–97; Peter A. Thomas, "Contrastive Subsistence Strategies and Land Use as Factors for Understanding Indian-White Relations in New England," *Ethnohistory* 23 (1976), 1–18; Yasu Kawashima, "Legal Origins of the Indian

Reservation in Colonial Massachusetts," *American Journal of Legal History* 13 (1969), 42–56; and "Jurisdiction of the Colonial Courts over the Indians in Massachusetts, 1689–1763," *New England Quarterly* 42 (1969), 532–50; James P. Ronda, "Red and White at the Bench: Indians and the Law in Plymouth County, 1620–1691," *Essex Institute Historical Collections* 110 (1974), 200–15; Lyle Koehler, "Red-White Relations and Justice in the Courts of Seventeenth-Century New England," *American Indian Culture and Research Journal* 3 (1979), 1–31. John Sainsbury, "Miantonomo's Death and New England Politics, 1630–1645," *Rhode Island History* 20 (1971), 11–23; G. E. Thomas, "Puritans, Indians, and the Concept of Race," *New England Quarterly* 48 (1975), 3–27; and William Burton and Richard Lowenthal, "Uncas: The First of the Mohegans," *American Ethnologist* 1 (1974), 589–99.

No Indian group in eastern North America has been more studied by historians and anthropologists than the Iroquois, whose geographical position placed them in close contact for two centuries with European settlers from France, Holland, and England. Both anthropologists and historians are represented in the following selection, which represents only an introduction to Iroquois studies: William N. Fenton, "Problems Arising from the Historic Northeastern Position of the Iroquois," in *Essays in Historical Anthropology of North America* (Washington, D.C., 1940); William N. Fenton, ed., *Symposium on Local Diversity in Iroquois Culture* (Washington, D.C., 1951); George T. Hunt, *The Wars of the Iroquois: A Study in Intertribal Relations* (Madison, Wis., 1940); Karl H. Schleiger, "Epidemics and Indian Middlemen: Rethinking the Wars of the Iroquois, 1609–1653," *Ethnohistory* 23 (1976), 129–45; Allen W. Trelease, *Indian Affairs in Colonial New York: The Seventeenth Century* (Ithaca, N.Y., 1960); Anthony F. C. Wallace, *The Death and Rebirth of the Seneca* (New York, 1969); William N. Fenton, "The Lore of the Longhouse: Myth, Ritual, and Red Power," *Anthropological Quarterly* 48 (1975), 131–47. James T. Flexner, *Mohawk Baronet: Sir William Johnson of New York* (New York, 1959); Barbara Graymont, *The Iroquois in the American Revolution* (Syracuse, N.Y., 1972); Francis Jennings, "The Constitutional Evolution of the Covenant Chain," *Proceedings of the American Philosophical Society* 115 (1971), 88–96; Georgiana C. Nammack, *Fraud, Politics, and the Dispossession of the Indians: The Iroquois Land Frontier in the Colonial Period* (Norman, Okla., 1969); and Arthur C. Parker, *History of the Seneca Indians* (Port Washington, N.Y., 1967).

Of special interest to students of Indian-European relations, because it casts grave doubts on the widely enunciated thesis that conflict was inevitable between cultural groups as widely separate as Algonkians and Europeans, is the interaction of the Pennsylvania Quakers and the Delaware (Lenni Lenape) Indians. Both the early Quaker contacts with the Delawares and the subsequent breakdown of amicable relations are detailed in the following selections: Thomas E. Drake, "Penn's Experiment in Race Relations," *Pennsylvania Magazine of History and Biography* 68 (1944), 372–87; Francis Jennings, "The Delaware Interregnum," *Pennsylvania Magazine of History and Biography* 89 (1965), 174–98; Rayner W. Kelsey, *Friends and the Indians, 1655–1917* (Philadelphia, 1917); W. W. Newcomb, Jr., *The Culture and Acculturation of the Delaware Indians* (Ann Arbor, Mich., 1956); Theodore G. Thayer, "The Friendly Association," *Pennsylvania Magazine of History and Biography* 67 (1943), 356–76; Frederick B. Tolles, "Nonviolent Contact: The Quakers and the Indians," *Proceedings of the American Philosophical Society* 107 (1963), 93–101; Sherman P. Uhler, *Pennsylvania's Indian Relations to 1754* (Allentown, Pa., 1951); Anthony F. C. Wallace, *King of the Delawares: Teedyuscung, 1700–1763* (Philadelphia, 1949); Paul A. W. Wallace, *Indians in Pennsylvania* (Harrisburg, Pa., 1961); C. A. Weslager, *The Delaware Indians: A History* (New Brunswick, N.J., 1972); and Charles E. Hunter, "The Delaware Nativist Revival of the Mid-Eighteenth Century," *Ethnohistory* 18 (1971), 39–50.

Because it was not settled until the last third of the seventeenth century the Southeast was the last zone of Anglo-Indian contact in the colonization of North America. But interaction between the English settlers of the Carolinas and Georgia with the Creeks and Cherokees, the two most powerful tribes of this region, is among the most instructive examples of culture contact, because these powerful tribes, like the Iroquois, maintained their political power and cultural integrity long after the small coastal tribes had been decimated or subordinated. This complex confrontation, which involved shifting alliances between the three European powers contending for advantage in the area and the two Indian powers seeking preeminence, must be followed in both historical and anthropological accounts. The best are: John P. Brown, *Old Frontiers: The Story of the Cherokee Indians from Earliest Times to the Date of Their Removal to the West* (Kingsport, Tenn., 1938); David H. Corkran, *The Cherokee Frontier: Conflict and Survival, 1740–62* (Norman, Okla., 1962); and *The Creek Frontier, 1540–1783* (Norman, Okla., 1967); John P. Corry, *Indian Affairs in Georgia, 1732–56* (Philadelphia, 1936); R. S. Cotterill, *The Southern Indians: The Story of the Civilized Tribes before Removal* (Norman, Okla., 1954); E. Merton Coulter, "Mary Musgrove, 'Queen of the Creeks': A Chapter of Early Georgia Troubles," *Georgia Historical Quarterly* 11 (1927), 1–30; Verner W. Crane, *The Southern Frontier, 1670–1732* (Ann Arbor, Mich., 1929); Frederick Gearing, *Priests and Warriors: Social Structures for Cherokee Politics in the 18th Century* (Menasha, Wis., 1962); Mary R. Haas, "Creek Inter-town Relations," *American Anthropologist* 42 (1940), 479–89; Charles M. Hudson, ed., *Red, White and Black: Symposium on Indians in the Old South* (Athens, Ga., 1971); Robert L. Meriwether, *The Expansion of South Carolina, 1729–1765* (Kingsport, Tenn., 1940); Chapman J. Milling, *Red Carolinians* (Chapel Hill, N.C., 1940); James Mooney, *Myths of the Cherokee* (Washington, D.C., 1900); Morris E. Opler, "The Creek 'Town' and the

Problem of Creek Indian Political Reorganization," in Edward H. Spicer, ed., *Human Problems in Technological Change: A Casebook* (New York, 1952); Hale G. Smith, *The European and the Indian: European-Indian Contacts in Georgia and Florida* (Gainesville, Fla., 1956); Alexander Spoehr, *Changing Kinship Systems: A Study in the Acculturation of the Creeks, Cherokees, and Choctaws* (Chicago, 1947); John R. Swanton, *The Indians of the Southeastern United States* (Washington, D.C., 1946); *Indian Tribes of Lower Mississippi Valley and Adjacent Coast of the Gulf of Mexico* (Washington, D.C., 1911); and *Early History of the Creek Indians and Their Neighbors* (Washington, D.C., 1922); Charles Hudson, *The Southeastern Indians* (Knoxville, Tenn., 1976); Philip Reid, *A Law of Blood: The Primitive Law of the Cherokee Nation* (New York, 1970), and *A Better Kind of Hatchet: Law, Trade, and Diplomacy in the Cherokee Nation during the Early Years of European Contact* (State College, Pa., 1976); and Rennard Strickland, *Fire and the Spirits: Cherokee Law From Clan to Court* (Norman, Okla., 1975).

Valuable accounts of smaller coastal tribes in the South include John T. Juricek, "The Westo Indians," *Ethnohistory* 11 (1964), 134–73; James W. Covington, "Apalachee Indians, 1704–1763," *Florida Historical Quarterly* 50 (1972), 366–84; William C. Sturtevant, "Spanish-Indian Relations in Southeastern North America," *Ethnohistory* 9 (1962), 41–94; George L. Hicks, "Cultural Persistence Versus Local Adaptation: Frank G. Speck's Catawba Indians," *Ethnohistory* 12 (1965), 343–54; and Charles M. Hudson, *The Catawba Nation* (Athens, Ga., 1970).

In the national imagination and in popular history warfare has always stood out as the crucial element in Indian-white relations. But three aspects of the acculturative process—disease, trade, and religion—deserve much greater emphasis. Of the three, trade is especially important, for along the trade routes went not only material goods but also microorganisms and ideology. For various aspects of the Indian trade and for different assessments of its conduct the following are significant: Harold A. Innis, *The Fur Trade in Canada* (New Haven, 1930); Francis X. Moloney, *The Fur Trade in New England, 1620–1676* (Cambridge, Mass., 1931); Walter O'Meara, *Daughters of the Country: The Women of the Fur Traders and Mountain Men* (New York, 1959); Lewis O. Saum, *The Fur Trader and the Indian* (Seattle, 1965); Malvina Bolus, ed., *People and Pelts: Second North American Fur Trade Conference* (Winnipeg, 1972); *Aspects of the Fur Trade: Selected Papers* (St. Paul, Minn., 1967); Conrad Heidenreich and Arthur J. Ray, *The Early Fur Trade: A Study in Cultural Interaction* (Toronto, 1976); Thomas E. Norton, *The Fur Trade in Colonial New York, 1686–1776* (Madison, Wis., 1974); and Calvin Martin, *Keepers of the Game: Indian-Animal Relationships and the Fur Trade* (Berkeley and Los Angeles, 1979). More specialized studies include Allen W. Trelease, "The Iroquois and the Western Fur Trade: A Problem of Interpretation," *Mississippi Valley Historical*

Review 49 (1962), 32–51; Bruce Trigger, "The Jesuits and the Fur Trade," *Ethnohistory* 12 (1965), 30–53; Francis Jennings, "The Indian Trade of the Susquehanna Valley," *Proceedings of the American Philosophical Society* 110 (1966), 406–424; John C. McManus, "An Economic Analysis of Indian Behavior in the North American Fur Trade," *Journal of Economic History* 32 (1972), 36–53; and Harold Hickerson, "Fur Trade Colonialism and the North American Indians," *Ethnohistory* 1 (1973), 15–44.

On the role of disease in Indian-European relations, see P. M. Ashburn, *The Ranks of Death: A Medical History of the Conquest of America,* ed. Frank D. Ashburn (New York, 1947); Alfred W. Crosby, Jr., *The Columbian Exchange: Biological and Cultural Consequences of 1492* (Westport, Conn., 1972); John Duffy, "Smallpox and the Indians in the American Colonies," *Bulletin of the History of Medicine* 25 (1951), 324–41; E. Wagner and Allen E. Stearn, *The Effect of Smallpox on the Destiny of the Amerindian* (Boston, 1945); and Sherburne F. Cook, "The Significance of Disease in the Extinction of the New England Indians," *Human Biology* 45 (1973), 485–508. Alcohol, another form of disease brought by Europeans to Indian societies in the view of many historians and anthropologists, is re-examined in Nancy Oestreich Lurie, "The World's Oldest On-Going Protest Demonstration: North American Indian Drinking Patterns," *Pacific Historical Review* 40 (1971), 311–32 and Craig MacAndrew and Robert B. Edgerton, *Drunken Comportment: A Social Explanation* (Chicago, 1969).

English missionary activity, which must be seen in a political as well as religious context, is analyzed in G. Gordon Brown, "Missions and Cultural Diffusion," *American Journal of Sociology* 50 (1944), 214–19; W. Stitt Robinson, "Indian Education and Missions in Colonial Virginia," *Journal of Southern History* 18 (1952): 152–68; Francis Jennings, "Goals and Functions of the Puritan Missions to the Indians," *Ethnohistory* 18 (1971), 197–212; Frank J. Klingberg, *Anglican Humanitarianism in Colonial New York* (Philadelphia, 1940); Elma Gray, *Wilderness Christians: The Moravian Mission to the Delaware Indians* (Ithaca, N.Y., 1956); John F. Freeman, "The Indian Convert: Themes and Variations," *Ethnohistory* 12 (1965), 113–28; James P. Ronda, "The European Indian: Jesuit Civilization Planning in New France," *Church History* 41 (1972), 385–95; and " 'We Are Well As We Are': An Indian Critique of Seventeenth-Century Christian Missions," *William and Mary Quarterly* 34 (1977), 66–82; Robert Conkling, "Legitimacy and Conversion in Social Change: The Case of the French Missionaries and the Northeastern Algonkian," *Ethnohistory* 21 (1974), 1–24; Neal Salisbury, "Red Indians: The 'Praying Indians' of Massachusetts Bay and John Eliot," *William and Mary Quarterly* 31 (1974), 27–54, and "Prospero in New England: The Puritan Missionary as Colonist," in William Cowan, ed., *Papers of the Sixth Algonquian Conference,* 1974 National Museum of Man, *Mercury Series* (Ottawa, 1975), 253–73; James Axtell, "The European Failure to Convert the Indians: An Autopsy," *ibid.,* 274–90; and Kenneth M. Morrison, "Towards a History of Intimate Encounters: Algonkian Folklore, Jesuit Missionaries, and Kiwakwe, The Cannibal Giant," *American Indian Culture and Research Journal* 3 (1979), 51–80, and "That Art of Coyning Christians: John Eliot and the Praying Indians of Massachusetts," *Ethnohistory* 21 (1974), 77–92.

Acculturation, of course, was a two-way process. On "Indianization" of European colonists, some especially valuable works are: Erwin H. Ackerknecht, "White Indians," *Bulletin of the History of Medicine* 15 (1944), 18–35; Marius Barbeau, "Indian Captivities," *Proceedings of the American Philosophical Society* 94 (1950), 522–48; Thomas A. Boyd, *Simon Girty: The White Savage* (New York, 1928); Felix S. Cohen, "Americanizing the White Man," in Lucy Kramer Cohen, ed., *The Legal Conscience: Selected Papers of Felix S. Cohen* (New Haven, 1960); A. Irving Hallowell, "The Backwash of the Frontier: The Impact of the Indian on American Culture," in Walker D. Wyman and Clifton B. Kroeber, eds., *The Frontier in Perspective* (Madison, Wis., 1957); and "American Indians, White and Black: The Phenomenon of Transculturalization," *Current Anthropology* 4 (1963), 519–31; J. Norman Heard, *White into Red: A Study of the Assimilation of White Persons Captured by Indians* (Metuchen, N.J., 1973); Roy H. Pearce, "The Significance of the Captivity Narrative," *American Literature* 19 (1947), 1–20; and *Savagism and Civilization: A Study of the Indian and the American Mind* (Baltimore, 1965); James Axtell, "The White Indians of Colonial America," *William and Mary Quarterly* 32 (1975), 55–88; and Theda Perdue, "People Without a Place: Aboriginal Cherokee Bondage," *Indian Historian* 9 (1976), 31–37.

AFRO-AMERICAN HISTORY

Afro-American history begins in Africa, and students who wish to learn more about the Atlantic slave trade and the initial phases of the enslavement process should first gain a basic understanding of African cultures at the time of initial contact with Europeans. A good place to begin is with Basil Davidson, *The African Genius: An Introduction to African Social and Cultural History* (Boston, 1969); J. F. A. Ajayi and Michael Crowder, eds., *History of West Africa*, I (London, 1971); and J. D. Fage, *A History of West Africa*, 4th ed. (London, 1969).

The slave trade should be considered in an international context. Among the many contributions to the literature of this commerce, which was to play such a crucial role in the development of colonial societies in the New World, the following are especially important: Basil Davidson, *The African Slave Trade: Pre-Colonial History, 1450–1850* (Boston, 1961); Philip D. Curtin, *The Atlantic Slave Trade: A Census* (Madison, Wis., 1969); J. E. Inikori, "Measuring the Atlantic Slave Trade: An Assessment of Curtin and Anstey,"

Journal of African History 17 (1976), 197–224, and "Discussion: Measuring the Atlantic Slave Trade," by Philip D. Curtin, Roger Anstey, and J. E. Inikori, *ibid.*, 595–627; Walter Rodney, *West Africa and the Atlantic Slave Trade* (Nairobi, 1969); Richard N. Bean, *The British Transatlantic Slave Trade, 1650–1775* (New York, 1975); Martin Kilson and Robert I. Rotberg, eds., *The African Diaspora* (Cambridge, 1976); Richard S. Sheridan, "Africa and the Caribbean in the Atlantic Slave Trade," *American Historical Review* 77 (1972), 15–35; Herbert Klein, *The Middle Passage: Comparative Studies in the Atlantic Slave Trade* (Princeton, N.J., 1978); and Henry A. Gemery and Jan S. Hoogendorn, eds., *The Uncommon Market: Essays in the Economic History of the Atlantic Slave Trade* (New York, 1979). A comprehensive bibliographical discussion of the slave trade can be found in Peter H. Wood, " 'I Did the Best I Could for My Day': The Study of Early Black History during the Second Reconstruction, 1960–1976," *William and Mary Quarterly* 35 (1978), 199–206.

Some general works on slavery which deal with the origins of the labor system in the New World are Eric Williams, *Capitalism and Slavery* (Chapel Hill, N.C., 1944); Roger T. Anstey, "Capitalism and Slavery: A Critique," *Economic History Review*, 21 (1968), 307–20; David Brion Davis, *The Problem of Slavery in Western Culture* (Ithaca, N.Y., 1966); Stanley M. Elkins, *Slavery: A Problem in American Institutional and Intellectual Life* (Chicago, 1959); Oscar and Mary F. Handlin, "Origins of the Southern Labor System," *William and Mary Quarterly* 7 (1950), 199–222; Robert C. Haywood, "Mercantilism and Colonial Slave Labor, 1700–1763," *Journal of Southern History* 23 (1957), 454–69; C. L. R. James, "The Atlantic Slave Trade and Slavery: Some Interpretations of Their Significance in the Development of the United States and the Western World," *Amistad* 1 (1970), 119–64; Evsey D. Domar, "The Causes of Slavery and Serfdom: A Hypothesis," *Journal of Economic History* 30 (1970), 18–32; Stanley L. Engerman, "Some Considerations Relating to Property Rights in Man," *ibid.* 33 (1973), 43–65; and Carville Earle, "A Staple Interpretation of Slavery and Free Labor," *Geographical Review* 68 (1978), 51–65.

General histories of slavery in the United States are legion, but most of them focus on nineteenth-century slavery in the South and do not trace the evolution of slavery from the colonial period. A general framework for studying slavery can be gained from studying the work of U. B. Phillips, Kenneth Stampp, John W. Blassingame, and Eugene Genovese. A general corrective to their indifference to geographical and temporal variations in the history of slavery is provided by Ira Berlin, "Time, Space, and the Evolution of Afro-American Society on British Mainland North America," *American Historical Review* 85 (1980), 44–78.

Since slavery differed significantly, depending on geography, ecology, settlement patterns, and other factors, regional studies of the institution are invaluable. The Chesapeake colonies of Maryland and Virginia are especially important because it was there that slavery took deepest root in colonial soil in the seventeenth century. A great burst of scholarship is now adding greatly to our understanding of the evolution of Chesapeake slavery delineated in older works, such as Thad W. Tate, Jr., *The Negro in Eighteenth-Century Williamsburg* (Williamsburg, 1965); Wesley F. Craven, *White, Red, and Black: The Seventeenth-Century Virginian* (Charlottesville, Va., 1971); Jonathan L. Alpert, "The Origin of Slavery in the United States: The Maryland Precedent," *American Journal of Legal History* 14 (1970), 189–221; and Adele Hast, "The Legal Status of the Negro in Virginia, 1705–1765," *Journal of Negro History* 54 (1969), 217–39. Among the rich new work of demographic and social historians is Carville V. Earle, *The Evolution of a Tidewater Settlement System: All Hallow's Parish, Maryland, 1650–1783* (Chicago, 1975); Allan Kulikoff, "Black Society and the Economics of Slavery," *Maryland Historical Magazine* 70 (1975), 203–10; "The Origins of Afro-American Society in Tidewater Maryland and Virginia, 1700–1790," *William and Mary Quarterly* 35 (1978), 226–59; and "A 'Prolifick' People: Black Population Growth in the Chesapeake Colonies, 1700–1790," *Southern Studies* 16 (1977), 391–428; Russell Menard, "The Maryland Slave Population, 1658–1730: A Demographic Profile of Blacks in Four Counties," *William and Mary Quarterly* 32 (1975), 29–54; and "From Servants to Slaves: The Transformation of the Chesapeake Labor System," *Southern Studies* 16 (1977), 355–90; T. H. Breen, "A Changing Labor Force and Race Relations in Virginia 1660–1710," *Journal of Social History* 7 (1973), 3–25; and Ronald L. Lewis, "Slavery on Chesapeake Iron Plantations before the American Revolution," *Journal of Negro History* 59 (1974), 242–54; and "The Use and Extent of Slave Labor in the Chesapeake Iron Industry: The Colonial Era," *Labor History* 17 (1976), 388–412.

Slavery in the Carolinas has also attracted the attention of a new generation of scholars. Most important are Peter H. Wood, *Black Majority: Negroes in Colonial South Carolina from 1670 through the Stono Rebellion* (New York, 1974); M. Eugene Sirmans, "The Legal Status of the Slave in South Carolina, 1670–1740," *Journal of Southern History* 28 (1962), 426–73; Daniel C. Littlefield, *Rice and Slaves: Ethnicity and the Slave Trade in Colonial South Carolina* (Baton Rouge, La., 1981); and Philip Morgan, "Black Society in the Lowcountry, 1760–1810," in Ira Berlin and Ronald Hoffman, eds., *Slavery in the Revolutionary Era* (Charlottesville, Va., 1982).

Among the studies of northern slavery in the colonial period, the most important are Lorenzo J. Greene, *The Negro in Colonial New England, 1620–1776* (New York, 1942); Winthrop D. Jordan, "The Influence of the West Indies on the Origins of New England Slavery," *William and Mary Quarterly* 18 (1961), 243–50; Edgar J. McManus, *Black Bondage in the North* (Syracuse, N.Y., 1973); and *Negro Slavery in New York* (Syracuse, N.Y., 1966); Simeon F. Moss, "The Persistence of Slavery and Involuntary Servitude in a Free State (1685–1866)," *Journal of Negro History* 35 (1950),

289–314; Gary B. Nash, "Slaves and Slaveholders in Colonial Philadelphia," *William and Mary Quarterly* 30 (1973), 223–56; Edward R. Turner, *The Negro in Pennsylvania: Slavery, Servitude, Freedom, 1639–1861* (Washington, D.C., 1911); Richard C. Twombly and Robert H. Moore, "Black Puritans: The Negro in Seventeenth-Century Massachusetts," *William and Mary Quarterly* 24 (1967), 224–42; Darold D. Wax, "Quaker Merchants and the Slave Trade in Colonial Pennsylvania," *Pennsylvania Magazine of History and Biography* 86 (1962), 143–59; David Kobrin, *The Black Minority in Early New York* (Albany, 1971); Joyce D. Goodfriend, "Burghers and Blacks: The Evolution of a Slave Society at New Amsterdam," *New York History* 59 (1978), 125–44; and Joseph P. Reidy, " 'Negro Election Day' and Black Community Life in New England, 1750–1860," *Marxist Perspectives* 1 (1978), 102–17.

Comparative studies of slavery in the last generation have done more to increase our understanding of American slavery than almost any other conceptual approach to the history of this institution. Thus students will want to examine slavery outside of North America, both in English colonies in the West Indies and in the colonies of Spain, Portugal, France, and Holland. The field of comparative slave studies is growing enormously and only a fraction of the many studies can be mentioned here. But of special importance are studies that compare two or more slave societies, such as Frank Tannenbaum's pioneering *Slave and Citizen: The Negro in the Americas* (New York, 1956); Marvin Harris, *Patterns of Race in the Americas* (New York, 1964); Herbert S. Klein, *Slavery in the Americas: A Comparative Study of Virginia and Cuba* (Chicago, 1967), Carl N. Degler, *Neither Black Nor White: Slavery and Race Relations in Brazil and the United States* (New York, 1971); H. Hoetink, *Slavery and Race Relations in the Americas* (New York, 1973); Stanley L. Engerman and Eugene Genovese, *Race and Slavery in the Western Hemisphere: Quantitative Studies* (Princeton, N.J., 1975); Ann M. Pescatello, ed., *Old Roots in New Lands: Historical and Anthropological Perspectives on Black Experiences in the Americas* (Westport, Conn. 1977); and Vera Rubin and Arthur Tuden, eds., *Comparative Perspectives on Slavery in New World Plantation Societies*, Annals of the New York Academy of Sciences, v. 292 (New York, 1977).

Valuable studies of seventeenth- and eighteenth-century slavery in individual colonies outside North America are Ronald H. Chilcote, ed., *Protest and Resistance in Angola and Brazil* (Berkeley, Calif., 1972); Harry J. Bennett, *Bondsmen and Bishops: Slavery and Apprenticeship on the Codrington Plantations of Barbados, 1710–1838* (Berkeley, Calif., 1958); Richard S. Dunn, *Sugar and Slaves: The Rise of the Planter Class in the British West Indies, 1624–1713* (Chapel Hill, N.C., 1972); Colin A. Palmer, *Slaves of the White God: Blacks in Mexico, 1570–1650* (Cambridge, Mass., 1976); Florestan Fernandes, *The Negro in Brazilian Society* (New York, 1969); Elsa V. Goveia, *Slave Society in the British Leeward Islands at the*

End of the Eighteenth Century (New Haven, 1965); Gwendolyn M. Hall, *Social Control in Slave Plantation Societies* (Baltimore, 1972); Orlando Patterson, *The Sociology of Slavery: An Analysis of the Origins, Development and Structure of Negro Slave Society in Jamaica* (London, 1967); Frank W. Pitman, "Slavery on the British West India Plantations in the Eighteenth Century," *Journal of Negro History* 11 (1926), 584–668; Michael Craton and James Walvin, *A Jamaican Plantation: A History of Worthy Park, 1670–1970* (Toronto, 1970); Michael Craton, *Searching for the Invisible Man: Slaves and Plantation Life in Jamaica* (Cambridge, Mass., 1978); Richard B. Sheridan, *Sugar and Slavery: An Economic History of the British West Indies, 1623–1775* (Baltimore, 1974); Edward Brathwaite, *The Development of Creole Society in Jamaica, 1770–1820* (Oxford, 1971).

The connections between racism and slavery are intimate. The major work in this area is Winthrop D. Jordan, *White Over Black: American Attitudes Toward the Negro, 1550–1812* (Chapel Hill, N.C., 1968). Jordan's book can be supplemented by Milton Cantor, "The Image of the Negro in Colonial Literature," *New England Quarterly* 36 (1963), 452–77; Carl N. Degler, "Slavery and the Genesis of American Race Prejudice," *Comparative Studies in History and Society* 2 (1959), 49–66; Roger Bastide, "Color, Racism, and Christianity," *Daedalus* 96 (1967), 312–27; and Ronald Sanders, *Lost Tribes and Promised Lands: The Origins of American Racism* (Boston, 1978). Also profitable are the psychoanalytical and anthropological approaches of Erik H. Erikson, "The Concept of Identity in Race Relations," *Daedalus* 95 (1966), 145–71 and John R. Swanton, "Notes on the Mental Assimilation of Races," *Journal of the Washington Academy of Sciences* 16 (1926), 493–502.

A number of special topics concerning the evolution of Afro-American society in colonial America deserve attention. Miscegenation and the status of the mulatto are of great importance. They are thoroughly treated in the previously mentioned work of Winthrop Jordan and Carl Degler and also in Carter G. Woodson, "The Beginnings of Miscegenation of the Whites and Blacks," *Journal of Negro History* 3 (1918), 335–53; Winthrop D. Jordan, "American Chiaroscuro: The Status and Definition of Mulattoes in the British Colonies," *William and Mary Quarterly* 19 (1962), 183–200; Edward B. Reuter, *The Mulatto in the United States* (Boston, 1918); Donald L. Horowitz, "Color Differentiation in the American Systems of Slavery," *Journal of Interdisciplinary History* 3 (1973), 509–41; A. Leon Higgenbotham, Jr., *In the Matter of Color: Race and the American Legal Process: The Colonial Period* (New York, 1978); and William M. Wiecek, "The Statutory Law of Slavery and Race in the Thirteen Mainland Colonies of British America," *William and Mary Quarterly* 34 (1977), 258–80.

Slave resistance is studied in many of the works already mentioned, but is the special concern of the following studies: Raymond A. Bauer and Alice H. Bauer, "Day to Day Resistance to Slavery," *Journal of Negro History* 27

(1942), 388–419; Thomas J. Davis, "The New York Slave Conspiracy of 1741 as Black Protest," *Journal of Negro History* 56 (1971), 17–30; Marion D. duB. Kilson, "Towards Freedom: An Analysis of Slave Revolts in the United States," *Phylon* 25 (1964), 175–87; Gerald W. Mullin, *Flight and Rebellion: Slave Resistance in Eighteenth-Century Virginia* (New York, 1972); Ferenc M. Szasz, "The New York Slave Revolt of 1741: A Re-Examination," *New York History* 48 (1967), 215–30; Darold D. Wax, "Negro Resistance to the Early American Slave Trade," *Journal of Negro History* 51 (1966), 1–15; Ann J. Lane, ed., *The Debate over Slavery: Stanley Elkins and His Critics* (Urbana, Ill., 1971); and Richard Price, ed., *Maroon Societies: Rebel Slave Communities in the Americas* (Garden City, N.Y., 1973).

Important works on the manumission of slaves and the role of the free Negro in colonial society, also studied in many of the more general histories mentioned above, include James H. Brewer, "Negro Property Owners in Seventeenth-Century Virginia," *William and Mary Quarterly* 12 (1955), 575–80; David W. Cohen and Jack P. Greene, eds., *Neither Slave Nor Free: The Freedman of African Descent in the Slave Societies of the New World* (Baltimore, 1972); C. Ashley Ellefson, "Free Jupiter and the Rest of the World: The Problems of a Free Negro in Colonial Maryland," *Maryland Historical Magazine* 66 (1971), 1–13; John H. Russell, *The Free Negro in Virginia, 1619–1865* (Baltimore, 1913); Ross M. Kimmell, "Free Blacks in Seventeenth-Century Maryland," *Maryland Historical Magazine* 71 (1976), 19–25; T. H. Breen and Stephen Innes, *"Myne Owne Ground": Race and Freedom on Virginia's Eastern Shore, 1640–1676* (New York, 1980); and Ira Berlin, *Slaves Without Masters: The Free Negro in the Antebellum South* (New York, 1974).

The best studies of early abolitionist thought are David B. Davis, *The Problem of Slavery in Western Culture* (Ithaca, N.Y., 1966) and *The Problem of Slavery in the Era of Revolution* (Ithaca, N.Y., 1975). Also valuable are Thomas E. Drake, *Quakers and Slavery in America* (New Haven, 1950); W. E. B. DuBois, *The Suppression of the African Slave Trade* (New York, 1896); and Arthur Zilversmit, *The First Emancipation: The Abolition of Slavery in the North* (Chicago, 1967).

The conversion of the African slave to the Christian religion, an important element in the acculturative experience, is studied in Denzil T. Clifton, "Anglicanism and Negro Slavery in Colonial America," *Historical Magazine of the Protestant-Episcopal Church* 39 (1970), 29–70; Marcus W. Jernegan, "Slavery and Conversion in the American Colonies," *American Historical Review* 21 (1915–16), 504–27; Jerome W. Jones, "The Established Virginia Church and the Conversion of Negroes and Indians, 1620–1760," *Journal of Negro History* 46 (1961), 12–23; Frank J. Klingberg, "The African Immigrant in Colonial Pennsylvania and Delaware," *Historical Magazine of the Protestant-Episcopal Church* 11 (1942), 126–53; Edgar L. Pennington, "Thomas Bray's Associates and Their Work Among the Negroes," *American Anti-*

quarian Society Proceedings, n.s. 48 (1938), 311–403; and Douglas C. Strange, " 'A Compassionate Mother to Her Poor Negro Slaves': The Lutheran Church and Negro Slavery in Early America," *Phylon* 29 (1968), 272–81.

Slave religion should be considered not only from the viewpoint of white proselytizing efforts but also from the vantage point of the forging by slaves of Black Christianity. This requires studying the cultural characteristics of African societies from which slaves were taken and the adaptation of these cultural traits in a new environment. A particularly valuable essay on this approach is Sidney W. Mintz and Richard Price, *An Anthropological Approach to the Afro-American Past: A Caribbean Perspective* (Philadelphia, 1976). Among the works by anthropologists, ethnomusicologists, and ethnohistorians that students can profitably consult are: Melville J. Herskovits, *The Myth of the Negro Past* (Boston, 1941) and *The New World Negro* (Bloomington, Ind., 1966); Roger Bastide, *African Civilizations in the New World* (New York, 1971); W. Robert Higgins, "The Geographical Origins of Negro Slaves in Colonial South Carolina," *South Atlantic Quarterly* 70 (1971), 34–47; Lawrence W. Levine, "Slave Songs and Slave Consciousness: An Exploration in Neglected Sources," in Tamara K. Hareven, ed., *Anonymous Americans: Explorations in Nineteenth-Century Social History* (Englewood Cliffs, N.J., 1971); John Lovell, Jr., *Black Song: The Forge and the Flame* (New York, 1972); John S. Mbiti, *African Religions and Philosophy* (New York, 1969); John Rublowsky, *Black Music in America* (New York, 1971); Eileen Southern, *The Music of Black Americans: A History* (New York, 1971); Lorenzo D. Turner, "African Survivals in the New World with Special Emphasis on the Arts," in John A. Davis, ed., *Africa from the Point of View of American Negro Scholars* (Paris, 1958); Norman E. Whitten, Jr., and John F. Szwed, eds., *Afro-American Anthropology: Contemporary Perspectives* (New York, 1970); Michael R. Bradley, "The Role of the Black Church in the Colonial Slavery Society," *Louisiana Studies* 14 (1975), 413–21; Leonard Barrett, *Soul-Force: African Heritage in Afro-American Religion* (New York, 1974); Henry Mitchell, *Black Belief: Folk Beliefs of Blacks in America and West Africa* (New York, 1975); Mechal Sobel, *Trabelin' On: The Slave Journey to an Afro-Baptist Faith* (Westport, Conn., 1978); and Albert Raboteau, *Slave Religion* (New York, 1978).

The slave family has been the subject of several important works. Most important are: Herbert Gutman, *The Black Family in Slavery and Freedom* (New York, 1976); Allan Kulikoff, "The Beginnings of the Afro-American Family in Maryland," in Aubrey C. Land, et al., eds., *Law, Society, and Politics in Early Maryland* (Baltimore, 1977); Stanley Engerman, "Studying the Black Family," *Journal of Family History* 3 (1978), 78–101; and Mary Beth Norton, et al., "The Afro-American Family in the Age of Revolution," in Ira Berlin and Ronald Hoffman, eds., *Slavery in the Revolutionary Era* (Charlottesville, Va., 1981).

Another aspect of intercultural contact in early America was that between African and Indians. Much remains to be done in this area, but some glimpses into the problem can be gained by consulting Laurence Foster, *Negro-Indian Relationships in the Southeast* (Philadelphia, 1935); Peter B. Hammond, "Afro-Americans, Indians, and Afro-Asians: Cultural Contacts Between Africa and the Peoples of Asia and Aboriginal America," in Gwendolan M. Carter and Ann Paden, eds., *Expanding Horizons in African Studies* (Evanston, Ill., 1969); John M. Lofton, Jr., "White, Indian, and Negro Contacts in Colonial South Carolina," *Southern Indian Studies* 1 (1949), 3–12; Kenneth W. Porter, *The Negro on the American Frontier* (New York, 1971); Richard Halliburton, Jr., *Red Over Black: Black Slavery Among the Cherokee Indians* (Westport, Conn., 1977); Theda Perdue, *Slavery and the Evolution of Cherokee Society, 1540–1866* (Knoxville, Tenn., 1979); William S. Willis, Jr., "Divide and Rule: Red, White and Black in the Southeast," *Journal of Negro History* 48 (1963), 157–76; and Daniel F. Littlefield, *Africans and Creeks From the Colonial Period to the Civil War* (Westport, Conn., 1976).

RIVALRY FOR NORTH AMERICA

International rivalry for the North American continent has been the subject of a vast literature, mostly cast in the genre of political or military history. Almost every item of importance is listed in the bibliography by Jack P. Greene listed earlier, and for the period just before the American Revolution, in John Shy, *The American Revolution* (Northbrook, Ill., 1973). Works that deal primarily with the role of Indian societies in this struggle for the eastern half of the continent and that have importance for social and cultural as well as political and military history are John R. Alden, *John Stuart and the Southern Colonial Frontier: A Study of Indian Relations, War, Trade, and Land Problems in the Southern Wilderness, 1754–1775* (Ann Arbor, Mich., 1944); Richmond P. Bond, *Queen Anne's American Kings* (Oxford, 1952); Julian P. Boyd, ed., *Indian Treaties Printed by Benjamin Franklin, 1736–1762* (Philadelphia, 1938); Kenneth Coleman, "The Southern Frontier: Georgia's Founding and the Expansion of South Carolina," *Georgia Historical Quarterly* 56 (1972), 163–74; Louis DeVorsey, Jr., *The Indian Boundary in the Southern Colonies, 1763–75* (Chapel Hill, N.C., 1966); Randolph C. Downes, *Council Fires on the Upper Ohio: A Narrative of Indian Affairs in the Upper Ohio Valley Until 1795* (Pittsburgh, 1940); Lawrence Henry Gipson, *The British Empire Before the American Revolution*, 14 vols., (New York, 1958–69); Charles S. Grant, "Pontiac's Rebellion and the British Troop Moves of 1763," *Mississippi Valley Historical Review* 40 (1953), 75–88; Wilbur R. Jacobs, *Diplomacy and Indian Gifts: Anglo-French Rivalry along the Ohio and Northwest Frontiers, 1748–1763* (Stanford, 1950); *Indians of the Southern Colonial Frontier: The Edmond Atkin Report and Plan of 1755* (Columbia, S.C., 1954); and "Wampum; The Protocol of Indian Diplomacy," *William and Mary Quarterly* 6 (1949), 596–604; Douglas E. Leach, *The Northern Colonial Frontier, 1607–1763* (New York, 1966); Charles H. McIlwain, ed., Introduction to *An Abridgement of the Indian Affairs . . . Transacted in the Colony of New York, from the Year 1678 to the Year 1751, by Peter Wraxall* (Cambridge, Mass., 1915); Peter Marshall, "Sir William Johnson and the Treaty of Fort Stanwix, 1768," *Journal of American Studies* 1 (1967), 149–79; David C. Skaggs, ed., *The Old Northwest in the American Revolution* (Madison, Wis., 1977); Howard H. Peckham, *Pontiac and the Indian Uprising* (Princeton, N.J., 1947); Dawson A. Phelps, "The Chickasaw, the English, and the French, 1699–1744," *Tennessee Historical Quarterly* 16 (1957), 117–33; Helen L. Shaw, *British Administration of the Southern Indians, 1756–1783* (Lancaster, Pa., 1931); Jack M. Sosin, *Whitehall and the Wilderness: The Middle West in British Colonial Policy, 1760–1775* (Lincoln, Neb., 1961); Paul A. W. Wallace, *Conrad Weiser, 1696–1760: Friend of Colonist and Mohawk* (Philadelphia, 1945); and Nicholas B. Wainwright, *George Croghan: Wilderness Diplomat* (Chapel Hill, N.C., 1959). For nativistic movements, which were an important part of the eighteenth-century Indian response to changing conditions of contact with European colonizers, see Ralph Linton, "Nativistic Movements," *American Anthropologist* 45 (1943), 230–40; Anthony F. C. Wallace, "Revitalization Movements: Some Theoretical Considerations for Their Comparative Study," *American Anthropologist* 58 (1956), 264–81; and Charles E. Hunter, "The Delaware Nativist Revival of the Mid-Eighteenth Century," *Ethnohistory* 18 (1971), 39–50.

SOCIAL AND POLITICAL CHANGE

For social and political change in the eighteenth-century colonies, students should consult the essays and bibliographies in Stanley N. Katz, ed., *Colonial America: Essays in Social and Political Development* (2nd edit., Boston, 1976); Richard Hofstadter, *America at 1750: A Social Portrait* (New York, 1971); and James A. Henretta, *The Evolution of American Society, 1700–1815* (Lexington, Mass., 1973). In addition, there are a number of more specialized studies, many of them based on close examination of individual communities.

Four pathbreaking community studies, published more than a decade ago, are: Richard L. Bushman, *From Puritan to Yankee: Character and the Social Order in Connecticut, 1690–1765* (Cambridge, Mass., 1967); John Demos, *A Little Commonwealth: Family Life in Plymouth Colony* (New York, 1970); Philip J. Greven, Jr., *Four Generations: Population, Land, and Family in Colonial Andover, Massachusetts* (Ithaca, N.Y., 1970); and Kenneth A. Lockridge, *A New England Town: The First Hundred Years* (New York, 1970).

More recent contributions to the social history of New England are: David G. Allen, *In English Ways: The Movement of Societies and the Transferal of English Local Law and Custom to Massachusetts Bay in the Seventeenth Century* (Chapel Hill, N.C., 1980); Paul Boyer and Steven Nissenbaum, *Salem Possessed: The Social Origins of Witchcraft* (Cambridge, Mass., 1974); T. H. Breen, *Puritans and Adventurers: Change and Persistence in Early America* (New York, 1980); Edward M. Cook, Jr., *The Fathers of the Towns: Leadership and Community Structure in Eighteenth-Century New England* (Baltimore, 1976); Bruce Daniels, *The Connecticut Town: Growth and Development, 1635–1790* (Middletown, Conn., 1979); Richard P. Gildrie, *Salem, Massachusetts, 1626–1683: A Covenant Community* (Charlottesville, Va., 1977); Robert A. Gross, *The Minutemen and Their World* (New York, 1976); Christopher M. Jedrey, *The World of John Cleaveland: Family and Community in Eighteenth-Century New England* (New York, 1979); Kenneth A. Lockridge, *Literacy in Colonial New England: An Enquiry into the Social Context of Literacy in the Early Modern West* (New York, 1975); and Paul R. Lucas, *Valley of Discord: Church and Society Along the Connecticut River, 1636–1725* (Hanover, N.H., 1976).

Social change in the Middle Colonies has been illuminated by Douglas Greenberg, *Crime and Law Enforcement in the Colony of New York, 1691–1776* (Ithaca, N.Y., 1976); Sung Bok Kim, *Landlord and Tenant in Colonial New York: Manorial Society, 1664–1775* (Chapel Hill, N.C., 1978); James T. Lemon, *The Best Poor Man's Country: A Geographical Study of Early Southeastern Pennsylvania* (Baltimore, 1972); Robert C. Ritchie, *The Duke's Province: A Study of New York Politics and Society, 1664–1691* (Chapel Hill, N.C., 1977); Alan Tully, *William Penn's Legacy: Politics and Social Structure in Provincial Pennsylvania, 1726–1755* (Baltimore, 1978); Philip L. White, *Beekmantown, New York: Forest Frontier to Farm Community* (Austin, Tex., 1979); Jerome H. Wood, Jr., *Conestoga Crossroads: Lancaster, Pennsylvania, 1730–1790* (Harrisburg, Pa., 1979); and Stephanie G. Wolf, *Urban Village: Population, Community, and Family Structure in Germantown, Pennsylvania, 1683–1800* (Princeton, N.J., 1977).

In addition to the references in the section on Afro-American history, the following are important in tracing social change in the colonial South: Richard R. Beeman, "Social Change and Cultural Conflict in Virginia: Lunenburg County, 1746 to 1774," *William and Mary Quarterly* 35 (1978), 455–76; Paul G.E. Clemens, *The Atlantic Economy and Colonial Maryland's Eastern Shore: From Tobacco to Grain* (Ithaca, N.Y., 1980); Carville Earle and Ronald Hoffman, "Urban Development in the Eighteenth-Century South," *Perspectives in American History* 10 (1976), 7–78; Thad W. Tate and David L. Ammerman, eds., *The Chesapeake in the Seventeenth Century: Essays on Anglo-American Society* (Chapel Hill, N.C., 1979); David C.

Skaggs, *Roots of Maryland Democracy, 1753–1776* (Westport, Conn., 1973); and Gregory A. Stiverson, *Poverty in a Land of Plenty: Tenancy in Eighteenth-Century Maryland* (Baltimore, 1978).

For economic life and values, see J. E. Crowley, *This Sheba Self: The Conceptualization of Economic Life in Eighteenth-Century America* (Baltimore, 1974); and James A. Henretta, "Families and Farms: Mentalité in Pre-Industrial America," *William and Mary Quarterly* 35 (1978), 3–32. The cities are studied in Gary B. Nash, *The Urban Crucible: Social Change, Political Consciousness, and the Origins of the American Revolution* (Cambridge, Mass., 1979); Jacob M. Price, "Economic Function and the Growth of American Port Towns in the Eighteenth Century," *Perspectives in American History* 8 (1974), 7–78; and Carville Earle, "The First English Towns of North America," *Geographical Review* 67 (1977), 34–50.

The Great Awakening is examined in J. M. Bumsted and John Van de Wetering, *What Must I Do to Be Saved? The Great Awakening in Colonial America* (Hinsdale, Ill., 1976); Alan Heimert, *Religion and the American Mind from the Great Awakening to the Revolution* (Cambridge, Mass., 1966); Harry S. Stout, "Religion, Communications, and the Ideological Origins of the American Revolution," *William and Mary Quarterly* 34 (1977) 519–41; Rhys Isaac, "Problems of the Anglican Establishment in Virginia in the Era of the Great Awakening and the Parsons' Cause," *William and Mary Quarterly* 30 (1973), 3–32; Patricia J. Tracy, *Jonathan Edwards, Pastor: Religion and Society in Eighteenth-Century Northampton* (New York, 1979); and William G. McLoughlin, "'Enthusiasm for Liberty': The Great Awakening as the Key to the Revolution," *American Antiquarian Society Proceedings* 87 (1977), 69–95.

INDEX

Abenaki (Indian tribe), 76, 120
Abolitionism, 267–72
Adams, John, 201
Adoption, of Indian children into white
    families, 280
Africa, prehistory of, 142–43
African backwardness and cultural im-
    poverishment, myth of, 142
African-Indian contact, 285–86
    in South Carolina, 286–89
African slave trade, 144, 145, 148
    capture and transport of slaves,
        166–170
    competition among European nations
        for, 147
    forcible recruitment of slaves in, 146
    importance of, 141–42
    and sugar, 146
Agricultural revolution, 10–11
Agriculture, early, 10
Albany, 90, 93
    fur trade, 94–95
Albany Congress of 1754, 249, 251
Alcohol, 94, 97, 294
    as factor in Indian culture, 242–44

as weapon against Indians, 295
Algonkian Indian tribes of New Eng-
    land, 75–76
American colonies, condition of (1763),
    264–67
Amherst, Jeffrey, 255, 260
Anglican Church, 34, 65, 187
Anglo-French-Spanish in Southeast,
    231–35
Antinomianism, 73
Archdale, John, 132
Argall, Samuel, 105
Assimilation, 284
Atkin, Edmond, 251, 297
Atkins, John, 168
Attucks, Crispus, 2
Ayllon, Lucas Vasquez de, 111
Aylmer, John, 1

Bacon, Nathaniel, 121, 123, 124
Bacon, Thomas, 188
Bacon's Rebellion, 121–25
Barbados, 142, 149, 162

Barlow, Arthur, 44
Barnes, Richard, 52
Barnwell, John, 133
Barracoons, 166
Belcher, Andrew, 211
Benezet, Anthony, 268
Benin, kingdom of, 143
Bering Straits, in early settlement, 7–8
Berkeley, William, 121, 123, 124
Beverley, Robert, 106, 276
Bienville, Jean de, 110
Black codes. *See* Slave codes
Black culture, 185–86, 196–97
  the family, 192–96
  religion, 186–90
  work, 191–92
Bosomworth, Mary Musgrove, 241
Bosomworth, Thomas, 278
Braddock, James, 250
Bradford, William, 77, 85
Brant, Joseph, 278
Braudel, Fernand, 208
Brazil, 31, 88, 89, 142, 152, 153
  and production of sugar, 146
Brickell, John, 297
Bull, William, 255
Byrd, William, 106, 218, 276

Cabot, John, 32
Cabot, Sebastian, 38
Cahokia, 14
Cameron, Alexander, 278
Canary Islands, 145
Cape Cod, 70
Carter, Landon, 191
Cartier, Jacques, 18
Catawba (Indian tribe), 131–32
Catholic Church, 31, 34, 64, 154
  attitude toward non-Christian people,
    274
  in New France, 107–8
  in New Spain, 112–13
Catholicism, 31–32
Cayuga (Indian tribe), 17
Champlain, Samuel de, 105
Charles II, 147
Charleston, 128, 138
Chavez, Caesar, 2
Cherokee (Indian tribe), 136, 233
  diplomacy of, 234–35
  and escaped slaves, 289

political organization of, 239–42
  in Seven Years War, 254–55
Chesapeake colonies, 46–49
  and Bacon's Rebellion, 121–26
  English-Indian relations in, 53
  reorganization of, 49–50
  and tobacco, 50–51
  See also Jamestown colony; Virginia
Chickasaw (Indian tribe), 137
Chief Brims, 231, 232
Choctaws (Indian tribe), 132, 137, 235
Christian instruction, problem of,
  187–89
Coffles, 130, 166
Colbert, Jean Baptiste, 106
Colden, Cadwallader, 208–9
Colleton, John, 127
Colonization of the Americas, religious
  motive in, 31–32
Columbus, Christopher, 30, 37
Company of New France, 105
Concubinage, 284
Cooper, Anthony Ashley, 127
Coronado, Francisco de, 112
Cotton, John, 71, 209
Counterblast to Tobacco, 51
Creeks (Indian tribe), 128, 132, 235
  diplomacy of, 230–34
  political organization of, 239–42
  in Seven Years War, 256–57
  in Yamasee War, 134–37
Crevecoeur, Michel de, 279–80
Croghan, George, 261
Cultural interaction in colonial America,
  291–98
Culture, definition of, 4
Curacao, 89
Currency Act of 1764, 266

Dale, Thomas, 105
Davenport, James, 220–21
Davis, Angela, 195–96
Deerskins, trade in, 129–30, 131, 132
Degler, Carl, 284
Delaware (Indian tribe), 95, 96, 250
  migration of, 99–104
  and "Walking Purchase," 102
Deloria, Vine, Jr., 2
Depression of 1760, 267
DeSoto, Hernandez, 111

Diphtheria, 60
Diseases, as weapon against Indians, 17, 60, 65, 76, 79, 80, 96, 109, 233, 239, 294, 295
Divide and rule, English policy of, 138
Downing, Emanuel, 295
Drake, Francis, 44
DuBois, W. E. B., 194
Dutch, in the New World, 88
  and African slave trade, 89, 147
  and Indian fur trade, 90–91, 94–95
  and Indian trade of New England, 84, 89–90
Dutch West Indian Company, 88, 91, 92, 95, 150

Early life, in North America, 7–8
Early Native American cultures, 11–16
Easton, Treaty of, 252
Economic activity, principal forms of, 296
Edwards, Jonathan, 222
Egalitarianism in colonial America, 214–15
Eighteenth-century America, 200–201
  agricultural society in, 206–7
  changing social structure in, 213–18
  competitive, individualistic attitude of, 207–9
  diversity of immigrants, 202
  economic life in the cities, 210–13
  indentured servants, 203–5
  Protestant work ethic in, 207
Eliot, John, 71, 116
Elizabeth, Queen, 43, 45
Ellison, Ralph, 3
Elmina Castle, 89
Emancipation, 153
England, and colonies, 32–41
  early settlements, 43–66, 70–79
  involvement in slave trade, 147
English colonization, beginnings of, 34–36
English vs. Spanish system of colonization, 64–66
English village life, 68
Eurocentrism, 2
Evans, Lewis, 183
"Every man alone," concept of, 69

Five nations, 17, 109, 227–28, 229
Forestalling, 212
Fort Rosalie, 110
France, and colonies, 35–36
  first settlements, 104–5
  war with Natchez Indians, 110
Franklin, Benjamin, 3, 181, 199, 203, 210, 214–15
Frazier, E. Franklin, 194
Free blacks, need for, 160–62
French and Indian War. See Seven Years War
Fur trade, 36, 65, 89–90, 98
  in Carolina, 129–30, 132
  as factor in Indian culture, 236–38
  in New England, 86
  in New France, 107

Galloway, Joseph, 181, 272
Gates, Thomas, 57
German Protestants, 98
Ghana, kingdom of, 142
Goncalvez, Antam, 142
Gookin, Daniel, 116
Gorton, Samuel, 116
Graffenreid, Baron de, 133
Grant, Ulysses, 2
Gray, Robert, 39, 40
Great Awakening, the, 188, 219–22, 291

Hackensack (Indian tribe), 92
Hakluyt, Richard, 34, 39
Harvey, John, 63
Hawkins, John, 32
Heckewelder, John, 26
Hiawatha, 18
Hispaniola, 30
History and Present State of Virginia, The, 276
Hopi culture, 11
Hopkins, Samuel, 268
Hubbard, William, 85
Huguenots, 225
Hurons (Indian tribe), 90–91, 107, 228, 239
Hutchinson, Anne, 73
  trial of, 74

Iberville, Pierre Le Moyne, 137
Indentured servants, 51–53, 149–50
Indian ethos, 25–26
Indian factionalism, as cause of eventual
    defeat, 139–40
Indian languages, 9
Indian slave trade, in Carolina, 130–32,
    134–37, 138
Indian society, 296
    attitude toward slaves, 290
    cultural persistence of certain traits,
        244–246
    practice of adoption in, 280
    transformation of, 235–44
    values of, 296–97
Indian tribes of eastern North America,
    14–17
    process of decimation, dispossession,
        and decline, 138–40
Indigo, 175
Individualism, as mode of behavior, 26,
    69
Industrial Revolution, 141
Intercultural mixing, 275, 298
Interracial marriage, 65, 86, 105–6,
    150–51, 153, 162–63, 193, 241
    official policy in English colonies,
        277
    prohibited in various states, 282.
    See also Miscegenation
Intertribal hostility, as key to English
    success, 137, 138
Iroquois (Indian tribe), 17–24, 239
    alliance with Pennsylvania, 100,
        102–3
    child rearing, 21–22
    diplomacy, 227–30
    and fur trade, 90–91, 109
    kinship groups, 20
    strategy in Seven Years War, 253
Iroquois League, 133
    organization of, 17–19

Jamaica, 111, 149, 162
    comparison with Virginia, 294
James I, 45, 51, 70
Jamestown colony, 45–46
    early difficulties of, 46–47, 48
    relations with Indians, 53, 58–60
    war with Indians, 61–62, 63–64
Jefferson, Thomas, 270
Jennings, Francis, 238

Johnson, William, 252, 261, 263,
    275–76
Jordan, Winthrop, 282

Kieft, Willem, 91, 92
King Philip. *See* Metacom
Kongo, kingdom of, 143

Land companies, 248
"Land lopers," 122
Land possession, Puritan theories of,
    79–80
Land speculation, 215
LaSalle, Robert de, 110
Las Casas, Bartholome de, 38
Lawson, John, 245
Lay exhorting, 221
League of the Iroquois, 17–19
Leeward Islands, 149, 162
Lenni Lenapes. *See* Delaware (Indian
    tribe)
Letters from an American Farmer, 279
Levine, Lawrence, 190
Locke, John, 127
Logan, James, 100, 102
London, growth of, in 17th century, 68
Lurie, Nancy, 59

McDonald, John, 278
McGillivray, Alexander, 278
Madeira Islands, 145, 146
Mahicans (Indian tribe), 89, 90
Mali, empire of, 143
Martin, Calvin, 26
Martyr, Peter, 111
Massachuset (Indian tribe), 76, 80
Massachusetts Bay Company, 78
Massachusetts colony, early settlement
    of, 71–74
Mather, Cotton, 85, 181
Mather, Richard, 71
Maule, Robert, 244–45
Mayhew, Thomas, 116
Mestizos, 274, 278–79
    in Portuguese and Spanish colonies,
        284
Metacom, 117, 120
    and war with Puritans, 118–20

Metacom's War, 116–20
Methodist Church, 188
Mintz, Sidney, 5
Miscegenation, 193–94, 273–75
  in English colonies, 153, 275–90
  in French colonies, 105–6
  in Portuguese Brazil, 153
  public attitudes toward, 282.
  See also Interracial marriage
Mississippian culture, 13–14
Mittelberger, Gottlieb, 204, 215
Mohawks (Indian tribe), 17, 90, 120,
  252
  relations with Dutch, 93
Mohegan (Indian tribe), 116
Montreal, 90, 109
Mooney, James, 17
Moore, James, 134
Moore, Thomas, 131
Morgan, Edmund, 52
Morton, Thomas, 78
Moundbuilder culture, 13, 14
Mulattoes, 274
  status of, in English Jamaica, 285
Mustee, 274, 290

Narragansett (Indian tribe), 76, 77, 83,
  116
  in Metacom's War, 119–20
Natchez (Indian tribe), 110
Native Americans, 11–16
  European images of, 36–41
Navigation Acts, 266
Neesnummin, John, 117
Negro Election Day, 178
Nemattanew (Jack of the Feathers), 60,
  61
Neolin (Indian prophet), 261–62
New Amsterdam, 89, 93
  relations with local Indians, 91–93,
  94
New England colony, 70
  religious orthodoxy in, 71
New England Confederation, 116
  and Metacom's War, 116–20
Newfoundland fisheries, 32, 70
New France, 104, 105
  evangelization in, 107–8
  expansionist policy in, 225
  in Mississippi Valley, 110
  racial intermixture in, 106, 277
  sovereignty in, 108

New Netherland. *See* New Amsterdam
Newport, Christopher, 46, 53
Nicholls, Richard, 93
Nigeria, 142
North Carolina, settlement of, 133
  war with Tuscarora Indians, 133–34
  war with Yamasee Indians, 134–37
Nova Scotia, 106

Occum, Samson, 280
Oglethorpe, James, 233
Oneida (Indian tribe), 17
Onondaga (Indian tribe), 17
Opechancanough, 60–61, 63
Orinoco River, 37
Ottawa (Indian tribe), 228

Paine, Thomas, 245–46
Parker, Ely, 2
Pawtucket (Indian tribe), 76, 80
Peace of Paris, 258
Pearce, Roy H., 82
Peckham, George, 39, 40, 41
Penn, William, 96
  and Indians, 97–98
Pennsylvania colony
  dispossession of Delawares, 100–104
  founding of, 96–98
  Indian tribal migration to, 99
Pequot (Indian tribe), 76, 83
  and battle at Mystic Fort, 84–85
  and Dutch, 84
  resistance to acculturation, 86
Pequot War, 84–86
Percy, George, 57
Philadelphia, 97, 98, 99
Phips, William, 210
Pilgrims, 76–77
Pitt, William, 253
Pocahontas, 56, 58
  marriage of, 276–77
Political organization, as factor in In-
  dian culture, 239–41
Politics, in late colonial period, 267
Pontiac's Revolt, 262–63
Poor relief, 216
Popé's Rebellion, 113
Population of North America, in pre-
  contact period, 17
Port Royal, settlement of, 104, 105

Portugal, and colonies, 31, 35, 88, 89, 154
  involvement in slave trade, 143, 144, 147
Pottery-making, 16
Powhatan, 55
  relations with Jamestown settlers, 56–58
Powhatan Confederacy, 55, 56–59, 64, 121
Pownall, Thomas, 297
"Praying Indians," 116–17
Presbyterian Church, 188
Priber, Gottlieb, 234–35
Proclamation of 1763, 258–59, 262–63
Progress, European idea of, 29–30
Protestantism, 31–32, 188–89
  attitude toward savages, 274
  attitude toward slaves, 155
Protestantism vs. Catholicism, 32, 33, 67–68
Protestant work ethic, 207
Pueblo (Indian tribe), 112, 113
Pueblo Bonita, 11
Pueblo culture, 11
Puritanism, 67–70
Puritans, 70
  and Indians, 75–79
  and Metacom's War, 116–20
  and Pequot War, 84–86
  sense of mission, 81–83
  settlement in New England, 71–74, 77–79
  theories of land possession, 79–81

Quakerism, 95
Quakers, 95, 98, 104
Quebec, 104
Queen Ann's War, 230

Racial groups, classification of, 4–5
Racial mixing between Indians and Europeans, 275–80
Ragueneau, Father, 23–24, 107
Raleigh, Walter, colonization efforts of, 43–45
Regional variations in slavery, in America
  Carolina and Georgia low country, 174–77

Chesapeake Bay area, 173–74
  in the North, 177–78
Reversion to savagery, 279
Rhode Island, 73, 74
Rice, 175
Roanoke Island settlement, 34, 40, 43–45
Robinson, John, 22, 78
Rolfe, John, 52, 58, 61
  marriage of, 276–77
Roman law, as protection of slave, 154, 274
Royal Adventurers to Africa, 147
Royal African Company, 147
Rum, in colonial times, 242, 295

Sachems and sagamores, as political leaders, 75, 117
Sagadahoc settlement, 34
St. Augustine, founding of, 111–12
St. Eustatius, 89
St. Martin, 89
Salem, 80
Salisbury, Neal, 75
Santa Fe, founding of, 112
Savannah (city), 132
Savannah (Indian tribe), extirpation of, 131–32
Scarlet fever, 60
Scots-Irish, 98
Seneca (Indian tribe), 17, 260
Sequeira, Ruy do, 144
Serfdom, 144
Settlement, flaws in English plan of, 47–49
Seven Years War, 248, 250–51
  Indian strategy in, 251–57
Sexual politics, in English colonies, 284–85
Shawnee (Indian tribe), 130, 131
Shepard, Thomas, 71
Shirley, William, 183
Siberia, 7
Slave and Citizen, 153
Slave codes, 150–51, 157, 184, 289
Slave labor in Southern colonies
  adjustment to slave life, 170–72
  institutionalization of, 151–52
  maximization of profit as factor in, 156, 159
  reasons for shift to, 149–50

Slavery, as worldwide phenomenon, 144–45
  differing factors in, 155–60
  in English colonies, 147
  in Southern colonies, 150–52
Slavery in North America vs. South America, 152–63
Slaves and slavery in America, 170–72
  and assimilation, 292–93
  between 1760 and 1770, 271–72
  Christianization of, 291
  education of, 292
  and miscegenation, 277–78
  regional variations in, 172–78
  resistance and rebellion, 178–85
Smallpox, 79, 294–95
Smith, John, 46, 47, 49, 55–56, 57, 61
Society, definition of, 4
Society for the Propagation of the Gospel, 244, 292
Society of Friends. See Quakers
South Carolina, colonization of, 126–27
  constitution of, 127
  relations with Indians, 128–32
Spain, and colonies, 31, 35, 64–65, 154
  and conversion of Indians, 112–13
  early settlements, 111
  in Florida, 111–12
  involvement in slave trade, 145
  in New Mexico, 112
Spanish Armada, 33
Spanish Colonie, The, 38
Speculum oris, 169
Spirituals, 189–90
Squanto, 77
Stamp Act of 1765, 266
Standish, Miles, 77–78
Stono revolt, the, 287, 288
Sugar, 146
  and sugar plantations in Caribbean, 149
Susquehannocks (Indian tribe), 98, 126, 228
  at war with Virginians, 122–25
Swiss Mennonites, 98

Tannenbaum, Frank, 153, 155
Tennant, Gilbert, 220
Tierra del Fuego, 9
Timbuktu, 143
Tobacco, 50–52, 60, 63, 243
Transculturation, 4

True Report, of the late discoveries, . . . of the Newfound Landes, 40–41
Tuscarora (Indian tribe), 132–34, 288

Underhill, John, 239

Vacuum domicilium, legal theory of, 79, 80
Velasco, Alonso de, 57
Verrazzano, Giovanni da, 35, 37, 104
Violence, as means of ensuring social stability, 151, 157
Virginia, 45–48, 142
  Bacon's Rebellion, 121–25
  census of 1669, 64
  comparison with Jamaica, 294
  growth of, 63, 125
  and policy of genocide, 61–62
Virginia Company, 45–46, 47, 50–58, 61
Voltaire, 97

"Walking Purchase," 102
Wallace, Anthony, 18
Wampanoag (Indian tribe), 76, 77, 116
  at war with Puritans, 117–20
Warfare, as factor in Indian culture, 238–39
Wars for empire in North America, 223–24, 225–27
Wax, Murray, 25
Way to Wealth, The, 208
West Indies, 51, 111
Westos (Indian tribe), 128
  destruction of, 130
Whitaker, Alexander, 59
White-black intermixture, in colonial America, 280–85
Whitefield, George, 219–20
White Indians, 280
White racial prejudice, 152
Williams, Roger, 73, 208
  on Indian warfare, 239
  and land question, 80–81
Winthrop, John, 71, 72, 73
  theory of land, 79–80, 81
Woodmason, Charles, 218, 245

Woodward, Henry, 129
Woolman, John, 268, 269
World view, Native American vs. European, 25–27

Yamasee (Indian tribe), 134–37, 288
Yellow fever, 60

Zuni culture, 11